Alvin M. Josephy, Jr.

The Longest Trail

Alvin M. Josephy, Jr., was born in 1915 in New York City. He went to school at Horace Mann and Harvard, worked as a screenwriter in Hollywood, as a print and radio journalist in New York, and as a World War II Marine Corps combat correspondent in the Pacific; his recording of the amphibious landing at Guam was broadcast nationwide. After the war he became an editor at *Time* magazine and then *American Heritage*. On assignment with *Time* in Idaho in the early 1950s, he encountered the Nez Perce tribe of Indians. That meeting changed his life—and that of many others. Fifty years of books and articles on American Indian and western history followed. He was also a technical advisor on the film *Little Big Man*, a noted book and magazine editor, and an advocate for Indians. Josephy worked with Stewart Udall in the Kennedy administration, wrote an influential Indian "white paper" for the Nixon administration, and served as chair of the founding board of the National Museum of the American Indian in Washington, D.C. Many of his books remain in print. He and his wife, Betty, bought a small ranch in the heart of Nez Perce Country in eastern Oregon in 1963, where the family spent summers for more than forty years. Josephy died in 2005, a year after Betty's passing.

The Longest Trail

Arrival of the Nez Perce at the Walla Walla Treaty, May 1855.
(Drawing by Gustav Sohon. Photo courtesy of the
Washington State Historical Society.)

The Longest Trail

WRITINGS ON AMERICAN INDIAN
HISTORY, CULTURE, AND POLITICS

Alvin M. Josephy, Jr.

Edited by Marc Jaffe and Rich Wandschneider

VINTAGE BOOKS
A Division of Penguin Random House LLC
New York

A VINTAGE ORIGINAL, OCTOBER 2015

Vintage Books and colophon are registered trademarks of
Penguin Random House LLC.

Pages 495–496 constitute an extension of the copyright page.

The Library of Congress Cataloging-in-Publication Data
Josephy, Alvin M., 1915–2005.
[Works. Selections]
The longest trail : writings on American Indian history, culture,
and politics / by Alvin M. Josephy, Jr. ; edited by Marc Jaffe and
Rich Wandschneider.
pages cm
1. Indians of North America—History.
2. Indians of North America—Social life and customs.
3. Indians of North America—Politics and government.
I. Jaffe, Marc, editor.   II. Wandschneider, Rich, editor.   III. Title.
E77.J788 2015   970.004'97—dc23   2015010197

Vintage Books Trade Paperback ISBN: 978-0-345-80691-8
eBook ISBN: 978-0-345-80692-5

Author photograph courtesy of Knopf Publishing Group
Map design by Robert Bull
Book design by Jaclyn Whalen

www.vintagebooks.com

Printed in the United States of America
10 9 8 7 6 5 4 3 2 1

Contents

PART III.
THE MIRACLE OF INDIAN SURVIVAL

Foreword

A Man of Honor: Alvin Josephy, an Appreciation

Alvin Josephy's work seeped into my life and foreshadowed my path in ways neither of us could have anticipated. My awareness of him began as a child, in my grandparents' living room on the Umatilla Reservation, when he visited with Grandpa, Gilbert E. Conner, the only living grandson of Ollokot, younger brother of Young Joseph. In 1926, Grandpa had been secretary of the "Remnants Committee," an assemblage representing remnants of the families involved in the 1877 war, including Yellow Wolf and Josiah Red Wolf. Alvin and Grandpa spent hours discussing the genealogy and intricate history of the descendants of Wellamotkin, father of Old Joseph.

That Alvin sought to represent our kinship and geographic relationships was indicative of his attention to detail. Notably, an illustration in *The Nez Perce Indians and the Opening of the Northwest*, the book that grew from those original interviews, represents village headmen and not modern Tribal identities—an apt and accurate depiction of our pre- and early-contact societal structure. It was white leaders who insisted on "head chiefs" and distinct tribal boundaries.

Decades later, I would come to appreciate that Alvin had conducted research in an unprecedented manner among western historians at that point in time, as he listened studiously to numerous Cayuse, Nez Perce, and Palouse elders on the Nez Perce, Colville, and Umatilla reservations. He trusted the oral accounts they provided.

I remember him telling me then that we—Tribal members— needed to write our own histories. He lamented that he had been told stories and given material that he could not use because it would be dismissed as hearsay if he used it in his work. But, if we recounted our oral history in the first-person narrative, it would be genuine, authentic.

The year that Alvin's *Red Power* was published I joined other Tribal and some non-Indian students in forming "Na- numa Natitayt," the first Indian club at our high school. When I took my first college anthropology class, *Red Power* was required reading. When the *United States v. Washington* deci- sion on treaty fishing rights was announced, I worked with my colleagues at "Indians Into Communications" in Seattle on a special newspaper edition and interviewed lead attor- ney Mason Morisset for a televised special on the case. Shortly thereafter, *Now That the Buffalo's Gone* was published with the chapter "The Great Northwest Fishing War," detailing the long history leading up to the Boldt Decision. For Alvin, west- ern history—especially that regarding Indians—was still un- folding.

During one of his visits, Alvin told me he would send me a proof of his autobiography, *A Walk Toward Oregon*. I said it was kind of him but not necessary. He said he hoped that he'd gotten the part about his relationships with Tribal people right. I was puzzled. He said he had always been somewhat struck by the fact that Indian people welcomed him into their homes and trusted him with their stories—when they had been given no good reason to continue to trust white men. I told him that our old people relied on their intuition, assessing character, discerning who had a good heart and who did not. Clearly, they had decided he meant well by them. Little did they realize in the 1950s and '60s that he would later influence the Nixon administration's support for the Indian Self-Determination Act of 1975, an act that would pivot the course of our future.

In 1999, I was in Washington, D.C., for the groundbreaking of the National Museum of the American Indian (NMAI). In 2000, when Alvin visited Tamástslikt Cultural Institute for a book signing, he paid our permanent exhibit galleries an extraordinary compliment. He said, "This feels Tribal. I hope our museum will." I was back in Washington in 2004 with the Umatilla delegation in the incredible grand procession on opening day. Alvin, as the founding chair of the NMAI Board of Trustees, was front and center in both the groundbreaking and the opening ceremonies. Roughly two decades after his term, I had the privilege of chairing the NMAI Board.

My last occasion to work with Alvin came with *Lewis and Clark Through Indian Eyes*, his own last book. The only instruction Alvin gave the Indian contributors was to say what we wanted to say from a Tribal point of view. I struggled with the piece and was relieved when my mother helped me frame what I wanted to say by sharing things her father had told her. I was also calmed by the notion that Alvin Josephy would review and prepare the writing for publication. As an undergraduate journalism student, I had come to value editing. Alvin didn't change a word. He did exactly what he said he would do: let us each tell our stories in our own words.

Alvin was a man of his word. He was a man of honor who wielded influence with humility. He cared deeply about the future of Indian people. In his lifetime, he contributed much to help shape that future, seeking no acclaim for the work. And, perhaps for me the most important measure of his affinity, he loved our country in Northeast Oregon.

Sísaawipam
Roberta Conner
Pendleton, Oregon
September 2013

The Longest Trail

Introduction

Why an anthology of Josephy writings on American Indians now, a decade after his death and three, four, and five decades after most of the material was written? The answer is wrapped in his multiple writing personae and in his early conversion to Indian advocacy. In his 2000 memoir, *A Walk Toward Oregon*, he says that by 1959, well into research on the Nez Perce but before his first book on Indians was published, he and his wife, Betty, had become advocates for American Indians.

It all began with a chance assignment from Henry Luce himself to Alvin, then a *Time* staff writer, to do a story on Idaho. The assignment—ironically from a man widely known for his antipathy to Indians—brought this New York bred east erner together with a number of Indians who "influenced and changed" the rest of his life. It inspired a twelve-year investigation of the Nez Perce tribe and the historical context of the Nez Perce War, a subject of little interest to historians at the time. *The Nez Perce Indians and the Opening of the Northwest*, published in 1965, quickly established itself as a seminal work and the cornerstone of Josephy's accomplishments as a historian of the American West and of the American Indian.

From his initial focus on the Nez Perce, Alvin's interaction with Indians of other tribes in the Northwest and then throughout the hemisphere led to a flurry of research and writing. Books and articles about Indians past and present began to

flow, beginning with *The Patriot Chiefs* in 1961 (he had interrupted work on the Nez Perce history to write this book), continuing with the classic *Indian Heritage of America*, a National
Book Award finalist, and ending with the elaborately illustrated
500 Nations: An Illustrated History of North American Indians.
Articles appeared in *Life*, *American Heritage*, *Audubon*, and
many other publications, both academic and those meant for
the general public.

Alvin Josephy was a friend and mentor to the editors of
this volume for more than thirty years. And in that time we
learned much about the intensity and commitment that lay
behind an exterior of quiet reserve. In 2001, in Olympia, Washington, while on a tour with Alvin in connection with the publication of his memoir, we learned that he had discovered the
extraordinary Gustavus Sohon drawings of Northwest Indians,
forgotten in state archives, as he researched his book on the
Nez Perce tribe. These are some of the only images of important tribal leaders of the mid-nineteenth century and are now
widely published. In Lewiston, Idaho, Nez Perce Indians—
friends and the sons and daughters of friends—came to say
hello and thank him for his work and friendship.

Also on that book tour across Oregon, Idaho, and Washington, veterans of World War II in the Pacific came to say that they
too had been at Guadalcanal, Guam, or Iwo Jima. Some had
read his first book, *The Long and the Short and the Tall: The
Story of a Marine Combat Unit in the Pacific*, published in 1946,
shortly after the war's end. Others had already picked up the
new memoir and read the chapter that was the signal event in
their own lives. Almost sixty years on, they quietly mouthed the
names of beaches and battles, which sometimes brought them

to tears. Alvin listened and responded, nodding and trading a few words, and signed their books—perhaps with a "Semper Fi," the Marine Corps motto. (Once, on the Pine Ridge Reservation in South Dakota in dark Indian days, a Marine Corps emblem on a humble shack led to conversation and friendship—Alvin, like many of his Indian friends, was forever a marine.)

It is important to an understanding of Josephy's writing career that he came to Indian affairs less than a decade after his time in the Pacific. He had covered the war from foxholes and wrote hundreds of stories about the troops in the front lines. He trusted the interview method and the stories that followed. When a young Nez Perce Indian told him some raw truths about his heritage, Josephy saw a "great American epic" that had been largely omitted from the narrative of "American" history. When he found first-person accounts of Indian life recorded by an eccentric Washington rancher named Lucullus McWhorter, published by a small press in Idaho, he decided that he would tell the Nez Perce story as part of the broader history of the Pacific Northwest.

Alvin had told us on publication of his first book on Indians, *The Patriot Chiefs*, that he found it most often under "Natural History" on bookstore shelves, and that he had determined then to begin his personal campaign to move Indians into American history on bookshelves and in American minds. He knew that the full, authentic story of Indian Country must be told from the Indian point of view, as well as from documents and narratives from a white world. On the tour for his memoir, he still found some of his books misplaced under "Insects and Dinosaurs," thus *The Longest Trail* is one more effort for Alvin to help "get it right."

Other ideas that inform this book are here as well. The title *The Patriot Chiefs* was, Indians told Josephy over the years, the first time anyone had called their ancestors, who had fought for their lands, families, and cultures, "patriots." Indians did not "vanish," as has been often predicted—and sometimes proclaimed as government policy—but are part of America still, living on reservations and in towns and cities across the country. The fact of their survival as Indians and members of named Indian tribes is a kind of miracle. And their participation in American life today, in accordance with treaties signed by their ancestors and white governments thirsty for settlement land and "peace" with tribes, is a matter of fact and consequence to all of us, especially as Indian lands and treaties involve the nation's waters, forests, and fish—our natural resources.

Who really was Alvin Josephy? When asked how Alvin identified himself, a family member said simply, "He identified himself as a writer." And a writer he certainly was—screenwriter, novelist, newspaper, radio, and magazine journalist, historian. Josephy first put pencil, pen, and typewriter to paper as a professional in his teenage years. Then, after an economy-forced departure from Harvard College during the Depression, it was on to Hollywood, to the *New York Herald Tribune* (among other journalistic venues), to the Marine Corps as a combat correspondent, to Time Inc., to American Heritage as an editor of books and magazines—these last at a time when he was writing respected history about Indians and the West (though without benefit of PhD or collegiate lectern). As he moved into the publishing world as a principal editor at American Heritage Publishing Company, there came a different challenge for his devotion to words—and pictures as well. The task called for little writing but entailed commissioning of other writers to put words on paper, suggesting ideas for articles and books, worrying about deadlines and an array of administrative details, and driving for higher book sales and magazine circulation. Alvin clearly was good at his job. He was responsible for the highly successful series of American Heritage book publications, and by the 1970s had become editor-in-chief of *American Heritage*, as well as supervising all the company's magazines.

Josephy had become a respected writer and editor on Indian and western issues, but unlike most other historians and journalists, his activities led to strong personal relationships with the people he wrote about, and then to full-throated activism on behalf of American Indian rights and Indian social, political, and economic progress. His first appearance on the national stage was the preparation of a report on Indian affairs at the request of the Nixon administration. That report (which appears in this volume in abbreviated form) has been credited as a key influence in Nixon's proposal to change the entire direction of federal policy toward the Indians, from Eisenhower's "termination" of Indian reservations and treaties in the 1950s to the concept of self-determination for Indian peoples. The Nixon presidential legacy is shadowed by scandal and resignation, but under his administration, urged on by Alvin Josephy, Indians began a slow but steady progress never thought possible before that time.

For Josephy, activism was a way of life, and he operated at many levels. At the request of Governor Nelson Rockefeller,

Josephy joined others in righting a sinking ship at the Heye Museum of the American Indian in New York City, and eventually helped steer its consolidation with the Smithsonian Institution in Washington, D.C. Josephy was the founding board chair of the National Museum of the American Indian, which has sites both in New York and on the National Mall in Washington, D.C. On a more local and personal level, he often acted as an informal travel guide, for example, writing a four-page letter charting the most historically important views along the route from Boise, Idaho, to Wallowa Lake, Oregon (as well as the best place to stop for pancakes). It was written for the benefit of three New York City visitors to the opening session of a literary event called the Fishtrap Gathering, in 1988. The event and the organization, Fishtrap, which he helped form, continue to this day.

While Josephy's activism on behalf of American Indians never flagged, from the 1960s to the end of his life, yet another persona developed on a more or less parallel track. In his autobiography Josephy writes that during his work on a Heritage book about Yellowstone Park, "I became aware of a strange, redemptive change that had come over me." The impact of the writings of men like Wallace Stegner, Peter Matthiessen, Justice William O. Douglas, and the poet Paul Engle, and the images of the photographers Edward Weston and Ansel Adams, merged with his empathy for the Indian identification with the natural world, as well as with his own love for the "unspoiled parts of the West." Josephy turned his back on the "unrestrained exploitation of the earth," which he had so strenuously promoted as a Time Inc. journalist. Over time he became a "conservationist," or what is called in early twenty-first-century terminology an "environmentalist." This new commitment was reflected not only in his writing (three examples of which appear in this volume), but also in practical political involvement as a close advisor to President Kennedy's secretary of the interior, Stewart Udall. In later years, Josephy was known not only to have clashed with forces such as power and coal companies, but also to have been in close relationships with writers such as Edward Abbey (of *Monkey Wrench Gang* fame); William Kittredge, dean of environmental writers in the West; and the well-known southwestern writer and environmentalist Jack Loeffler.

There we have him. Alvin M. Josephy, Jr.—writer, editor, historian, activist, environmentalist. But one still may ask—how did the son of a cultured, upper-middle-class German-Jewish New York family become a devoted citizen and distinguished historian of the American West and defender of a tiny population of threatened Native Americans? The answer may come from two directions. First, the character of the man. He had a powerful intelligence, wide-ranging curiosity, relentless (some would say insufferable) perseverance, and a surfeit of what a famous sociologist, Pitirim Sorokin, called an "instinct for combinations" (this last being the ability and desire to bring things together, people of varying types and dispositions or ideas of disparate nature, all toward a positive result). Second, Alvin Josephy's innate motivation, perhaps a hundred generations in the making, was to help the world to a better place.

As editors, we learned much about Alvin Josephy and about American Indians in the preparation of this book. In the end, we hope it helps others learn what Indians have thought and done over five hundred years of American history. We all must continue to learn even more about how and why it is important for Indian voices to be heard, for Indians to be involved in national conversations—about resources, religion, and politics—today, and for generations to come.

Marc Jaffe
Williamstown, Massachusetts

Rich Wandschneider
Joseph, Oregon
November 2014

Editors' Note

The editors have provided headnotes for each of the chapters in this volume in order to identify properly each selection and set it in context as much as possible.

There remains the question of bringing certain facts and comments into the present. In some instances footnotes have been provided, but in a few cases, especially the closing pages of chapter 13, the "Michigan speech," we have allowed the text to stand as historically accurate.

In addition, we have invited contributions from authoritative American Indian voices to provide contemporary views of Josephy's writings.

"The artist, Peter Rindisbacher, titled this picture *Indian Women in Tent*, but the group seems to include a white man (second from left) and a half-blood man and boy (at right) together with Indian or half-blood women. The French-speaking half-blood hunters at Red River generally dressed themselves and their families in white man's clothes, but in their ornamentation and in many of their ways of living they were like Indians. The half-blood at right smokes a long Indian pipe whose red pipestone bowl piece probably came from the Sioux country in Minnesota."—Alvin Josephy, "The Boy Artist of Red River," in *American Heritage*, February 1970. (Photo used by permission of West Point Museum Collection, United States Military Academy.)

I

PUTTING AMERICAN INDIANS INTO AMERICAN HISTORY

Listening to Indians

A Commentary by Clifford Trafzer

In late July 1944, Alvin Josephy waded ashore on the Pacific island of Guam with the attacking force of U.S. Marines. His recording of that walk, under intense fire, remains the only such eyewitness radio account of an amphibious landing in World War II. Josephy may have met Indians before the war, but his encounter with Navajos on Guam was significant in the context of his involvement with the Indian world thereafter. These Navajos were members of the Code Talkers, who gained fame as communications personnel using a never-broken code based on the Diné language. As he describes in his memoir, *A Walk Toward Oregon,* Josephy's encounter with the Navajos taught him the hard truth behind the myths about the famous Kit Carson and his Indian-fighting exploits. Most telling, however, for Josephy, was a Navajo response to one marine who questioned the Indians' patriotism. "We're fighting for our country, too."

Josephy's connection to Indians was taken up again when, as briefly referred to in the introduction to this volume, he met Bill Stevens, a Nimípu, or Nez Perce Indian, on the reservation near Lewiston, Idaho, while on assignment with *Time* magazine. In that small town on the banks of the Clearwater and Snake Rivers, Stevens shared stories about his tribe's history and the government's theft of Nez Perce land. Josephy wanted to know more. Thus began his research into the history of the Nez Perce people that culminated in a masterpiece, *The Nez Perce Indians and the Opening of the Northwest.*

Unlike most historians of his time, Josephy listened and learned from Nez Perce people, and came to understand that in order to write about Native Americans he had to learn about their cultures, religions, kinship structures, and relationships with newcomers. He studied the people from the inside out rather than the outside in.

During the 1950s and 1960s, most historians examined tribal people as if under a magnifying glass. They did not enter American Indian worlds through oral histories, ceremony, families, feasts, powwows, songs, and stories. They felt no obligation to know the culture and spirit of Indian people, but wrote from documents written by non-Indian trappers, explorers, missionaries, agents, soldiers, politicians, and newspaper editors. Josephy certainly used written sources, but he also conducted oral histories and listened to the testimony of Yellow Wolf, Mourning Dove, Five Wounds, and Sanclow (Mary Moses), as well as L. V. McWhorter, William Brown, Andrew Pambrun, George Kuykendall, and others. He listened and learned from Native Americans and then wrote their histories, excerpts from which are offered in the following pages.

Even today, most Americans know little about American Indian cultural history, and what they do know often comes from outdated school textbooks and from television and movie stereotypes. Today, even though the History Channel, PBS stations, and FNX (First Nation's Experience) offer far

more authentic documentaries about Native Americans—
and American Indian authors, filmmakers, and journalists
have opened their diverse worlds—basic misunderstandings
still exist. And in the Age of Indian Gaming the general public
lives in the mistaken belief that all Indians are rich with casino
wealth and still receive government checks.

Josephy was ahead of his time in throwing aside the Euro-
centric context within which most history about native peoples in the Americas was being written and understood. As he
points out, white settlers' values, including the accumulation
of wealth, empire, architecture, roads, conquests, and written
records, were derived from Europe. Although the Inca, Maya,
Olmec, Aztec, and others also built empires, most Native
Americans lived in worlds based on spirit, family, foods, village, or band life, with a reverence toward the natural world.
Most important, Josephy challenged the destructive image of
Native Americans as lazy, stupid, backward, uncivilized, and
savage. Many whites still assumed Indians were without an
understanding of government, economies, education, or belief
in God. Non-Indians still portrayed Indians as childlike wor-
shippers of Satan who posed a threat to Christ and His white
children. It was too often thought that the United States offered
Indians democracy and the light of civilization—things, ironically, already known to Native Americans.

The seven excerpts from Josephy's writing, which compose
the first part of this volume, demonstrate the broad scope of
his knowledge, as well as his deep understanding of the place
of Indian peoples and their leaders in American history. They
open windows and shed light on a world too often clouded by
myth and sheer ignorance.

First, in the opening chapter of *500 Nations*, Josephy explores Native Americans' rich oral literature about how their worlds came to be and how to live the good life. Their versions of creation conflicted with God giving mankind "dominion" over plants, animals, places, and resources; Indian songs and stories explained that man is only part of creation, not the ruler of animate and inanimate things. Josephy reminds us that before 1492, Native Americans lived in towns, villages, and communities all across North and South America. For thousands of years before the arrival of Europeans, Native Americans had enjoyed successful modes of government, education, the military, religion, medicine, trade, and agriculture. He describes the Mississippian, Anasazi, and Hohokam cultures, which disappeared, and the Haudenosaunee, who remain today in parts of the Northeast and whose political structure inspired the Founding Fathers of colonial times.

In his essay centered on Indian-white relations in the region bordering Long Island Sound—presently Connecticut, Rhode Island, and parts of Massachusetts—during the seventeenth century, Josephy describes typically shifting patterns of peaceful coexistence descending into divisiveness, violence, and war, all motivated by fear and hatred on the part of whites along with the inevitable pressures of the settlers' need for more and more land. Perhaps the most definitive episode of the history of such conflict was the Pequot War, in which white forces persuaded Indian tribes to join in attacks on the powerful Pequots. The war culminated in a massacre at a major Pequot village on the Mystic River. The invaders killed men, women, and children; set dogs on those who fled; and set the village aflame. Puritans and Pilgrims sold survivors into slavery and eased their guilt by comparing their campaign to David's wars in the Old Testament.

In the third excerpt we move to a biographical profile. Josephy points to Tecumseh, the early nineteenth-century Shawnee leader, as "the greatest Indian," among the nine patriot chiefs in his volume of the same title. The reasons are clear—and instructive for an understanding of the achievements possible for nations in the face of an encroaching white society. Tecumseh had the political vision to see, and fear, that if Indian people did not halt American expansionism, their lands, especially those north of the Ohio River, would be lost forever. That vision and the force of his personality led him to the formation of an intertribal confederacy unlike any seen before or since. Tecumseh and his allies fought valiantly on the side of the British in the War of 1812, but lost his life and his cause at the Battle of the Thames in Upper Canada. What he did not lose was his place in American history.

In his essay on the Hudson's Bay Company, Josephy details the development and expansion of an enterprise of fur trappers and traders in the northern regions of the American West, including present-day Canada. Despite the huge impact of the company on the economic and cultural life of Indians, its story is in a curious way no more than a sidebar in standard treatments of American Indians. Josephy points to one of the great ironies of American Indian history: that the entity offering in principle and in fact the fairest treatment of native peoples was an organization whose motivation was nothing other than more and more profit. It was capitalism in its purest form.

Josephy is at his best in the final excerpts in Part I, describing the decline of Indian power from the 1850s diplomatic submission to the Nez Perce military surrender in 1877.

In 1853, the United States split the Oregon Territory, creating a second half—Washington Territory. President Franklin

Pierce had appointed Isaac I. Stevens governor and superintendent of Indian affairs, and as surveyor of a northern railroad
route. Stevens arrived in Olympia, Washington, full of himself
and convinced he could liquidate Indian title to the lands,
and place Indians on reservations in short order. He coerced
coastal and Puget Sound tribes to sign treaties and forged
the names of Chief Leschi and his brothers on the Medicine
Creek Treaty. Deep tensions arose among coastal tribes who
reported their discontent to relatives on the eastern side of the
Cascade Mountains, where, at the Walla Walla Council, Indian
leaders emphasized their spiritual relationship with the earth,
explaining that they could not sell their land. In the end, they
capitulated, fearing that if they did not sign, the government
would steal all their land. Reluctant chiefs, including Chief Old
Joseph, signed the 1855 Nez Perce Treaty.

The Walla Walla Council and treaties had many consequences for the tribes. They lost millions of acres and billions
of dollars' worth of resources. The United States sent agents
to manage reservations and limit Indian movement across the
Plateau and mountains. And when miners discovered gold—
crucial to the Union cause in the Civil War—and overran the
Nez Perce Reservation, the government officials' answer was
to shrink the Nez Perce Reservation to one-tenth its original
size, reducing it by 6,932,270 acres. At a Lapwai Council in
1863, the Nez Perce Chief Lawyer and fifty-one of his followers
signed what "non-treaty" bands—non-signers—soon called
the "Thief Treaty," and the Commissioners sent it to Washington where the Senate and President Abraham Lincoln signed
it into law.

For many years after 1863, many Nez Perce leaders refused
to acknowledge the Thief Treaty, and Chief Joseph's band

lived quietly in the Wallowas. But with the end of the Civil War and Custer's debacle at the Little Bighorn, General William T. Sherman ordered his field commanders to place all non-reservation Indians onto reservations. Negotiations took place between agents and chiefs, Chief Joseph of the Nez Perce tried again and again to use diplomacy and patience to resolve differences. But in the end, General Oliver O. Howard showed the Indians "the rifle," threatening them to either move onto the Idaho reservation or face war. Chief Joseph later explained, "We were like deer. They were like the grizzly bears." The result, though not inevitable, due to the extraordinary endurance and military creativity of Chief Joseph's fleeing band, was that the grizzly caught the deer just miles short of escape into Canada.

After the Nez Perce War, the Bannock, Cheyenne, Apache, Ute, and others fought American politics of concentration, reservations, and assimilation. They resisted the government that sought to destroy Native American economies, religions, political systems, and family structures. Then came Wovoka, the Paiute Ghost Dance Prophet, who urged his people to remain native but live in peace with whites. He asked them to dance and sing in four day intervals to hasten a spiritual event and return to their old lives with plenty of game, seeds, vegetables, and fruit. Tribes across the American West adopted elements of the Ghost Dance and added to the prophet's doctrine. This last breath of resistance was peaceful, but ended with the impact of bullets on December 29, 1890. The 7th Cavalry had its answer to the defeat at the Little Bighorn in the massacre at Wounded Knee. The cause of Indian survival had an answer as well. Wounded Knee serves as a symbol of American treatment of Native Americans, confining them on reservations, suppressing religion, and forcing assimilationist policies.

Neither soldiers nor government officials could conquer or destroy Native Americans. They survived reservation agents, boarding school superintendents, and entrepreneurs eager to steal Indian lands and resources. Indians did not vanish as whites had predicted. Indians did not assimilate, but they acculturated into American society, where they have made their mark in many ways on their native soil. Alvin Josephy spent his life doing what he could to work with and for American Indian people, providing a voice for Indians in the hope of changing the way non-Indians presented the history of Native America. His work offered an important step for Indian people to follow. Now they would write their own stories and help build a new history centered on Native Americans and their interpretations of the past. After recounting his life history, Nez Perce Chief Yellow Wolf explained: "Nobody to help us tell our side—the whites told only one side. Told it to please themselves." Then along came Alvin Josephy.

1

A Continent Awakes

◇◇

Alvin Josephy was invited by Kevin Costner, Jim Wilson, and Jack Leustig to write 500 Nations, *published in 1994. The resulting elaborately illustrated volume "adheres closely" to the narrative of their similarly titled eight-hour television series, which ran in 1995. At the same time, the book serves well as a brilliant, readable, and authoritative narrative history of the Indian nations of North America. This first chapter tells the earlier story of these nations, beginning with their creation myths, then describes the highly developed and sophisticated civilizations of the Olmecs and Mayas. The story then moves north to the hunting tribes of the Great Plains, and on to the agricultural and trade-based societies of the mound building Hopewellians and Mississippians. From there Josephy takes us to the Iroquois, whose longhouses were perhaps the very birthplace of American democracy. And finally, we reach the Southwest, where the agriculturally sophisticated Hohokams and the mysterious Anasazi, along with others, survive as the Pueblos, Zunis, and Hopis of today.*

This chapter is a summary account but establishes a necessary background that clearly sets the stage for the story to come.

———————

On an unusually mild December day in 1890, a small band of hungry, desperate Miniconjou Sioux—one hundred twenty men and two hundred thirty women and children, led by their ailing chief, Big Foot—hurried across the hills of South Dakota's Pine Ridge Indian Reservation. The Miniconjous, some on ponies, others in aged wagons or trudging beside their travois, were tired from their long flight.

Fear drove them on. American armies were searching for them, intent on arresting Indians who continued to practice the banned Ghost Dance religion, which the whites believed was whipping them up for war. Long since defeated militarily and penned on reservations, many of the demoralized and helpless Plains tribes had turned to this new religion, which had reached them through Wovoka, a Paiute Indian holy man in far-off Nevada. Wovoka's message was peaceful: with certain dances, songs, and prayers, the tribes could bring back their dead ancestors, the vanished hosts of buffalo, and the old ways of life that had existed before the coming of the white man. To government agents and the army, the dancing Indians seemed, instead, to be preparing for an uprising. Two weeks before, Indian police, working for a fearful reservation agent, had murdered the great Hunkpapa Sioux chief Sitting Bull, whom the government regarded mistakenly as one of the leaders of the new religion. Then the army had sought to arrest Big Foot, whose Miniconjou band included many of the most devout Ghost Dancers.

In alarm, Big Foot and his people had abandoned their village on the Cheyenne River Sioux Reservation and fled for one hundred fifty miles across the plains and the silent, wintry Badlands, through snow and icy windstorms. Evading pursuing armies, they hoped to find safety on the Pine Ridge Reservation among Oglala Sioux followers of the aging Chief Red Cloud, who had invited them to come. During the journey, Big Foot, whom the Sioux knew as a quiet, generous man of peace and wisdom, often called on to settle quarrels among the bands, was stricken with pneumonia. His people put him in one of the lurching horse-drawn wagons, wrapped like a mummy in an old overcoat, a scarf, and a blanket. Blood dripped from his nose and froze on the floor of the open wagon bed, and the fugitive Miniconjous knew he was dying in the cold.

Now, having reached Pine Ridge, they were close to where they expected to reach Red Cloud's Oglalas. On this day, December 28, fate ran against them. Early in the afternoon, they topped a ridge. Spread across the lower ground, barring their way about two miles distant, was a long skirmish line of dismounted cavalrymen of the late Lieutenant Colonel George Armstrong Custer's old regiment, the 7th U.S. Cavalry, reconstituted after its disastrous defeat by Northern Cheyennes and Sioux—including the Miniconjous—fourteen years earlier at the battle of the Little Bighorn. Army-employed Oglala scouts had given notice to the military of the arrival of Big Foot's band on the Pine Ridge Reservation.

The Miniconjous debated what to do. They did not want to fight but decided that there was nowhere to go but straight ahead toward where they would find Red Cloud's people. Hoping they could parley peacefully with the soldiers, they attached a white cloth to a pole and raised it on the wagon that was carrying the sick chief. The women and children were fearful, and the men were tense but determined to defend the families. As the little band moved down the slope toward the waiting soldiers, the young warriors spread out to the right and left, forming a protective battle line opposite the troops.

At the bottom of the ridge, the Indians halted, and several went forward to ask the troops' commander, Major Samuel M. Whitside, for a parley. Whitside refused, demanding instead to see Big Foot. The chief's wagon was driven forward, and Whitside, leaning over from his horse, saw that the Indian was sick. The officer reached down and shook the chief's hand, then through an interpreter reassured him that if he surrendered, there would be no fighting. According to Whitside's account, Big Foot agreed to surrender and with his people accompany the troops across the hills to where the cavalrymen had their camp—to Chankpe Opi Wakpala, said the Sioux interpreter, Wounded Knee Creek. That was all right, Big Foot nodded. It was in the direction where his people were going anyway.

So they set off together, troops and Indians, both of them watchful and on edge, and that night they camped together sleeplessly at Wounded Knee Creek. The next morning, a random shot started a panic. By noon, it was over. The mild-mannered chief, Big Foot, and almost two hundred fifty members of his band were dead, some of them lying in heaps where the soldiers had first surrounded them and where Hotchkiss guns had mowed them down. Others were strewn across the frozen campgrounds and in the ravines where screaming survivors had tried to flee from the frenzied hatred of the troops. More than fifty additional Miniconjous, some of whom would not survive, were wounded, and still others who had got away were thought to have died or been wounded. The frightened cavalrymen had also suffered, many by their own cross fire. The army counted twenty-five dead of its own and thirty-seven soldiers and two civilians (an interpreter and a priest) wounded.

In the smoke and agony of the massacre at Wounded

Knee on that morning of December 29, 1890, there died the last tortured hope of freedom among the Indian nations of North America. That night it turned suddenly cold, and the snow began to fall gently and covered the fallen bodies. It was the end of a long story of dreams and drama and courage, one that had involved many different peoples of hundreds of Indian nations and had begun in myths and shadows when humans were new-made and still young, fifteen thousand or more years ago. . . .

Creation

In the nineteenth century, most of the Sioux people like the Miniconjous lived on the Great Plains, and it was there that the last of the great battles and confrontations took place between the expanding whites and the resisting Indians whom they were dispossessing. Largely because of the romance and color of the mounted Plains tribes and the skills and fierce determination of their chiefs and warriors, which dime novels, Wild West shows, and movies publicized far and wide, the Great Plains came to be associated in the minds of non-Indian peoples throughout the world as the land of the North American Indians.

What is little understood even today, however, is that almost every community in Canada, the United States, and Mexico was once an Indian community, and those communities before the arrival of the whites were part of hundreds of unique Indian nations that blanketed the entire continent. They reached from the Atlantic to the Pacific and from Central America to the Arctic, with borders between many of them that dated back to far before the time of the Roman Empire. Including Mexico and the Caribbean, it was a continent of perhaps as many as forty million people, some nomadic, but most of them permanently settled in communities that ranged in size up to cities as large and sophisticated as any in the world at that time. Every part of the land and all of the natural world within it was sacred to one Indian nation or another.

Not unlike today, the most dense populations were along the coasts and the major rivers, around the Great Lakes, and in Mexico, Florida, and the Caribbean islands and California. Six hundred distinct languages were spoken by the different communities, bands, and chiefdoms that made up the nations. There were Indian kings and prophets, artisans and architects, sculptors and poets, mathematicians and doctors. Land and water trade networks interconnected the continent, spreading commodities and ideas. In medicine, sports, military service, dance, religion, diplomacy, art, and a dozen other fields, Indian children could dream of personal accomplishments. And not unlike today, also, all of these possibilities existed in a different way in each nation. Traditions, environment, and form of government all played a role in giving each nation an individual identity and directing it along an individual path. Some were committed by thousands of years of tradition to perfecting an unchanging way of life. Others built massive armies and military empires.

From the very first arrival of Europeans in the Western Hemisphere, the whites marveled at what they saw and wondered where it had all come from. Who were the peoples of these Indian nations, they asked, and where did they originate? The question tantalized generations of non-Indian scholars and scientists, some of whom spent lifetimes trying to prove that the Indians were descendants of seafaring Phoenicians or Chinese, pyramid-building Egyptians, one of the Lost Tribes of Israel, Welshmen, or even survivors of Plato's legendary lost continent of Atlantis.

The question of their origin never puzzled most Indian nations. All human societies have possessed versions of their own beginnings, and the Indians of North America have been no different. Stories of natural or supernatural creation on their own land or of emergence from another, lower world or of migration from elsewhere have existed among all Indian tribes and, like the white man's biblical narrative of Genesis, have been clung to as matters of faith and spiritual truth.

Among the Nez Perce and other Indian peoples of the mountainous Northwest, generations of grandparents told children stories of a time when the world was inhabited only by animals, all of whom spoke like humans and had human-like characteristics. Living by one of the waterways was a fierce monster who kept all the animals in fear by devouring them. Finally, the bold and courageous Coyote, the tribe's culture hero, jumped down the monster's throat and killed him by sawing up his heart with a flint. When the monster was dead, Coyote cut its body into small pieces, creating from each part a different tribe. In each case, the group telling the story related that it had sprung from the monster's heart or blood, which had made it the bravest and wisest of all the tribes.

In the desert Southwest, Hopi, Zuni, and Pueblo descendants of the Anasazis and other radiant pre-Columbian societies possess a body of sacred-origin stories. Some of them tell of the emergence of their people through a hole, known as *sipapu*, from an underground lake. Others relate in great detail the climb of their ancestors toward perfection through three underworlds and their final emergence through *sipapu* into the present, or fourth, world. All of them then tell of migrations to the sites that became their homes in this world.

The most common origin stories, however, illustrate a close spiritual bond between the Indians and all of creation within their universe. The Creator, the Master of Life, the Great Spirit, Wakan Tanka—whatever terms the various Native American groups used—breathed life into humans and bound their spirits to those of all else in their universe. "My strength, my blood is from the fish, from the roots and berries . . . and game," said a Yakima man. "I . . . did not come here. I was put here by the Creator." At the same time, Taos Pueblo elders told their young,

> When Earth was still young and giants still roamed the land, a great sickness came upon them. All of them died except for a small boy. One day while he was playing, a snake bit him. The boy cried and cried. The blood came out, and finally he died. With his tears our lakes became. With his blood the red clay became. With his body our mountains became, and that was how Earth became.

Most tribes believed that the people of their nation were created on their land, and their land, where they were created, was the center of the world. But there was a symbiosis between the land and the people. Because of their spiritual attachment, one gave life to the other, and it behooved humans to keep that attachment in balance and harmony by proper conduct and thoughts, lest it harm the people's well-being.

As might be expected, traditional tribal versions of the Indians' origins differ greatly from the beliefs of modern-day science. In contrast to the certainties of the Indians' stories, however, the scientists themselves are still far from possessing all the answers. Since no remains of a pre–Homo sapiens type of man have ever been discovered in the Americas, it is assumed that humans did not evolve there, as they did on other continents, but arrived in the Western Hemisphere after the development of modern man. Most of the scientists and scholars also agree—from archaeological findings in Siberia, Mongolia, and North America, and studies in linguistics, physical anthropology, and other disciplines—that the Indians came in one or more migrations from eastern Asia, crossing a land bridge to Alaska that appeared from time to time during the Ice Age when the formation of huge glaciers caused the sea levels to fall by as much as three hundred feet.

So far, scientists do not agree on much more, including the date of the arrival of the first migrants from Asia. It is thought that the land bridge across what is now the Bering Strait existed sometime between seventy thousand and thirty thousand years ago; again from twenty-five thousand to fifteen thousand years ago; and once or twice more between approximately fourteen thousand and ten thousand years ago. During any of these periods, small bands of Asian hunters and their families, following herds of mastodons and other large Ice Age game animals across the land bridge or along its coasts, could have reached Alaska. From archaeological discoveries, all that is known definitely is that people were living in all parts of North and South America by at least twelve thousand years ago—long before the time of Egypt, Phoenicia, China, Israel, or any other nation known to history. Indeed, gaining increasing acceptance, but still controversial, are finds from Alaska to Chile and from Pennsylvania to California suggesting the presence of people in the Americas even earlier—perhaps as long as thirty-five thousand, or even fifty thousand, years ago.

Whether the ancestors of the Indian nations came in one wave or in separate movements at different times during the Ice Age, once they entered Alaska, they and their descendants continued to hunt the mastodons and other big-game animals, killing them in group attacks with spears, clubs, and ingenious spear-throwing shafts called *atlatls*, but living also by fishing and gathering wild foods. Gradually, they moved with the animals along ice-free routes on the Alaskan coasts, up the Yukon and other river valleys, and south along the chains of the Rocky Mountains, through natural corridors that existed from time to time between the massive glaciers. Eventually, reaching the vast tundra and forest environments south of the ice sheets, the bands spread toward the Atlantic Coast and to Central and South America.

In their movements, the people often sheltered themselves in caves or beneath overhanging rocks. But it would be wrong to think of them as stereotypical "cavemen," with stooped shoulders, heavy brows, and dull, brutish features. Physically, they were fully developed modern people, intelligent, sensitive, and already endowed with spiritual impulses that bound them as relatives under a common creator to their natural surroundings and to the various plant and animal sources of their food. In a material way, they were also more advanced than is generally thought. Their chipped stone tools, weapons, and utensils were among the most efficient in the world at that time; in addition, they were adept at fashioning trim hide clothing and basketry sandals, painting various possessions, and making personal adornments and religious objects from stone, horns, bones, walrus-tusk ivory, shells, and other natural materials.

Although their population at first was sparse, here and there the bands came in contact with one another, combined, divided into new groups, or drove one another into less hospitable and accessible areas. Until about ten thousand years ago, these bands shared North America with the great mammoths, mastodons, outsize bison and bears, giant sloths, small prehistoric horses, and other animals of the Ice Age. Then the Ice Age came to an end, the great glaciers receded, and the earth was re-formed. The tundra and evergreen forests at the southern edge of the ice sheets moved north, following the retreating glaciers, and were replaced by great grassland prairies, hardwood forests, and arid plains and plateaus. Jungles grew in Mexico, and virgin woodlands covered North America from the Atlantic Coast to the center of the continent. And in two thousand years, all the mastodons, giant sloths, miniature horses, saber-toothed tigers, and many other animals of the Ice Age became extinct.

In most parts of the continent, the humans studied the smaller creatures that had survived with them and, changing their hunting methods and the size of their spear points, hunted deer, antelope, and other small animals, at the same time relying more on fish and shellfish and the gathering of nuts, berries, grass, seeds, and wild vegetables and fruits. With the passage of time, different groups came to identify themselves with special parts of the land, understanding in some cases that it was the place of their ancestors' origin or in others that the Creator or other supernatural beings meant them to live there. Century after century, they established spiritual harmony with their particular territory, learning to understand and take care of its resources so that the resources, in turn, would take care of them.

In time, as population increased and the ancient Indians adapted to the different environments, cultural and physical variations began to appear among them. Those along the coasts developed maritime-oriented cultures with economies based largely on their ability to harvest fish and collect shellfish. In the eastern forests and California, woodland peoples learned to use fire to clear the land for new growth that would increase the yield of deer and other animals. In the Canadian North, caribou hunters traveled on snowshoes and employed mannequins to herd frightened animals into corrals. In the Great Basin of the West, one of the harshest and poorest regions on the continent, nomadic bands, living on anything that was edible, including pine nuts and desert reptiles, established a satisfactory and stable way of life that lasted for thousands of years, into the nineteenth century. And in Mexico and river valleys in the East, hunters and gatherers began to turn into part-time farmers, learning below the Rio Grande how to grow corn, beans, and squash and in the eastern woodlands cultivating such edible plants as sunflowers, sumpweed, and goosefoot. In every part of the continent the ancient Indian peoples continued to build relationships with their land, harmonizing their needs with what their natural worlds could provide them, and their spiritual life with the spirits of all of the universe about them.

The Buffalo

Most Indian nations of North America lived in the equivalent of what Christianity would call the Garden of Eden—the place of creation—the place of plenty, the single place on earth most perfect for them. For every nation that place was unique.

"The Crow country is a good country," said Arapooish, a leader of the Crow Indians of Montana, to white men in the nineteenth century. "The Great Spirit put it exactly in the right place; while you are in it you fare well; whenever you are out of it, whichever way you travel, you fare worse. . . . The Crow country is exactly in the right place. Everything good is to be found there. There is no place like Crow country."

On the northern Great Plains, long before Arapooish's time, the ancient peoples lived on a vast homeland of grass cut by occasional rivers and streams lined by trees and underbrush. Small extended families of fewer than twenty-five people moved in seasonal rounds of hunting game and gathering berries, nuts, seeds, and roots. They had no horses; they were people on foot, depending on experience and intelligence to guide them. But among the many foods and natural resources available to them, one animal above all others—the bison— truly provided for them.

"The great Father of Life who made us and gave us this land to live upon, made the buffalo . . . to afford us sustenance," said a warrior of the northern Plains. "Their meat is our only food; with their skins we clothe ourselves and build our lodges. They are our only means of life—food, fuel, and clothing." He, like Arapooish, was talking to whites in the nineteenth century, but he might have been speaking as well for his ancestors of thousands of years before. The ancient Indians of the northern Plains studied, revered, and established strong spiritual relationships between themselves and the buffalo, associating the animal directly with the Creator and centering most of their religious life around the great shaggy beast. And no wonder. No animal, the Indians said, ever gave so much of itself to people. There was almost no part of the buffalo that Plains Indian nations did not use: the tongue and flesh for food; the rawhide for shields, buckets, moccasins, rattles, drums, bullboats, ropes, splints, thongs, and containers; the hair for headdresses, ornaments, and ropes; the tail for brushes; the horns for cups, fire carriers, and ladles; the hooves for glue and rattles; the skull for ceremonies and rituals; the beard for ornamentation; the bladder for sinews, pouches, and bags; the muscles for thread, glue, and sinews; the paunch for the lining of cups, basins, and buckets; the scrotum for rattles; the stomach for medicines and the lining of containers; the bones for clubs, sleds, game dice, knives, scrapers, awls, digging sticks, and other implements and utensils; the chips for fuel; and the hide for clothing, robes, cradles, bags, lodge covers, dolls, and a hundred other products.

For people in small bands who had to move on foot, hunting the large, aggressive buffalo that traveled in huge herds and stampeded easily could be especially dangerous and not always successful. There were more effective ways to hunt, and for that many Plains bands would come together in tribal gatherings near a herd. Cooperatively, they would lay out drive lanes, like avenues across the plains, lining them with piles of rocks and brush behind which their hunters could hide. The drive lanes were funnel-shaped, with their wide mouths near the herd and the narrow ends leading into a stout-walled corral or pound, or to the abrupt edge of a steep cliff or bluff over which the stampeding animals could be driven to their death. The killing site was known to the Indians as a *piskun*, meaning a deep-blood-kettle, and later-coming whites called the cliff-type hunting sites buffalo jumps.

In southern Alberta is a famous one, used by the people of the northern Plains for more than five thousand years. It is called the Head-Smashed-In Buffalo Jump for an unfortunate Indian of long ago who, legend says, became trapped against the base of the cliff and was crushed under the weight of the falling animals. Today, Head-Smashed-In is a vivid example of what the many buffalo jumps on the northern Plains were like and how they were used.

First, the peoples' shamans, or spiritual leaders, went out on the plains and, employing *iniskims*, small, buffalo-shaped stones that were believed to have the power to attract the bison herds, called to the buffalo to come toward the drive lanes. As the herd moved slowly toward the lanes, the hunters who were hiding emerged suddenly from behind the rocks and brush and, shouting and waving robes, panicked the animals into a thundering rush down the funnel and over the cliff or into the corral or pound. Indians lining the kill areas at the foot of the cliff easily dispatched the stunned and injured animals that had not died in the fall, and Indian women hurried to skin and butcher the slaughtered bison, making use of virtually everything. At one time, the cliff at Head-Smashed-In was a sheer drop of more than sixty feet, but talus from the crumbling cliff edge and the bones of hundreds of thousands of animals who plunged blindly to their death have piled up century after century until the fall is less than thirty-five feet.

The mass hunts were hard work and often dangerous, but they were also a spiritual communion between the people and the bounty, who were giving their lives to sustain the Indians.

While the skillful method that drove the bison into pounds or over the cliffs was impressive and could mean the difference between the people's well-being and starvation, an equally notable accomplishment was the Indians' ability to coordinate the gatherings for the cooperative hunt. Small bands, scattered over thousands of square miles of High Plains country, had to be brought together—had to know where and when to meet. How it was achieved is still debated. Some believe that an answer may lie in remarkable creations in stone found in various parts of the northern Plains and known as medicine wheels.

Formed by piles of rocks laid out on the ground in a pattern of concentric circles or ovals intersected by spokes radiating out from a central cairn, the medicine wheels were undoubtedly sacred sites, used by northern Plains peoples for vision quests, prayers, and other spiritual purposes. But they may also have allowed the users to create an annual calendar based on the relation of the spokes to the positions of the sun or certain stars. It would have been easy to keep track of the time for traveling to communal hunts, as well as for other things, such as when berries would ripen in a particular valley or when waterfowl would return to a certain lake.

In addition, some archaeologists have speculated that the reckoning of time by the northern Plains bands may not have been the only use of the wheels. Hunting and gathering peoples traveling in small groups needed an intimate knowledge of their territory. The medicine wheels, most of which were located on high points that provided expansive views, may have offered people the ability to familiarize themselves with the land the Creator had given them. Spokes pointed out toward major landmarks and toward other medicine wheels on far-off peaks. Year after year and from one generation to another through the course of centuries, hunters could have used the wheels to learn the shape of their world and, by studying several wheels, construct a mental picture of thousands of square miles of territory. When traveling great distances, for example to the tribal hunts, they would have been able to read the landscape and know where they were and where they were going.

In that sense, the wheels could have been pathfinders and maps as well as calendars. Whatever roles they actually played in the lives of the ancient peoples, however, Indian nations of the northern Plains still hold them sacred. It is hard to imagine otherwise. In their silence and timelessness, the medicine wheels have connected people with the supernatural, the land, and with one another through uncounted generations.

The City of the North: Cahokia

The heart of the continent is bisected by the Mississippi, one of the world's great rivers. With its hundreds of tributaries, some as major as the Ohio, the Missouri, the Tennessee, the Arkansas, and the Red, the Mississippi's network links a third of North America by water. Along these rivers and across much of the center of the continent there developed, beginning about AD 700, one of the most spectacular and least known of the great North American Indian civilizations, that of the Mississippians, given that name by archaeologists because their culture appears to have originated along the bottomlands of the middle Mississippi and the lower Ohio, Illinois, and Tennessee Rivers. Known also as Temple Mound Builders for the religious structures that surmounted their huge, flat-topped earthen mounds, they had evolved over many centuries and were the stunning climax of other mound-building societies that had preceded them.

As early as 1500 BC, Indians in some parts of the northeastern woodlands had adopted the practice of burying their dead, along with personal ornaments, tools, and other grave goods, on ridges, knolls, and other elevated sites. Later, some groups began raising dome-shaped mounds of earth above the burials. By about 1000 BC, this simple burial-mound practice, reflecting spiritual motives, developed into the more sophisticated Adena culture, spreading among peoples in the Ohio Valley, New York, and New England who, though they still hunted and gathered wild foods, had domesticated local plants like sumpweed, marsh elder, squash, and sunflowers and had settled down in permanent or semi-permanent villages. Without maize, the population was still small, but the Adena Indians built circular earthworks and large mounds and turned out as well many utilitarian and artistic objects, often of mica and copper.

About AD 200, maize finally reached some of the mound-building peoples, diffusing north, probably from the Southwest or Mexico. Population increased, and a new, vital mound-building culture, the Hopewell (named for the owner of one of its principal sites in the Ohio Valley), replaced the Adena and spread among proliferating Indian farming villages along the rivers of the Midwest and East. Flourishing until about AD 500, the Hopewellian civilization was far more complex than the Adena. Large ceremonial centers, with elaborately constructed earthen walls, contained conical or dome-shaped burial mounds up to thirty feet or more in height and two hundred feet in circumference. Religious leaders and the elite dwelled in the centers, surrounded by the nearby farming settlements and the round or oval-shaped wigwams of the general population.

One of the most distinctive achievements of the Hopewellians was the creation of an amazing trade network that was almost continent-wide and brought to the Hopewellian centers objects and materials from the Atlantic Coast to the Rocky Mountains and from the Great Lakes to the Gulf of Mexico. Hopewellian artists and artisans flourished, using the materials received from the trade to turn out a wealth of articles, including sacred and ceremonial objects, pendants, necklaces, armbands, and other decorative items; panpipes and rattles, tools, spoons and other utensils; and stone pipe bowls sculptured beautifully in the form of humans and animals. Fashioned from copper, bone, antler, stone, and shell, many of the objects were buried in the mounds with their deceased owners.

The mounds and other evidence suggest that Hopewellians had a highly developed social system that included a class structure, with rulers of hereditary rank and privileges; a strong religious system; specialists like artists, traders, and metalworkers; and organized direction over cooperative labor. After AD 500, the Hopewell star faded. It is not known what happened, or why. Perhaps the trade network on which so much had depended collapsed. At any rate, artistic abilities declined, fewer large burial mounds were constructed, and in various places people took to building instead enormous effigy mounds, probably with spiritual functions or meanings, in the shape of birds, animals, serpents, and humans. All along the river valleys, new groups with changing ideas and cultures of their own were emerging. By AD 700, one of them, the Mississippians, with a population increasing rapidly from the harvests of a new, highly productive strain of corn, took over.

Few cultures compare with the endurance and continuity of that of the Mississippians, which lasted for nine hundred years. During its long existence, great Mississippian urban centers—Ocmulgee, Etowah, Moundville, Spiro, and others—arose, from the Atlantic Coast to Arkansas and Oklahoma. Within the centers, earthen mounds, many of them much bigger than any yet seen, were topped by temples or homes of rulers or religious leaders and served as settings for public rituals and spectacles. Unlike the Adena and Hopewellian mounds, few of those constructed by the Mississippians were for burials. Like the Hopewellians, the Mississippians put together great trade networks that connected them with many different nations. Over the networks, through the countries of peoples speaking different languages, traveled the commerce of the Mississippian world by Indian traders in dugouts or canoes or on foot. Pottery, weaving, and copper came from the Great Lakes; obsidian from the Yellowstone country in the far west; mica and crystal from the Appalachians; gold and silver from Canada; and conch shells from the Gulf of Mexico.

By the year 1000, much of the continent was again interconnected by trade. At its center, and at the center of the Mississippian world, three miles from the Mississippi River, across from the site of present-day St. Louis, one powerful city, Cahokia, stood alone. It was the largest urban community in the history of what would be the United States prior to the nineteenth century. Only in 1800 did the population of Philadelphia finally surpass the historic size of the Indian Cahokia. For almost seven hundred years, it was inhabited, and for three hundred years, from AD 850 to AD 1150, it was the heart of the Mississippian civilization.

The elite walled city of five square miles, containing more than a hundred large and small truncated pyramids and earthen mounds, was renowned over tens of thousands of square miles. At its peak, perhaps more than ten thousand people lived within the city in homes of wattle and daub, with thousands more dwelling in outlying villages along the Mississippi River's bottomlands. Farmers, fishermen, hunters, artisans, builders, traders, and other specialists supplied the needs of an elite class of war chiefs and political and religious officials and their families and retainers who inhabited the city. At the top of the social system was Cahokia's absolute ruler, a revered chieftain known as the Great Sun, who dwelled with his relatives on the flattened top of Cahokia's biggest mound. Now called Monks Mound, it was ten stories high and had an earthen base far larger than that of any pyramid in Egypt or Mexico. From this forbidden holy estate, elevated toward the sky above the bustling urban center, Cahokia's hereditary monarch, the head of both state and religion, ruled like a god over all aspects of Mississippian life.

While centuries passed and other nations and civilizations around the world rose and fell, Cahokia lived on, and the Mississippian civilization spread its influences among scores of Indian societies, sometimes peacefully and sometimes by violence. Large, opulent centers of the Temple Mound Builders appeared from Florida to Texas, bound together loosely by common rituals, art motifs, symbols, and practices like the purification rites involving the use of a powerful emetic known as the Black Drink.

In time, Cahokia came to an end. By the sixteenth century,

when invading Spanish conquistadors marched through the Mississippians' country, this once-great Indian urban center on the Mississippi River had become a ghost city of overgrown mounds. Perhaps it had outgrown its ability to feed itself, forcing its population to disperse and migrate elsewhere. But across the South, the Europeans found many Temple Mound Building nations still flourishing—Timucuas, Cherokees, Coosas, Muskokees, Mobiles, Choctaws, Chickasaws, Quapaws, and others—and in the country of the lower Mississippi as late as the eighteenth century they encountered a regal Indian atop a grand mound who was carried on a litter and was venerated as a god, the Great Sun of the Natchez nation. He was the last major mound builder.

The influence of the Mississippians was felt most strongly across the southeastern part of what is now the United States. In the Northeast and in the area of the Great Lakes, meanwhile, the demise of the preceding Hopewellian civilization about AD 500–700 had been followed by the ascendance of a number of different regional and local groups. Among them were the ancestors of the Iroquois, a family of Indian nations destined for greatness.

The Haudenosaunee: Dawn of Democracy

Whenever the statesmen of the League shall assemble for the purpose of holding a council, the Onondaga statesmen shall open it by expressing their gratitude to their cousin statesmen, and greeting them, and they shall make an address and offer thanks to the earth where men dwell, to the streams of water, the pools and the lakes, to the maize and the fruits, to the medicinal herbs and trees, to the forest trees for their usefulness, and to the animals that serve as food and give their pelts for clothing, to the great winds and the lesser winds, to the Thunderers; to the Sun, the mighty warrior; to the moon, to the messengers of the Creator who reveal his wishes, and to the Great Creator who dwells in the heavens above who gives all the things useful to men, and who is the source and the ruler of health and life.

Then shall the Onondaga statesmen declare the Council open. . . . All the business . . . shall be conducted by the two combined bodies of Confederate statesmen. First the question shall be passed upon by the Mohawk and Seneca statesmen, then it shall be discussed and passed by the Oneida and Cayuga statesmen. Their decision shall then be referred to the Onondaga statesmen, the Firekeepers, for final judgment.

> —*From the Great Law of Peace of the League of the Haudenosaunee, or Iroquois*

Surrounded in large part by Algonquian-speaking people, five nations of the Haudenosaunee or Iroquois—the Mohawks, Onondagas, Cayugas, Oneidas, and Senecas—lived side by side in long parallel bands of territory running north-south in the valleys along the lakes of what is upper New York State. By AD 1000, they had been well established for centuries. Skillfully managing the natural bounty of the region, they hunted, fished, gathered nuts, berries, and other wild foods, and cultivated increasingly productive gardens, principally of corn, beans, and squash.

The tribes were divided into clans that served as extended

families, with clan membership passing from mother to child. Within the clans, the children were taught by elders, the needy and the sick were cared for, and community responsibilities were defined. When persons were ready to marry, they had to do so outside of their own clan—an injunction that tended to weave the entire tribe together into a single great family. The clans lived in large bark-covered longhouses, barrel roofed, like the Quonset huts of World War II, and extending up to two hundred feet in length and twenty-five feet in width. A single longhouse could shelter ten or a dozen families through a harsh winter, each one with its own private space and a fire that it shared with others. The family sections contained raised platforms covered with reed mats or pelts that served as seats during the day and beds at night. Articles of clothing were hung on the walls or, with food and supplies, were stored in bark bins and baskets.

Theirs was a world in which each person, man and woman, had an important function. Men were hunters and warriors, providers and protectors of the community. Women owned the houses, gathered wild foods, cooked, made baskets and clothing, and cared for the children. Spiritual life, strong and pervasive throughout the society, was highly organized. It included a priesthood of men and women, Keepers of the Faith, who supervised religious rites and various secret organizations that performed curing and other ceremonies. Like many Indians, the Iroquois believed that the spirits of all humans were joined to those of the objects and forces of nature, and, in addition, that a human's own inner spiritual power, called *orenda*, combated the powers of evil that could harm the individual as well as the rest of the people. Although an individual's *orenda* was small, it contributed to the total *orenda* possessed by a family group or clan. When a person died, the group's total *orenda* was reduced and was often replenished by the adoption of a captive or a member of another tribe to acquire his or her *orenda*.

Bravery and fortitude were highly respected virtues among the Iroquois. When a man died in warfare against an enemy, it was the clan, not just the parents or wife of the fighting man, that mourned the loss. In addition, the clan was held responsible for avenging the warrior's death. Generations ago, prior to the coming of the white man, an unending cycle of raid and counter-raid, death and revenge, began to run out of control among the five Haudenosaunee nations. The fabric of their civilization was on the verge of being torn apart by the feuds and warfare among them. Attempts to break the cycle of violence had been thwarted repeatedly by a sinister Onondaga war priest named Thadodaho, who in Iroquois legend was a monstrous figure with snakes for hair, hands like turtle claws, and the feet of a bear. Committed to warfare and the death and destruction of his enemies, he opposed all efforts to achieve peace. One year, a visionary Huron elder named Deganawida appeared in the Iroquois territory, preaching a powerful message of peace. In his travels, he met an Onondaga man named Hiawatha, who was himself caught in the violence of the time. Hiawatha listened to the message of Deganawida. The Peace Maker, as Deganawida was coming known, conceived of thirteen laws by which people and nations could live in peace and unity—a democracy where the needs of all would be accommodated without violence and bloodshed. To a modern American, it would suggest a society functioning under values and laws similar to those of the Ten Commandments and the U.S. Constitution combined. Each of its laws included a moral structure:

> In all of your . . . acts, self-interest shall be cast away. . . .
> Look and listen for the welfare of the whole people, and
> have always in view not only the present, but also the
> coming generations . . . the unborn of the future Nation.

Hiawatha became a supporter of the Peace Maker and his Great Law and, because of his strong oratorical skills, was its principal spokesman, constructing, according to legend, the first wampum belt, a beaded system of coded information employed in reciting the Great Law. Then, with this system for recording and expressing their beliefs, both Deganawida the Peace Maker and Hiawatha took the word to each of the most powerful leaders among the five tribes. The simple truth and justice of the new law was undeniable, and soon only one chief, Thadodaho, stood as an obstacle to regional peace. Hiawatha went to the village of the violent leader and, using all his skills of persuasion, expressed the dream of peace. So moving was the message that, as legend has it, Thadodaho was transformed from a demon into a man, and finally to a champion of the Great Law. The Haudenosaunee, or Iroquois, Confederacy had begun. The Peace Maker then planted as a symbol of peace a great white pine tree.

> Under the shade of this Tree of Great Peace . . . there
> shall you sit and watch the Fire of the League of Five
> Nations. . . . Roots have spread out from the Tree of Great
> Peace. . . . These are the Great White Roots, and their

nature is Peace and Strength. If any man or any nation
shall obey the laws of the Great Peace . . . they may trace
back the roots to the Tree. . . . They shall be welcomed to
take shelter beneath the Great Evergreen Tree.

To administer the law, the Haudenosaunee imposed an
order and a structure on their world. They envisioned the
combined territory of the five nations as a gigantic longhouse
that stretched two hundred fifty miles across the present-day
state of New York. The Great Longhouse's central aisle was
the Haudenosaunee Trail, the principal route of communication between the different members of the League. The eastern end of the domain was guarded by the Mohawks, who
were declared the Keepers of the Eastern Door. The Senecas
watched over the western door, and the Onondagas, located
at the center, were the Keepers of the Fire for all five member
nations of the Great Longhouse.

The posts conceived as supporting the Great Longhouse
symbolically represented the tribal chiefs, who among the Iroquois attained their position in a unique way. In each nation,
the women of every clan selected the most respected woman
among them to be the clan mother. The clan mothers, in turn,
appointed the male chiefs to represent the clans at the Grand
Council. In this way, the men most trusted by their people for
wisdom, integrity, vision, fairness, oratorical ability, and other
statesmanlike qualities were given the responsibility of the
Great Law:

With endless patience, they shall carry out their duty. Their
firmness shall be tempered with a tenderness for their peo-
ple. Neither anger nor fury shall find lodging in their minds,

and all their words and actions shall be marked by calm
deliberation.

The structure of the Haudenosaunee government, allowing
different states to coexist under one rule of law, was a concept
in democracy. The Grand Council met at the Haudenosaunee
capital of Onondaga. The Oneidas and Cayugas, the younger
brothers in the League, sat to the west of the council fire; the
elder brothers, the Mohawks and Senecas, sat to the east, with
the Onondagas to the north. Decisions were made by the representatives of each nation, who first reached consensus among
themselves; then the brothers on the east and west would confer until they reached consensus. After that was accomplished,
the elder brothers passed their decision to the younger brothers. If the younger brothers could accept the decision, the permanent leader of the council, an Onondaga, would announce
consensus. If, on the other hand, the younger brothers could
not accept the decision of the elder brothers, the Onondaga
would cast the deciding vote and break the deadlock.

The system worked. The confederacy envisioned by the
Peace Maker and Hiawatha, together with the republican
and democratic principles that lay at the heart of its form
of self-government, influenced enlightened seventeenth- and
eighteenth-century white philosophers and writers in the colonies and Europe who were seeking just ways for their own
people to be governed. In 1754 Benjamin Franklin's Albany
Plan of Union for the British colonies drew inspiration from
the example of the Iroquois League. Later, the structure of the
League had an indirect influence, through the studies of the
political philosophers by the Founding Fathers of the United
States, not only on the union of the colonies, but on the gov-

ernment of the United States as it was constituted in 1789. In the method, for instance, by which Congress reaches consensus on bills through compromise meetings of House and Senate conferees, one may recognize similarities to the way in which the Iroquois League functioned.

The new United States did not go as far as the Haudenosaunees, for, unlike the Indians, it did not accord equality to all men and both genders among its people. While the United States and other nations of the world struggled during later generations to rectify such inequities, the Great Law of the Haudenosaunee remained unchanged and still guides the Grand Council of the People of the Longhouse—one of the world's oldest continuing democracies—to this day.

The Anasazis

Far off in the American Southwest, Indian peoples, in the meantime, had developed still other high cultures and civilizations totally unlike those of the Mound Builders or the politically astute Iroquois in the Northeast. Among them were the ancestors of the present-day Pueblos, Zunis, and Hopis of New Mexico and Arizona. Still among some of the most traditional Indians in the Americas, most of them—as expressed by a modern-day Bluebird chief of one of the Hopi villages—continue to observe the spiritual beliefs and practices of their forefathers of thousands of years ago:

> *Our religious teachings are based upon the proper care of*
> *our land and the people who live upon it. We must not*
> *lose the way of life of our religion. . . . We believe in that;*

we live it, day by day. . . . We the leaders of the traditional
Hopi . . . want our way of life to continue on; for ourselves,
for our children, and for their children who come after.

The forefathers of the modern-day tribes were themselves descendants of some of the earliest-known peoples in the Americas—nomadic groups who had hunted mastodons and other big-game animals across much of the Southwest during the Ice Age. Later, when the glaciers retreated and those animals disappeared, the people developed a different culture, suited to the more arid conditions. Based on fishing and the hunting of small animals and birds, but most important on the gathering of all manner of edible, wild-growing foods, their lifeway is known to archaeologists as the Desert Culture. Spread far and wide through the dry country of the West and into northern Mexico, it lasted in various places, particularly in the desert areas of the Great Basin, for almost ten thousand years.

In some areas, however, beginning about 1000 BC, agricultural knowledge and skills were introduced from Mexico, and during the following two thousand years, three major civilizations of farming peoples arose in parts of the region. The first, the Mogollon, developed in the forested mountain country along the present Arizona–New Mexico border. Some of the Mogollon Indians, who lived in New Mexico's Mimbres Valley from approximately AD 750 to 1250, were expert potters, whose works, painted with exquisite natural figures or geometric designs, have been acclaimed by art critics and collectors as among the most beautiful produced anywhere in the world, including ancient Greece. When the Indian owner of a pot died, holes were punched through it to "kill" the spirit of its painted figures, and the pot was buried in the owner's grave, where archaeologists and modern-day pot hunters and grave robbers have found them.

The origin of a second civilization, the Hohokams, which was centered in the hot, lower desert country of southern Arizona, is still something of a puzzle. Archaeologists are not yet decided on whether the Hohokams were a migrant group who brought their culture with them from Mexico, or whether they evolved locally from previous Desert Culture Indians.* Flourishing from approximately 300 BC to AD 1450, they were highly skilled farmers who seem to have introduced irrigation agriculture to the arid West, building hundreds of miles of canals to carry water from the Salt and other rivers to their fields of maize, beans, squash, and cotton around present-day Phoenix and Tucson. The Hohokams maintained trade networks with tribes in northern Mexico, including peoples who lived along the Gulf of California, produced many articles of artistic beauty, and constructed ball courts similar to those used much farther south by the Mayas and other nations of Mesoamerica. Their end is also in doubt, although it is widely believed that they were the ancestors of today's O'Odham (Pima and Papago) Indian nations of the Southwest.

---

* Eds. note: "Early archaeologists proposed that Hohokam culture developed in Mexico and moved into what is now Arizona. In the 1990s, a major archaeological dig along the Santa Cruz River in Tucson resulted in a startling discovery. Archaeologists identified a culture and people that were ancestors of the Hohokam. Called the Early Agricultural Period, this early group grew corn, lived in sedentary villages all year round, and developed sophisticated irrigation canals. This group might have occupied southern Arizona as early as 2000 BC! Originating as archaic hunters and gatherers who lived on wild plants and animals, these peoples settled in permanent communities and produced their own food instead of living a more mobile life and gathering what nature provided."—Arizona Museum of Natural History, available at www.azmnh .org/arch/hohokam.aspx.

By AD 900, a third, and greater, civilization, encompassing some influences from both the Mogollons and Hohokams,
had arisen on the Colorado Plateau in the high Four Corners
country of southern Utah and Colorado, northern Arizona and
New Mexico. Today, their Hopi descendants refer to them as
the Hisatsinom, but they are better known by the name the
Navajos gave them, the Anasazis, meaning "Ancient Enemies."

For hundreds of years, the earliest Anasazis lived in subterranean pit houses, sunken homes with stonework walls
and broad, strong roofs, providing protection from the searing
summer sun and the bitter winter cold of the western environment. In time, they began to adapt their aboveground storage houses into living quarters, retaining the underground pit
houses as spiritual centers, known as kivas, used for religious
teaching and rituals and as meeting places for clans. In the
center of the circular kivas was a hole, symbolizing *sipapu*,
the place of origin through which their ancestors had emerged
into this world. Here in the kivas, the Anasazi clan leaders formalized a theocratic society and a faith that have guided and
protected the Puebloan peoples to this day.

Gradually, the Anasazi society expanded. Indian villages
joined together to harness water with earthen dams, reser-
voirs, and irrigation systems, turning parts of the high desert
into gardens of corn and other crops. Where there was no surface water, they utilized moisture deposited deep down in the
sandy soil during seasons of flood and developed plants with
roots deep enough to reach these invisible pools. Well-fed,
stable populations increased and experienced a flowering of
culture and art.

The Anasazis' abilities at basket making, which had been
evolving for more than a thousand years, were joined by

another skill—that of pottery making. With every generation, the beautifully crafted and painted pots improved in durability and variety. Religion and trade unified the region, and as the movement of goods and ideas increased, the Anasazi leadership planned a new strategy.

In the very center of their world was a vast and treeless region that supported little habitation. In this harsh environment in northwestern New Mexico's Chaco Canyon, they constructed a center for their civilization—a place where traders exchanged goods and spiritual pilgrimages ended. They built more than four hundred miles of roads and broad avenues leading to the canyon from the different regions of their country. The roads were unique and distinctive, perfectly straight lanes that passed through or over obstructions rather than around them. At distant points along the roads, signal stations were erected and fires maintained to communicate across the vast stretches of the desert and to guide travelers at night. On the roads, the Indians hauled the timber and resources to build and maintain twelve towns in the canyon, having a population of five thousand or more. Carried along also were new ideas gleaned from other peoples that would help the development of the new Chacoan civilization.

Like the Gothic cathedrals, whose construction in Europe began a hundred years later, beautifully crafted great kivas were built throughout the Anasazis' territory. Chaco's were huge and magnificent, many of them able to hold more than five hundred people. Tons of timbers, making up the vast roofs and support systems, had to be transported from far distances without the use of beasts of burden. Within the great kivas, the Anasazi clans kept alive the ancient underground heritage.

Grand as the various towns and structures in Chaco Canyon

were, none compared with the largest single building the Anasazis ever constructed, Pueblo Bonito, the architectural jewel
of the canyon. At the peak of its occupation, Pueblo Bonito
housed over a thousand residents in more than six hundred
rooms—craftsmen, merchants, and government and religious
leaders and their families. The main plaza was constructed as
a great amphitheater with some sections looming five stories
above the canyon floor. It was the busy heart of Anasazi religion and trade. The commerce in one stone, turquoise, more
valuable to traders who came up from Mexico than gold or
jade, was the engine of Pueblo Bonito's wealth and power.
Here, the raw stone would arrive from distant mines for the
craftsmen of Pueblo Bonito to cut and shape into small tiles.
Once prepared, the turquoise tiles would be shipped south to
the merchant centers in the heart of Mexico. There they would
be transformed into extraordinary jeweled creations. For a
hundred years the precious North American stone flowed out
of the canyon while goods and technology flowed in from
throughout the Southwest, California, and Mexico.

Chaco was the center of a sophisticated and creative civilization, but its wealth and power were fleeting. We do not
know exactly what made its populations move after two centuries. Turquoise began trading heavily from other locations in
Arizona and Nevada. Its abundance may have devalued it. At
the same time, Chaco's major turquoise consumer, Tollan, the
Toltec capital in Mexico, fell to civil strife. More likely, a terrible
fifty-year-long series of droughts, beginning about AD 1130,
which dried up the water sources, was a deciding factor in the
abandonment of Chaco Canyon. By the thirteenth century, it
was deserted, and the great turquoise road over the Mexican
High Sierra was abandoned with it.

Despite the demise of the powerful capital, the hush over Chaco Canyon did not mean the end of Anasazi society. In fact, it was now expanding and flourishing anew in the surrounding Four Corners region. To the north, high on the pine-studded mesas and in the fertile valleys of southern Colorado, a large population had become concentrated around Mesa Verde. As Chaco Canyon was being abandoned, the Mesa Verde Indians, many of whom migrated from Chaco itself, started to move their dwelling sites, seeking the protection of recesses in the steep cliffs that dropped from the top of the mesas. While the adjacent Montezuma Valley had a population of thirty thousand, the Cliff Dwellers of Mesa Verde numbered only three thousand but lived in some of the most stunning and enduring buildings of all time, built in the recesses of the cliff walls. The largest of them has been called the Cliff Palace.

Among the Anasazis, there were, in fact, no palaces or special buildings set aside for the powerful or wealthy. All lived alike, the religious and civil leaders, the farmers, the pottery makers, hunters, stonemasons, healers, and spinners and weavers of fine cotton. At Mesa Verde, the people farmed the mesa top, reaching their town by climbing the sheer cliff walls with finger- and toeholds.

In time the cliff towns, too, were given up. By AD 1300 entire regions had been abandoned by the Anasazis. One can only speculate why scores of towns and thousands of square miles in the Southwest were suddenly emptied of people. The Anasazis' lucrative trade with Mexico had evaporated, droughts may have crippled their economies, and it is possible that peace itself had come to an end as the Navajo and Apache nations, Athapascan peoples at the end of an epic migration from northwestern Canada and Alaska, moved into the region.

The question of the abandonment of the cliff towns may always be a mystery.

Once more, the Anasazi people themselves did not disappear. By the tens of thousands, they moved again—most of them to the east and the Rio Grande Valley, to Alcanfor, Taos, Piro, and many other towns, where the Spaniards came upon them two centuries later and called them Pueblo Indians. Others went to the Hopi and Zuni towns in present-day Arizona and New Mexico and merged with the population of those nations. The Navajos eventually took over the heart of the traditional Anasazi country, while most of the Apache peoples established themselves in the more southerly areas that Mogollons and Hohokams had once dominated.

The period of the ancient ones came to an abrupt end, and the modern Southwest world began. The traditions that live today among the various Puebloan peoples and were encountered by the Spaniards in the sixteenth century are the resonance of the Anasazi heritage that reaches back through generations to places like Chaco Canyon and Mesa Verde.

2

Indians of the Sound

◇◇

Pawtucket, Quinnipiac, Niantic. These are currently the names of a baseball team, a respected university, and a small town on the Connecticut coastline near New London. They are also the names of three of the many thriving Indian tribes in seventeenth-century New York, Connecticut, Massachusetts, and Rhode Island in the region around the Long Island Sound.

Of the approximately twenty-five thousand Indians in this region in the 1600s, only a few remain, living among the general population or on tiny reservations. Thus tribal names survive, but historians have paid relatively little attention to the story of that decimation, with the exception perhaps of King Philip's War, the major military episode of the period. Mythology, though, has paid special attention to the Thanksgiving turkey and its fixin's.

Josephy goes a long way toward filling the gap, even in this single essay, originally published in two parts in On the Sound *magazine in 1972. He offers the essential facts of the story but, more important, he foreshadows in one paragraph the more than two centuries of "incremental genocide" to come. He writes: "The Massachusetts settlers' fanatical views regarding relations between themselves and Indians were the beginning of a pattern that has characterized*

*Indian-white relations everywhere in the United States until today.
The invading white was the superior human; he had the duty, divinely directed or otherwise, to exercise that superiority; and all Indians were held guilty collectively for the offenses of an individual."*

During the night of August 11–12, 1676, in the woods of a
peninsula in Narragansett Bay, an army of English colonists surrounded the camp of the unsuspecting Wampanoag
Indian chieftain, Metacom—known to them as King Philip. At
dawn the attackers charged into the camp, slew Philip and his
few remaining followers, and brought to a close the desperate
war that this native American patriot, the second son of the
Pilgrims' friend, Massasoit, had led for fourteen months to try
to end the white man's threat to Indian life, liberty, and lands
in New England.

Although the war had been fought principally north and
east of Long Island Sound, the future of the Sound's many
tribes—most of them already shattered and decimated by
white settlers, and the victims of some of the most terrible
massacres in American history—hung in the balance. There
were intimate connections among all the tribes, and a victory
by Philip would inevitably have spread the conflict westward
along the Sound to New York and all across the length of Long
Island. The Wampanoag chief's failure, instead, meant final
doom for all the Indians of the Sound.

Along the shores of Westchester County, Connecticut, and
Rhode Island, and in many parts of Long Island, Indians continued to exist. But their power to oppose the expansion of the
whites and threaten their mushrooming settlements was gone
forever. Their hunting grounds, fishing stations, and village
sites now disappeared even faster than before. Their organiza-

tions, spiritual resources, and beliefs in themselves and their values withered and died. The Indian population dwindled quickly from disease, oppression, and the lack of a will to live. Their chapter in the white man's version of the history of the Sound was finished, and their future, as the conquerors took over their lands, was one of extinction. By the beginning of the nineteenth century they were so invisible and unknown that most Americans, including leaders of more westerly Indian tribes that were still strong, assumed that they were completely gone.

"Where today are the Pequot? Where the Narragansett, the Mohican, the Pokanoket and many other once powerful tribes of our people?" demanded Tecumseh, the midwestern Shawnee chief in 1811. "They have vanished before the avarice and oppression of the white man, as snow before a summer sun." And in 1826, the publication of James Fenimore Cooper's *The Last of the Mohicans* established firmly in the American consciousness that, indeed, this once numerous Connecticut people no longer existed as an organized entity.

But they have survived—in small numbers and small pockets: Pequots, Mohicans, Narragansetts, Montauks, Shinnecocks, Patchogues, and others. And among them today there is pride, not alone in the satisfaction that, despite everything, they are still here, but because they are the descendants of great and strong peoples who were the first Americans, who were here for thousands of years before the white man came, and who, when the whites did arrive, met them with nobility, dignity, and extraordinary courage.

The history of the Indians of the Sound reaches back for at least twelve thousand years, to the period of the Ice Age. As the great glaciers retreated, the first men—having long since come down more westerly parts of the continent from Alaska and turned east to cross southerly portions of what is now the United States—moved north through the forests that arose in the glaciers' wake and entered the area of Long Island and southern New England, probably about 10,500 BC. They were principally hunters of big-game animals that are now extinct—mammoths, mastodons, and giant Pleistocene beaver, elk, and caribou—and they traveled and lived in small family groups, leaving behind them as evidence of their presence fluted, Clovis-type spear points with which they hunted.

As the Ice Age animals gradually vanished, the people turned to hunting smaller game, to fishing and to the use of shellfish, as well as to more reliance on the gathering of wild vegetables. The climate continued to warm, and the spruce and fir trees of the region gave way to forests of hardwoods. More peoples arrived, population increased, and groups of one hundred or more made their living together within territories that had fixed limits. Numerous archaeological finds have provided a picture of these groups of an Early, Middle, and Late Archaic Period following a seasonal round of movements within their individual territories, from hunting grounds to fishing sites to wild food–gathering areas.

In the Late Archaic Period (roughly about thirty-five hundred years ago), additional peoples seem to have come to the borders of the Sound from inland and to have developed a life oriented to fishing and the gathering of shellfish. New peoples came after them, introducing various skills and crafts, including the making of stone pots and carved soapstone vessels, as well as more sophisticated ways of life that had developed elsewhere. After 1000 BC, in periods designated by archaeologists as Early, Middle, and Late Woodland, life became richer and more complex. Increasing numbers of settlements appeared on the fringes of bays, inlets, coves, and creeks, and banks of shell mounds, which were once common sights along almost all of the Sound, reflected the importance of shellfish, particularly oysters and quahogs, in the peoples' diets. Toward the end of the Early Woodland Period, about 400 BC, agriculture came to the area. It had spread north from Mexico from group to group, via the Mississippi and Ohio River valleys, and gradually it wrought great changes among the Indians who adopted it.

People lived a more settled life, establishing permanent or semi-permanent villages near their fields of corn, beans, squash, pumpkins, and tobacco. For the first time, there was surplus food to store for later use. Population increased and became more concentrated, and the larger groups, in turn, required increasingly complex and intricate social organizations. Where once a father or elder had guided a family or small group, there now arose a need for the orderly leadership and social, political, and religious structuring of very large bodies of people. At the same time, the more abundant food supply provided people with leisure time in which they could make things that satisfied their aesthetic tastes. They had acquired the skill of making pottery about 1000 BC, and they now turned out stone and ceramic smoking pipes and pots of various styles. In addition, they fashioned gorgets of shell and personal adornments of copper, which came to them from the Great Lakes area through an extensive trade network that linked tribes throughout much of the Northeast.

During this period, contact was established and maintained between the shore-dwellers of southern New England and the Indians of Long Island. The people used several types of canoes, making most of them by hollowing out the trunks of fallen trees with stone adzes and the use of fire. By the time the white men arrived, one of them reported seeing Indian craft carrying eighty men plying the Sound. On Long Island, among the settlements of people who were principally semi-sedentary, shellfish and wild food–gatherers, complex burial rituals were developed. Abundant finds of ancient Indian cemeteries on Long Island once led archaeologists to believe that Indians of southern New England crossed the Sound to bury their dead on Long Island, but that has now been disproved.

In the Middle Woodland Period, between approximately 380 BC and AD 325, new migrants appeared in the area, coming from the greatly advanced Adena and Hopewell mound-building centers of the Ohio River Valley, and moving into eastern New York, southern New England, and up the valley of the Connecticut River. They brought with them many new ideas for the making of tools, implements, utensils, and ornamental objects, as well as improved methods of agriculture. But people still hunted, fished, and gathered nuts, berries, and other wild foods.

By about AD 1200, the tribes and ways of life that the white man would meet in the region of the Sound were beginning to take final form. Groups had continued to increase in size; villages were becoming larger; conical and dome-shaped wigwams of straight or bent poles covered with mats, hides, or strips of bark were being used; and distinctive bark-covered longhouses with barrel-shaped roofs were being shared for communal living or for social and religious activities. Toward the end of this period, in the final centuries before the arrival of the Dutch and English, many of the Indian villages were given the protection of palisades—high walls of poles con-

structed in rectangular or circular shape around the settlements. Their use reflected the existence of warfare among
many of the groups, and particularly the fear by some of them
of raiding Iroquoian Mohawk war bands who ranged far from
their homeland in northeastern New York.

The political grouping of friends and enemies was one of
the characteristics that marked the history of the Sound Indians just before and after the arrival of the white men in the
early seventeenth century. Although no accurate estimate of
the Indian population along the Sound about AD 1600 is now
possible, the best guesses suggest that there were at least
twenty-five thousand Indians in southern New England and
on Long Island. About six thousand may have lived on Long
Island and the rest along the coast from Westchester County
to the beginning of Cape Cod.

They were members of the Algonquian language family,
related to the peoples of numerous tribes from Canada and
the Great Lakes almost to the Gulf of Mexico, and all spoke
somewhat similar dialects and could understand one another.
Each tribal group, composed in most cases of a number of different villages, acknowledged the leadership of a *sachem*, usually a particularly wise or brave man, who counseled rather
than commanded the people. Under him were *sagamores*,
who were also men whose wisdom or courage had won them
followings in their villages. Tribal decisions were usually made
after serious debates in tribal councils, and while the decisions
had to be unanimous before they were acted upon, they were
not necessarily binding on every member of the tribe. An individual could disagree and follow his own course of conduct, as
long as it did not harm the rest of the people.

Along the coast of western Connecticut, inland on the

west side of the Connecticut River, and in a part of present-day southeastern New York, numerous sachemdoms had united— principally for mutual action against the raiding parties of Mohawks and other enemies—into a loose confederation, known (for one of their principal tribes) as the Wappinger Confederacy. The member tribes who dwelled along the Sound included, from west to east, the Wecquaesgeek in part of present-day Westchester County; the very numerous villages of the Siwanoy sachemdom that extended from Westchester through Greenwich, Stamford, and Norwalk, almost to Bridgeport; the Tankiteke, who occupied a small part of the coast west of Bridgeport but extended inland; the Paugusset of Bridgeport, Stratford, Waterbury, and their vicinities; the Menunkatuck around Guilford and Madison; and the Hammonasset in the region of Saybrook and Clinton. Altogether, the Wappingers are believed to have numbered almost five thousand in 1600.

East of the Hammonasset lived the Western Niantics, whose territory extended eastward past present-day Lyme and Niantic until it met the lands of the Pequots. The latter, numbering about twenty-two hundred people, dwelled on both sides of the lower Thames River and extended eastward to present-day Stonington and the country of the Eastern Niantics, who occupied the rest of coastal Connecticut and a small part of Rhode Island. North of the Pequots, centering at one time about present-day Norwich, but expanding at various times to include much of eastern and central Connecticut, were the Mohegans, also estimated to number about twenty-two hundred.

At the time of the white man's arrival, the Pequots and Mohegans were living as one people under the Pequot *sachem*

Wopigwooit. Some time just before, it is believed, they had left the area of northwestern Connecticut and the adjoining area of New York east of the Hudson, where they may have been a part of a larger body of people known as Mahicans (Wolves). They had moved southeastwardly, conquering and establishing domination over a number of Wappinger tribes in central Connecticut, including the Hartford area, and eventually slicing into the Niantic country at the mouth of the Thames River, and splitting the Niantics into two groups. The Pequots were warlike and militarily the strongest of all the tribes in the area, and they soon crossed Long Island Sound to assert their domination over many of the tribes on Long Island and on the islands in the Sound.

The Niantics, who lived as uneasy neighbors of the Pequots, were related to the Narragansetts, whose large population of about four thousand dwelled in southern Rhode Island, principally around present-day Kingston. The Narragansetts were also wary of the Pequots, but their main enemies were the tribes of the Wampanoag Confederacy, whose people occupied the eastern side of Narragansett Bay, much of southeastern Massachusetts exclusive of Cape Cod, and Martha's Vineyard and Nantucket. Before the arrival of the Pilgrims in 1620, several Wampanoag villages had been victimized by English sea traders who kidnapped a number of Indians for sale as slaves in Spain and the Mediterranean. But far more disastrously, the white seamen had introduced a sickness that reached epidemic proportions among the Indians and depopulated a large part of the Wampanoag country just before the Pilgrims landed. The site of Plymouth was one such area that had been emptied of Indians. Nevertheless, Massasoit, the *sachem* of the Wampanoags, whose home village was at Mount Hope

in Narragansett Bay, became a warm friend of the English—
principally because he valued them as the source of guns and
European goods, and because they provided him with security
against the more powerful Narragansetts.

Another loose confederation, the Montauk Confederacy,
united all of the thirteen tribes of Long Island. From west to
east they were the Canarsie of Brooklyn; the Rockaway, Mer-
rick, Massapequa, Secatogue, Patchogue, Shinnecock, and
Montauk tribes that stretched in that order along the southern
shore of the island; and the Matinecock, Nesaquake, Setauket,
Corchaug, and Manhasset tribes along the northern shore.
Although the actual Montauk tribe dwelled on its fringes on
the most easterly tip of the island, early white history designated the entire confederacy the Montauk. Probably this dis-
tinction was conferred on the Montauk's *sachem* because of
the power he could command—but possibly also because
he was the first Long Island *sachem* the English knew and
the leader whom they came to favor and acknowledge as the
grand sachem over all the Long Island native peoples. Of all
the confederacy's members, only the Canarsie, in the extreme
west, were troubled by Mohawks. Until the Dutch persuaded
them to stop, they paid an annual tribute of dried clams and
wampum to the Mohawks, who never seem to have exerted
domination farther east on the island. But all the other Montauk
Confederacy members had been subjugated by the Pequots
and, at one time or another, were also threatened by Niantic
and Narragansett war parties from across the Sound.

Despite tribal enmities, Indian warfare was nothing like
that which the Europeans introduced. Battles were more in
the nature of swift and sudden raids of short duration, carried
out for prisoners or booty, or for revenge, by comparatively

small numbers of warriors. Casualties were usually light, and often no one was killed, although a great number of arrows were discharged back and forth. Many fights ended in truces and treaties of peace, in which one side would acknowledge the superiority of the other, promise to side with it against all enemies, and agree to pay some form of annual tribute as a token of its subjection. Prisoners were frequently taken, but many of them were adopted into the villages of the captors and, in time, became full-fledged members of their captors' tribes. Other prisoners were fiendishly tortured according to the Indians' code of war, which regarded the torturing process as an honorable opportunity to let a brave man demonstrate the full measure of his courage. All-out war, however, with the object of exterminating a whole people, was unknown until the Dutch and English appalled and terrified the tribes by introducing savage racial warfare, encouraging at the same time as an approved part of that warfare the taking of enemy heads, hands, and scalps. Contemporary white observers never knew of a battle between Indians in which the number of killed exceeded thirty, and the practice of scalping, according to the best evidence, was introduced to the Northeast Indians by the Dutch of New Netherlands, who gave bounties for heads but accepted scalps because they were easier to carry.

The first Dutch arrivals, like the first English, found the Indians friendly and anxious to be helpful. The Dutch navigator Adriaen Block was the first white man to explore the Sound. In 1614, five years after Henry Hudson found the Indians along the river named after him to be "loving kind" and six years before the Pilgrims came to Plymouth and received help from the Wampanoags in getting through their first year, Block sailed from the East River through Hell Gate (which he named) and entered the Sound, coasting along the shores of both Long Island and southern New England as far as Narragansett Bay. Indian villages, often lying at the mouths of streams, were half-hidden in the dense forests that clothed both shores. At various places, warriors came out in clusters of canoes to greet him. They wore breechclouts, leggings, moccasins, and sometimes shirts of deerskin, ornamented with designs fashioned with porcupine quills or wampum, and the heads of many of them were entirely plucked free of hair or shaved, save for a long strip that was allowed to grow and stand up stiffly (with the aid of bear grease) from the forehead to the back of the neck. Some of the men also grew a "scalp lock" that hung down at the back of the head to taunt an enemy, while others let their hair grow long, tying it in braids and wearing a headband of wampum to keep the bangs out of their eyes. Block noted them and their country favorably, and fur traders from New Amsterdam soon followed him into the Sound to do business with the tribes.

Long Island was known to the peoples of both coasts as Matouac or Sewanhakie (land of shells). It was the principal supplier of periwinkle and quahog shells used in the making of wampum, which almost every tribe in the Northeast greatly valued. Some of the tribes on Long Island were among the most expert makers of wampum, cutting small pieces of shells and boring them so that, like beads, they could be strung in belts as objects of ornamentation, or sewn decoratively on clothing and personal possessions such as tobacco pouches. White wampum was the more common; black or purplish wampum was twice as valuable. Belts strung of wampum were often used as mnemonic devices, helping individuals recall messages or important events to large Indian gatherings. Other belts were carried by emissaries to councils and presented by one side to the other as symbols guaranteeing the intent or word of the donor. Smaller wampum bands were worn around the head or on other parts of the body, and the great demand for wampum made it a medium of exchange among the different tribes. In time, both the Dutch and English standardized its value and used it as money both within the colonies and in dealings with the Indians. Through most of the seventeenth century, Indians on the Sound sold pieces of their lands to the whites for so many fathoms of wampum, as well as for manufactured goods.

Trouble between the whites and Indians on the Sound was not long in coming. The acquisition of European manufactured goods by the Pequots and other tribes that traded beaver to the Dutch on the Connecticut coast aroused the envy of Wappinger Confederacy groups in the interior, and in 1631 one of their *sachems* from the area of present-day Hartford visited Plymouth and asked the English to come over and trade with his people on the Connecticut River. The Plymouth settlers were unable to respond at once, but in 1633 Dutchmen from New Amsterdam sailed up the Connecticut River and built a fortified trading post at Hartford. The local tribe had been conquered by the Pequots, and the Dutch wisely purchased the site for their post from the Pequot *sachem* Wopigwooit. However, the Pequots soon took offense at the good fortune of their subjects who were now receiving the benefits of the white man's trade, and a series of quarrels and threats ended with the killing of two local Indians by the Pequots.

The Dutch placed the blame for the friction directly on Wopigwooit himself, and, hoping to restore peace, seized him aboard one of their trading vessels and murdered him, compounding the crime by asking a large ransom from the Indians for the life of their *sachem* and, after receiving it, returning him to them dead. It brought turmoil to the Indians' country. Sassacus, who succeeded Wopigwooit as *sachem* of the Pequots, waged a desultory war of revenge against all Dutch traders, but, in turn, was harassed by a jealous and powerful Indian rival who had wanted to become the new *sachem*. He was a courageous but conniving Mohegan leader named Uncas, and in time he proved to be a notorious troublemaker between the whites and almost every tribe in the area, as well as a traitor who assisted the whites in their wars against the tribes. The Mohegans were the northernmost of the various Pequot groups, and in the midst of his angry fight with the Dutch, Sassacus had to put down a rebellion by Uncas and his followers.

The Pequots had other troubles. Narragansetts pushed them out of Rhode Island, and in the fall of 1633, Pequots, and perhaps some Niantics, failing to differentiate between the Dutch and the English, and maddened by Wopigwooit's cruel death, killed an English trader, Captain John Stone, and nine companions on the Connecticut River. At the same time, other Englishmen from Plymouth Colony established a trading post on the same river at present-day Windsor, this time buying the land from the local Indians. Despite the fact that it was an insult to the Pequots, who regarded the sellers as their subjects, the English managed to smooth Sassacus's feelings by promising to send traders to his people. A treaty between the Pequots and the English in November 1634 brought temporary peace to the Hartford area, and English traders and colonists crossed to the Connecticut River, buying more land from the Indians and establishing the town of Wethersfield. But the English failed to live up to their promises to the Pequots, and for two years no traders visited their villages near the coast.

In the spring of 1636, another English trader, John Oldham, and two white boys were killed off Block Island, which was occupied by Manhasset Indians who were subject to the Pequots. When news of Oldham's death reached Boston, it created a storm. Memories of the murder of Captain Stone were reawakened, and the English were soon accusing the Pequots of harboring some of Oldham's killers. A wild-eyed expedition of ninety men under John Endecott was dispatched to exterminate the Indians of Block Island and to demand satisfaction from the Pequots, even though there was no evidence of their implication in the affair. At Block Island Endecott's men were able to find and kill only one man. After burning and destroying the Indians' villages, property, and cornfields, they sailed to the newly established Connecticut fort at Saybrook, where its commander, Lion Gardiner, pleaded with them not to attack the Pequots. "You have come to raise a nest of wasps about our ears," he said, "and then you will flee away."

The hotheaded Endecott refused to listen to Gardiner. Marching impulsively against the Pequots, he delivered an ultimatum to one of their ambassadors, demanding a thousand fathoms of wampum or twenty children of their principal men as hostages. The ambassador disappeared, and Endecott tried unsuccessfully to draw the Indians into battle. When they evaded him, he burned their villages and destroyed their property, and returned exultingly to Boston.

The Massachusetts settlers' fanatical views regarding relations between themselves and Indians were the beginning of a pattern that has characterized Indian-white relations everywhere in the United States until today. The invading white was the superior human; he had the duty, divinely directed or otherwise, to exercise that superiority; and all Indians were held guilty collectively for the offenses of an individual.

Gardiner's warning to Endecott was soon realized. The irate Pequots laid siege to Saybrook, attacked Wethersfield, and killed thirty English settlers. The colonists in Massachusetts and Connecticut responded with shocked fury, terming the Pequots agents of Satan who, according to God's will, should be wiped from the earth. In something close to a religiously inspired crusade, encouraged by the colonists' ministers, expeditions from the upper Connecticut River and Massachusetts set off for the Pequot country. The English were joined by many Indian enemies and rivals of Sassacus and the Pequots, including Uncas and a band of Mohegans, as well as parties of Narragansetts and Niantics. On June 5, 1637, the army surrounded a fortified Pequot village at Mystic, trapping more than six hundred Indians inside. The English and their allies rushed in and fought a brief hand-to-hand battle with the Pequots. Then they set fire to the village, withdrew, and encircling the fort killed the terrified Pequots as they tried to escape from the flames. No one knows how many Pequots perished in the massacre, but the English claimed that only seven Indians escaped from the carnage and another seven were taken prisoner.

The other Pequots, who were gathered in a second village, were stunned by the ferocity of the English and decided to separate and flee in different directions. Sassacus and a group of several hundred Indians hurried up the Connecticut River, turned west, and finally hid in a swamp near present-day Fairfield. Another group tried to hide in their own country, but its members were discovered by Narragansetts, who led the English to them. When the Pequots surrendered, the colonists, commanded by Israel Stoughton, killed all the men in cold blood and sent the women and children to Boston to be sold as slaves. Another English expedition, accompanied by the traitorous Uncas, then set off on the trail of Sassacus and his body of refugees. Along the way, they overtook Pequot stragglers and killed them without mercy. At Fairfield, they surrounded Sassacus and his people in their hiding place in the swamp and carried out another massacre. This time, however, they accepted the surrender of some two hundred Indians and consigned them to slavery. Sassacus and some of his people escaped and tried to flee to the Mohawks. Instead of finding safety, they were slain by the Mohawks.

For months, the English encouraged the Mohegans, Niantics, and Narragansetts to kill any Pequots they found and send their heads and hands to the colonial authorities. Nevertheless, many Pequots managed to survive. Some crossed to Long Island, some fled to the Iroquois, and others traveled far south or into the interior of the continent, finding safety with remote tribes. Still others eventually received an unexpected welcome from Uncas, as well as from the Niantic *sachem* Ninigret and the Narragansetts, all of whom decided that they could build up their own ranks by adopting Pequot survivors into their tribes. The English soon suspected that their allies were harboring Pequots, but they could do nothing about it. On October 1, 1638, the English signed a tripartite treaty with Uncas and the Narragansetts, agreeing to divide some two hundred surviving Pequots among the Mohegans, Narragansetts, and Niantics. The Pequots were forbidden to live in their home country, and they were no longer even to be referred to as Pequots. As far as the English were concerned, the tribe was extinct, and its lands were the property of the whites.

That did not finish the Pequots. They continued to live among the alien groups until 1655 when they were once again recognized as a separate people and given two small settlements of their own in southeastern Connecticut. On occasion, over the years, they had land conflicts with encroaching whites and were moved to different locations. Their population slowly declined, and with the loss of their hunting grounds their poverty became chronic. Some of them fought for the English colonists during the French and Indian War, and later others became whalers. From time to time, groups moved elsewhere, particularly to the Oneida country in upper New York. But always there were Pequots where they had been when the English had struck them in 1637, and they are still there today, living in the southern part of Connecticut's New London County.

The destruction of the Pequots in 1637 threw fear into all the tribes of the Sound. With the return of peace, English colonization of their lands began in earnest, and the whites found most Indians anxious to sell them parts of their countries and have friendly Englishmen living close to them, providing them with manufactured trade goods, and sheltering them against their enemies with their power.

The English who had tracked the *sachem* Sassacus west of the Connecticut River to the Fairfield swamp had come on many promising sites for settlement, and organizations were now formed to establish colonies along that part of the Connecticut coast. In 1638, the Quinnipiacs traded a large part of their land from Milford to Madison, including the site of present-day New Haven, for an assortment of European goods that included English cloth coats, spoons, hatchets, hoes, knives, porringers, and French scissors. Other Indians willingly sold their lands at Milford, Derby, Fairfield, Guilford, Norwalk, and part of Stamford (then called Rippowams). By 1642, English settlements dotted almost all the northern shore of the Sound, although around the new villages and tiny forts there were still sizeable populations of Indians, growing corn and other crops outside their towns, and hunting, fishing, and gathering shell-fish as they had for generations.

In that year, another war between the Indians and whites broke out—this time starting in the Dutch settlement at New Amsterdam and spreading to the Sound. Once again, it stemmed from the arrogance and hotheadedness of a white man. Director-general Willem Kieft of the Dutch West India Company, like John Endecott of Boston, hated the Indians with the zeal of a fanatic. When he took charge of New Amsterdam in 1638, he astounded the local Manhattes of the Wappinger Confederacy by ordering them to pay an annual tax in furs, corn, or wampum because, as he told them, their presence in the area forced the Dutch to spend money on defensive forts. His actions angered the Indians, but for several years there was peace, although minor conflicts between individual Indians and Dutch settlers were common.

The Dutch, meanwhile, grew out of Manhattan into all the present-day boroughs of New York City and across the Hudson River to the future site of Jersey City. In Brooklyn their way was cleared for them by a war party of Mohawks, who almost wiped out the Canarsies when that tribe, on the advice of the Dutch, stopped paying tribute to the upper New York State Indians. In Astoria, in Queens County, the Dutch made a large land purchase in 1640 for a barrel of beef and a few trinkets. A year or so later they did even better in Westchester and western Connecticut, paying a total of twelve glasses, twelve knives, and six cloth coats to the Siwanoy *sachem* Ponus for a huge tract of land that included Pound Ridge, part of Bedford, Greenwich, Stamford, Darien, and New Canaan.

Trouble finally erupted in 1642. At Pavonia, on the west side of the Hudson River, an aggrieved Indian killed a Dutch settler. The episode infuriated Kieft, who tried in vain to force the Indians to deliver the murderer to him. The next year he got his revenge. Two bands totaling almost one thousand terrified Indians came streaming suddenly south, seeking protection from their enemies, the Mohawks, who were pursuing them. The refugees were members of the Wappinger Confederacy and had had nothing to do with the slaying of the year before. One band entered Manhattan and for two weeks was fed and sheltered by the inhabitants. Then its members established a camp slightly north of the Dutch village. The other band nestled under the protection of the Dutch in Pavonia.

Kieft's year of frustration now came to the surface. Despite the objection of some of the settlers, he ordered simultaneous surprise attacks on both Indian villages. His directions were carried out. At midnight Dutch forces struck at both Indian camps. The frightened and helpless Indians ran in all directions, and most of them got away in the darkness. But one hundred twenty were slain in the two attacks, and the Dutch cut off their heads and carried them back to New Amsterdam.

The massacres opened another wasps' nest. Soon war bands of all the tribes of the Wappinger Confederacy were striking at Dutch and English settlements from Staten Island to the Connecticut River. At Pelham Bay in Westchester, the controversial religious dissenter Anne Hutchinson (for whom the Hutchinson River was named) and seventeen others were killed. Dutch settlers were driven out of the Bronx and Kings and Queens counties. Manhattan filled with refugees, and food supplies ran dangerously low. The English settlers in Connecticut, threatened now by Wappinger Confederacy tribes, blamed the Dutch for the war, but had to join them nevertheless in common defense.

Through much of 1643, Dutch and English expeditions fought indecisively against the Indians. One group landed at Greenwich, Connecticut, marched through the countryside searching for a hostile Siwanoy *sachem* known as Mayn Mayano, but failed to find him. Instead, they came on an Indian village of men, women, and children, killed all the men, and took the other people back to Manhattan as prisoners. Another expedition ranged through Brooklyn and Queens, killing one hundred twenty Indians at Hempstead and sending many others scurrying for safety across Long Island Sound.

Finally, in February 1644, Captain John Underhill, a veteran of the Pequot War who now lived under Dutch hegemony in Greenwich, arrived in Manhattan with word of the discovery of an encampment of five hundred Indians near Stamford. With a force of one hundred thirty Dutch and fifty English soldiers, Underhill sailed back to Greenwich. He was held up temporarily by a snowstorm, but the next night found and surrounded the Indian encampment at Strickland's Plain, known also as Horse Neck. After a furious fight, Underhill gave orders to set fire to the village. In a repetition of what had occurred at the Pequot fort at Mystic, Indians tried to escape from the flames, only to be shot down by the whites. Once again, there was a massacre. In the morning more than five hundred bodies of Indian men, women, and children crimsoned the snow. Eight Indians were said to have escaped.

The slaughter of Siwanoys and their allies virtually ended the war, although minor raids and conflicts continued for another year, and the Dutch paid for enemy scalps as had been their wont since they had first settled on Manhattan Island. Formal peace finally returned with the signing of a treaty in August 1645. The affair broke the spirit and power of the Wappinger tribes of the western Connecticut coast, most of whom in the following decades moved north and west to merge with the shattered remnants of other tribes and seek safety in areas where Indians were still secure. The other Wappinger groups hung on as the white population expanded and engulfed them. They tasted all the bitter experiences of defeated and powerless Indians, losing their lands—sometimes in honest transactions, more often through fraud and theft—suffering from poverty, disease, prejudice, and alcohol, and finally becoming truly "vanishing Americans." Their numbers decreased steadily until by the twentieth century, from Greenwich to the Connecticut River, the peoples of the once-powerful Wappinger sachemdoms were regarded as all but extinct.

On Long Island, meanwhile, Indian-white relations had been more peaceful. During the Pequot War, Lion Gardiner, the commander at Saybrook, had become friendly with the Montauk *sachem* Wyandanch who, with three brothers, headed the Montauk Confederacy on Long Island. The Montauk groups had been in the habit of paying their conquerors, the Pequots, an annual tribute of twenty fathoms of wampum for each tribe in the confederacy. The Montauks had sided with the English in the war, and although, after it ended, Wyandanch agreed to pay the English the same tribute he had given the Pequots, he regarded the white men as friends and allies rather than enemies. In 1639 he sold Gardiner the Manhassets' island of Manchonoke (the present-day Gardiners Island), and a year later traded some of the Shinnecock land at Agawam (today's Southampton) to a colonizing group of about forty families, most of them from Lynn, Massachusetts. Other land sales by Long Island Indians soon followed, notably at Huntington in 1646, East Hampton in 1648, and Setauket in 1655.

Principally because of their fear of Connecticut tribes, the Indians of the Montauk Confederacy were friendly to the whites, considering their presence as protection against the stronger groups across the Sound. The different Long Island tribes showed the settlers how they made wampum with "muxes," or awls (from which came the phrase, *muxing* or *mucking* around); introduced them to *sarnp*, a corn porridge, as the Massachusetts Indians had introduced the Pilgrims to succotash; and taught them how to go whaling offshore in small boats. At first the whites hired Indians to go whaling for them, but soon whites went along with the Indians. It was the start of what eventually became an important colonial industry, and in its heyday, in the nineteenth century, Long Island Indians were still among the crews of many of the large American whaling vessels.

On more than one occasion, the whites were able to return the Indians' friendship by acts of their own. In 1650 they deterred Uncas, the Mohegan, from attacking the tribe of a Long Island *sachem* named Mohansic. Instead, Uncas complained to the English that Mohansic had "bewitched" him, hoping that the English would execute the *sachem*. The English dismissed the charge. Three years later the Niantic *sachem* Ninigret tried to enlist the support of the Shinnecocks and Montauks in a quarrel he was having with the whites. Wyandanch informed Gardiner of Ninigret's proposal. The latter, in a rage, sent a series of expeditions across the Sound to punish Wyandanch. Gardiner and the settlers at East Hampton provided protection to the terrified Long Island Indians for several years, and when peace returned Wyandanch in gratitude presented Gardiner with the area of present-day Smithtown.

Wyandanch died in 1659, but Indian land sales continued. Two men from East Hampton bought a large tract of land at Montauk for one hundred pounds sterling in 1660. In 1664, Governor John Winthrop, Jr., of Connecticut purchased Fishers Island, and in 1683 a group of settlers, including many from Islip, England, bought sixty square miles around present-day Islip, Long Island.

Meanwhile, another, and more fearful enemy of the Indian—the white man's diseases—had begun to wreak havoc among the Long Island tribes. Epidemics of measles, smallpox, and virus infections broke out from time to time for almost a century, raging from one end of the island to the other. They wiped out whole villages and brought a steady decline in the Indian population. By 1741, disease, rather than war, had cleared almost all of Long Island to white settlement. Only four hundred Indians remained from the estimated original total of six thousand. The Indian population stabilized then, and even increased. The remnants were widely scattered in small pockets and many of them became almost indistinguishable from the neighboring whites. Efforts were made to Christianize and assimilate them. From 1749 to 1761 a celebrated Mohegan preacher, Samson Occom, who had been instructed by Eleazer Wheelock, the founder of Dartmouth College, worked in the Long Island Indian communities trying to make converts to Christianity. He married a descendant of Wyandanch, became a Montauk himself, and eventually led a band of followers away from Long Island to the Oneidas' country in upper New York State.

Despite their isolation and small numbers, the surviving Long Island Indians continued to cling to their Indianness. In the mid-nineteenth century, P. T. Barnum induced the *sachem* of the Montauk tribe to appear in public billed as the "King of the Montauks." When the *sachem*, whose name was Stephen Pharoah, died in 1878, the press called him the last "king" of his people, and in 1910 a Long Island judge, ruling on a case, declared that there no longer existed a Montauk tribe. But he was wrong: there are still Montauks living on eastern Long Island. According to the 1970 census, in fact, there were 1,044 Indians in Suffolk County,* many of them showing the strains of whites or blacks who married their ancestors. Just west of Southampton, one hundred fifty Shinnecocks live on their own reservation. A smaller number of Poosepatucks, descendants of the Patchogues, occupy another reservation near Mastic. And concentrations of descendants of other Long Island tribesmen dwell in Babylon, Brookhaven, Huntington, Islip, Riverhead, Hicksville, Sag Harbor, and East Hampton.

North of the Sound, the history of the tribes east of the Wappingers was a mournful one after the Pequot War. The Mohegans, Niantics, and Narragansetts all jockeyed against each other to fill the power vacuum left by the Pequots. The

* Eds. note: It is difficult to make exact comparisons. The 2010 U.S. Census gives the Suffolk County population as 1,493,000, with 3.4 percent being Indian. The Census provides a precise 2010 population for the Shinnecock Reservation: 662.

master intriguer was Uncas, who time and again raised suspicions among the English that the other tribes were plotting
against the whites. Ambitious, jealous, and venal, he played
the role of the great and good friend of the English and was
not averse to doing the work of the colonists against Indians
of his own and other tribes that the English considered their
enemies. In 1643 he captured Miantinomo, the Narragansett
sachem, persuaded the English to allow him to kill the prisoner, and then did so, cutting a piece from the dead Narragansett's shoulder and announcing that it was "the sweetest meat
I ever ate."

Until 1683, when death took him at nearly eighty, Uncas
feuded with every Indian group and was detested by all of
them. Even the English grew irritated with his jealousies and
troublemaking. But he had served the whites well by under-
mining and preventing effective Indian resistance to the colonists' expansion, and when he died, he willed much of the
Mohegans' land to the English.

He lived long enough to help the English end the last serious Indian threat in New England. In 1675, King Philip of the
Wampanoags finally succeeded in uniting with the Narragansetts and other New England tribes in a desperate attempt to rid
the region of whites. At first Philip had remarkable successes,
defeating English forces and burning numerous towns and
settlements in Massachusetts, Rhode Island, and Connecticut.
But among his enemies were Mohegans and Pequots, sent
into the conflict by Uncas to aid the colonists. In December
1675 they were among a force of one thousand colonists who
trapped the Narragansetts on an island in a wild marsh known
as the Great Swamp near West Kings in southern Rhode
Island. There was another massacre. More than six hundred

Narragansett men, women, and children perished; "terribly Barbikew'd," exulted Cotton Mather, the Boston divine. The carnage ended the power of the Narragansetts. Their *sachem*, Canonchet, escaped and fought on, until he was captured the following April. The Mohegans, with the permission of the English, cut off his head and quartered him.

With the death of Philip in August 1676 the last flicker of freedom died for the Indians of the Sound. The war that he had fought made stronger for the whites an image they had formed of Indians during the Pequot and Dutch wars. All three had been Indian wars of resistance, and they had been waged desperately and fiercely by both sides. But the whites now regarded the Indians as savage enemies who had to be assimilated or exterminated. The two races could not live side by side in peace. The wars fought along the Sound set the rules for an uncompromising interracial warfare that moved westward, from frontier to frontier, for the next two hundred years.

During those two centuries, the conquered and broken Wampanoags and Narragansetts, as well as the Mohegans and Niantics, struggled to maintain their existences and identities in the white man's world. Without the power to resist, they were dispossessed of their lands and pressed into smaller and smaller communities. Strict laws regulated their conduct, and white advisors supervised their affairs. In time, more and more of them became assimilated and lived like the whites, although generally in abject poverty. Their numbers declined, and many of their settlements disappeared. The survivors, however, remembered their Indian heritage, and passed it from one generation to the next. Their descendants are still in their ancestral homelands: Wampanoags in many parts of southeastern Massachusetts; Narragansetts in every section of

Rhode Island; Mohegans along the Thames River in Connecticut; and Niantics in the vicinity of the town that bears their name.

They left a rich heritage to all Americans: foods, words, canoes, medicines, ways of the wilderness, nobility of conduct and spirit, belief in the individual's worth, and much more. And on the maps of the lands that border the Sound are their names: Montauk, Narragansett, Mohansic, Pawtucket, Patchogue, Mianus, Canonchet, Quinnipiac, Wyandanch. It was all Indian land.

3

Tecumseh, the Greatest Indian

◇◇◇

*In the long chain of Indian history, from the mysteries of the Ana-
sazi to the tragedy of Wounded Knee, to the legal triumphs of the
twenty-first century, Tecumseh was one of the most influential Indians. He was a peerless orator, statesman, warrior, and visionary.
He remains in history not only as a powerful individual leader but
also as an equally powerful symbol of an effort to bring a disparate
group of nations into one. This is his story, told by Josephy in his first
book on Indians,* The Patriot Chiefs *(1961).*

In its issue of December 2, 1820, the *Indiana Centinel* of Vincennes, Indiana, published a letter praising a late and much
hated enemy. "Every schoolboy in the Union now knows that
Tecumseh was a great man," it read. "He was truly great—and
his greatness was his own, unassisted by science or the aids of
education. As a statesman, a warrior and a patriot, take him all
in all, we shall not look upon his like again."

Seven years earlier, frontier communities throughout the
territory of the Old Northwest had exulted over the death of
the "yaller devil" who had tried to bar white men from the rich
lands north of the Ohio River. But with the disappearance of

danger, thoughtful citizens, like the *Centinel*'s correspondent, had at last begun to realize that a native of soaring greatness had been in their midst. Along the waterways and dirt roads of Ohio and Indiana, settlers who still shuddered with memories of the warfare that had wrested the region from the Indians talked of Tecumseh with admiration, and agreed with the verdict of their own hero, General William Henry Harrison, who had led them against the war chief. Tecumseh, Harrison had reported to Washington, was "one of those uncommon geniuses, which spring up occasionally to produce revolutions and overturn the established order of things. If it were not for the vicinity of the United States, he would perhaps be the founder of an Empire that would rival in glory that of Mexico or Peru."

Today, one hundred fifty years after his death, Tecumseh, as made clear by Glenn Tucker, his most recent and ablest biographer in his book *Tecumseh: Vision of Glory*, still looms as the greatest native leader in the long, tragic resistance of the Indians of the United States. A brilliant orator and warrior and a brave and distinguished patriot of his people, he was intelligent, learned, and wise, and was noted, even among his white enemies, for his integrity and humanity. But, unlike all previous native leaders, he looked beyond the mere resistance by a tribe or group of tribes to white encroachments; and here lay his unique greatness. He was a Shawnee, but he considered himself an Indian first, and fought to give all Indians a national, rather than a tribal, consciousness, and to unite them in defense of a common homeland where all might continue to dwell under their own laws and leaders.

In modern days, world opinion which endorses the right of self-determination of peoples might have supported before the United Nations his dream of a country of, by, and for Indians. But the crisis he faced came too early in history, and he failed. His failure meant considerably more than that the main theater of his struggle, Indiana (originally "the country of Indians"), became a white rather than an Indian state. It threw all the tribes back upon their separate resources, as they had been since the beginning of their conflict with white men, and re-established a pattern in which individual tribes or regional confederacies sought hopelessly to cope alone with the invaders. More important, it ended for all time the possibility that an Indian free state or nation might be created within territory won or purchased by the United States from other white governments.

Tecumseh's story was a tragedy, for in the end it was a white man's war between the United States and Great Britain that obscured his nationalist cause and made the Americans feel that they were merely fighting a military auxiliary of their enemies. The true nature of his struggle was apparent only after his death, but before that day, his uncompromising leadership, fiery courage, and tireless energy brought the Indians startlingly close to victory.

Tecumseh was born in March 1768, in one of the villages that formed a large, straggling settlement of Indian wigwams and bark cabins called Old Piqua on the bluffs above Ohio's Mad River, northeast of present-day Dayton. His father, a Shawnee war chief named Puckeshinwa, was a proud, intelligent man who had been born in Florida, and his mother, Methoataske, probably a Creek Indian, was from eastern Alabama. Their birthplaces, far from Ohio, reflected the long, nomadic history of the Shawnees. Their restless, confused wanderings, marked by numerous alliances with other tribes and constant guerilla warfare against advancing whites, had made them more conscious than most natives of the similarity and urgency of the racial struggles being waged against the settlers on many different fronts. To them, the major enemies of all Indians were the English colonists, and from the time of the French and Indian War, when they sided with the French, they were in constant conflict with frontier settlers and with puni- tive English and colonial expeditions that were sent against them. After the American Revolution, their great numbers and continued resistance made them a prime target of the settlers.

Two events of his childhood and youth intensified Tecum- seh's personal animosity toward the white invaders. One was the brutal murder of his father by frontiersmen near Old Piqua, though by treaty they were forbidden to come north of the Ohio. This episode filled Tecumseh with horror and hate, and he resolved to become a warrior like his father and be "a fire spreading over the hill and valley, consuming the race of dark souls." Then, a few years later, white men also treacherously murdered Cornstalk, a Shawnee war leader, who had become the youth's idol.

After the death of Puckeshinwa, a chief named Blackfish, who ruled the Indian town of Old Chillicothe, a few miles from Old Piqua, had adopted Tecumseh into his family, and the boy had traveled back and forth between the two villages, receiv- ing at both places education in personal conduct, oratory, and tribal lore. The murder of Cornstalk enraged Blackfish, and under his leadership the Shawnees commenced a new war of revenge. In 1778, Blackfish invaded Kentucky, struck at some of the settlements, and captured Daniel Boone and twenty-six other whites. He brought the noted frontiersman back to Old Chillicothe, where Tecumseh saw him. Later, Boone escaped.

In 1780, an American army under George Rogers Clark drove the natives from both Old Chillicothe and Old Piqua. The two cities were burned, and farther west on the Miami River the defeated Shawnees, Tecumseh with them, built another city, also called Piqua, which meant "town that rises from the ashes." Conflict continued, and two years later Tecumseh, as a youthful observer rather than a warrior, accompanied a group of British and Indians in another invasion of Kentucky. Without taking part in the fighting, he watched the Indians try in vain to capture one of the settlements and then saw them administer a severe drubbing to an army of Kentuckians on the Licking River. Soon afterward, he got into his first battle, fighting by the side of his brother Cheeseekau in a small skirmish in Ohio. Cheeseekau was wounded, and Tecumseh was unnerved and fled from the battlefield. That night, he upbraided himself for his cowardice; it would be the last time anywhere that he would show fear.

With the end of the Revolution, the British withdrew offensive forces from along the Ohio River, and the Indians at last accepted as permanent the loss of their hunting grounds to the south. But there was still little peace for them. The flood of westward-moving settlers was increasing, and the newcomers now had their eyes on the rich Indian lands north of the river.

Once more, border warfare blazed. Still in his middle teens, Tecumseh joined a band of Shawnees that tried to halt the white invasion by intercepting settlers' flatboats that came down the Ohio from Pennsylvania. For a while, the Indians made the route so hazardous that river traffic almost ceased.

After one battle on the river, the Indians captured a settler and burned him at the stake. Tecumseh, then about fifteen years old, watched the spectacle with horror. Suddenly he leapt to his feet and made an eloquent appeal that shamed the Indians for their inhumanity. This revulsion at vengeful cruelty was to be a notable part of his personality throughout his life; it was one of the sources of the admiration that white men eventually acquired for him.

In time, Tecumseh became the leader of his own band of warriors. The border conflict in the Northwest Territory had by now become critical for the settlers. In 1790 and 1791 two U.S. Army detachments—one under Josiah Harmar, the second under Arthur St. Clair—were sent out to protect the whites. Both were thrown back by Indians under a Miami war chief named Little Turtle. St. Clair's defeat, in which Tecumseh particularly distinguished himself, was one of the worst routs ever suffered by an American army, and for a while it spread terror among the whites in the Northwest Territory and halted the flow of new settlers.

Tecumseh followed the victory by leading raids against white frontiersmen in both Ohio and Kentucky. In 1792, upon the death in battle of his brother Cheeseekau, Tecumseh became leader of all the Shawnee warriors in the south. In 1793, he broke off his forays against settlers there to hurry north and help defend the Ohio country against an invasion by a new American army, this one commanded by Major General Anthony Wayne.

The Shawnee Blue Jacket was now in command of all the Indian forces in the Northwest Territory. Tecumseh and his followers were assigned as scouts to follow the American army as it moved north. Wayne advanced from Cincinnati in October 1793. Eighty miles north, at Greenville, he erected a fort and paused for the winter. But in June Wayne started forward again toward the Maumee River in northwestern Ohio. He had three thousand men with him, but Blue Jacket with fourteen hundred warriors decided to engage him.

On August 20, 1794, the two forces met in a large clearing along the Maumee River where a tornado had blown down many big trees. Tecumseh's scouts began the fight by firing on Wayne's advance guard, and in the battle that followed, Tecumseh added to his reputation among the Indians by his boldness and courage. Throughout the fight among the fallen trees, he was seen wherever the action was most desperate, and even after his rifle jammed and became unusable, he continued to lead and inspire his companions. At the height of the battle, another of his brothers was killed, but there was no time for grief. Wayne's sharpshooters kept the Indians pinned down behind the trees, his cavalry thrashed at them, and at length the infantry launched a frenzied bayonet charge across the timbers. It scattered the natives and ended the battle that became known as Fallen Timbers. Wayne destroyed every Indian village he could find, built Fort Wayne at the head of the Maumee in Indiana, and retired for the winter to Greenville.

The following spring he invited the vanquished warriors to a peace meeting. Nearly one thousand of them responded, representing twelve different tribes of the Northwest Territory; after two months of pressure, their chiefs reluctantly signed the Treaty of Greenville, which ceded to the United States for sale to settlers almost two-thirds of Ohio, including the Shawnee sites of Old Piqua and Old Chillicothe on the Mad River; a triangular tract in southeastern Indiana; and sixteen strategically located areas in the Northwest, including the sites of Detroit, Toledo, Peoria, and Chicago. In return, the Indians divided among themselves about $20,000 in goods and received the promise of $9,500 in annuities.

Tecumseh had refused to attend the council, and after the treaty provisions became known, he split with Blue Jacket and announced that he would not accept what the chiefs had done. Nevertheless, as settlers moved into the ceded territory, he recognized the hopelessness of resistance, and withdrew westward with his followers into Indiana. His anger and opposition to the treaty furthered his reputation among both Indians and whites, and as large numbers of disgruntled warriors began to give him their loyalty and call him their chief, he became the dominant native leader in the Old Northwest.

He was twenty-seven years old now, five feet, ten inches tall, a powerful and handsome man with a proud and aggressive bearing. Though there is no definitely established contemporary portrait of him, white men who knew him described him as hard and fiery, a man who would announce with great authority, "I am Tecumseh," and if challenged, would menacingly touch the stem of his tomahawk. At the same time, he had a complex personality in which many forces were apparently in conflict, for he could also be tender and sentimental, thoughtful and kind, or even playful and good-humored, depending on his mood.

In 1796, he married a half-breed woman named Manete, who is described merely as an "old woman." She bore Tecumseh a son, but soon afterward he quarreled with her and they parted. Toward the end of the century, during a visit to an older sister, Tecumapease, who had remained near Old Chillicothe, he met a sensitive young white girl named Rebecca Galloway, the daughter of an intelligent pioneer farmer who had once been a hunter for George Rogers Clark. She was blond and beautiful, he was magnetic and interesting, and a strange, romantic attachment developed between them. In time, as

Tecumseh continued to call on her, she taught him to speak better English and read to him from the Bible, Shakespeare, and history books.

Tecumseh broadened in dramatic fashion under Rebecca's sympathetic tutoring. He absorbed the history of Alexander the Great and other leaders of white civilization, pondered over biblical philosophy, and thirsted for even more knowledge that would make him better equipped to understand and deal with the Americans. His regard for the blond, blue-eyed girl also increased, and eventually he asked her father if he might marry her. Mr. Galloway respected Tecumseh and advised him to ask Rebecca. Tecumseh did so, and the girl said that she would be willing if he would agree to give up his Indian ways and live with her as a white man. The decision was painful for Tecumseh, and he took a month to make up his mind. Finally, in sadness, he returned to Rebecca and told her that he could not abandon his people. He said good-bye to her, left, and never saw her again. But the memory of her loveliness and guidance stayed with him, and he never took another wife.

The peace envisioned for the Northwest Territory by Wayne's treaty lasted little more than a decade and was never more than a truce. As Tecumseh had foreseen, the line established at Greenville between the races could not halt conflict. Though the Indians acknowledged white possession of southern Ohio, many of them continued to live and hunt on their former lands, and they were in constant friction with frontier settlers. Moreover, as whites continued to come down the Ohio River, they began to press for the opening of new Indian lands, and in 1800, as if preparing to slice another large piece from the natives' domain, the government established administrative machinery for a Territory of Indiana, west of Ohio.

During this period, another tragedy struck the Indians. Traders and settlers brought liquor into the region in huge quantities, and native bands in close contact with the whites could not resist it. They traded land, possessions, and their services for the alcohol, and almost overnight large segments of once-proud and dignified tribes became demoralized in drunkenness and disease. As poverty and death claimed the natives, whole bands disappeared, and the weakened survivors clung together in ragged misery.

Tribes like the Shawnees, which remained farthest from contact with the traders, managed to retain their independence and strength. Tecumseh himself refused to drink whiskey and preached angrily against its use by his followers. One Shawnee, however, who became noted among his people as a depraved drunk, was Tecumseh's younger brother, Laulewasika. A loud-mouthed idler and loafer, he had lost an eye in an accident and wore a handkerchief over the empty socket. For years he drank heavily and lived in laziness. Then, in 1805, he was suddenly influenced by the great religious revival taking place among white settlers on the frontier, and particularly by itinerant Shaker preachers, whose jerking, dancing, and excessive physical activity stirred mystical forces within him.

During a frightening epidemic of sickness among the Shawnees, Laulewasika was overcome by a "deep and awful sense" of his own wickedness and fell into the first of many trances, during which he thought he met the Indian Master of Life. The latter showed him the horrible torments and sufferings of persons doomed by drink, and then pointed out another path, "beautiful, sweet, and pleasant," reserved for abstainers. Laulewasika's regeneration was instantaneous. He began to preach against the use of liquor, and the intensity of his words drew followers to him. As he continued to have trances and commune with the Master of Life, he changed his name to Tenskwatawa, "The Open Door," which he took from the saying of Jesus, "I am the door."

He allied himself with Tecumseh and gradually, under the war chief's influence, broadened his doctrine of abstinence into an anti-white code that urged Indians to return to the ways of their fathers and end intertribal wars. Moving to Greenville, Ohio, at the very place where the chiefs had signed their treaty with Wayne in 1795, the two brothers built a large frame meetinghouse and fifty or sixty cabins for their converts.

The Prophet's emotional appeals traveled quickly across the Northwest Territory, and he soon gained followers from almost every tribe. His growing influence and the dangerous concentration of natives around him disturbed Governor Harrison at his territorial headquarters in Vincennes, and he began to scoff publicly at the Prophet, hoping that ridicule would undermine the natives' belief in him. But Harrison made little progress. Then, in April 1806, he challenged Tenskwatawa to perform a miracle. "If he is really a prophet," he wrote to one group of Indians, "ask him to cause the sun to stand still, the moon to alter its course, the rivers to cease to flow, or the dead to rise from their graves. If he does these things, you may then believe he has been sent from God."

Harrison's challenge was disastrous. From some white source, perhaps a British agent in the north, the Prophet learned that a total eclipse of the sun would occur on June 16. In a bold and boastful response to Harrison, he proclaimed to the Indians that he would make the sun darken, and on the designated day a huge crowd of natives assembled at Greenville. Moving into their midst, Tenskwatawa pointed commandingly at the sun, and at 11:32 a.m. the moon, apparently responding to his order, began to darken its face. The Indians were stricken with awe. As night descended over the gathering, the Prophet called to the Master of Life to bring back the sun. In a moment, light began to reappear. With the return of full daylight, the Prophet's reputation and power were assured.

Word of the "miracle" electrified the tribes of the Northwest Territory, and as far away as Minnesota entire bands gave their loyalty to the Shawnee's code. In the Northwest Territory particularly, the Prophet's preachings inspired the natives with new pride and purpose and, as Tecumseh hoped, helped to strengthen the feeling of unity among them. Moreover, as Tenskwatawa's personal power increased, he began to stir his followers with demagogic appeals against Christianized Indians and others who weakened the native cause by their friendship for the whites. Several hundred Indians were killed before Tecumseh personally stopped the purge.

The developments following the eclipse alarmed Harrison, whose agents sent him reports of various tribes that had deposed their old chiefs and gone over to the Prophet. Tension between Great Britain and the United States, ever present since the end of the Revolution, had reached a critical point again, and Harrison and most western settlers were certain that the British in Canada were the real troublemakers behind Tenskwatawa. Gradually, Tecumseh felt the increasing animosity toward the natives, and recognized what its ultimate consequences would be: in their fear of the British, the Americans would again attack the Indians and try to drive them out of more of their lands. He saw only one hope—all the tribes must be brought together to fight as a single people in defense of their common lands.

To avoid premature conflict, he ordered Tenskwatawa to evacuate Greenville, which was too close to settlers in Ohio, and move his center westward to a tract of land in Indiana on the west bank of the Tippecanoe River. There, in May 1808, at the stream's confluence with the Wabash River, Tenskwatawa and the families of eighty of his followers raised the mission house and bark dwellings of a new Prophet's Town. As soon as it was established, Tecumseh and his brother, with several companions and attendants, set out on horseback to unite the tribes for defense.

At village after village in the Northwest Territory, exciting the people with the presence of the Prophet and himself, Tecumseh appealed for their support with thrilling and patriotic oratory. At many places, chiefs who had signed the Treaty of Greenville and wanted no more war with the Americans opposed him, and he suffered many rebuffs. Elsewhere, whole tribes responded with enthusiasm to his speeches, or divided their loyalties between their old chiefs and eager young warriors who agreed with Tecumseh's appeals.

Tecumseh next turned south and west, and in 1809, accompanied by a small band of followers, visited dozens of tribes, from the Seminoles in Florida to the Osages in Missouri. He received attention and sympathy and made many friends; among most of the peoples he visited, he managed to sow the seeds of future action against the Americans. Before the end of the year, he was back in the north and heading into New York State, where he tried in vain to enlist the Iroquois tribes in his alliance. No matter: from Lake Superior to the Gulf of Mexico, he had laid the groundwork for the common defense of the Indians' country by the greatest military alliance in native history.

While he was away, the situation had worsened in Indiana. The war scare had abated, but additional pressures were threatening the natives. There were now more than twenty thousand Americans in southern Indiana, and if they were to receive statehood, for which they were clamoring, they would have to secure more Indian land on which to support a larger white population. The politically ambitious Governor Harrison was as aggressive as any of the settlers, and during the summer of 1809 he decided to force the Indians into a new cession. He sent his agents to Little Turtle and a host of the older and weaker chiefs and, armed with maps of central Indiana, met them at Fort Wayne in September. Harrison's letters reveal that he had little conscience in his dealings with the Indians and that he was not above deceit. He "mellowed" the chiefs with alcohol, and after he had placed considerable pressure on them, they proved obliging. For $7,000 in cash and an annuity of $1,750 they ceded three million acres of land in Indiana, much of it owned by tribes that were not even represented at Fort Wayne.

The new cession enraged Tecumseh. While he had been away trying to unite the Indians in defense of the country they still owned, Indians behind his back had sold more of it. He circulated word that Indian country was the common property of all the tribes, and that he and his allies would refuse to recognize the latest piece of treachery. Angry Indians who agreed with him flocked to the Tippecanoe, and in the spring of 1810, Tecumseh had a force of one thousand warriors at the Prophet's Town, training to repel, if necessary, any attempt by Americans to settle the newly ceded lands. Early in August, ignoring Harrison's invitation to visit the President of the United States in Washington, Tecumseh and the Prophet set off determinedly to see the Governor at Vincennes.

The council was tense and dramatic. In a grove near the Governor's mansion, Tecumseh and Harrison faced one another, both strong, willful leaders of national forces that had met in head-on collision. The two men were proud and suspicious, and as their followers stood nervously in the background, eyeing each other for signs of treachery, the air bristled with hostility. Tecumseh spoke first, beginning slowly, but soon pouring out his words in such swift and passionate flights of oratory that the interpreter had difficulty following.

The Shawnee first reviewed the history of Indian-white relations in the Ohio Valley, and reminded Harrison of every wrong suffered by the natives at the hands of the Americans. Now, he told the Governor, he was trying to unite the Indians, but the American leader was fomenting enmities among them. Tecumseh's words were lofty and eloquent, but we have only the interpreter's stilted translation of his ideas.

> You endeavor to make distinctions. You endeavor to prevent the Indians from doing what we, their leaders, wish them to do —unite and consider their land the common property . . I am a Shawnee. My forefathers were warriors. Their son is a warrior. From them I take only my existence. From my tribe I take nothing. I have made myself what I am. And I would that I could make the red people as great as the conceptions of my mind, when I think of the Great Spirit that rules over all. I would not then come to Governor Harrison to ask him to tear the treaty. But I would say to him, Brother, you have liberty to return to your own country.

Several times Tecumseh turned to his dream of uniting the tribes in order to halt the whites. "The way, the only way to stop this evil," he told Harrison, "is for all the red men to unite in claiming a common and equal right in the land, as it was at first, and should be now—for it never was divided, but belongs to all. No tribe has a right to sell, even to each other, much less to strangers, who demand all, and will take no less. . . ." "Sell a country," he interrupted himself at one point. "Why not sell the air, the clouds, and the great sea, as well as the earth? Did not the Great Spirit make them all for the use of his children?"

Toward the end of his speech, he apparently tried to nettle Harrison. "How can we have confidence in the white people?" he asked him. "When Jesus Christ came upon the earth, you killed Him, and nailed Him to a cross. You thought He was dead, but you were mistaken. You have Shakers among you, and you laugh and make light of their worship." Finally, he pointed to the United States as a model for the natives. "The States," he said, "have set the example of forming a union among all the fires [states]—why should they censure the Indians for following it?" Then, declining Harrison's offer of a chair, he sat down proudly on the ground.

Harrison began his reply by insisting that Tecumseh had no right to contest the sale of land in Indiana, because the Shawnee homeland had been in Georgia. The Indian chief stirred angrily, recognizing the deliberate evasion of his thesis that Indian land everywhere belonged to all natives. As Harrison went on, he became more impatient, and tension among the onlookers began to mount. Suddenly Harrison asserted that the United States had always been fair and just in its dealings with Indians. Tecumseh leaped to his feet and shouted, "It is false! He lies!" As he poured his wrath on Harrison, the Governor unsheathed his sword and started forward. Several whites aimed their guns, and the Indians behind Tecumseh drew their tomahawks. For an instant, a fight seemed imminent. Then Harrison coolly adjourned the council.

The next morning, Tecumseh's temper had subsided, and he sent his apologies to Harrison. The Governor accepted them, and visited the chief's camp. Tecumseh was in a good mood, and the two men sat down together on a bench. Gradually, the Indian kept pushing against Harrison, forcing the American to move closer to one end. Finally, as Harrison was about to be shoved off, he objected, and Tecumseh laughed, pointing out that that was what the American settlers were doing to the Indians.

Harrison's attitude served notice that he intended to keep pressing for more Indian land, and Tecumseh knew that to stop him, he had to hurry his alliances and strengthen the natives' will to resist. Once more, the Shawnee leader made rapid visits to the tribes of Ohio, Indiana, and Michigan, delivering passionate pleas for his confederation. On November 15, 1810, he even crossed to the Canadian side of the Detroit River and, at the British post of Fort Malden, addressed a council of Potawatomis, Ottawas, Sauk, Foxes, and Winnebagos. The next year Harrison, believing that the best defense was vigorous offense, decided the time had come to smash the Prophet's Town and scatter the leaders of Indian opposition.

All he needed was an overt act by the natives to justify his invasion of the Indians' country, and in July 1811 he gained his excuse when Potawatomis killed some white men in Illinois. Harrison claimed at once that they were followers of the Prophet and demanded that the Shawnees on the Tippecanoe surrender them to him for justice. In reply, Tecumseh and the Prophet again visited Vincennes for a personal meeting with the American leader. They refused to deliver the Potawatomis, and once more the council ended in an impasse. The Prophet returned to his center on the Tippecanoe, and Tecumseh, accompanied by twenty-four warriors, set off down the Wabash River, bound on a second attempt to unite the southern tribes behind him.

Tecumseh's second southern journey was a heroic and memorable effort that in five months took him down the Ohio and Mississippi Rivers to the present site of Memphis, through Tennessee to Mississippi, Alabama, Georgia, and Florida, back north again across Georgia to the Carolinas, through the full length of Tennessee to the Ozark Mountains of Arkansas and Missouri, north into Iowa, and eventually back home. Once more, he hurried from village to village, pleading for a united war against the Americans.

His words "fell in avalanches from his lips," one who heard him said. "His eyes burned with supernatural lustre, and his whole frame trembled with emotion. His voice resounded over the multitude—now sinking in low and musical whispers, now rising to the highest key, hurling out his words like a succession of thunderbolts. . . . I have heard many great orators, but I never saw one with the vocal powers of Tecumseh." Wearing only a breechclout and moccasins, with lines of red war paint beneath his eyes, the Shawnee stood alone with his followers amid vast, encircling throngs and cried to the Indians to stop their intertribal wars, to unite in a single nation as the United States had done, and to fight together for all their land before it was too late. Old chiefs listened to him uneasily and argued back. They would not unite with old, hereditary enemies. They would not give up their autonomy to strangers. The kind of union that Tecumseh talked about was for white men, not Indians. And besides, it was already too late.

In historic debates with the greatest chiefs of the South, Tecumseh continued to plead his cause. "Where today are the Pequot?" Tecumseh cried to one audience.

> Where the Narragansett, the Mohican, the Pokanoket and many other once powerful tribes of our people? They have vanished before the avarice and oppression of the white man, as snow before a summer sun. . . . Will we let ourselves be destroyed in our turn without making an effort worthy of our race? Shall we, without a struggle, give up our homes, our country bequeathed to us by the Great Spirit, the graves of our dead and everything that is dear and sacred to us? I know you will cry with me, Never! Never!

Again and again, young warriors shouted their approval, and small groups promised to strike the Americans when Tecumseh gave them the signal. But the older leaders were wary and afraid. Some of them were receiving annuities and gifts from the Americans; some saw only ruin in Tecumseh's plans; and some thought that their people could do well enough by themselves. Only the Creeks and Seminoles, already smoldering with hatred for the Americans, provided the Shawnee with hope.

Disappointed by his failures in the South, Tecumseh returned to the Tippecanoe River early in 1812, only to be met by news of a more stunning setback at home. During the Shawnee leader's absence, Harrison had finally struck at the Prophet's Town. At the head of an army of almost one thousand men, the Governor had marched up the Wabash River, and on the night of November 6, 1811, had camped near the Indian settlement at the mouth of the Tippecanoe. The ominous arrival of the hostile force alarmed the Indians, and at first, without Tecumseh to direct them, they were undecided about what to do. A band of Winnebagos, bolder than the others, argued for an immediate attack on the invading whites, and finally won Tenskwatawa's approval.

In the early hours of morning, some four hundred fifty natives crawled through the darkness toward the Americans. Harrison had placed his men in an unbroken line around the three sides of his triangular-shaped camp, and shortly before four o'clock, a sentry on the northern perimeter saw an Indian moving in the gloom and shot him. In an instant, the whooping natives were on their feet, charging toward the whites. The Americans met them with blazing musketry, and only a few of the Indians were able to crash into the camp, where Harrison's men battled them in hand-to-hand struggles. The rest were chased back, and though they launched a series of rushes at other sides of the camp, they failed to break through.

As the sky lightened, the Indians finally withdrew among the trees, and kept up a desultory fire from cover during the day. By the second day, they had all vanished, and Harrison burned the Prophet's Town.

The number of Indians dead in the battle was never known, though it was estimated to be between twenty-five and forty. Harrison lost sixty-one killed and one hundred twenty-seven wounded, but on his return to the settlements, he announced that he had won a great victory and wrote to the Secretary of War that "the Indians have never sustained so severe a defeat since their acquaintance with the white people." The importance of the battle was soon exaggerated beyond reality; in 1840 the magic of its memory still worked well enough to help elect Harrison to the presidency.

Tecumseh reached the Tippecanoe in late February or early March 1812, and seethed with rage as he viewed what had happened behind his back. His anger was directed against his brother, who had failed to prevent the battle. The southern trip had shown Tecumseh that his confederation was far from ready for the united movement he had planned to lead, and the clash on the Tippecanoe would now set off exactly the kind of border war he had tried to avoid. The tribes would rise individually seeking vengeance, and once more the Americans would deal with them piecemeal. Tecumseh banished the Prophet, but meanwhile the isolated uprisings Tecumseh feared had already begun. Irate bands, crying for revenge, fell on settlers in Indiana and Illinois. They raided independently of one another and without plan, but the panic they aroused united the Americans against all the natives, and strengthened the settlers' conviction that the British and Tecumseh were directing the new attacks. Frontier feelings flamed against both the English and the Indians, and as frightened settlers abandoned their homes and fled south to safety, angry militia units built new forts and blockhouses north of the Ohio River. In Ohio, a large American army under Brigadier General William Hull began to march north to Detroit, while in Vincennes Harrison prepared for the decisive war for which Tecumseh was not yet ready.

During the spring, the tension on the frontier spread to Washington, where it helped to precipitate the War of 1812. On June 18, the United States, under the pressure of Henry Clay and other "War Hawk" legislators from Kentucky and the West, began the war against Great Britain. Almost immediately, both the British and the Americans sent agents among the tribes, appealing for their help in the struggle. Several of the older chiefs, who had opposed Tecumseh and maintained their loyalty to the United States, argued the American case before their tribesmen. But in a large council called by the Americans at Fort Wayne, Tecumseh defied them. "Here is a chance . . ." he cried scornfully, "yes, a chance such as will never occur again—for us Indians of North America to form ourselves into one great combination."

His words fired his listeners, and twice he dramatically broke in two the peace pipes which an American envoy handed him. Then, gathering a large party of Shawnees, Delawares, Kickapoos, and Potawatomis, he marched off to Fort Malden and announced his allegiance to the British. Other bands, remembering his visits and ardent appeals of the past, soon began to join him. Wyandots, Chippewas, and Sioux came from Canada, Michigan, and Minnesota, while an old acquaintance, Black Hawk, who would himself one day lead a war against the whites, moved across the northern wilderness from Illinois and Wisconsin and arrived with a war party of Sauk, Foxes, and Winnebagos. Elsewhere, Indian runners and British agents carried word that Tecumseh had finally declared war on the Americans, and the response of many tribes showed that the Shawnee's travels had not been entirely in vain. Though they fought without Tecumseh's guiding direction, and not as the united Indian people he had envisioned, bands rose against the Americans on every front, driving settlers, traders, and armed forces into retreat in the Northwest, the upper Mississippi, and the Deep South. Before the war ended, the Americans had stopped them, but the costly months of their hostility were scarred by massacres, the disruption of commerce, and the desolation of settlements from the outskirts of St. Louis to the Creek country of Alabama and Georgia.

On the Canadian side of the Detroit River, Tecumseh soon
had a native army of between one thousand and three thousand men. The American General Hull established his headquarters at the town of Detroit, and on July 12 launched an
invasion of Canada. Crossing the river with three thousand
men, he prepared to attack the three-hundred-man British garrison at Fort Malden. Hull was an elderly hero of the Revolution
who had become weak and timid with age. His advance guard
won a preliminary skirmish with a small mixed body of Indians and British, but soon afterward, Tecumseh and one hundred fifty warriors ambushed another of his scouting parties,
then slipped behind Hull and cut off one of his supply columns
coming north from Ohio.

Hull panicked, and when he further learned that Chippewa allies of Tecumseh had assisted in the British capture
of Michilimackinac in northern Michigan and were probably
canoeing south to attack Detroit, he hastily abandoned his
invasion of Canada and recrossed the river to the American
shore. His officers and men were appalled by his cowardice,
but the threat of Indian strength now hung heavy over them
all. On August 8, an earlier relief column having been cut to
ribbons, Hull sent a new force of six hundred men to try to rescue the cut-off supply expedition, under Captain Henry Brush,
now pinned down behind the River Raisin. By this time some
British troops had also crossed the river, and at Monguaga, a
few miles south of Detroit, they joined Tecumseh's Indians and
helped to intercept the new American relief column. A furious
battle ensued, during which Tecumseh fought with conspicu-
ous bravery and received a wound in the leg, but the British
and Indians were eventually forced to abandon the field and
withdraw to the Canadian side of the river. Still, the mauled

American troops dared move no farther south, and Brush's supply convoy remained in hiding south of the River Raisin.

On August 13, Major General Isaac Brock arrived at Malden with three hundred British reinforcements from the east. Brock, the Lieutenant Governor of Canada, was an able and resolute military leader, a huge man well over six feet tall, with a powerful physique and a gentle and considerate nature. He had heard great praise of Tecumseh and had already formed a high opinion of the Indian chief. On the night he reached Malden he read Hull's dispatches, which Tecumseh had captured, and realized from them the extent of the American commander's fears and weaknesses. When Tecumseh came in to be introduced to him, Brock asked the Shawnee leader for his opinion of what they ought to do next. Tecumseh pleased him by urging an immediate attack on Detroit. Only one British officer supported the Indian's view, but at four o'clock in the morning, Brock decided to follow Tecumseh's advice, and sent a message across the river, calling on Hull to surrender. The American refused, and as British guns opened fire on Detroit, Tecumseh's Indians embarked for the American shore.

At the same time, Brock allowed one of his couriers to be captured by the Americans. The courier shattered Hull's nerves by reporting that five thousand Indians were arriving from the upper Lakes to join Tecumseh. Hull had still been occupied in trying to rescue Brush's convoy and had just dispatched a third force of three hundred fifty men to bring it in. Tecumseh's men landed between Detroit and the new expedition, and once more the American relief column was brought to a halt when its leaders realized what had happened. As the men wheeled about to march against the Indians in their rear,

Tecumseh ranged his warriors around the fort and tried a ruse. Marching his men in single file, he moved them three times out of the woods and across a clearing in full view of the fort's defenders, so that it looked like the expected Chippewa reinforcements had arrived from the north. The stratagem had its desired effect: without a struggle, Hull raised a white flag and surrendered Detroit.

The American commander's ignominious action shocked the United States. His capitulation even included Brush's beleaguered column, but those men, learning what had happened, turned around in fright and raced safely back to the Ohio settlements. The fall of Detroit spread new panic across the frontier, but in the fallen city, the helpless members of the garrison soon found themselves turning from contempt for Hull to appreciation for Tecumseh. Though he had fought as an Indian, stripped to leggings and breechclout, the Shawnee chief dressed proudly in white men's clothes for his entrance into Detroit, and his friendly and dignified conduct gradually won the admiration of the prisoners, many of whom had fearfully expected to be massacred.

The dramatic victory, meanwhile, had given the Shawnee leader new hope that he might, after all, achieve his dream of an Indian nation. Additional tribes were entering the war and were striking at other American strongholds. Potawatomis had captured Fort Dearborn, and aided even by a band of Miamis, who had long opposed Tecumseh's appeal for unity, were laying siege to Fort Wayne. If victories continued the Americans might well be forced to recognize an Indian country. In the fall of 1812, Tecumseh made another tour to the South, principally to see the Creeks, who had promised to support his cause.

Soon after he returned north, part of the Creek Confederation commenced a war across the South that cost the Americans thousands of lives and millions of dollars.

By April of 1813, Tecumseh was once again back at Malden. On his way home, he had picked up six hundred recruits from among the Illinois tribes, and now had three thousand natives under his command, one of the largest Indian armies ever assembled. During the Shawnee's absence, however, General Brock had been killed in action on the Niagara border, and Colonel Henry Procter, a petulant, small-minded officer, had taken command at Malden. He was a fat, haughty man who was disdainful of Indians, and Tecumseh let him know quickly that he considered him a poor substitute for the bold, imaginative Brock.

In January, Procter and a force of Indians had gained a notable victory at the River Raisin over an army of eight hundred fifty Kentuckians, killing or capturing the entire American force. Procter had assured the Americans that he would not allow the Indians to harm the prisoners, but when some of the natives got drunk, he looked the other way and did nothing to halt their butchery of all wounded and defenseless captives. When Tecumseh learned about it, he criticized the British commander for weakness in not having controlled the natives. If the Indians were ever to gain recognition of their own state, he told both the British and tribal leaders, they must gain the respect of white men for their humanity and civilized conduct.

The grisly massacre had also aroused the American West to a spirit of no-quarter revenge, and by the time Tecumseh returned from the South, his old adversary, General William Henry Harrison, was marching toward Detroit with a new army to avenge the savagery at the River Raisin. On the Maumee River, near the site of Wayne's victory of Fallen Timbers, Harrison paused to build a new post called Fort Meigs; suddenly, on April 25, 1813, he found himself besieged by an army of British and Indians, which had come south from Malden under Procter and Tecumseh. A brigade of eleven hundred Kentuckians was on its way through the wilderness to reinforce Harrison's army, and a little more than a week after the siege had begun, the new force made its appearance on the river. In an effort to break through the British lines and get into the fort, the Kentuckians divided their forces and moved down both banks of the river; but before they could reach the fort, some eight hundred troops were surrounded and almost annihilated by Tecumseh's Indians. Almost five hundred Americans were killed, and one hundred fifty captured.

While Tecumseh remained at the siege lines, some of the English and Indians marched the prisoners downriver to Procter's headquarters at the British Fort Miami. Once more when the Indians began to murder the captives, Procter did nothing to restrain them. This time, however, a native carried word of what was happening to Tecumseh, and in a wild rage the Shawnee leader galloped to the British camp and hurled himself into the scene of massacre. The Indians had already killed more than twenty captives, and were tomahawking and scalping others when Tecumseh arrived. He knocked down one Indian with his sword, grabbed another by the throat, and lunged at the rest. As the natives drew back, he shouted at them, "Are there no men here?" The carnage stopped abruptly, and the Shawnee chief hastened to see Procter. When he demanded to know why the natives had again been allowed to kill prisoners, Procter answered lamely, "Your Indians cannot be controlled. They cannot be commanded." His reply filled the Shawnee with contempt. "You are unfit to command," he sneered at the British leader. "Go and put on petticoats." Then he added bitterly, "I conquer to save, and you to murder."

A couple of days later, over Tecumseh's objection, Procter lifted the siege of Fort Meigs. The Indian leader was disgusted and two months later forced the British commander to surround the post once more. But Procter was weak and indecisive, and soon afterward he again abandoned the attempt to take the American fort. As opportunities continued to slip away from Procter, the Indians lost faith in his leadership. Finally, on September 13, disaster struck them all in a naval battle on Lake Erie. At Put-in-Bay, an American fleet under Commodore Oliver Hazard Perry swept the British from the lake, and cut off Procter's army from its eastern supply bases.

Aware of his isolation and fearing Harrison, who was now beginning to move against him with a heavily reinforced army, the British commander decided to abandon the Detroit region and withdraw along the northern shore of Lake Erie to join other English troops on the Niagara frontier, leaving the Indians to shift for themselves.

Procter's duplicity inflamed Tecumseh. Gathering his Indians together on the Fort Malden parade ground, he humiliated the British commander in front of the other white officers, told the natives that the English were flying from the enemy, and later called Procter "a miserable old squaw."

That same day, Procter began his withdrawal, and in time Tecumseh and his Indians were forced to follow him. The Shawnee was crushed. He had managed to wring from the British general a promise to retreat only as far as the Thames River, about fifty miles away, but as the natives trooped off, leaving behind them the country Tecumseh had worked so hard and so long to save for his people, the chief's spirits flagged, and he was overcome with gloom. "We are now going to follow the British," he told one of his warriors, "and I feel certain that we shall never return."

On September 27, Harrison's army crossed Lake Erie to Canada and commenced its pursuit of the British. Procter led the retreating army. Tecumseh with the Indians, including a band of Sioux from far-off Minnesota, brought up the rear, holding off advance units of the Americans while denouncing Procter for refusing to stand and fight.

On the night of October 4, he went into camp with the British near the present town of Thamesville, a short distance up the Thames River. They had now reached the line that Procter had promised to hold. But that night, as if he had accepted the final defeat of everything he had lived and fought for, Tecumseh had a premonition of death. As he sat by his fire with his closest Indian lieutenants, all of them men who had followed him loyally for years, he said calmly: "Brother warriors, we are about to enter an engagement from which I shall not return. My body will remain on the field of battle."

The next morning, Procter again wanted to retreat, and Tecumseh had another bitter quarrel with him, this time threatening to shoot him with a rifle. Finally, the British commander agreed to honor his promise and make a stand at their present location. But it was Tecumseh, the Indian, who suddenly became the leader of the entire army. While Procter issued faint-hearted orders to his British and Canadian units, Tecumseh selected a defensive position where the main highway ran between the Thames River and a wooded swamp. Organizing the field of combat, the Shawnee placed the British in a line across the highway, with the river and swamp protecting the left and right flanks respectively. On the other side of the swamp, he divided the Indians into two groups, putting one of them under his own command as an extension of the British line, and placing the other in a larger swamp that paralleled the highway, and from which the warriors could sweep the road with flanking fire.

As the British and Indians took their positions, Tecumseh hunted up Procter and, in a forgiving mood, tried to reassure him. "Father," he said, "have a big heart! Tell your young men to be firm and all will be well." Then the Indian moved along the British line, inspecting the positions of the men and pausing to raise their spirits with friendly words. "He pressed the hand of each officer as he passed," a British major related after the battle. "[He] made some remark in Shawnee—which was sufficiently understood by the expressive signs accompanying, and then passed away forever from our view."

At four in the afternoon the Americans appeared down the road. Harrison's force of thirty-five hundred troops included fifteen hundred mounted Kentuckians under Colonel Richard Johnson, and two infantry divisions. Against him were seven hundred British troops and slightly more than one thousand Indians. Harrison had scouted the English positions and decided to attack with his cavalrymen, sending the infantry after them in close support. As a bugle sounded the charge, Johnson's Kentuckians galloped forward, shouting, "Remember the River Raisin." Johnson himself led one battalion against Tecumseh's Indians and sent the rest of his men toward the British lines, which were barring the road. Those horsemen smashed headlong into the English units, and the terrified British gave way at once. Procter, who had been waiting in the rear, jumped in his carriage and fled from the battlefield. His troops, cut to pieces, threw up their hands and surrendered in a body.

On the British right flank, meanwhile, Tecumseh's Indians met Johnson's charge with a blaze of musketry that threw the Americans back, and forced the horsemen to dismount and fight from behind trees. At the same time a division of infantry advanced on the run to support the cavalry. They spotted the Indians in the swamp that flanked the road and veered off to attack them. As the Americans pressed into the woods and through the miry underbrush, the battle mounted. Over the din, many men could hear Tecumseh's huge voice, shouting at the Indians to turn back the Americans. "He yelled like a tiger, and urged his braves to the attack," one of the Kentuckians later said.

Other men caught glimpses of the Shawnee leader, running among the Indians with a bandage still tied around one arm, injured in an earlier skirmish. Now American bullets hit him again and again. Blood poured from his mouth and ran down his body, but the great warrior staggered desperately among the trees, still crying to his Indians to hold. The dream of an Indian nation was slipping fast, and as twilight came, it disappeared entirely. Suddenly, the Americans realized that they no longer heard Tecumseh's voice, or saw his reckless figure. As darkness halted the battle, the Indians slipped away through the swamp, and the Americans dug in along the road.

In the morning, Harrison's men hunted in vain for Tecumseh's body. Somehow, during the night, it had vanished, and though several of the Shawnee chieftain's closest followers said later that they had taken it away in the darkness and buried it secretly, some white men wondered for years whether Tecumseh was still alive. The Americans captured no Indians during the battle, but the struggle on the Thames River scattered the warriors and ended further serious resistance in the Northwest Territory.

Tecumseh's dream, unrecognized by his enemies, disappeared with his body. No new native leader arose to unite the tribes, and in a few years the advancing tide of civilization completed the demoralization and decay of the proud peoples who had once called the country of the Northwest Territory their home. In time, the pitiful survivors, reduced to poverty and sickness, were forcibly dispossessed of what little land remained to them and were removed to reservations on the west side of the Mississippi River. Many of them, as Tecumseh had foreseen, were moved again and again to make way for new advances of the whites. Today, across the state of Oklahoma, the dispersed descendants of the Shawnee chief's warriors live among other and more numerous tribes, ignored and forgotten by most Americans. To them, however, belongs the pride of knowing that one of their people was the greatest of all the American Indian leaders, a majestic figure who might have given all the Indians a nation of their own.

4

The Hudson's Bay Company and the American Indians

◇◇◇

This essay first appeared as a three-part article in the 1971 Brand Book, a publication of the New York Posse of the Westerners, a loosely formed national organization of historians, journalists, editors, booksellers, and just plain Western "buffs." (The New York Posse, one of Alvin Josephy's favorite organizations, normally held its meetings in a conference room overlooking the huge, highly polished copper equipment in Jacob Ruppert's old brewery on the Upper East Side.) The articles were republished in 1972 in the magazine The American West.

Displayed here is the wide range and intensity of Josephy's research and his interest in all aspects of Indian history and culture, in this case the two centuries of the Hudson's Bay Company's dominance of the fur trade in most of Canada as well as parts of what is the United States today. Further, it is a unique historical case study of the impact on a native population, both positive and, ultimately negative, of a purely capitalist, profit-driven enterprise, quite apart from military or political pressures.

Beginning in the fifteenth century the peoples of Western Europe, equipped with superior technology and armament, sailed out of their ports and established dominion over the native inhabitants of large parts of the rest of the world. Engaging in conflict for monopolistic positions among themselves, they exploited, changed, and destroyed native societies with which they dealt, and, in the process, enriched the economies of their own countries and acquired the wherewithal to increase further their technological superiority over the peoples they dominated.

The Hudson's Bay Company was an institution of that outward surge from Europe. Men, of course, act within the context of the morality and the just and allowable behavior of their own times and cultures, and it is less than honest to attempt to judge events of the past solely in terms of a later day's ideas of right and wrong. Nevertheless, the relations between the Hudson's Bay Company and the American Indians can be seen fairly and truly only from a perspective that recognizes the imperialistic dynamics of the company during its fur trade heyday from 1670 to 1870—the time span with which this study is concerned.

By a Royal Charter granted May 2, 1670, the *Governor and Company of Adventurers of England trading into Hudson's Bay*, became the "true and absolute Lordes and Proprietors" of a vast portion of present-day Canada, all of it, save a small fringe of the Hudson Bay shoreline, unexplored and unknown, but surmised to be inhabited by many native peoples who would provide the new company with furs.

Within this huge territory, which was given the name of Rupert's Land, the company was granted ownership of the land and of mineral and fishing rights, as well as the exclusive right to trade with the natives. Though responsible for its actions to the Crown, the Parliament, and British public opinion, the company, as "Lordes" of the grant, was free to rule, administer, and police the native populations in any way that seemed necessary and possible.

Later, in the nineteenth century, the company acquired additional rights to all the territory west and northwest of Rupert's Land. This, in effect, spread its authority across the homelands and hunting and fishing grounds of all the native inhabitants of British North America outside the boundaries of Canada, as Canada was constituted prior to 1867.

All of this was consistent with traditional European practice. Sovereignty was claimed by discovery or conquest; lands and rights were granted to individuals and groups by the governments of the nations claiming sovereignty. Native sovereignty was rarely, if ever, considered, though occasionally more than lip service was paid to the recognition that because the Indians owned the land, their title to it had "to be extinguished." Thus, in 1668, Captain Zachariah Gillam, commander of the *Nonsuch* of the adventurers first trading expedition to Hudson Bay, even before the Charter had been granted, is said to have made a treaty with Indians in James Bay, formally purchasing Rupert's River "and the Lands thereabouts." How binding this was, and how seriously it served as a precedent for further company land acquisitions from natives, will be discussed later.

It cannot be known how many Indians and Eskimos were under the Hudson's Bay Company's stewardship or influence. The maximum number may have been considerably more than two hundred fifty thousand. They included the members of a great number of different tribes of many language families and varying environments and cultures. In the so-called Arctic cultural region, stretching from the coasts of Labrador and Hudson Bay, across northern Canada to the present boundary with Alaska, were numerous groups of Eskimos. In the sub-arctic regions were Algonquian-speaking tribes, living generally south and east of Hudson Bay, and including Naskapi, Montagnais, and Cree, though the latter also circled about the southern end of Hudson Bay and extended northwestward to the Churchill River and westward beyond the north side of Lake Winnipeg.

West of Hudson's Bay, stretching across the vast subarctic north, were a host of Athapascan-speaking tribes, including the Chipewyan, Beaver, Dogrib, Carrier, Hare, Sekani, Nahani, Slave, Tahltan, Tuchone, Yellowknife, and Kutchin. In the woodland country farther south, from the northern side of the Great Lakes to the Canadian plains, were other Algonquian-speakers, including Ojibwas (also called Chippewas and, in the case of some of their bands, Saulteurs) and Ottawas. On the Canadian plains were more Crees, as well as Athapascan-speaking Sarcis, Siouan-speaking Assiniboines, and Atsinas (known by several names, including Gros Ventres), Piegans, Bloods, and Blackfoot, all of the Algonquian language family.

As Hudson's Bay Company trade pushed westward beyond the bounds of Rupert's Land, a huge number of additional tribes inhabiting the Rocky Mountains, the western Plateau and Columbia Basin, and the Northwest Coast came under company domination or influence. They included such diverse peoples as the sea-oriented Haidas and Tlingits of the coast, the horse-mounted Kutenais, Nez Perce, and Flatheads of the Plateau, the Shoshonis and Paiutes of the Oregon and Idaho Great Basin region, and the Chinooks and neighboring fishing tribes of the lower Columbia River.

The map shows the extent of the Hudson's Bay Company's "charter" from the Crown—originally all lands draining into Hudson's Bay—and much of the territory worked by Hudson's Bay traders, the Northwest Company, and free traders and trappers as the fur trade moved west.

All of these peoples, with their differing cultural backgrounds, languages, and social, political, and religious systems, were at one time or another engaged in trade with the officers and servants of the Hudson's Bay Company, who, in addition, were free to impose upon them whatever authority they considered appropriate and practicable. In that light, it is a remarkable testament to the company, and its policies and personnel, that its members were able to cope, usually on company terms, so successfully and harmoniously for so long a period of time with so many different peoples of varied cultures. The reason is not hard to discover, for it must be said further that, in comparison with the domination exerted over native peoples by many other Europeans in North America and elsewhere, the Hudson's Bay Company pursued its long-range goals with an unusual degree of self-discipline, characterized by a steadfast commitment to restraint and, in general, a conscientious regard for humane and principled dealings with the natives.

The company did not come to the New World to conquer or dispossess the Indians. It did not covet their land, hunting grounds, or fishing stations. It did not mean to disrupt them, undermine their beliefs, destroy their means of existence, shatter their organizations and ways of life, or change them into white men. It did not come with threats of death or of conflict. It was a commercial enterprise, in business to make a profit buying furs peaceably from the natives at prices that would bring the highest rewards to its stockholders. Since the Indians provided the furs, common sense dictated policies that would draw the natives with their pelts, in increasing numbers and without interruption, to company posts and traders.

To further the goal of maximum trade and profits, company policies regarding relations with the Indians were sternly dictated and monitored by the Committee in London and were fairly consistent. From the start, the traders at the Bay were instructed to use a "mild and benevolent approach" to the Indians and to treat them in such a manner as to encourage their wish to continue to provide furs to the company and also bring in the trade of other Indians from their own and additional tribes.

"Draw downe the Indians by fayre and gentle meancs to trade with us," the Committee directed Henry Sergeant, the new Governor at James Bay in 1683, exhorting him also to use justice and humanity in dealing with the natives. Again, in the 1730s, the *Letters Outward* to the traders at the Bay were filled with instructions to "use" the natives "very civilly" and "at all times to Trade upon an Equal Foundation." This was not rhetoric, but practical policy, laid down decade after decade in directions to company officers at the various posts. The company needed and desired friendly natives, not enemies. It was not "the intention or the interest of the Company to create Contentions" with the Indians, the London Committee wrote to personnel in the field in 1805.

Officers and servants who conducted themselves or the trade in such a way as to violate these instructions and offend the native suppliers of furs usually received reproof, stern punishment, or recall by the Committee. In the 1720s, reports of "irregularities and debaucheries, disgusting and terrifying the Natives from coming to trade" resulted in the disciplining of the leadership at Albany Fort and the recall of some of its personnel. Similarly, on occasions when a company post or company personnel were attacked by Indians, the Committee was quick to suspect that the natives had been responding to ill-usage by traders or servants who had violated orders from home. Explanations were demanded, and little sympathy was given offenders.

An uninterrupted, orderly trade required, in addition, peace among the tribes, and almost from the beginning the Committee included peacemaking activities as one of the capstones of its Indian policy. The Indians, as well as the whites, sought monopolistic positions for themselves in the trade. A tribe, dealing directly with the whites and acquiring the white men's guns and manufactured goods, wished to be the only tribe in that fortunate position, and certainly did not relish equal good fortune for its enemies. With the guns received from the whites, it would gain superiority over its rivals, who would not have guns. Even when it had no hostile intent against another tribe, it wished to play the favored position of middleman, turning a profit for itself, as it were, by trading to the other tribes the goods it had received from the whites.

Since this ran counter to the interests of the company—which desired the trade of all tribes that could provide it with furs—diplomacy, goodwill, and tact had to be called upon regularly. During its first years at the Bay, the company traded principally with Crees, who had been expanding aggressively toward the north and west. With trade guns, the Crees became more of a menace to their enemies, all of whom were rapidly perceived by the company to be potential suppliers of furs. As early as 1690, the company realized that it had to get to the interior tribes, make peace between them and the Crees, and persuade them that they would receive the same fair treatment that the Crees were receiving at the company's trading posts on the Bay. Missions like those of Henry Kelsey, who in 1690–92 journeyed inland to the Canadian plains and tried to make peace between the Crees and Assiniboines, and William Stuart, who, in a heroic trip to the Northwest in 1715–16, actually did achieve peace between the Crees and their traditional enemies, the Chipewyans, were notable episodes in a continuing peacemaking effort on the company's part.

The policy could not, and did not, always succeed. One of the more destructive results of the fur trade—resulting sometimes simply from the presence of the Hudson's Bay Company as a source of supply of guns and a fountainhead of friction, but more often from competition between different white fur gatherers, including members of the Hudson's Bay Company— was accelerated warfare between the tribes. Beyond the control of peacemaking company traders, Ojibwas with guns drove the unarmed Sioux out of their Minnesota homelands and onto the Plains, thus causing a wave of collisions of one tribe against another. In the north and northwest, Chipewyans enrolled in the trade stepped up their terrorization of Eskimos, and in the west, newly armed Blackfeet raided the Kutenais and Shoshonis, scattering people into and beyond the Rockies.

As Hudson's Bay Company men reached each tribe, they tried to bring peace. Sometimes their efforts achieved success, and sometimes they were able to establish, at best, only a temporary and uneasy period of truce. On many occasions, the peacemakers themselves fell victims of the very tribes they had armed. Hudson's Bay Company officers and servants, again and again, felt the angry enmity of Atsinas and Blackfeet who tried to halt their trade with tribes west of the Rocky Mountains.

The very nature of the Hudson's Bay Company, with its tight direction and control over personnel, aided the Committee in assuring a maximum observance of its Indian policy by the men in the field. To minimize friction, to establish and maintain the Indians' respect for the whites, and to avoid private, competitive trade by individuals, strict rules were issued from time to time. Men at the posts were forbidden to mix with the natives, take native wives, give alcohol to the natives, or behave in any fashion that would arouse native contempt for them. Rigid regulations defined how trade was to be conducted at the posts. Indians were often barred from certain parts of the establishments; large numbers of Indians were rarely admitted to the posts at one time. Frequently all trade was conducted with business-like formality through a small window or hole in the wall.

In actual practice, some of the rules were more frequently violated than observed. Private trade with Indians, particularly by ships' captains and top company officials at the posts, was a constant headache to the Committee. Furthermore, asking men in the long and lonely isolation of wilderness trading houses to ignore the social company of Indian women was unrealistic. Most men managed to find ways to fraternize with the Indians around the posts. Not a few of the governors and chief factors of the company, including such men of authority and influence as George Simpson, James Isham, Andrew Graham, John McLoughlin, and David Thompson, took Indian wives and raised families of half-blood children. One of the latter, Moses Norton, the part-Cree son of Governor Richard Norton, even became chief factor at Churchill in the 1760s, while many other half bloods also rose to positions of prominence in the company's ranks. Finally, the company's history was spotted with episodes that reflected more serious violations of rules: murders, armed attacks by Indians, and the burning of posts often resulted from alcoholic binges, the cheating of natives, or incidents of overfamiliarity.

In a further attempt to ensure fair and consistent dealings with the Indians, the company also utilized the rigid *Standard of Trade*, a price list of how many beaver pelts it expected to receive for each item of trade, such as ten skins for a gun and so forth. The Standard was intended to show all the Indians that they were treated alike, that there was no chance for haggling, that they could get no better deal at one post as against another, and that the company was an honorable one that made plain its prices and stuck to them. At the same time, the Standard reflected the tight organizational control of the company: the men were all employees who followed rules and had no freedom to risk problems and difficulties by setting their own prices or varying them as they saw fit.

In practice, especially when the traders were faced by competitors for the Indians' furs, the rigidity of the Standard disappeared. Sometimes the traders' complaints and advice induced the Committee to agree to changes in the price list or to differences in prices from post to post. Sometimes the traders simply felt they had to make the changes themselves on the spot, and sometimes they got completely around the Standard by giving added "presents" to the Indians or—in a nefarious practice that became known as the *Overplus of Trade*— by paying the Indians less than the called-for price, or short measures.

When the Overplus practice became known in London, the traders pleaded that they used the difference, which they had saved the company, to make presents to Indians or to provide credit to Indian fur suppliers (itself a practice on which the Committee generally frowned). There is evidence that the Committee tolerated the Overplus practice, even though it must have known that it constituted the defrauding of Indians. In the mid-eighteenth century, for example, one Richard White, a clerk for seven years at Albany Fort, told a Parliamentary investigating committee that some of the governors "have their Measure for Powder too short, and don't fill even that short Measure above half full; that the Profits gained by this Method are distinguished by the name of the Overplus Trade, which signifies the Number of Skins which are gained more than are paid for on the footing of the Standard; that the Company knows of this practice . . . and either the Governor, or the Company, takes all the Profits of the Overplus trade."*

Although the Charter gave it a monopoly position in Rupert's Land, the Hudson's Bay Company was rarely without competition—often of the bitterest and most violent sort—throughout the entire 1670–1870 period. At one time or another, the competitors included British interlopers in Rupert's Land; French traders from the St. Lawrence, sometimes supported by French naval power; Canadians out of Montreal and Quebec; New England colonial traders; American fur companies

---

* This manuscript was read by representatives of the Hudson's Bay Company, and at my request, one of them graciously furnished me with a critique of some of its points. Although they do not quarrel with any of the factual material, and in the main merely stress company feeling concerning certain of my interpretations, I am including them in acknowledgment of the company's interest in the article, and for the further interest they may have for the reader.

"The Overplus," said the company representative, "usually effected by short measure, was in the main, I believe, used for gifts or liquor for the Indians, a customary preliminary to trading and one used by the competitors, in fact a reserve for which there was no provision in the accounts of trade. There were no doubt abuses by unscrupulous individuals who lined their own pockets, but the impression left is that the Company was just making an extra profit at the expense of the Indian."

and free trappers and traders; and Russians on the Northwest Coast. Inevitably, the circumstances of competition demanded flexibility, and even change, in the company's relations with the Indians.

To draw fur-supplying Indians to themselves and away from competitors, and to retain the loyalty of natives in the face of seduction by others, the company's traders relied principally on their ability to supply the Indians with a more reliable and better grade of trade goods than were offered by their rivals. In this they received determined support from the members of the London Committee, who directed the purchasing and shipping of quality goods which the natives desired, and which would not disappoint them. Brazil tobacco, the kind most favored by the natives, was purchased in Portugal. High-quality cloth and manufactured goods were shopped for in Great Britain. In 1780 the first of the famous Hudson's Bay Company "point" blankets were introduced to the Indians; their superiority over the blankets offered by other traders was recognized so quickly by the natives that after 1789 they became one of the more popular articles of the company's trade.

In many instances, the offering of better-quality goods kept competition at a disadvantage. But often it was not enough. The Indians welcomed competition among the whites, shopping around not only for the best goods, but the best prices. At such times, the Hudson's Bay Company traders were forced into improvisations that represented violations of a normally conducted trade. The Standard of Trade was eroded, as prices paid to Indians were raised at individual posts in order to outbid competition. The relaxing of the Standard, in time, worked as well against the Indians, for once the prices were raised, they could also be lowered. Thus, when competition disappeared, traders had no hesitancy in lowering their prices abruptly, sometimes to well below their original levels. When that occurred, Indians, who had become dependent on trade, had no choice but to accept the new prices.

Even the flexibility in prices often failed the company. Its traders then fell back, though sometimes reluctantly, on using the ultimate, and most reprehensible, lure of the fur trade. Like a thread running through the records of the Hudson's Bay Company is the sustained sentiment among the members of the London Committee against the use of alcohol at the posts overseas. Moderate use by the men was sometimes permitted, but it was not to be given to the natives. Nevertheless, it was recognized both at home and in the field that alcohol was a need the Indians possessed when they possessed no others; if the competition used it—and it did—and it was the only way to procure furs for the company, then its use had to be permitted.

As early as 1668 the records show that company ships took brandy with them to the Bay, although it may be that it was solely for the use of the whites. However, the company traders soon realized that the French had long been using it in exchange for furs. Soon there were incidents of its employment by the English. Competition gradually increased brandy's use by both sides. After 1706, the Hudson's Bay Company was sending gin and West Indian rum as well as brandy to its posts on the Bay. The result was the debauchment of the Indians, a conscience-less process that quickened during the company's competition with the Montreal-based "Pedlars" south of James Bay after 1763 and on the Saskatchewan after 1770.

The liquor produced the furs, usually at cheap prices, but it demoralized tribes, destroyed their standards, self-respect, independence, and health, provoked individuals into violence against each other and the whites, and led to endless turmoil and all sorts of difficulties for the hapless traders—who saw no way to stop using it as long as the competition employed it. "Brandy Brandy is the cry," wrote Humphrey Martin from Albany River in the early 1770s.

At times, the use of alcohol, tolerated by the London Com mittee, which looked the other way, made a mockery of the company's best intentions of "fayre and gentle" treatment of the Indians. In 1777 Matthew Cocking, totally frustrated in his attempts to wean Indians away from Canadian competitors on the Saskatchewan, concluded that liquor had to be used. Thereafter, the alcoholic floodgates were opened in the western trade. The debauchment of the Plains tribes proceeded with little restraint, providing, decade after decade, one of the more shameful chapters in the relationship of white men with North American Indians.

In its use of alcohol, the Hudson's Bay Company was probably more restrained than its rivals, the Pedlars, or later the North West Company, the Russians, and various groups of American traders. The London Committee offered steady reminders that it deplored its use and earnestly desired that it not be employed. Its sentiments were echoed by its more responsible officers in the field, and men like George Simpson and John McLoughlin took the initiative in trying to secure pacts with rival traders to stop the liquor traffic. They did, on their own, halt the use of alcohol whenever competition slackened or disappeared. But as late as the 1860s the Hudson's Bay

Company felt it had to permit the reintroduction of liquor in the trade because new competitors had started using it again on the Pacific Coast and the Central Plains.*

Withal, Hudson's Bay Company policy, as planned and directed in London, and carried out by officers and servants in the field, had, in general, the desired results for the company as a profit-making institution. Not all of the company's men were good, and not all of its orders and instructions were faithfully observed. But, in one way or another, it got on better with the Indians than its rivals, holding their loyalty through the years and outstaying all competition. At times, even competitors admitted as much, though none perhaps so generously as Colin Robertson, a former North West Company clerk who, when seeking to join the Hudson's Bay Company after 1804, commended it for "the mode you employ in transacting business with the natives of this Country, where your Candour and Generosity so far eclipses that of the Canadian Merchant that every impartial man must regret that you have not that footing in the North which your Conduct together with the natural advantages you possess entitles you to."

When a decade later intense rivalry developed between the Hudson's Bay Company and the North West Company in the Athabaska country, Robertson's observation received confirmation: despite aggressive, and often violent Nor'Wester competition, the Indians, by and large, gave their loyalty to the

* HBC: "Liquor had not been an Indian trade item, but was certainly used as an inducement to trade in the preliminaries. It was, if my recollection is correct, supplied to other Europeans at a post, teachers, physicians, missionaries, and so forth. In British Columbia in the 1860s the HBC was not in a privileged position, just a trading company in the colony."

Hudson's Bay Company. The North West Company, according to one of its own men, Simon McGillivray, Jr., lost "character, reputation and fame" among the natives, and the conflict weakened that organization and contributed to its eventual demise.

So much for the London-directed policies of the Hudson's Bay Company. The achievement of the company's goal, however, the acquisition of furs to sell for annual profits, rested, as must be clear by now, on intimate and personal day-to-day relationships between two sets of humans, the traders and the Indians. From their first arrival at the Bay, the white men, few in number and alone and isolated in an alien land, needed the Indians. The latter supplied not only furs, but food that kept alive the men at the posts and those who traveled in the interior. Along the Bay, groups of Indians—they came to be known as Home Guards—settled around the posts and for many years provided the whites with huge stores of geese, partridge, and other wildfowl. There and elsewhere, Indians also brought in fish and wild game, and in the buffalo country entire bands supplied the company with its annual need of the pemmican that provisioned the journeys to the fur lands of the north and far west. In addition, the natives were essential as ambassadors to other tribes, and as guides, interpreters, translators, and companions and allies in the wilderness.

On numerous occasions, Hudson's Bay Company men were the first whites to be seen by Indians. Almost without exception, initial contacts were friendly. Since the traders' presence generally raised no threat that was discernible to the natives, but, on the contrary, made possible the Indians' acquisition of guns and other products which they keenly desired, goodwill could reign. The long record of relationships between the races was, on the whole, one of tranquility.*

In the "community of interests" of buyer and seller in the fur trade, many diaries and journals of the traders bear witness to the friendship and help the Indians gave them. The natives' contributions, in fact, were often decisive to the explorations and other achievements that are usually credited to the whites alone. But today they are frequently overlooked even in assessments of the fur-gathering successes of the traders. It should not be forgotten that the Indians showed the whites the canoe routes, trails, and passes of the continent, often going along with the fur men, sharing hardships and perils with them, and frequently entering country of their own mortal enemies. One thinks immediately of the loyal Crees who traveled with Anthony Henday to the Blackfeet in 1754, of the "sociable, kind and sensible" Matonabbee, who led Samuel Hearne to the Coppermine River in 1772–73, and of the Chipewyans who suffered and almost perished with David Thompson during his dangerous journey to Athabaska Lake in 1796. Nor should it be forgotten that the Indians showed the whites how to build and travel in canoes and how to make and use different types of snowshoes, and that they instructed them in fishing and hunting techniques and in adapting themselves to wilderness life. They introduced the traders, moreover, to arts and skills of woodcraft, to pemmican, and to many articles of clothing,

---

*   Eds. note: Indians across the continent had long-established trade networks, and trading furs was, as Vine Deloria, Jr., points out in *Indians of the Pacific Northwest*, a natural step. Indians were more likely to understand trading mentality than later settler mentalities.

including moccasins, fur mittens and caps, capotes, and skin leggings, all of which the whites adopted.

In general, the men of the Hudson's Bay Company were no different in their personal attitudes toward Indians than other white fur traders. The officers and servants, as already noted, were responsible to an organized company that not only controlled and checked their conduct, but, to a degree anyway, influenced their attitudes. In addition, many of the officers were men of character who tried to keep the country free of unprincipled and troublemaking whites and, by example as well as command, guided the relationships between their employees and the Indians. But the individual feelings of the men were those of any like number of white men engaged in the fur trade.

Always working against the Indians was the inexorable truth that their cultures were totally different from that of the whites. Save for an occasional trader like David Thompson, few of the fur men deviated from the usual pattern of Europeans who regarded the native cultures and peoples as inferior. Even most of those who took Indian wives and raised families of half bloods looked down on the Indians. Governor George Simpson referred to his half-blood wife, who bore him a child, as a "bit of brown." Often factors and traders left their native families behind them when they returned to civilization, where they took new wives as if they were their first.*

Many of the Hudson's Bay Company men were well educated and talented. Some showed a great curiosity about the

* HBC: "It is true that many traders left their native families (and they may have been happier in Rupert's Land than in Scotland), but they usually made provision for them, and often had the children well educated."

Indians. A few learned native languages, studied their ways, probed them about their beliefs and histories, and came to recognize and appreciate the values of the varied native peoples they met. Some, like Henry Kelsey, compiled dictionaries of native languages. Others wrote long accounts of tribal ways and customs, which are extremely valuable today to students of ethnology, for they describe the lives of tribes before the white men had corrupted them.

But most fur men were indifferent to Indian customs and welfare. They were engaged in a business. What interest they showed in the Indians was usually a reflection simply of their recognition that their lives and fortunes depended on the natives. Most of the men, including some who, like Philip Tumor, Andrew Graham, and Alexander Ross, occasionally praised and professed sympathy for the Indians, were harassed and frustrated by native traits that they did not understand or appreciate, and filled their diaries and writings with vilifications of the natives, terming them *scoundrels*, *rogues*, and *rascals*, and characterizing them as *treacherous*, *fickle*, *deceitful*, *dishonest*, *slanderous*, *capricious*, *cunning*, *gluttonous*, and *perfidious.**

Other traders, more perceptive, recognized that differences in culture, ignorance of accepted Indian ways, and failures of communication caused the frustrations. After they had given vent to angry feelings, they often admitted that they really had not meant all that they had said.

No man heaped greater invective on the natives than Peter Skene Ogden, who on one occasion when things were going

---

* HBC: "This list of vilifications is marvelous, but here it would be likely to be picked up out of context and claimed as the view of the Company towards the Indians whom they have 'always exploited.' "

badly for his brigade in the Snake country, wrote furiously, "Acting for myself, I will not hesitate to say I would willingly sacrifice a year or two to exterminate the whole Snake tribe, women and children excepted. In so doing I could fully justify myself before God and man. Those who live at a distance are of a different opinion. My reply to them is this: Come out and suffer and judge for yourselves if forbearance has not been carried beyond bounds ordained by Scripture and surely this is the only guide a Christian sh'd follow." Yet at other times Ogden wrote with understanding and compassion for the Indians, and after the uprising by the Cayuse Indians at the Whitman mission in the Oregon Territory in 1847, he was so well respected by the Indians that he was able to effect the rescue of the survivors.

At the same time, the imperialistic nature of the company's daily intercourse with the natives was never in any doubt. The Indians were not treated as equals, but were cajoled, manipulated, exploited, and sometimes bullied. Many a governor, factor, and trader, though outwardly friendly to them, held them in contempt. "Treat them civilly not Useing to much familliarity with them for that will make them prove Saucy & impudent," James Knight cautioned his men in 1717. "Impudent" was an overused characterization of the Indians by the traders, and through the years they overlooked no opportunity to make the Indians know that the whites, not the Indians, set the rules of the relations between them.

The high-handedness of the buyer in the sellers' country began early. In 1686, Governor Sergeant flogged an Indian at Albany Fort, and the flogging of natives became so common a punishment at posts thereafter that when the American missionary Henry Spalding began flogging Nez Perce Indians in

Oregon in the 1830s, he thought it was the proper way for a white man to deal with Indians, since the Hudson's Bay Company flogged them at nearby Fort Walla Walla.*

Generally, the traders' policy was aimed at deterring trouble by the Indians by making them aware that the whites would retaliate with stern punishment. Trouble, in the usual sense, would mean the murder of a white man, an attack on a post, a theft, or some other serious action which constituted an affront to the traders, despite the fact that they were in the Indians' country and the Indians' act might have been in retaliation for a white man's affront to them. Thus, when Indians felt they had good cause to burn down Henley House on Albany River in 1755 and murder its master, who had given them grievous offense, four Indians who confessed the action were put in irons, tried, and hanged.

Wherever it was practicable, the company extended the enforcement of its version of what constituted justice. In time, trouble meriting punishment came to include infractions of rules of trade and conduct around the posts, insults and "impudence" to the whites, threats, and even Indian misconduct to other Indians. Although the effect in some areas was to make Indians docile, and even servile, a situation the traders did not find unpleasant, company authorities, with a sense of the white man's superiority, continued to justify their right to punish Indians by asserting that only force or fear of force made Indians act "properly." The Indians, said George Simp-

* HBC: "I would question that flogging natives was a very common practice at posts. Offending the dignity of an Indian usually meant retaliation or an end to trade—both undesirable results. It was a brutal age and Company employees were flogged at times, probably more often than Indians. I believe Dr. McLoughlin was very free with his stick, which may have set a bad example in Oregon."

son, were "solely prevented from committing the most atrocious crimes by a fear of the consequences." He advocated ruling them with a "rod of iron," and saw that the traders under him followed suit.

From the company's point of view, it worked. Indians, made accountable for their breaches of the codes of conduct the traders gave them, saw that they could not win. The company held the upper hand, for it could halt trade with everybody, thus turning the anger of other Indians against the native or group of natives that had caused the difficulty. As a result, the Indians often policed themselves, forcing everyone to abide by the traders' rules, and surrendering to the whites anyone who caused offense.

The policy worked nowhere better than in the Columbia River district, where John McLoughlin established so great a degree of respect from the various tribes that a trader could boast that he could walk anywhere in the district unarmed and feel a perfect sense of security. The measure of the effectiveness of the company's dominion over the natives was seen only a few years later, when the same country went under American rule, and the Indians erupted in bitter warfare against the newly arrived settlers. "I am of opinion," wrote the Hudson's Bay Company's James Douglas, "that there must have been some great mismanagement on the part of the American authorities or it is hardly credible that the natives of Oregon, whose character has been softened and improved by fifty years of commercial intercourse with the establishments of the Hudson's Bay Company, would otherwise exhibit so determined a Spirit of hostility against any white people."

The "softening" of the Indians had another entirely practical effect. It made the Indians easier to exploit. The company had a long history of pleading to Parliament for the continuation and extension of its monopoly position, arguing, with a large degree of correctness, that competition debauched and harmed the Indians, whereas a single company such as itself could conduct trade in an orderly manner, with due regard for the Indians' welfare. There was much to be said for this, since competition had clearly disrupted and corrupted many tribes. But monopoly made the Indian something of a pawn for the monopolist, and on many occasions, also, the Hudson's Bay Company had had to defend itself in England against charges that it was exploiting the natives. As early as 1698 the company had been accused of cheating the Indians at the Bay and driving them into the arms of the French. More serious charges of the same nature were made in 1749, and from the 1830s till the 1860s accusations that the company was exploiting the Indians were common.

There was more than a little truth to them. By its nature, the fur trade broke down the old ways of the Indians and made them dependent on the traders. Indians who substituted guns for bows and arrows became helpless when arms and powder were denied them. The problem was evident in 1672, when three Indians approached the English at Rupert's River to beg for provisions. By 1726, one generation after the Hudson's Bay Company had begun to trade at the Bay, it reported that "many thousand Families of the Natives for want of the supply they Annually receive from us, of Guns, Powder, and Shott, wherewith they kill the Beavor, Buffalo, and several other Beasts of that Country, the Flesh whereof is their food, will by the disappointment of the not arrival of the said ships, be starved before the next Year." The numbers of Indians dependent on the trade increased each year; only conscience, self-restraint, and the weak voice of public opinion need limit a monopoly's ability to exploit them.

In 1831 Governor Simpson unabashedly directed his men to encourage the Indians' dependency. "The best and most effectual way of encouraging the natives to industry," he told them, "is by paying them liberally for their skins, by which means our supplies in due time become so necessary to them as to make them in a certain measure dependent on us." Simpson, who was the greatest efficiency expert for the reaping of profits that the company ever had in North America, was also one of its most compelling voices for monopoly position. He knew the advantages of dependency to a monopoly, for he was first and always a businessman. "Philanthropy is not the exclusive object of our visits to these Northern Regions," he once said.*

On the whole, through the years, the company did well in its trade with the Indians, but one may argue about the extent to which its profits represented exploitation of the natives. It had good years and bad, and often it suffered from competition, losses at sea, interruptions from war, and other difficulties not connected with the exchange of trade goods with the Indians for furs. Statistics on profits as against the cost of trade goods to the company are available for certain periods; sometimes they tell the whole story, sometimes they do not. In the decade of the 1720s, the company made an annual average profit of about 10,000 pounds, based on average annual gross sales of about 27,000 pounds. But it is not clear how much of the 17,000 in average costs went for the purchase of trade goods. In the

---

* HBC: " 'Exploitation of the natives' by the HBC is an ever-recurring theme in newspapers and magazines in Canada, and this would add grist to the mill. There is no reference to some of the contributions the Company made to the natives' welfare, much of which was reported in the 1857 Parliamentary Report."

decade 1739–48 the record is more precise. Average annual profits were about 6,350 pounds on average annual gross sales of 27,000 pounds; the cost of trade goods averaged about 3,700 pounds per year. Stores, equipment, and various other charges were the costs that ate into sales receipts.[*]

Between 1830 and 1839 the company made an annual average profit of 20,500 pounds; between 1840 and 1857 the average yearly profit was 65,573 pounds. Trade goods in 1843 cost the company 6,500 pounds; in 1853, 14,000; and in 1857, 30,800. In the latter year, the 30,800 in trade goods bought furs that the company sold for 116,225 pounds. The company always got its money's worth from the Indians. In the later years, the Indians, as well as the Metis and others who purchased supplies from the company at Red River, became increasingly dissatisfied with the low prices paid for furs and the high prices charged for trade goods and supplies.

On other scores, the fur trade proved disastrous for the Indians, although the Hudson's Bay Company was only one of the contributors. Every competitor in the trade shares the blame. Chief among the catastrophes were the epidemic diseases that the white man spread among the Indians. In 1781, and at least twice again in the nineteenth century, smallpox wiped out great numbers of Indians in the fur country and on the plains. During the 1830s, respiratory diseases caused the deaths of tens of thousands of Indians along the lower Columbia, all but emptying the area of its red-man population. Measles, "inter-

---

[*]   HBC: "Out of the gross sales also had to come provisions, maintenance of factories, clothing, wages; and shipping at times meant the complete loss of ship and cargo. Moreover there were the many years when no dividends were paid (I do not know what the sales were, but they evidently kept the Company going): 1670–1684, 1685–1687, 1690–1718 (28 years), 1783–1785, 1809–1814."

mittent fever," and other illnesses struck again and again at tribes, demoralizing and weakening them and hastening the end of their power and freedom.

Fur trade wars between nations, as well as among competing private companies, enlisted tribes as allies of the rival whites, pitting Indians against Indians, and causing the destruction of tribes, the ejection of native peoples from their homelands, and anguish and death for thousands of Indians. When the home country of one tribe was trapped clear of beaver, the trade induced the Indians to move greedily into someone else's territory, setting off more strife. The destruction and impoverishment by alcohol has already been noted; the liquor weakened family, clan, and tribal ties and made the Indians slaves to the trading posts. Old systems and societies crumbled; Indian values and lifestyles were abandoned. Trapping broke up the group and community orientation of the natives and, bringing in its place, prestige, favoritism, and rewards to the best fur suppliers, introduced jealousies and factions.

Most of all, the cumulative impact of all these destructive forces impaired the Indians' ability to cope with the more aggressive whites who followed the fur men into the Indian country, seeking timber, mineral wealth, and land. With the withering of the fur trade and the abandonment of posts, the Indians, dependent for so long on the trade, were left impoverished and helpless, without a means of support, a source of needed goods, or even the ability to secure their lands.*

---

* HBC: "This sounds more like the French-British rivalry in eastern Canada and New England. It seems an unreasonable exaggeration to blame the fur trade for 'pitting Indians against Indians, destruction of tribes, ejection from homelands, death for thousands . . . slaves to the trading posts'." (The author cannot agree with this observation; history details just those conclusions.)

In the long run, the latter was to be the most enduring and damaging effect of the fur trade. Mention has been made of the purchase of Indians' land at Rupert's River by Captain Zachariah Gillam of the adventurers' first expedition to the Bay in 1668. The company itself encouraged such local transactions but, in the context of international rivalries, considered them important more for the right of possession they established against rival white claims than as formalities owed the Indians.

From time to time through the years, traders continued to make treaties with individual groups of natives, purchasing small areas of land. But many posts were established without formal acknowledgment of Indian land ownership. By and large, with the exception of a disputed purchase by the Earl of Selkirk of land for colonists at Red River in 1817, and the acquisition of tracts on Vancouver Island after 1849, the company extinguished little of the natives' title to Rupert's Land or the territory northwest and west of that domain. In 1869, when the Hudson's Bay Company surrendered back to the Crown all of Rupert's Land, it won agreement from Canada that it would be exempt from responsibility for claims by Indians to the lands it surrendered. By washing its hands of the matter, it bequeathed to Canada an injustice still unrectified.*

In the latter part of the nineteenth century a series of government treaties won land cessions from some of the Indians of the former Rupert's Land and placed many of the natives on reserves. But much was left undone. Indians in British Colum-

---

* Eds. note: The Dene Nation of central and northwestern Canada has argued with some legal success that treaties were viewed by the Indians as agreements of "peace and friendship," and not as agreements to give up aboriginal land. In any case, negotiations over Indian land rights in Canada are ongoing.

bia and northern Quebec still have no treaty rights to any of their lands. Similarly, though the Indians of the Northwest Territory and Yukon were long ago promised treaty recognition of their lands, the Canadian government's promises were never kept, and the natives are still without their rights.*

The issue is bound to surface as present-day Indians become increasingly insistent on recognition of their rights. And their long-deferred quest for justice, harking back to the almost-forgotten times of the greatest days of the Hudson's Bay Company's fur trade with their ancestors, will undoubtedly add an important and valuable point of view to the assessment of the company's relations with the Indians—that of the native peoples themselves.†

---

* HBC: "I don't think the HBC ever made claim to lands, merely established squatters' rights at its posts. 'Bequeathing to Canada an injustice still unrectified' is very harsh and hardly seems justified. The HBC acquired its land as part of the compensation for transferring Rupert's Land to the Crown, thence to Canada. Relieving the Company of responsibility for compensation to Indians referred to land for settlement subsequent to the Deed of Surrender, as I read it." (The author reiterates that the Canadian non-Indian population today holds title to considerable western and northern Canadian land for which Indians were never paid.)

† HBC: "Quest for justice, harking back to the . . . days of the HBC's fur trade certainly puts the Company in an extremely unfavourable light." (Events already occurring in Indian affairs in Canada, the author believes, are already justifying the article's conclusion.)

5

"A Most Satisfactory Council"

◇◇

Described by Isaac Stevens, first governor of the newly organized Washington Territory, as "a most satisfying council," the 1855 meeting with Indian tribes on the Walla Walla River and the treaty that resulted from it gave him all that he wanted. For the Indians, however, it was destined to be one of the most disastrous markers in what is called by today's Indians the Trail of Broken Treaties. Josephy's account of the event unfolds in almost dramatic form, based as it is on a substantial written record of speeches and statements on both sides.* Historical characters are developed in full—from the ambitious Stevens to Lawyer, the self-important Nez Perce leader, to the warrior Looking Glass, initially a fiery opponent who reluctantly accepted a final submission. The Stevens treaty story, published originally in American Heritage *magazine in 1965, is emblematic of most, if not all, confrontational Indian-white governmental relations that preceded and followed it, a story necessary for a full understanding of those contentious dealings over a period of centuries.*

* Eds. note: All quotations from the minutes of the Walla Walla Council are from the L. V. McWhorter Manuscript Collection, Washington State University Library, 201, no. 48, and are used with the kind permission of the University Library at Pullman.

The meeting had been called by Isaac I. Stevens, an impatient, politically ambitious West Pointer and Mexican War veteran who had arrived in the Northwest in 1853 as the first governor of the newly created Washington Territory. In addition, he was the territory's Superintendent of Indian Affairs and the leader of the most northerly of four Pacific Railroad Survey groups dispatched by the War Department to find the most feasible route for a railroad to the Pacific.

A dynamo of a man, still only thirty-seven years old, Stevens saw all three of his jobs complementing each other toward a single grand end. As a governor who wanted to build up the population and prosperity of the territory, he was intent on winning congressional approval for the railroad route he had charted from St. Paul to Puget Sound. That meant clearing the Indian owners away from the proposed route: buying what part of their land he wanted, tucking the natives away on reservations, and ensuring the safety of the right of way for railroad builders and travelers. At the same time, the Indian cessions would increase the territory's public domain and make land available for more settlers. Stevens bore no ill will against Indians, and even fancied that he admired and respected them. But as an instrument of advancing American civilization, he had a job to accomplish, and with a flair for publicity, he expected to win notice in the national capital for what he would achieve.

During the winter of 1854–55, Stevens concentrated on the area west of the Cascades, where the demands of the settlers for land were the most urgent. In four land-purchasing treaties—which he forced on the Indians in rapid-fire succession by promises, cajolery, threats, and fraud—he permanently extinguished native title to almost the entire country

bordering Puget Sound. Then he turned his attention to the
territory east of the Cascades, sending agents to tribes in that
region to make arrangements for a treaty-making council to be
held at the end of May 1855.

Few whites yet lived in the vast interior of eastern Washington, northeastern Oregon, and northern Idaho, but already the
country was marked by conflict and unrest. It was inhabited by
great horse-owning tribes, including the Yakimas, Klickitats,
Palouse, Nez Perce, Umatillas, Cayuse, Walla Wallas, and Spokans, as well as by many bands that lived along the Columbia
River and its tributaries. Large numbers of the horse owners
roamed long distances eastward to hunt buffalo on the plains,
but in their home villages all the tribes shared a plateau culture
that was based on such foods as fish, roots, and small game.

Lewis and Clark had been the first white men in this country, and for many years after the explorers' departure, the
natives had gotten on peaceably with British and American
fur traders. Missionaries had entered the region in the 1830s
and pioneer settlers, on their way to the lower Columbia, had
passed through it after 1841. The increasing numbers of whites
had frightened the Indians. The Cayuse, for example, when
struck by measles in 1847, feared a white plot to wipe them
out; they turned on their missionaries, the Marcus Whitmans,
and murdered them.

In a punitive expedition, Americans from the Willamette
Valley had moved impetuously up the Columbia, hitting many
tribes and embroiling much of the interior area in war. By 1850,
the whites had withdrawn again to the west side of the Cascades, but great damage had been done. All the inland tribes
were uneasy, certain that the Americans would return and
take their land away from them. When Isaac Stevens had gone

through the country in 1853, exploring for a railroad route, the alarm had risen, and rumors had flown from tribe to tribe that the new American "chief" was going to seize their lands. Then, during the winter of 1854–55, reports of the coercion of the Puget Sound tribes had come from anguished Indian friends west of the Cascades.

Although the arrival of Stevens' agents in the interior in the spring of 1855 was thus half expected, it caused confusion and disunity among the tribes over what to do. The purpose of the meeting was not told to them, but they were certain that they would be asked to sell some of their lands. Concern spread from band to band, and hurried intertribal councils were called. Kamiakin, a Yakima leader who had welcomed Catholic priests on his land but treasured fiercely his independence and freedom, urged the tribes to refuse to sell any of their country to the whites and to unite in resistance if the refusal should lead to war. Other Yakimas, including two rival leaders, Owhi and Teias, sometimes written Te-I-as, did not wish to give up land either, but they were more timorous than Kamiakin and feared an American attack. Peopeo Moxmox, the elderly headman of the Walla Wallas, leaned toward support of Kamiakin. But he had been a longtime friend of fur traders and had served with Fremont during the conquest of California in the 1840s. Although a white man had murdered his son and had gone unpunished, Peopeo Moxmox had no hatred for Americans and wanted no war; he agreed that the Indians should resist, but he believed they could fend off Stevens peaceably by persuasive arguments in the council.

Cayuse headmen, including Five Crows and Young Chief, were more fearful. They wanted no land-surrendering treaty, but they and their people had been badly hurt after the killing of the Whitmans, and they hoped for no further fighting with the Americans. A small and fragmented tribe since their punishment, they looked for leadership to the Nez Perce, the most powerful tribe in the interior, numbering at the time more than three thousand people. But they, too, were divided. The majority was led by a man named Lawyer, a former buffalo hunter converted to Christianity by Protestant missionaries and appointed by government agents as head chief of the tribe. The appointment was contrary to tribal tradition, which recognized the autonomy of every band under its own headman, and it rankled many Nez Perce. Some headmen, like Timothy and Utsinmalikin, were staunchly loyal to Lawyer: others, like Old Joseph (father of the later and celebrated Chief Joseph), James, Metat Waptass, and Red Wolf, sometimes accepted Lawyer as spokesman for all and sometimes did not. A great hunting and war leader, Looking Glass (father of one of the fighting leaders of the Nez Perce War of 1877), had little use for Lawyer and frequently opposed him. Ever since the killing of the Whitmans, the Nez Perce headmen had tugged and pulled over whether to help the other tribes resist the Americans or to be friendly with the whites and keep their own villages and people out of trouble. Lawyer, firmly convinced that the Indians would have to adopt the white men's ways and accept American domination if they were to survive, had counseled friendship, or at least neutrality, and had so far prevailed. But Looking Glass now angrily supported Kamiakin and was ready to fight the Americans if necessary; many of the other Nez Perce leaders were not quite sure what to do.

As May approached, the headmen of all the tribes gradually came to agreement: they would meet Stevens and listen, at least, to what he proposed. Then it would be seen whether the choice, after all, was sell or fight.

The proposed council site was on the Walla Walla River near the present city of the same name, about midway between the Yakima River country of Kamiakin's people and the center of the Nez Perce nation near present-day Lewiston, Idaho. Joined by Joel Palmer, Superintendent of Indian Affairs for Oregon, who had jurisdiction over the Oregon bands called to the council, Stevens and a large entourage, including a guard of forty-seven soldiers from The Dalles, journeyed up the Columbia past basalt cliffs and barren plains to the Walla Walla River. On May 21, the party reached the council grounds, where an advance group had erected tents, a log storehouse to hold presents for the Indians, and two arbors of poles and boughs, one to serve as a council chamber, the other, according to Stevens' son and biographer, Hazard, "as a banqueting-hall for distinguished chiefs, so that, as in civilized lands, gastronomy might aid diplomacy."

Then, as the chiefs dismounted and joined the commissioners' party in a reviewing group at the council's flagpole, the rest of the Nez Perce started toward them and circled the pole. They made a colorful sight, "a thousand warriors," wrote Hazard Stevens, drawing on his father's journal, "mounted on fine horses and riding at a gallop, two abreast, naked to the breech-clout, their faces covered with white, red, and yellow paint in fanciful designs, and decked with plumes and feathers and trinkets fluttering in the sunshine." They put on a series of equestrian displays for the commissioners, "charging at full gallop . . . firing their guns, brandishing their shields, beating their drums, and yelling their war-whoops," and then, after a war dance, filed off to a location a half-mile away that had been selected for their camp. Stevens was pleased by the grand show, but he missed part of its significance. It was the Indians' way not only of according him a salute but of demonstrating that they were strong and unafraid, and expected to be treated as a powerful people.

Still, some of the most important Nez Perce were not there. Looking Glass and many of the tribe's ablest warriors and hunters were in buffalo country. Stevens must have been delighted to receive that information. In the absence of Looking Glass, there was less chance of his encountering difficulty with the more tractable head chief, Lawyer, who, in his opinion, was "wise, enlightened, and magnanimous . . . head and shoulders above the other chiefs, whether in intellect, nobility of soul, or influence."

To the members of the council who were meeting the missionary-educated Nez Perce for the first time, Lawyer and his people were remarkable Indians. "There is an odd mixture of this world and the next in some of the Nez Perces,—an equal love for fighting and [religious] devotion, the wildest Indian traits with a strictness in some religious rites which might shame those 'who profess and call themselves Christians,'" wrote Lieutenant Lawrence Kip, a member of Stevens' military escort. "They have prayers in their lodges every morning and evening—service several times on Sunday—and nothing will induce them on that day to engage in any trading." Later, after the council began, Kip was impressed when he learned that "two or three of the half-civilized Nez Perces, who could write, were keeping a minute account of all that transpired at those meetings." Nevertheless, there was still a gap between those friendly Indians and the whites. When Lieutenant Archibald

Gracie, who commanded the military escort, strove to test Lawyer by asking him if he would welcome having Gracie make a brief visit to the Nez Perce country, the head chief evaded the question and then answered only, "Perhaps so." It was a measure of the narrow line Lawyer was trying to walk between accommodating the whites and retaining his hold over his people, but Lieutenant Gracie did not recognize it.

When the Cayuse, Walla Wallas, and Umatillas arrived, they were less friendly than the Nez Perce, and, Hazard Stevens wrote, "went into camp without any parade or salutations." Peopeo Moxmox reflected the deep distrust of these tribes by sending word to Stevens that they had brought their own provisions with them and did not want any from the whites. Even the messenger refused to accept any tobacco for his chief, "a very unfriendly sign," and rode off muttering, "You will find out by and by why we won't take provisions." Soon afterward, Young Chief and several of the other Cayuse leading men rode into Stevens' camp and, refusing to smoke, "shook hands in a very cold manner." Nevertheless, Stevens wrote in his diary, "The haughty carriage of these chiefs and their manly character have, for the first time in my Indian experience, realized the descriptions of the writers of fiction."

Fathers Eugene Chirouse, who had a mission in the Walla Walla Valley, and Charles Pandosy, who had one among the Yakimas, also appeared, reporting to Stevens that all the Indians they knew, except Kamiakin, were well disposed toward the whites. Some Indians had told them, "Kamiakin will come with his young men with powder and ball." Stevens added Kamiakin to a list of potential "malcontents," as he called them, that included Peopeo Moxmox and Young Chief; but when the Yakima leader arrived with his brother Siloam, Owhi, and a number of warriors, he shook hands in a friendly manner and sat down for a smoke, although he refused tobacco from the commissioners.

The day before the council opened, Peopeo Moxmox, having insisted that he, Young Chief, Lawyer, and Kamiakin do all the talking for the Indians, asked Stevens for more than one interpreter, "that they might know they translated truly." When Stevens agreed to the request, the old Walla Walla chief looked around the area at young Nez Perce who loitered about and said with scorn, "I do not wish my boys running around the camp of the whites like these young men."

The line between distrust and hostility was a thin one. Stevens had come to the council certain that "a few determined spirits, if not controlled, might embolden all not well disposed, and defeat the negotiations. Should this spirit be shown," he wrote in his journal, "they must be seized; the well affected would then govern in the deliberations." Still, he was an optimist, certain that he could win over men like Peopeo Moxmox without using force. Palmer and some of the others were not so sure. And if it came to force, forty-seven troopers were slim security against several thousand Indians. There was always Lawyer, however, who Stevens understood would keep the Nez Perce friendly to the Americans. Through him Stevens counted on a large force of native allies. The governor cultivated the Nez Perce chiefs and at a banquet for thirty of them piled their tin plates to the brim "again and again." A mess was maintained for them throughout the council, "and every day was well attended."

Before the council started, a number of other Indians arrived, including members of several bands that lived along the Columbia, a headman of the Palouses who reported that his people "were indifferent to the matter," and Spokan Garry, a Christianized Spokan leader from northeastern Washington who came as an observer. Altogether, some five thousand Indians had finally gathered. On the morning the council was to begin, the commissioners visited Lawyer, who was in great pain from an old wound he had received helping American trappers fight Gros Ventres at Pierre's Hole in southeastern Idaho more than twenty years before. While they were with Lawyer, Utsinmalikin appeared and told the commissioners that Peopeo Moxmox, Kamiakin, and the Cayuse had asked him and two other Nez Perce chiefs to come to their camp for a council. He claimed he had rebuffed them angrily. "Why do you come here and ask three chiefs to come to a council, while to the head chief [Lawyer] and the rest you say nothing?" he reported having said. The news confirmed to the commissioners that the malcontents were already at work plotting some conspiracy; but it seemed evident also that the friendly Lawyer was still in firm control of the Nez Perce, and there were as many of them as of all the other Indians together.

The council met in front of an arbor erected near Stevens' tent. Stevens and Palmer sat on a bench, and the Indians gathered around them on the ground in a large circle. The chiefs sat in the front row, with about a thousand of their people ranged behind them. As the white men spoke, William Craig* and the other interpreters translated each sentence to Indian criers, who announced it in loud voices to the assemblage. After the interpreters were sworn in on the first day, it began to rain and the council was adjourned. The next day Stevens opened the proceedings with a speech, praising the individual

---

* Eds. note: Former fur trader, married to a Nez Perce woman.

tribes for their friendship to whites and for their accomplishments in adopting some of the ways of life of the white man. "I went back to the Great Father last year to say that you had been good, you have been kind, he must do something for you," he told the Indians. Getting to what that "something" was took him through a long and tortuous explanation. There were bad white men, he said, who made trouble for Indians. But east of the mountains, the Great Father had taken measures to protect his Indian children from the bad white men. He had guided the red men "across a great river into a fine country," where he could take care of them, away from the troublemaking white men. Stevens even named the Great Father, Andrew Jackson, although he omitted references to the coercion, misery, starvation, and deaths of the "trail of tears" that marked the enforced removal of Indians from their homelands east of the Mississippi. But some of the northwestern Indians were not as uninformed as he thought they were. Delawares, Iroquois, and Plains Indians had been telling them for fifteen years of what had happened to the eastern Indians. As they sat and listened to Stevens, the Governor was already beginning to lose ground.

He went on. The Great Father had done wonderful things for the Indians whom he had moved to new homes. In fact, they were so happy, Stevens said, that he wanted to do the same thing for the western tribes. "This brings us now to the question, What shall we do at this council? We want you and ourselves to agree upon tracts of lands where you shall live; in those tracts of land we want each man who will work to have his own land, his own horses, his own cattle, and his home for himself and his children." Among the Indians who were absorbing this, he was now in trouble. He may have recognized that he was moving too fast, for he checked himself and switched quickly to a long list of things he wanted to give to the Indians: schools, blacksmiths and carpenters, plows, wagons, saw mills, grist mills, and instructors who would teach them to spin, weave, make clothes, and become mechanics, farmers, doctors, and lawyers. Then suddenly it was out: "Now we want you to agree with us to such a state of things: You to have your tract with all these things; the rest to be the Great Father's for his white children." There must have been an awful pause, for according to the minutes, Stevens immediately reverted to his litany of gifts: "Besides all these things, these shops, these mills and these schools which I have mentioned, we must pay you for the land which you give to the Great Father," he summed up, finally saying, "I am tired of speaking; you are tired of listening. I will speak tomorrow."

Palmer must already have sensed that the Indians were not reacting well, for he interjected: "It is not expected that we can come together with one day's talk; nor do we expect you can understand with what has been said all that we want. . . . Sometimes when people have a matter to settle, they commence way off; but as they understand each other they come together. With us, if we commenced way off, I hope we are a little nearer now, and by and by I hope we shall come quite together." The minutes show that the Indians made no reply, and the council was adjourned until the next day.

On May 31, Stevens made another speech, repeating several times the many things the Great Father wished to give the Indians. "We want you to have schools and mills and shops and farms . . . there will be blankets and cloth for leggings . . . we want in your houses plates and cups and brass and tin kettles, frying pans to cook your meat and bake ovens to bake your bread; you will have your own smiths, your own wheelwrights, your own carpenters, your own physicians and lawyers and other learned men. . . ." He went on, appearing as if he had a compulsion to keep talking about gifts but obviously doing everything possible to postpone coming to the main point, the acquisition of the Indians' lands. None of what he was saying could have been helpful to him. Save perhaps for Lawyer and a few other headmen, the Indians had not the slightest interest in abandoning their own ways and adopting the white man's culture. Few of them saw the desirability of acquiring all that Stevens was offering them, but they could see clearly that he was bargaining with promises of gifts—if they sold him what they did not wish to sell.

Eventually, Stevens changed his tack and told them that he planned to make a treaty also with their enemies, the Blackfoot tribes on the Montana plains, and end the Blackfoot menace to their buffalo-hunting parties. The Blackfeet would be friends of the western tribes, but Stevens would want the western tribes to be models for the Blackfeet and teach them how to settle down on prosperous farms like white men. This the western tribes could do to help Stevens.

He then called on Palmer, who spoke as if he did not know what to say. Launching into a talk on "the course pursued by the government towards the Indians on the other side of the mountains," he gave a long, rambling, and distorted version of the history of Indian-white relations in the East, commencing with Columbus. It was a hodgepodge of colonial and midwestern episodes, showing, if anything, Palmer's ignorance of what he was talking about. However, it led abruptly to a relevant point, which Palmer recognized was worth emphasizing for several moments: there had always been bad white men, frontier troublemakers, from whom the Indians had needed protection, and there were such bad men now in the North-west scheming "to get your horses," and do other evil things to the Indians. "It is these men . . . who would rob you of your property," he said, suddenly adding a new idea, "who are giving you advice not to treat with us. Whose councils do you prefer to take? These men who would rob you, or ours who come to befriend you?" These men, he concluded, even married Indian women, in order to steal the Indians' horses. "All such men need watching . . . who are your friends, such men, or myself and my brother [Stevens] who have come here to act for your good?" On that note, the council adjourned till the next day.

But the council did not meet the next day, "as the Indians," Lieutenant Kip wrote, "wished [time] to consider the proposals." It is obvious that in the private meetings among the head-men, the purpose of the white commissioners was clear to all, and Kamiakin and Peopeo Moxmox must have found it easy to muster support for their policy of opposition. The talk of history, presents, and other matters that had clothed the commissioners' central point—their hope that the Indians would give up some of their country—must, in fact, have angered men like Kamiakin, who would have characterized it as the glibness of crooked tongues.

At any rate, when the council convened again on June 2, Palmer knew that the Indians' opposition was hardening, and he made a more forthright appeal to them, stating that, "Like grasshoppers on the plains," the white settlers were coming to this country, and no one would be able to stop them. It simply could not be done, any more than one could "stop the waters of the Columbia River from flowing." But the land, like the air, the water, the fish, and the game, was "made for the white man and the red man," and that was why the commissioners wished to have the Indians choose the lands they wanted to keep for themselves before the settlers arrived. "We did not come here to scare you or to drive you away, but we came here to talk to you like men . . . if we enter into a treaty now we can select a good country for you; but if we wait till the country is filled up with whites, where will we find such a place? . . . If we make a treaty with you . . . you can rely on all its provisions being carried out strictly."

When Palmer was done, Stevens announced that the time had come for the Indians to be heard. There was a pause. "We are tired," said Five Crows, the Cayuse half brother of the Nez Perce Joseph. Palmer assured him that the whites had nothing more to say, and Five Crows then spoke briefly. The Father in Heaven had made the earth, and had made man of earth, but he had given man no gardens to plow, he pointed out to the commissioners—a comment on Stevens' talk about turning the Indians into farmers.

The session ended tensely. The old Walla Walla had been blunt. Moreover, he had embarrassed Lawyer by stating that he knew Craig was putting pressure on the Nez Perce for an immediate answer, without giving them time to think. "The whole has been prearranged," he said.

What happened among the Indians that evening will probably never be clear. Long after the entire council was over, Stevens claimed that Lawyer had come to his tent alone after midnight. The Nez Perce chief said he had just learned that during the day the Cayuse had formed a plot to massacre all the whites at the council, and that the Yakimas and Walla Wallas were now about to join them. The conspirators did not trust

the Nez Perce, said Lawyer, and he announced to Stevens, "I
will come with my family and pitch my lodge in the midst of
your camp, that those Cayuse may see that you and your party
are under the protection of the head chief of the Nez Perce."
Lawyer did move into Stevens' camp, but his story, if indeed
that is what he told Stevens, is questionable. Stevens made no
mention of it in the contemporary records of the council, and
the Indians have always laughed at his later report of the plot.
They have insisted that there was no such plan, that Lawyer
would not have been so stupid as to move his family to the site
of an intended attack, and that more likely the truth of what
had happened was that after Peopeo Moxmox's speech, many
of the Nez Perce had turned against Lawyer, and he had left his
people for his own safety.

There is no doubt that Lawyer was in a difficult position
and that he was frightened. On Monday, June 4, when the
council reconvened, Stevens called on him to talk. He spoke
in a confused manner, trying not to offend Stevens, but at the
same time attempting not to arouse the ire of his Indian listeners. After posing somewhat as an intermediary, and telling
Stevens that the Indians were poor and did not want to lose
their lands, he pleaded, "There are a good many men here
who wish to speak. Let them speak."

But no one had much to say. Kamiakin stated that he was
afraid of the white man; Utsinmalikin said he agreed with
Lawyer; Stickus, a Cayuse normally friendly to the Americans, asked Stevens to speak plainly; and Peopeo Moxmox
demanded that the commissioners mention the specific lands
they were talking about. "You have spoken for lands generally.
You have not spoken of any particular ones." Then Tipyahla-
nah Ka-ou-pu—"Eagle of the Morning Light"—rose to review

the history of Nez Perce relations with the white men, telling the commissioners of a "brother" whom the Astorian fur
traders had hanged many years before "for no offense" at the
mouth of the Palouse River. "This I say to my brother here that
he may think of it," he said bitterly. He also told them of the
Hat, "my Father," who had gone to the States with a missionary
in 1837 and had been killed during the trip by Sioux Indians,
though the missionary had been spared. "His body was never
returned . . . this is another thing to think of."

When the Eagle of the Morning Light sat down, no other
Indian wished to speak, and Stevens rose hesitantly to answer
Peopeo Moxmox's question and make clear the specifics of
the treaty. Feeling his way carefully, he announced that he
had two reservations in mind, one in the Nez Perce country,
from Oregon's Blue Mountains to the Bitterroots of Idaho and
from the Palouse River to the Grande Ronde and Salmon Rivers, and the other in the Yakima country between the Yakima
and Columbia Rivers. On the first reservation he proposed that
the Spokans, Cayuse, Walla Wallas, and Umatillas move in
with the Nez Perce, and on the second reservation he hoped
to gather all the tribes and bands along the Columbia River
from The Dalles to the Okanogan and Colville valleys far in
the north. Both schemes had been carefully worked out and
were already delineated on maps which he showed the Indians. He did not, however, tell them his purposes, which were
to select lands for them that no white man yet wanted, and
to clear all the areas that the settlers were already eyeing or
entering or that he would have to secure for the building of a
railroad and wagon routes. Thus, he planned to have the Indians vacate regions like the Umatilla, Walla Walla, and Colville
valleys, as well as the Spokan and Palouse countries and the

Yakima River Valley through which his projected northern railroad would run.

He spent the next two days explaining the reservations more fully, tracing their boundaries on his map, and describing the payments the government would give the tribes for their lands. But he made little headway. With the exception of Lawyer and a few of the Nez Perce headmen whose homelands would be untouched because they would be part of the Nez Perce Reservation, the Indians reacted coldly and with bitterness. "There is evidently a more hostile feeling towards the whites getting up among some of the tribes," Lieutenant Kip noted on one of the evenings, adding that when he and Lieutenant Gracie attempted to visit the Cayuse camp, a group of young warriors stood in their way and motioned them to leave.

In addition to having to surrender much land, none of the tribes liked the prospect of being forced to live together like a single people. Few of the Columbia River bands that were supposed to move in with the Yakimas were even present at the council, and no one could speak for them. But the Yakimas wanted none of them on their lands. Similarly, the Cayuse, Walla Wallas, and Umatillas had no intention of moving onto Nez Perce lands, and few of the Nez Perce looked forward to welcoming them. Spokan Garry, merely a witness at the council, sat glumly, worrying about how to inform his people that they would have to join the Nez Perce; Joseph and Chief Plenty Bears, Nez Perce leaders from the Wallowa and Grande Ronde River districts, were concerned that they would have to sell their parts of the Nez Perce domain.

Lawyer conferred privately with the commissioners at night and, after ascertaining that he would receive added benefits and payments befitting his position as head chief, he worked

on Spotted Eagle, James, Red Wolf, Timothy, and some of
the other Nez Perce headmen and won their approval of the
treaty. On June 7, he got up in the council meeting and again
played the role of politician and diplomat for Stevens, making
a long speech about the history of Indians and white men. In
the course of it, he amused everyone with a recital of the story
of Columbus and the egg, which the missionaries must have
taught him, and then, inadvertently perhaps, revealed that Jim
Simonds, a Delaware Indian who lived with the Nez Perce, had
related to them how the white men had come steadily pushing against the Indians all across the continent, and now "they
are here." In closing, he expressed his approval of the treaty,
but reminded Stevens that the Indians were poor people, and
begged him to "take care of us well."

The spokesmen for the other tribes were smoldering. All
of the Cayuse made known their opposition to abandoning
their own country and moving in with the Nez Perce. Young
Chief, a Cayuse who had already lived through many crises,
was angry. What Lawyer could see well, "us Indians" could
not see:

The reason . . . is I do not see the offer you have made us
yet. If I had the money in my hand then I would see. . . . I
wonder if this ground has anything to say? I wonder if the
ground is listening to what is said? . . . I hear what this earth
says. The earth says, God has placed me here. The earth
says that God tells me to take care of the Indians on this
earth. The earth says to the Indians that stop on the earth,
feed them right. God named the roots that he should feed
the Indians on. The water speaks the same way: God says,

feed the Indians upon the earth. The grass says the same thing: feed the horses and cattle. The earth and water and grass say, God has given our names and we are told those names. Neither the Indians or the whites have a right to change those names. The earth says, God has placed me here to produce all that grows upon me. . . . The same way the earth says it was from her man was made. . . . God said, you Indians who take care of a certain portion of the country should not trade it off unless you get a fair price.

There it was: the Indians' sacred belief in the Earth Mother, a deeply held feeling, already vitiated somewhat by some of the leaders who were trying to adjust to white culture. But Stevens could not see it. Five Crows supported Young Chief, and Peopeo Moxmox—now fighting for the valley of his ancestors, the land where his forebear, the great Yellepit, had welcomed Lewis and Clark and the British explorer David Thompson—told the commissioners that they were treating him as if he were a child or a feather. He wanted to go slower, to have time to think. "I request another meeting," he asked. "It is not only by one meeting that we can come to a decision."

Kamiakin, also feeling the pressure that the whites, with Lawyer's help, were beginning to place upon him, had nothing to say. But Owhi, like Young Chief, reminded the commissioners that God had made the earth and given it to the Indians. Could the Indians now steal it and sell it? "God made our bodies from the earth. . . . What shall I do? Shall I give the lands that are a part of my body?" When the Yakima had finished, Stevens again asked Kamiakin to talk. It is possible that Kamiakin was thinking of the many unrepresented

Columbia River bands that would be moved onto the Yakima Reservation if he agreed to the treaty. He had no right to speak in their names. "What have I to be talking about?" he said to Stevens.

The tempo was speeding up, and the Indians could sense the hurry. Howlish Wompoon, a Cayuse, glared at Palmer. "I have listened to your speech without any impression. . . . The Nez Perce have given you their land. You want us to go there. . . . I cannot think of leaving this land. Your words since you came here have been crooked. That is all I have to say."

For a moment Palmer tried hurriedly to answer the different objections. Then Five Crows spoke again, looking at the Nez Perce in anger. "Listen to me, you chiefs. We have been as one people with the Nez Perce heretofore. This day we are divided." At that point, Stevens took over, maintaining the pressure on the Indians that Palmer had begun. "I must say a few words. My Brother and I have talked straight. Have all of you talked straight? . . . The treaty will have to be drawn up tonight. You can see it tomorrow. The Nez Perces must not be put off any longer. This business must be dispatched." The council then adjourned.

That night Lieutenant Kip wrote that in all the Indian camps except that of the Nez Perce there was violent confusion. "The Cayuse and other tribes were very much incensed against the Nez Perce." But the next day, the commissioners found that the pressure was working. At the council, Young Chief suddenly began to give in. "The reason why we could not understand you," he said to Stevens and Palmer, "was that you selected this country for us to live in without our having any voice in the matter. . . . Wait, we may come to an agreement." He pleaded, however, for more time to consider a division of the country between the whites and the Indians. He did not want to abandon his own homeland: "The land where my forefathers are buried should be mine. That is the place that I am speaking for. We shall talk about it," and his words seemed suddenly almost begging: "We shall then know, my brothers, that is what I have to show you, that is what I love— the place we get our roots to live upon—the salmon comes up the stream—. That is all."

He sat down, but Palmer had good news for him. The night before, as a result of the opposition by the Cayuse, Walla Wallas, and Umatillas to going onto the Nez Perce Reservation, the commissioners had changed their plans, and Palmer now offered them a single reservation of their own, centering on the Umatilla Valley. In a long speech aimed directly at the recalcitrant headmen, he made many new promises of things the government would do for them personally if they accepted this reservation: "We will build a good house for Peopeo Moxmox, and a good house for the chief of the Cayuses . . . we will plow and fence ten acres of land for Peopeo Moxmox; we will plow and fence the same for the chief of the Cayuses . . . we will give him [Peopeo Moxmox] . . . $500 in money, we will give him three yoke of oxen, wagon and two plows . . . we give him a salary, and also the chief of the Cayuses $500 a year in money, this to continue for twenty years—the same as is to be given to the Lawyer." Moreover, "You will not be required to go onto the reservation till our chief the President and his council sees this paper and says it is good, and we build the houses, the mills and the blacksmith shop. . . . How long will it take you to decide?"

The new promises had their effect. The Walla Walla, Cayuse, and Umatilla spokesmen were won over, and Peopeo

Moxmox promised to go on the reservation as soon as his new house was built. Stevens was delighted, and ordered the treaties prepared for signature. Only Kamiakin and the Yakimas still held out. But suddenly, wrote Lieutenant Kip, "a new explosive element dropped into this little political caldron. Just before the Council adjourned, an Indian runner arrived with the news that Looking Glass, the war chief of the Nez Perce, was coming." It is probable that both Lawyer and Stevens were thrown into confusion. Stevens recovered quickly. "I am glad Looking Glass . . . is coming," he announced. "He is a friend of Kamiakin . . . he has come away from the Blackfeet . . . let his first glance be upon you sitting here. When he is close by two or three of us will go and take him by the hand and set him down by his chief in the presence of his friend Kamiakin. Let us now have Kamiakin's heart."

The Yakima's reply, at last, was one of submission. But it indicated that he had received a dressing down from the other Yakima chiefs, Teias and Owhi, who had told him that they intended on signing the treaty. The significance of what he had to say was apparently not noticed by Stevens and Palmer. Let the Americans settle down by the Yakima Valley wagon route, Kamiakin said. Let them settle about the road so that the Indians may go and see them. "I do not speak this for myself; it is my people's wish. Owhi and Te-i-as and the chiefs. I, Kamiakin, do not wish for goods for myself. The forest knows me. He knows my heart . . . I am tired. I am anxious to get back to my garden."

So Kamiakin capitulated, and after him Joseph, Red Wolf, and Skloom spoke. Joseph appealed to the commissioners to think of the future generations of Nez Perce, and to be certain to include his Wallowa land in the Nez Perce Reservation.

Red Wolf asked that William Craig be allowed to stay with the Nez Perce "because he understands us . . . when there is any news that comes into the country we can go to him and hear it straight." Skloom, Kamiakin's brother, asked merely that the Americans pay what the Yakimas' land was worth. Stevens agreed, and on a note of complete victory announced that the treaties would be signed the next day. Then he adjourned the council.

A few minutes later the Indians hurried off to meet Looking Glass, who came riding onto the council grounds with three elderly Nez Perce buffalo-hunting chiefs and a retinue of about twenty warriors. Their arrival created a commotion. All were in buffalo robes and were painted for war. They had been in fights with the Blackfeet and had heard of the council when they got back from the plains to Montana's Bitterroot Valley. Looking Glass had left most of his band behind to travel slowly, and with a small group had hastened across the Bitterroots by the Coeur d'Alene route. As Stevens and Palmer came up to meet them, they noticed that one of the warriors carried a staff from which dangled a Blackfoot scalp. Looking Glass received the commissioners coldly. He looked around at the Indians, and launched suddenly into a tirade: "My people, what have you done? While I was gone, you have sold my country. I have come home, and there is not left me a place on which to pitch my lodge. Go home to your lodges. I will talk to you."

All of Stevens' work fell suddenly apart. The seventy-year-old war chief—"old, irascible, and treacherous," Stevens called him—heaped scorn that night on the headmen who had agreed to sign the treaty. The next day, June 9, Lawyer told Stevens that Looking Glass would probably calm down in a day or two, but Stevens's determination had now risen, and he had no intention of letting Looking Glass defeat him at the last moment. Before the council started, the Governor met privately with Peopeo Moxmox and Kamiakin and won promises from them to abide by their word and sign the treaties. Then he asked Kamiakin for a list of the tribes over which he had authority as head chief. The Yakima, according to Stevens's secretary, James Doty, named a number of tribes, but the only one other than the Yakimas that Doty recorded at the time was the Palouse.

When the council reconvened, Stevens presented the Indians with finished versions of the treaties for the three reservations, all ready to be signed. With studied indifference to Looking Glass, he reviewed what the treaties said, reminding the chiefs that they did not have to move their people onto the reservations "for two or three years." Certain points were glossed over: Kamiakin, for instance, was to be considered the head chief of a long roster of Columbia River bands that were not present, but whose people Stevens wished to move onto the Yakima Reservation, out of the way of the whites. Stevens was talking quickly, and probably did not even reveal the role he was assigning Kamiakin, for the Yakima would not willingly have accepted it, and it is not likely that he had included those bands in the "list" he had given Stevens and Doty earlier that morning. All of them had their own headmen, and Kamiakin had nothing to do with their affairs. But Stevens brushed past the point and kept talking. He offered to read the treaties, article by article, but told the Indians that they had heard everything in them, "not once but two or three times." Then he asked if anyone still wanted to speak.

"I thought we had appointed Lawyer our head chief, and he was to do our talking," Billy replied.*

Stevens and Palmer both tried to argue with Looking Glass, but to no avail. The war chief argued for his line, not the one defined in the treaty. Stevens turned away from him to ask the tribes if they were ready to sign. "What the Looking Glass says, I say," said Young Chief. "I ask you whether you are ready to sign?" Stevens repeated, "The papers are drawn. We ask are you now ready to sign those papers and let them go to the President?"

". . . to the line I marked myself. Not to your line," Looking Glass insisted.

Stevens faced the old war chief. "I will say to the Looking Glass, we cannot agree."

"Why do you talk so much about it?" Palmer snapped angrily at the Nez Perce.

"It was my children that spoke yesterday, and now I come," said Looking Glass.

Stevens sat back resignedly, as Palmer argued with the old man. It did him no good. "I am not going to say any more today," Looking Glass said. Stevens finally adjourned the council, urging Looking Glass to think the matter over and talk to the other Nez Perce.

After the meeting, Peopeo Moxmox signed the treaty for the Walla Wallas. Stevens maintained that Kamiakin also signed,

* Eds. note: In a footnote on page 147 of *The Nez Perce Indians and the Opening of the Northwest*, Josephy says that "Samuel Temoni, whom she [Mrs. Whitman] described as old enough to hunt buffalo, may have been the Nez Perce later known as Salmon River Billy, who claimed that he had gone east with the Flatheads in 1835" to find Captain Clark and learn more about his religion.

having "yielded to the advice of the other [Yakima] chiefs." But Kamiakin later insisted that he only made a pledge of friendship by touching a little stick as it made a mark. Later in the evening, Lawyer came to see Stevens, and told him that he should have reminded Looking Glass that he, Lawyer, was the head chief, that the whole Nez Perce tribe had said in council that he was the head chief, and that the tribe had agreed to the treaty and had pledged its word. Stevens, he said, should have insisted that the Nez Perce live up to their pledge.

"In reply," Stevens wrote in his journal,* "I told the Lawyer . . . your authority will be sustained, and your people will be called upon to keep their word. . . . The Looking Glass will not be allowed to speak as head chief. You, and you alone, will be recognized. Should Looking Glass persist, the appeal will be made to your people. They must sign the treaty agreed to by them through you as head chief." Lawyer then went to the Nez Perce camp, and in a stormy council that lasted through most of the next day managed to muster enough support to reaffirm his position as head chief. Looking Glass apparently accepted his position as second to Lawyer in the council, and the headmen drew up a paper that pledged the tribe to honor its word to Governor Stevens.

Early on the morning of June 11, Stevens told Lawyer that he was about to call the council. "I shall call upon your people

---

* Josephy refers to the L. V. McWhorter papers at Washington State University as his source for Treaty minutes. As regards Stevens's personal statements that are not in the minutes, his correspondence is at Yale University Library, and journal quotations would have been included in Stevens's work by his secretary, James Doty. In 1978—well after Josephy wrote this piece—Ye Galleon Press reprinted the *Journal of Operations of Governor Isaac Ingalls Stevens of Washington Territory in 1855*, as taken down by Doty. The originals are at the University of Washington. Josephy's other source of information about Stevens is Hazard Stevens's 1900 book, *The Life of Isaac Ingalls Stevens*.

to keep their word, and upon you as head chief to sign first. We want no speeches. This will be the last day of the council." Lawyer assured him that that was the right course, and that was the way it finally happened. The council convened, Stevens reminded the Nez Perce that they had all originally agreed that Lawyer was their head chief and spokesman, and that Lawyer had given his word to the treaty. "I shall call upon Lawyer the head chief, and then I shall call on the other chiefs to sign. Will Lawyer now come forward."

Lawyer signed. Then Stevens called on Looking Glass and Joseph, and both of them stepped up and made their marks without a word. The other Nez Perce headmen followed in a line, and after them, the Cayuse signed their treaty.

"Thus ended in the most satisfactory manner this great council," Stevens wrote in his journal.

How satisfactory it soon became apparent. Stevens himself violated its terms at once, announcing through the newspapers of western Washington and Oregon that the treaties had opened for immediate settlement all Indian lands east of the Cascades except areas specifically reserved for the Indians. No treaty had yet been ratified in Washington, D.C.; no provisions had yet been made for moving the Indians; no terms had yet been carried out by the whites. It made no difference. Miners and settlers entered the Indians' lands. The tribes smoldered, thought of how they had been dictated to and then betrayed. Angry young Yakimas began to warn the trespassers. Killings followed, and by fall 1855, the entire country was aflame.

Armies scoured the lands of the Yakimas, Palouses, Walla Wallas, Cayuse, Umatillas, Spokans, Coeur d'Alenes, and numerous other peoples till the close of 1858. Both sides counted victories and losses, and both sides had a great number of dead and wounded. In the fighting, many of the headmen, including Peopeo Moxmox and Owhi, were killed. When the battles ended, the tribes had been smashed, the people had been herded onto reservations or driven into hiding (Kamiakin had retreated to exile in Canada), and most of the land they had fought to save was lost.

Some of the Nez Perce, still under Lawyer's domination, even helped the Americans. Looking Glass and his followers fussed and fumed, but Lawyer sent volunteers to fight the other tribes. The Nez Perce turn to fight Americans came twenty years later. Alone then, without allies, the generation of the young Chief Joseph fought to save its own homeland from a new generation of whites—and also lost.

Stevens lost too. Secretary of War Jefferson Davis, a southerner, would have nothing to do with a northern railroad route. His determination to build across the South created a stalemate until the Civil War. Then northerners, finally in control of Congress, chose the central route to the Pacific. By that time Stevens, a Union officer, was dead, killed at Chantilly in 1862.

6

Red Morning on the Minnesota

◇◇

Largely ignored by historians, at least until the 1991 publication of Josephy's landmark volume The Civil War in the American West, *events taking place in the area from "the western fringe of the Mississippi Valley to the Pacific" during the Civil War period had particular impact on the lives of Indian peoples.*

Josephy notes in his introduction: "During the four years of the Civil War . . . more Indian tribes were destroyed by whites and more land seized from them than in almost any comparable period of time in American history."

"Red Morning on the Minnesota," chapter 4 of The Civil War in the American West, *encapsulates a typical chain of events. Treaties established reservations that were then squeezed and diminished, accompanied by corruption in the delivery of promised food commodities and cash payments. These broken promises led to violent Indian resistance, in this case a full-scale bloody rebellion, and then white retaliation. Following severe losses on both sides, the Dakota were forced from Minnesota, joining the Lakota farther west and setting the stage for Custer and the final, post–Civil War Indian wars on the Great Plains.*

These Minnesota events, all occurring in the early years of the

178 PUTTING AMERICAN INDIANS INTO AMERICAN HISTORY

Civil War, remain an important flashpoint in the story of America's westward expansion and remind us that the West and Indians were integral to the conduct of the big war in the East.

August 18, 1862: In the stifling woods and fields of eastern Virginia, the scene of the great battles was shifting north, away from Richmond and toward Washington. The Union's costly Peninsula Campaign, which had reached to the eastern doorstep of Richmond, had ended in failure and withdrawal. Against the will of the North's controversial commander Major General George B. McClellan, the huge, frustrated Army of the Potomac was steaming back up the Potomac River and the Chesapeake Bay, ordered by the War Department to reinforce Major General John Pope's newly created Federal Army of Virginia for a combined assault against the Southern capital from a different direction. With McClellan gone from in front of Richmond, General Robert E. Lee's victorious Confederates were also heading north, intent on taking the war to the enemy and destroying Pope before McClellan could join him. The attention of both the North and the South was riveted on the drama of rapid movement that would lead in a few tense weeks to the defeat of Pope at the Second Battle of Bull Run, anxiety in the Federal capital, and the terrible collision and carnage at the Battle of Antietam.

One thousand miles to the northwest, a drama of a different scope and nature was exploding in the border state of Minnesota. To Mary Schwandt, a pretty teenage daughter of a family of German immigrants who had settled only recently on the fertile bottomlands of the Minnesota River, Monday, August 18, was the weekly washday. It was, she remembered, a "red morning. The great red sun came up in the eastern sky, tingeing all the clouds with crimson, and sending long, scarlet shafts of light up the green river valley and upon the golden bluffs on either side." Later, it made her recall the words of an old German soldiers' song, "O morning red! O morning red! You shine upon my early death!"

Forty miles down the river at New Ulm—a village established in the mid-1850s by German settlers on grassy terraces above the Minnesota—many of the nine hundred residents had risen early and gathered in the main street in festive mood. To loud cheering and huzzahs, a brass band and a party of recruiters, led by twenty-nine-year-old Henry Behnke, the clerk of the county's district court, rode out of town in a caravan of five wagons to tour the neighboring prairie of Milford Township in search of volunteers for the Union Army.

It was only four years since Minnesota—long a wilderness domain of Indians and fur traders—had become a state. Although much of its land was still the undeveloped hunting and trapping grounds of thousands of Sioux, Winnebago, and Chippewa Indians, its white population of fewer than 175,000, a third of them foreign-born, was second to that of no other state in enthusiasm for the Union cause. When Fort Sumter was attacked, Minnesota's Alexander Ramsey had been the first governor to wire an offer of troops to President Lincoln. In the months since then, the state had raised six infantry regiments and a number of smaller units, and more than five thousand Minnesotans had gone south to fight the rebels. Now, following the Peninsula Campaign and Lincoln's call on August 4 for three hundred thousand more men, enlistments were being drummed up for five additional Minnesota regiments.

In high spirits, Henry Behnke and his companions made

their way west among the pioneer farms and cabins on the prairie. Five miles from New Ulm, at a bridge that spanned a wooded ravine, they came suddenly on a man who had been shot and was lying in the road. As the recruiters pulled their wagons to a stop and jumped down to help him, a number of Sioux Indians, wearing breechclouts and war paint, rose from the nearby brush and opened fire on them. Several of the recruiters were killed instantly, and others were wounded. Without arms to defend themselves, the panicked survivors scrambled back into their wagons, turning two of them quickly to head back to town and scattering the Indians with two others by driving directly at them. The dead and wounded were put in the fifth wagon, and everyone but Behnke raced back toward New Ulm. The young court clerk had already run off on foot to the nearest house, where he borrowed a horse and rode across the countryside to warn his family and other settlers of the Indians' attack.

Word of the killings quickly reached New Ulm. Even before the wagons arrived back, a rider from the prairie, relaying Behnke's excited warning, galloped into the main street, crying, "The Indians are coming—they have murdered the recruiting party!" Believing that some drunken Indians were on a rampage, Sheriff Charles Roos ordered the town's schoolchildren sent to the safety of their homes, then collected a posse of thirty men with rifles and shotguns. At the same time, he directed the New Ulm militia to fall out for service and, if it seemed necessary, to be prepared to erect barricades in the center of town.

Starting up the road the recruiters had taken, the sheriff's party soon met the returning wagons. Pausing only long enough to learn the details of what had happened, the posse

continued toward Milford Township, intending to kill or capture the culprit Indians. The recruiters hurried on to New Ulm
with the dead and wounded, arriving to find the town in a state
of alarm and filled with rumors. Members of the militia, armed
with all sorts of weapons, ranging from guns to pitchforks and
axes, were gathering, and some of the streets were already
being barricaded with wagons, boxes, and barrels.

None of the citizens knew what was happening. Under the
influence of agents, missionaries, and friendly chiefs—and in
the presence of watchful troops at Fort Ridgely, some twenty
miles up the river from New Ulm— the Sioux of the Minnesota Valley had lived for years as peaceful neighbors of the settlers. But in their villages along the river, some of them were
known to be complaining of mistreatment by the whites, and
to many of the anxious, German-speaking burghers of New
Ulm, the unprovoked attack on the recruiting party suggested
that something large and serious was occurring.

In a few hours, their most awful fears were confirmed. A
townsman named Jacob Nix, who had ridden up the river on a
reconnaissance toward the Indian agency, came racing back,
shouting wildly that the Indians were "murdering everything."
Soon afterward, terror-stricken refugees began streaming
into New Ulm on horseback, in buggies, crowded into farm
wagons, or on foot, all fleeing from the Sioux and telling of
Indian murders, atrocities, rapes, and the burning of homes
and farms farther upriver. Neither New Ulm nor Fort Ridgely
would be safe, they warned. The entire Sioux nation had risen,
determined to kill all the settlers in the valley and drive every
white person out of Minnesota. Panicking many of New Ulm's
families into joining them, they continued their flight to Fort
Snelling and St. Paul, the state capital, both more than a hun-

dred miles away near the confluence of the Minnesota and Mississippi Rivers.

Late in the afternoon, Sheriff Roos and the members of his posse returned to town, haggard, filled with stories and hearsay of the widespread extent of the uprising, and certain that the Indians would soon attack New Ulm. Roos appointed Jacob Nix, who was known for his experience with firearms, *Platzkommandant* of the militia, with the rank of major, and set about helping organize the men into companies. That night, as pickets kept watch near signal fires and people continued to build barricades by the light of torches, Roos, Nix, and many of the leading citizens met to plan the town's defense. Among the group was Henry Behnke, who had packed his wife, two children, and several other people into a one-horse buggy and sent them down the valley. At the direction of the others at the meeting, Roos composed a message to Governor Ramsey, pleading for the immediate dispatch of one thousand reinforcements and ammunition to help defend the town. But the group realized that St. Paul was too far away for troops to reach New Ulm quickly. In the emergency, Behnke volunteered to ride to the nearer center, Traverse des Sioux, thirty miles away, to ask the valley's most prominent citizen, Judge Charles E. Flandrau, a former Indian agent and a member of the Minnesota Supreme Court, to raise local volunteers for New Ulm's assistance. Mounting a horse once more, the weary Behnke forded the Minnesota at midnight and started out in the darkness.

By the following afternoon, the first messages from the valley had reached St. Paul, and Governor Ramsey was aware that a formidable Indian uprising had struck his state. In truth, what was occurring was the largest Indian massacre of whites in the nation's history. More than two hundred people had already been murdered, and the figure would rise to above three hundred fifty. In addition, an unknown number had been taken captive by the Indians, and hundreds more were fleeing or in hiding. Entire counties of whites, and numerous towns and settlements were in peril. Among those slain in the bottomlands of the Minnesota River on the first day were five members of Mary Schwandt's family; trying to flee, Mary herself had been seized and taken to an Indian village.

Two days later, the enormous extent of the outbreak was known in Washington and the East. Although the news shocked the administration, raising the specter of a Confederate-fomented Indian diversion, the War Department was in desperate need of men and supplies for the eastern battlefronts and could not offer immediate help. But as increasingly desperate messages arrived at the White House, conveying the seriousness of Minnesota's plight, President Lincoln could not ignore the Union's loyal supporters on the northwestern frontier. On August 27, he acceded reluctantly to Governor Ramsey's request for a month's extension of the deadline for Minnesota's quota of new enlistments. Half the state's population were fugitives, Ramsey wired, and recruiting could not proceed. It was a period of confusion and military crisis for the North, and Lincoln's mind was on matters closer to the capital. Stonewall Jackson had somehow circled around Pope's position, seized the Army of Virginia's huge supply depot at Manassas Junction, and interrupted communications between the President and Pope. Nevertheless, Lincoln replied to Ramsey, "Attend to the Indians. If the draft cannot proceed of course it will not proceed. Necessity knows no law."

In New York, the *Tribune*'s stormy editor, Horace Greeley, assumed that the Minnesota massacre was a diabolical Southern conspiracy. "The Sioux have doubtless been stimulated if not bribed to plunder and slaughter their White neighbors by White and Red villains sent among them for this purpose by the Secessionists," he advised his readers. "They will have effected a temporary diversion in favor of the Confederacy, and that is all their concern." Stirred by a rash of rumors and reports of Indian unrest elsewhere in the West, many who agreed with Greeley worried that the outbreak in Minnesota was the start of a general uprising against the Federal government by western tribes, provoked and directed by Confederate agents to divert Union troops and resources. Even Lincoln was suspicious; three months later, in his annual message to Congress, he revealed that he had been given information "that a simultaneous attack was to be made upon the white settlements by all the tribes between the Mississippi river and the Rocky mountains."

Minnesota's Indian country, indeed, was not without its white agitators. In the Minnesota River Valley, a number of Copperhead Democrats—disgruntled traders, mixed-breeds, and former Indian agency employees who had lost jobs and influence with the change of administration in 1861—had occasionally magnified Union defeats and difficulties to the Indians, some of whom had been following the course of the white men's war with interest. But the Confederacy had had no contact with the Sioux, and fears of a plot of concerted action by the western tribes in support of the South were groundless. Although the existence of the Civil War was a factor in the uprising, it was of far less importance than other causes. By a combination of ineptitude and deceit, cultural and racial arrogance, and obscene cheating and greed, the Federal government and white traders and settlers in Minnesota had pushed large numbers of the Sioux—especially the proud young warriors—beyond their limits of endurance and brought the desperate revolt upon themselves.

The Indians who had risen up so suddenly were members of bands of the Eastern, or Santee, division of the Sioux, composed of four tribes, the Mdewakantons, Wahpekutes, Sissetons, and Wahpetons, with a total population of about sixty-five thousand. Calling themselves collectively Dakotas, which means "allies," they were related to the Yankton, Yanktonai, and Teton, or Lakota, Sioux tribes that lived farther west on the plains. In the Dakotas' homeland—the game-filled forests, prairies, and lakes of Minnesota, where they had dwelt for centuries—their early relations with whites had been generally amicable. French, British, and American traders had brought them guns and manufactured goods that they valued and wanted, and many of the whites, either by giving gifts or by taking Indian wives and having children with them, had been adopted into Dakota families and incorporated into the village societies. The resulting kinship bonds were important in Sioux life and had benefited both the traders and the Indians, for the kinsmen on both sides were expected to observe the virtues of generosity, sharing, and reciprocity and support each other and all their relatives with assistance, counsel, and favors.

In time, American soldiers, government agents, missionaries, and settlers began to appear in the Dakotas' country. The settlers pressed into Mdewakanton territory on the eastern side of the Mississippi River, and in 1837 that tribe made the first cession of their Minnesota landholdings. The idea for the sale was their agent's, but it took little urging to win the Indians' agreement. Game had almost disappeared from the area in question; fur profits had declined, and traders were halting credits to the Dakotas and repossessing traps and guns they had advanced to the Indians; and many of the tribesmen were feeling the economic pinch and worrying about the prospect of starvation. Their agent was not only genuinely concerned for their well-being; as a kinsman with a Mdewakanton wife and child, he was trusted by the Indians when he advised them to sell the land for the guarantee of government food annuities and assistance in becoming farmers. For some five million acres—all of the tribe's land east of the Mississippi—the government promised to pay the Indians $1 million, apportioned among annual deliveries of food and cash, the providing of farm equipment and instruction, an educational fund for schools, and a few smaller benefits.

The food annuities saved the Mdewakantons from starvation, but failures in the implementation of the rest of the treaty were a harbinger of a new era of broken government promises and unheeded Dakota complaints. The cash annuities were delayed; the farm program, launched ineptly among Indians who were culturally unprepared to take up farming, made little headway; and other commitments, including the educational fund, were all but forgotten. Eventually, the agent resigned, disgusted by the government's failure to respect the treaty's obligations.

In 1849, Minnesota became a Territory, and pressure arose for acquiring the Dakotas' lands west of the Mississippi. Appointed governor Alexander Ramsey, a Pennsylvanian, arrived in Minnesota with the intention of buying up all the Indians' lands in the Territory. Promises of new annuities and of meeting the unfulfilled obligations of the 1837 treaty were dangled in front of the village and band chiefs of all four Dakota tribes, and one by one they gave their assent to discussing the cession of their country.

Encouraged and pushed by supposedly friendly whites, each with a different motive—traders, whose respect for kinship obligations vanished suddenly with the prospect of pocketing much of the money paid to the Indians; missionaries, who wanted to herd the Dakotas into centers where they could more easily control and "civilize" them; and speculators and settlers' agents, hungry for the land west of the Mississippi—the Indians in 1851 met in treaty sessions with Governor Ramsey and another commissioner at Traverse des Sioux and Mendota. After considerable opposition by some of the chiefs, their resistance was overcome, and the Dakotas—offered a small reservation—were cajoled into ceding twenty-four million acres, including their ancestral villages and hunting grounds, and moving onto a narrow strip of land twenty miles wide and extending for one hundred fifty miles in a northwesterly direction along both sides of the Minnesota River. In return, the four tribes were promised slightly more than $3 million, most of it to be put in trust to yield funds for annuities and reservation development. The rest of the money, some $495,000, was earmarked for the immediate subsistence of the Indians, their removal costs, and the payment of debts they owed to the traders.

The treaties were barely signed when the government's Indian system—characterized by a mutually beneficial alliance among traders, politicians, and agents—began to cheat the Dakotas. With the connivance of Ramsey, almost all of the $495,000 that was supposed to be paid to the Indians for their immediate needs was diverted into the pockets of traders for debts which they claimed—often falsely—the Dakotas owed them. The largest sum, $145,000, went to the local representative of the American Fur Company, Henry Hastings Sibley (no relation to the Confederate general, Henry Hopkins Sibley, of the New Mexico Campaign). Governor Ramsey himself, along with his secretary, took a 10 to 15 percent fee out of the Indians' money for handling the transactions. "We were deceived, imposed upon and wronged," the chiefs protested in vain. Ramsey, who was later charged with fraud and the maladministration of the Indians' funds, was sharply criticized, but was exonerated of wrongdoing in a hearing by the United States Senate.

It was only the beginning. The Senate took its time ratifying the treaty, and when it did so, it eliminated the clause allowing the Indians to retain a reservation in Minnesota. Meanwhile, settlers, unwilling to wait for the ratification, poured across the Mississippi River, occupying Indian villages and farms, claiming hunting grounds, and quarreling with Dakotas who resisted. Despite the Indians' untenable position, the chiefs were told that they would have to sign approval of the Senate's change in the treaty before their annuities could start being paid to them. The Dakotas were outraged. "Now what have we?" demanded Little Crow, one of the most prominent of the Mdewakanton chiefs. "Why, we have neither our lands, where our fathers' bones are bleaching, nor have we anything." Wabasha, another Mdewakanton, who as his tribe's spokesman at Mendota had stoutly opposed the cession until a consensus of his fellow chiefs had persuaded him to go along with them, echoed Little Crow. "There is one more thing which our great father can do, that is, gather us all on the prairie and surround us with soldiers and shoot us down," he declared.

The Secretary of the Interior finally induced President Franklin Pierce to issue an executive order permitting the Indians to occupy the reservation area promised them by the treaty until the President deemed it necessary to move them elsewhere. The temporary nature of the solution was unsatisfactory to the Dakotas, but they had been tricked into having no alternative. Under pressure from the whites, they accepted the executive decree as better than nothing and moved gradually into villages along the Minnesota River. Two agencies were established among them for their supervision, the Upper, or Yellow Medicine, for the Wahpetons and Sissetons, and the Lower, or Redwood Creek, for the Mdewakantons and Wahpekutes. An agent was assigned to the narrow reservation, and in 1853 Fort Ridgely, an unstockaded cluster of buildings, was erected thirteen miles below the Lower Agency and garrisoned by three companies of the 6th Infantry.

In their new homes, the Indians' grievances mounted. Their promised annuities began to arrive, but the goods were frequently shoddy and the food rotten and unfit to eat. Often, what was owed to them was stolen by the traders or by grafting government personnel, who sold it to others or made the Indians buy it from them on credit at exorbitant prices. Well-meaning missionaries, who established themselves near the two agencies, also caused resentments. Under their tutelage, some of the Indians began living in log cabins and frame and brick houses, donned white men's clothing, became successful farmers, and, allowing their long hair to be cut as a symbol of their turning away from their fathers' spiritual beliefs, accepted Christianity. Inevitably, the missionaries' fervor and assumption of authority created conflict and schisms between those Indians who had decided to take the white men's road and those who wanted to maintain their old institutions and ways of life. Giving support to the missionaries against the traditionalists, the government agents and their employees showed favoritism to the farming Indians and angered the others by trying to change their lives, interfering with their journeys to old hunting grounds off the reservation and punishing young Indians who went on raids against the Dakotas' ancient enemies, the Chippewas.

The worst grievances of all resulted from the steady pressure and anti-Indian attitudes of the growing number of settlers, mostly German, Scandinavian, and Irish immigrants, who moved in aggressively around the Dakotas and began to covet the lands of the newly established reservation. "Many of the white men often abused the Indians and treated them unkindly," a Mdewakanton farming chief named Big Eagle explained later.

> Many of the whites always seemed to say by their manner when they saw an Indian, 'I am much better than you,' and the Indians did not like this . . . the Dakotas did not believe there were better men in the world than they. Then some of the white men abused the Indian women in a certain way and disgraced them, and surely there was no excuse for that. All these things made many Indians dislike the whites.

Insults and tensions increased, and only the efforts of village chiefs like Little Crow kept the young men in check. Nevertheless, in 1857, after a white man and his son murdered nearly a dozen Wahpekutes, mostly women and children, a small band of that tribe led by their angry chief, Inkpaduta, killed almost fifty settlers in southern Minnesota and northwestern Iowa. Other Dakota leaders were quick to dissociate themselves from Inkpaduta's people, whom they had previously ostracized and forced into becoming something of wandering outcasts because they had slain a principal chief of the tribe. But when Inkpaduta evaded a company of Federal troops sent from Fort Ridgely, as well as Indian search parties led by Little Crow, the example of the Wahpekutes' boldness—which in the end went unpunished—was not lost on the restless Dakotas.

At the same time, the panic produced by Inkpaduta's outburst caused many whites to demand the removal of all Sioux from the Territory and the opening of the reservation to settlers. Two of the Dakotas' agents, one of whom at the time was Charles Flandrau, offered a counterproposal. Land speculators themselves, with an eye on personal profits from the Indians' rich acreage along the Minnesota River, they suggested to their superiors that the Dakotas divide their communal tribal holdings and accept individual eighty-acre allotments on which each Indian family could live and farm for itself like the whites. After the allotments had been made, much of the reservation land would be left over and could be opened to white settlement.

Although the government thought well of the proposal, the tenuous nature of the Indians' possession of the reservation made it impractical. Individual Indians could not be expected to create personal improvements on land which the President might at any time take from them and give to whites. Nevertheless, in response to the growing clamor for the reservation's land, the government induced Little Crow and a group of other chiefs to journey to Washington in 1858 for another treaty meeting. There, they conferred with the Commissioner of Indian Affairs, Charles E. Mix, a high-handed Minnesotan with a record of participating with political and business cronies in schemes that defrauded Indians. Reminding the Dakotas that the President could end their reservation at any time and throw them on the mercy of the people of Minnesota, Mix browbeat the chiefs into giving up the ten-mile-wide strip on the northeast side of the Minnesota River—in effect, half of the reservation. To compensate them for the loss, he offered them permanent title to the strip on the southwest bank (on which allotments would then be practical), some small gifts of cash and material goods, including ceremonial swords and flags, and a promise that Congress would consider an additional payment to them. When finally ratified by the Senate, the treaty, which permitted the eighty-acre allotments, awarded the Indians $266,880 for the relinquished 889,000 acres, or about 30 cents an acre. But, again, when Congress' appropriated the money, the bulk of it went to traders to pay off debts which they claimed the Indians owed them. Eventually, the two lower tribes received almost nothing, and the two upper tribes got about $85,000. In contrast, $12,000 of the appropriation further enriched the veteran fur trader Henry Sibley, who was now the Democratic governor of Minnesota, which in 1858 had become a state.

In the following years, the allotment was forgotten, and the situation of the Dakotas, cramped on their diminished reservation, became worse. Frustration and anger lay just below the surface, but the presence of the soldiers at Fort Ridgely inhibited any serious display of Indian militancy and reassured the settlers that they had nothing to fear. Moreover, the influential village chiefs, the farming, or "cut-hair," Indians who were trying to follow the white men's road, and a large number of mixed-breed families with kinship bonds with whites formed a controlling element on the reservation, and each group was committed to coexisting peacefully with the settlers.

To the whites, the best known of the Dakota chiefs was Little Crow, who was also called by his own people Taoyateduta, which meant His Red Nation. About fifty years old, ambitious and vain (he had reputedly been bribed with a wagon for his role in winning the other chiefs' agreement to pay the 1858 treaty money to the traders), Little Crow was the hereditary chief of only one of the Mdewakanton villages. But he was forceful and courageous, was also a Dakota shaman, or holy man, and possessed strong oratorical powers and a domineering personality that won him influence over many of the other Indians. From time to time, among the Mdewakantons, his prestige had risen and fallen. On occasion, he had been that tribe's principal spokesman, but in the spring of 1862, the Mdewakanton elders—apparently to show their displeasure with his leading role in accepting the hated 1858 treaty and buckling under to the traders—angered him by electing a rival chief as their head speaker. The winner, a farming chief, had been helped by the influence of the agent, and the decision persuaded Little Crow that if he was to regain his political prestige, he would have to move closer to those who were following the white men's road. Professing warm friendship for the whites, he began to accommodate to their ways, cutting his hair to shoulder length, moving into a frame house that agency employees built for him, and evincing an interest in becoming less dependent on government food annuities by taking up farming. Garbed in a black frock coat with a velvet collar, he even showed up for services at one of the mission churches, although he had no intention of becoming a Christian.

When the Civil War began, companies of Minnesota volunteers occupied Fort Ridgely and the two other frontier posts
in Minnesota—Fort Abercrombie on the Red River and Fort
Ripley on the upper Mississippi—relieving the Regulars, who
went off to the battlefronts. As time went on, the Indians were
not unaware of Northern reverses and the Federal government's need for more troops. They noticed that the turnover
of the bluecoat companies was frequent at the forts as new
volunteer units arrived periodically to free their predecessors
for service with the Union armies. "We understood that the
South was getting the best of the fight, and it was said that the
North would be whipped," said the farming chief Big Eagle.

The notion that the Federal government, on which they
blamed their problems, was losing the war gained added
credibility when early in August 1862 the Indians' agent,
Major Thomas J. Galbraith, recruited a company of youthful
half-breeds and agency employees, named them the Renville
Rangers (for Minnesota's Renville County), and prepared to
take them to Fort Snelling for enlistment. "The Indians now
thought the whites must be pretty hard up for men to fight the
South, or they would not come so far out on the frontier and
take half-breeds," declared Eagle. "It began to be whispered
about that now would be a good time to go to war with the
whites and get back the lands."

Still, the settlers considered the Indians peaceful. But on
the reservation, a serious crisis was brewing. In 1861, cut-
worms had damaged the Indians' corn crops, totally destroying the plantings of the Sissetons. From December until April
1862, the Upper Agency doled out small amounts of flour and
pork to some of the Sissetons, but by May 1862 all of the tribes
were feeling the food pinch. In their predicament, an increas-

ing number of Indians turned to buying food on credit from the traders, who charged them exorbitant prices. As their debts mounted, the Dakotas began to worry that the traders would claim all their cash annuities at distribution time in the summer. In the soldiers' lodge, where the young traditionalist hunters and warriors met secretly to air their grievances and discuss what they might do, some of them proposed that they continue to buy food from the traders, running up as much credit as possible, and then refuse to pay the traders from their annuities. Learning of the talk, the wary traders abruptly stopped all credit to the Indians and, despite angry threats from the Dakotas, refused to sell them food.

The government cash and food annuities were scheduled to be given out at both agencies in June. By that time, many of the people were in dire straits. Moreover, Thomas S. Williamson, one of the missionaries near the Upper Agency, had become alarmed by reports that Yanktonai and other western Sioux were planning to journey there from the plains during the annuity distribution to demand payment for some of the lands ceded in 1851, which they claimed had belonged to them. The Yanktonais, Williamson wrote to agent Galbraith, were threatening that if they were not paid, they would "kill the Indians who dress like white people, and the white people, and burn the houses." Noting that "many men from Minnesota have gone to the war, and these distant Indians hear very exaggerated reports of this, which may lead them to think the frontier is wholly unprotected," Williamson urged Galbraith to have an adequate number of soldiers present to maintain order during the distribution.

On receipt of Williamson's warning, Galbraith wrote to his superior, Clark W. Thompson, the Superintendent of Indian

Affairs at St. Paul. Thompson, in turn, contacted Governor Ramsey, and on June 18 a detachment of Company C of the 5th Infantry Regiment of Minnesota Volunteers under Lieutenant Timothy J. Sheehan was ordered to march from Fort Ripley to reinforce Fort Ridgely on the reservation. Arriving there, Sheehan added a detachment of Company B of Fort Ridgely's garrison to his command and with the combined force of one hundred men and a twelve-pounder mountain howitzer moved up the reservation to the Yellow Medicine Agency, arriving there on July 2. Major Galbraith, meanwhile, had also gone to that agency, where he had found more than three thousand hungry Sissetons and Wahpetons waiting for him. On June 20, when the impatient chiefs demanded their cash and food annuities, Galbraith announced that the distribution would have to be delayed a month. Undecided whether to pay the cash annuities that year with gold or with the new wartime paper greenbacks, the Indian Office in Washington had held up the delivery of $71,000 for the Dakotas, and the paymaster would not arrive with the money until July. Galbraith had provisions locked up in his large brick warehouse, but, insisting that bookkeeping problems, as well as reservation custom, required him to make the food and cash distributions at the same time, he refused to open the warehouse. Telling the Sissetons and Wahpetons to go off and hunt and come back in a month, he left the agency.

On July 14, he returned. The number of Indians, now including some Yanktons and Yanktonais from the Plains, had increased, and all were on the verge of starvation. In the tension and anger, only the presence of Sheehan's troops preserved order. But the paymaster had not yet arrived, and Galbraith still refused to distribute the food. In later years, the

agent, red-haired and a hard drinker, was described by someone who had known him as being undiplomatic and arrogant
to the Indians, "half the time out of his head" from his "excessive use of liquor" and "wholly unfit to manage a turbulent
lot of savages, who had long-standing grievances and were
disposed to be ugly." His desire to simplify his bookkeeping
chores may have been the only reason for his stubbornness.
But it was also said that, because of the previous year's crop
failure, he was husbanding the provisions for the needs of the
whites at the agency until the 1862 crop was harvested. In
addition, he may have had a more sinister motive. Recognizing Indian contracts and claims as rich sources of graft, Minnesota's Senator Morton Wilkinson had managed to secure
the appointments of Galbraith and Thompson to their positions in the Indian Service, and the three men, along with their
fellow Minnesotan Charles Mix, the Commissioner of Indian
Affairs, were habitually elbow-deep in fraud. In January 1862,
for example, Galbraith had written to Thompson suggesting
that the superintendent get the Indian Office to cooperate in
a scheme to skim off money for the ring during the process-
ing of some Minnesota Indian claims. "The biggest swindle
please[s] them best if they but have a share in [it]," Galbraith
wrote Thompson, referring to the Indian Office. The commissioner, he added, "would aid you & I think old Mix would easily go in." It is not inconceivable that Galbraith, perhaps with
the others, had private plans also to make money from the
Dakotas' food annuities.

If so, the Indians upset the plans. On the morning of August
4, a large crowd of mounted Indians, led by the young men of
the soldiers' lodge, diverted Sheehan's troops while some of
their members broke open the warehouse door with hatch-

ets and began carrying away sacks of flour. Stopped finally by Sheehan's men and by the aiming of the howitzer at the warehouse door, the Dakotas complained bitterly that their women and children were starving and that they had a right to the food. Realizing that the desperate Indians would continue to try to seize the provisions that their agent was withholding from them, the lieutenant argued with Galbraith, finally persuading him to issue the Indians some pork and flour. In return, the Dakotas withdrew, promising that their chiefs would meet the following day in a peaceful council with the agent.

The next morning, Sheehan sent a message to Captain John S. Marsh, the commander of the garrison at Fort Ridgely, informing him of the tense situation at the Upper Agency and requesting him to come in person. At the same time, word of the excitement at Yellow Medicine reached the Lower Agency and the Mdewakanton villages, and Little Crow and Andrew J. Myrick, the most prominent trader at that agency, both hurried upriver to participate in the council. Joined by Stephen Return Riggs, one of the missionaries among the Sissetons and Wahpetons, Galbraith met with the Indians in a first session on August 5. He listened to their appeals for food but made no promises to them. The next day, the council was Little Crow, Myrick, the clerks who ran the traders' stores at Yellow Medicine, and a young missionary, John P. Williamson, the son of Thomas S. Williamson, the man who had written originally to Galbraith urging him to have troops at the agency during the annuity distributions.

Little Crow took over at once, assuming the role of spokesman for the Indians and trying to defuse the tension. Stressing the Dakotas' need for food, he suggested that if Galbraith could not open the warehouse, he should attempt to find a way to persuade the traders to help the hungry Indians until the annuities could be paid. "We have no food, but here are these stores, filled with food," he said. "We ask that you, the agent, make some arrangement by which we can get food from the stores, or else we may take our own way to keep ourselves from starving." Then, either as an explanation of the attack on the warehouse of August 4 or as a threat of what could lie ahead, he added almost in an offhand way, "When men are hungry they help themselves."

Taking this as a threat, the alarmed interpreter refused to translate it to the whites, but Williamson, the missionary, understood the Dakota tongue and, at Galbraith's urging, told the agent and the traders what Little Crow had said. Turning to Myrick and the group of storekeepers, Galbraith inquired, "Well, it's up to you now. What will you do?" The traders conferred among themselves, and one of them replied finally, "Whatever Myrick does, we will do." But Myrick was red with anger at Little Crow's remark and started to leave the council without a response. Stopped by Galbraith, who demanded an answer, he said deliberately, "So far as I am concerned, if they are hungry, let them eat grass." When his reply was translated, the Indians jumped up furiously and stormed from the meeting, shouting war whoops and angry threats.

To many of the outraged Dakotas, the affront was almost too much to bear. Myrick, the other traders and their employees, the storekeepers on the reservation, were all married to Dakota women, or were half-breeds, yet for months they had ignored their kinship obligations and, instead of extending generosity and help to their relatives, had denied their responsibilities to them. Now they had insulted them in their adversity. In the context of Sioux culture, such conduct was maddening and unpardonable.

That afternoon, Captain Marsh arrived from Fort Ridgely, sized up the dangerous situation, and with Little Crow's help, talked the offended leaders into attending another council the next day. Galbraith was now frightened. "If there is anything between the lids of the Bible that will meet this case," he pleaded with the missionary, Stephen Riggs, "I wish you would use it." It was Captain Marsh, however, rather than Riggs, who restored calm. When the meeting convened, Marsh turned angrily on Galbraith and the traders, ordering the agent to issue the annuity goods and provisions in the warehouse immediately and warning the traders and storekeepers that he would arrest them if they gave even the appearance of causing further dissatisfaction among the Indians. Although he objected to Marsh's order, Galbraith had to accept it, and the distribution of food to the Indians began at once, continuing for the next two days. At its conclusion, the Dakotas, with good feelings restored, went back to their villages to await word from Galbraith when their cash annuities arrived. On August 11, with their mission accomplished, the troops left the agency to return to Fort Ridgely.

Galbraith had turned, meanwhile, to recruiting his company of half-breeds and agency employees for enlistment at Fort Snelling. On August 15, he brought them down the reservation to the Lower Agency, where he met again with Little Crow, who had returned home. At the Upper Agency, in the presence of Captain Marsh, Galbraith had promised the Mdewakanton chief that he would also distribute the food and goods annuities to the two lower tribes. But at Redwood, he found that the harvest of an abundant corn crop was already under way and that the fear of starvation was disappearing. Satisfied that the emergency had passed, the agent told Little Crow that he had changed his mind and would make no distribution to the Mdewakantons and Wahpekutes until the cash annuities arrived. Although his broken promise angered Little Crow and the nonfarming traditionalists, Galbraith believed that they constituted a harmless minority, and he left for Fort Snelling with his recruits.

On Sunday, August 17, all was quiet on the reservation. In the morning, Little Crow, dressed in his best suit of white men's clothes, attended services in the Episcopal chapel at the Lower Agency and shook hands amiably with everyone. At almost the same time, north of the Minnesota River, four Indian youths from a Mdewakanton village on Rice Creek above the Lower Agency were returning ill-humoredly from an unsuccessful deer hunt in woods beyond the reservation's boundary. At the white settlement of Acton, one of them paused to take some eggs from the nest of a hen belonging to a local resident. One of his companions objected, telling him that they would all get in trouble over the stolen eggs. Accused of cowardice by the others, the objector replied angrily that he was not afraid to kill a white man. The taunts and boasts continued and soon led to tragedy. Deliberately picking a quarrel with the hen's owner, the youths followed him to the log home of his stepson, where a number of whites were gathered. The Indians seemed to forget their quarrel and, after some friendly conversation, persuaded the whites to join them in a target-shooting contest. Suddenly, in an emotional explosion of boldness and hatred, the youths turned their guns on the whites, killing five of them, including two women. Stealing horses, the Indians rode excitedly back to their village.

When they arrived home late that night, waking the people to announce proudly what they had done, there was consternation. Many of the Indians feared that now the cash annuities would not be paid, that the troops would come and punish everyone, and that the whites would demand the lives of the youths. The members of the soldiers' lodge in the village, however, called an immediate meeting and, after much discussion, approved the young men's action and decided that the time had come for a war against the whites and the retaking of their lands. Reminded by their village chief, Shakopee, that they would need the support of other Mdewakantons, and especially of the able and experienced Little Crow, they sent word of what had happened to trusted warriors in other villages and asked them to meet in council at Little Crow's home.

Before dawn, representatives and warriors of many of the Lower Agency villages, most of them eager for war, gathered at Little Crow's house to decide what to do. Sitting on his bed of blankets on the floor of his large downstairs room, Little Crow was at first surly. "Why do you come to me for advice?" he demanded. "Go to the man you elected speaker and let him tell you what to do." When the warriors ignored him and pleaded that he lead them against the whites, he refused. Having twice visited Washington with delegations and seen the strength of the United States, he knew the foolhardiness of starting a war against the Americans. "You are full of the white man's devil-water," he chided them. "You are like dogs in the Hot Moon when they run mad and snap at their own shadows. We are only little herds of buffalo left scattered . . . the white men are like the locusts when they fly so thick that the whole sky is a snowstorm. . . . Kill one-two-ten, and ten times ten will come to kill you."

But the warriors persisted, recounting their grievances against the whites. Gradually, the recital of their resentments and the argument that only he could lead them appealed to Little Crow's vanity, and he saw an opportunity to regain his prestige. He painted his face black and pulled a blanket over his head. Suddenly one of the hotheaded warriors called him a coward. Little Crow leaped to his feet and, knocking the warrior's headdress to the floor, announced that he would lead them. "Braves," he warned, "you are little children—you are fools. You will die like the rabbits when the hungry wolves hunt them in the Hard Moon. Taoyateduta is not a coward; he will die with you!"

Carefully excluded from the meeting, most of the farming chiefs and their people—the pantaloon-wearing cut-hairs—as well as the half-breeds and mixed-bloods, knew nothing of what was happening. At dawn on August 18, Little Crow, now in war garb, led a column of painted Mdewakantons to the Lower Agency. By seven o'clock they were in position. At a signal, they attacked, overrunning the buildings and shouting in Dakota, "Kill the whites! Kill all the whites!" Among the first victims was trader Myrick, who tried to escape the Indians by sliding down a lightning rod from a second-story window above his store. The Mdewakantons shot him as he raced toward some woods. Rolling his corpse on its back, they rammed a tuft of grass into its mouth.

Other war parties swept through the countryside, releasing their pent-up hatred in an orgy of killing, burning, and looting. Soon the uprising was joined by some of the Sisseton and

Wahpeton warriors, and the terror and pillage engulfed the Upper Agency and spread to white farms and homes opposite the full length of the reservation. The farming Indians and the half-breeds and mixed-bloods were as surprised as the whites. Most of them refused to participate in the war, and some of them risked their lives hiding white friends and relatives, helping them to escape, or protecting and caring for them when they were captured and brought to the Indian villages. Others chose the side of the hostiles and, shedding their white men's clothing, painted their faces and joined the warriors.

By ten o'clock on the morning of the uprising, the first refugees, some of them bleeding, burned, or mute with horror, reached Fort Ridgely on the eastern side of the river, thirteen miles downstream from the Lower Agency. The post's garrison consisted of two officers and seventy-six enlisted men of Company B of the 5th Minnesota Infantry. Its commander, Captain Marsh, had fought with a Wisconsin regiment at the First Battle of Bull Run, but he had had no experience in fighting Indians. He quickly sent off a messenger to overtake Lieutenant Sheehan, who with his fifty-man detachment of Company C had started back to Fort Ripley the day before. "The Indians are raising hell at the Lower Agency," he notified Sheehan, asking him to return at once to Fort Ridgely. Then, with forty-six men of Company B and the post's interpreter, he set out for the Redwood Agency, passing mutilated bodies, burning houses, and other evidence of the Indians' fury. Despite warnings by fleeing settlers whom he met on the road that the Sioux would overwhelm his small force, he hurried his men on boldly, reaching the Redwood Ferry crossing of the Minnesota. The Lower Agency was still a mile off, spread across the top of a bluff on the opposite side of the river.

The troops had passed the still-warm body of the ferryman, lying on the road along which he had been fleeing, but his flat-bottomed skiff attached to the ferry cable rested against the shore where he had left it. From the far bank, an Indian called to the soldiers to come across on the ferry. He was recognized as Shonka-sha, or White Dog, a farming Indian, whom the Upper Agency had once employed to teach other Indians to farm. But Galbraith, on assuming office, had replaced him with one of his own appointees, and although the whites considered White Dog a civilized and friendly Indian, he was filled with resentment at the loss of this job and prestige. Through the interpreter, he called to Marsh that the Indians had had some trouble with the traders, but that the captain could straighten it out. The Indians did not want to fight, he declared, but were at the agency and would like to hold a council with him. "Everything is right over here," he shouted. "There will be no trouble."

Apparently believing that the hideous uprising was the work of a single renegade group and that he could restore peace as he had done at Yellow Medicine, Marsh prepared to cross with his men on the ferry. Before he could do so, a sergeant named John F. Bishop, who had gone to the water's edge to get a drink, saw some Indians fording the river farther upstream and warned Marsh that the Dakotas might be trying to surround them. A moment later, Bishop also spied some riderless ponies switching their tails in the brush on the opposite shore. Suddenly fearing an ambush, Marsh ordered the interpreter to ask White Dog what the ponies were doing there if the Indians were all up at the agency. In an instant, White Dog raised his gun, the interpreter shouted, "Look out!" and a volley of gunfire from Indians hidden in the grass and bushes across the river struck the soldiers.

"About one-half of our men dropped dead where they had been standing," Bishop reported. A second later, the Indians who had forded the river above them gave "a fearful yell" and rushed in on the soldiers' rear, firing double-barreled shotguns and engaging Marsh's men in hand-to-hand fighting. Within moments, the command was cut to pieces, and the survivors were in flight through the tall grass and brush that lined the river. Some of the men, entering a thicket, held off the Indians, but when they began running out of ammunition, Marsh ordered them to swim across the river and try to escape through the timber on the other shore. Leading the way, Marsh suffered a cramp in a hole of deep, rushing water and, despite the efforts of some of his men to save him, drowned. "I will never forget the look that brave officer gave us just before he sank for the last time—will never forget how dark the next hour seemed to us, as we crouched underneath the bank of the Minnesota river, and talked over and decided what next best to do," said Sergeant Bishop, upon whom command had devolved.

Meanwhile, the Indians, thinking that Marsh and his men had swum across the river, abandoned their positions around the thicket. Hurrying back to their ford, they returned to the opposite shore, intending to set up another ambush. Shielded by an overhanging bank along the river, Bishop and the other survivors got away unobserved, making their way safely downriver and arriving back at Fort Ridgely after nightfall. Twenty-five men, including the interpreter, had lost their lives, and five more had been wounded. Only one Indian had been killed.

The disaster shocked Lieutenant Thomas P. Gere, an inexperienced nineteen-year-old officer whom Marsh had left in charge of the fort. Suffering from the mumps and with only twenty-two enlisted men in addition to Bishop and the ambush survivors fit for duty, the youthful lieutenant sent a hastily scrawled message to Fort Snelling and Governor Ramsey for immediate reinforcements. "The Indians are killing the settlers and plundering the country," he wrote. Changing horses several times and going partway by wagon, his courier, Private William J. Sturgis, made the 125-mile trip to Fort Snelling in eighteen hours. Along the way, he overtook Galbraith and his Renville Rangers and turned them back to reinforce Gere.

At Fort Ridgely, preparations were made to withstand an expected attack. Without a stockade, its cluster of detached buildings grouped around a parade ground was a tempting target for the Indians. Moreover, if the Dakotas overran it, the way would be open for them to fall on every downriver town and settlement as far as the gates of Fort Snelling. More than two hundred refugees, mostly frightened women and children, as well as many wounded being cared for by the post's surgeon and sutler, were already crowded into the fort's log hospital building, surgeons' quarters, and fieldstone barracks. During the day, also, a stagecoach had arrived at the post from St. Paul with kegs of gold coins—the Indians' long-delayed cash annuities. Had they come a day or two earlier, the uprising might not have occurred. Lieutenant Gere told no one about the gold and with the help of the stagecoach guards hid the kegs securely in one of the buildings.

With Gere unwell, much of the responsibility for the preparations for defense was assumed by a seasoned, full-bearded Regular, a massively built ordnance sergeant named John Jones, who had stayed at the fort to care for some artillery pieces left behind the year before when the U.S. troops were withdrawn. The pieces included two twelve-pounder mountain howitzers, a twenty-four-pounder howitzer, and a six-pounder field gun. Jones had trained some of Marsh's men to load and fire them, and he now formed crews to man all but the twenty-four-pounder and stationed them at three of the fort's corners.

Early the next morning, August 19, a large number of Indians on horseback, on foot, and in wagons, flushed with their successes, appeared on the prairie west of the post. With them were Little Crow and several other village chiefs, including Mankato and Big Eagle. The Indians delayed their attack, however, and in full view of the fearful defenders conducted a council. Little Crow and the leading chiefs, who understood the strategic importance of the fort, argued for the immediate elimination of the bluecoats. But the young Indians of the soldiers' lodge contended that their force was too small to assault the post. Too many warriors were still spread across the countryside, killing the settlers, feasting, and filling their wagons with plunder. For the present, they maintained, it would be easier and more rewarding to attack the German settlers at New Ulm, where there were stores to pillage and women to capture. The troops at the fort could wait, they insisted.

The warriors finally won their argument, and the Indians turned away from the post. Many of the young men rode off toward New Ulm farther down the river. The others, including the chiefs, who refused to join their attack on the women and children of the town, returned to Little Crow's village, which had become the headquarters for those who were fighting the war.

The Indians' decision was a fortunate one for the fort's defenders. Had the Dakotas attacked the weakly held post immediately that morning, they might well have overrun it. But

even as the Indians concluded their council, Gere's little force
received the welcome reinforcement of Lieutenant Sheehan
and his fifty-man Company C of the 5th Minnesota. Overtaken
by Marsh's courier the previous evening as the troops were
making camp, Sheehan had immediately struck his tents and
led his men back on a forced march through the night, covering the forty-two miles to Fort Ridgely in nine and a half hours.
As senior officer, Sheehan took command of the post. That
evening, Galbraith and about fifty members of his Renville
Rangers also arrived at the fort, having hurried back from the
downriver town of St. Peter, where they had obtained some
old Harper's Ferry muskets and a supply of powder and lead.
Including a number of refugees at the post who possessed
guns, Sheehan's defending force was now approximately one
hundred eighty.

At New Ulm, meanwhile, the Dakota war party, numbering
about one hundred mounted men, appeared on a high bluff
that rose behind the tableland on which the town was situated.
At about 3 p.m., the Indians dismounted and advanced down
the hill to a crest at its base, where they began firing into the
town. While the women and children crowded in fright in the
buildings and behind the barricades, Jacob Nix's militiamen
returned the fire, keeping the Indians at bay. Several small groups
of Dakotas made bold dashes at the buildings and barricades,
killing a few of the townspeople before they were driven back.
Other Indians were content to set some of the undefended outlying buildings on fire. An hour after the fighting started, a party
of seven volunteers arrived from Nicollet County and helped
some of Nix's men move forward from building to building and
force the Indians back. A severe thunderstorm with lightning
and crashing thunder finally drenched the area, and with the

sudden appearance of more reinforcements—a group of sixteen mounted men from St. Peter led by the sheriff of Nicollet
County—the Indians broke off the fight and rode away. The
Dakotas had killed seventeen townspeople, but eleven of them
were members of a hapless party whom they had intercepted
on the prairie outside of town. The Indians carried away their
own casualties, and their losses were not known.

After dark, Judge Charles Flandrau, whom Behnke had
aroused from sleep the night before at Traverse des Sioux,
reached New Ulm with a hastily recruited relief column of
125 volunteer farmers and townspeople from St. Peter and Le
Sueur, together with a group of doctors, including William W.
Mayo, whose sons later established a famous medical center
at Rochester, Minnesota. Other bodies of armed citizens continued to arrive at the town, and Flandrau, who was elected
overall commander, soon had almost three hundred men preparing defenses against a return of the Indians.

At a council in his village that night, Little Crow and a group
of other chiefs who were committed to the war against the
whites finally had their way about the need to capture Fort
Ridgely. The next morning—joined now by a large party of
about four hundred warriors—they started back to the post.
Following a plan of attack that Little Crow had worked out,
the Dakotas divided into four groups, and early in the afternoon, moving under the cover of deep, wooded ravines, began
to surround the fort. On its western side, Little Crow, riding a
black pony, tried to distract the troops' attention, circling con-
spicuously back and forth on the prairie as if he were seeking
a parley. Meanwhile, other Dakotas crept into position through
the trees and thick brush in the ravines.

At a signal of three volleys fired by the Indians on the

north, the attack began from that direction. Once the shooting started, according to a warrior named Lightning Blanket, "we paid no attention to the chiefs; everyone did as he pleased." At first, Sheehan formed his men on the parade ground, but when two of them were hit by Indian bullets, he ordered the others to seek cover among the buildings and fire at will. In the early fighting, the Dakotas charged the northeast corner of the post, taking possession of a row of outlying log huts. Several Indians slipped between two buildings, temporarily penetrating the fort's inner defenses before they were killed and the gap was closed. In the confusion, other Dakotas managed to run off most of the post's horses, mules, and cattle. Supported by infantrymen, the crews of Jones's two howitzers finally blasted the Indians out of the log huts and back to the shelter of the ravine.

The Indians on the other sides of the fort were slow in pressing the attack, and when they did, hitting hard at the post's southwest corner, the six-pounder field gun, manned by the redoubtable Jones, and the musketry of the Renville Rangers and some of Sheehan's men held them off. The battle settled down to several hours of long-range shooting and ineffectual attempts by the Indians to set the buildings on fire with burning arrows. On occasion, the Dakotas tried to edge forward, but the fearful explosions of the artillery shells that burst around them with flying pieces of metal sent them running back. Afraid of the guns, which they had never faced, the Indians finally abandoned the fight and withdrew at dusk.

Heavy rain that began at midnight and continued through the next day gave a respite to the fort and to New Ulm and let the forces at both places strengthen their defenses. At Fort Ridgely, Sergeant Jones added the twenty-four-pounder howitzer to his artillery and positioned it on the parade ground. Barricades of cord wood and sacks of oats were erected around the guns and between some of the inner buildings. At Little Crow's village, the frustrated Indians made bullets from supplies seized from the Lower Agency and from the traders' stores and discussed what to do next. Although Little Crow had appealed for allies from the Sissetons and Wahpetons in the upper part of the reservation, the leading chiefs and the majority of the people of those tribes wanted to stay out of the war. Some of them were friendly to the missionaries and other whites and had helped them escape from the Upper Agency. Many of the young men and hunting Indians, however, were of a different mind. They had had conflicts with the whites; the confrontation with Galbraith over the distribution of their annuities was still fresh in their memory; and they were excited by the news of the uprising at the Lower Agency. On the night of August 21, approximately four hundred Sisseton and Wahpeton warriors who had left their hunting camps on the prairie near Big Stone Lake at the head of the Minnesota River arrived in the Mdewakanton villages and announced their eagerness to join the fighting. Welcoming their appearance, which doubled the size of the Indian force, Little Crow and the other warring chiefs decided to renew the attack on Fort Ridgely the next day.

It was to be "a grand affair," said Big Eagle. With Little Crow riding toward the battlefield in a buggy driven by a mixed-blood friend, the Indians reached the vicinity of the fort just before noon on August 22. Camouflaging themselves by putting grass, leaves, and prairie wildflowers in their headbands, the Dakotas crept again through the ravines and encir-

cled the fort. The signal for the attack, which as before was
to come from those on the northern side of the post, almost
miscarried. Before the Indians on the other sides were in position, a mail courier from New Ulm was seen approaching the
fort from the north. As he came up, three Indians fired at him,
killing him, but inadvertently also giving the agreed-upon signal for the Dakotas' attack. With what Lieutenant Gere called
"demoniac yells," Indians sprang up from the ravines and tall
grass, shooting their weapons as they ran forward. Returning their fire from behind the barricades and from windows
in the scattered buildings, the defenders halted the Indians
everywhere and forced them back beyond the explosions of
the howitzer shells. Rallied by their war leaders, the Dakotas came forward again. This time, some of them managed
to occupy the sutler's house and the stables on the southwest corner of the post. Jones's artillery shells soon dislodged
them, but set the buildings and the grass on fire. Elsewhere,
the Indians' flaming arrows began to hit other buildings. The
roofs were still damp from the recent rain, and the few fires
that were started were quickly extinguished by volunteers
who chopped away at the burning sections of the roofs. But
the sudden flare-up of flames and the billowing clouds of
smoke alternately reddened and darkened the battleground,
making it seem at times that the post was being consumed
by fire.

The fierce battle lasted through the afternoon. The Indians made repeated attacks, trying to shoot into the windows
through which the soldiers were firing. "The hail of bullets,
the whizzing of arrows, and the blood-curdling war-whoop
were incessant," Gere reported. Again and again, Jones's artil-

lery roared, and the Indians tried to pick off the gunners. "The [Dakotas'] fire in front of Jones's gun had become so hot and accurate as to splinter almost every lineal foot of timber along the top of his barricades," Gere said.

Trying to dodge a shell burst, Little Crow struck his head painfully on a rock, and Chief Mankato finally gathered a large number of the warriors and led them in a massed charge against the southwest corner of the fort. A barrage of double charges of canister from a mountain howitzer and the twenty-four-pounder, which was newly brought into action, landed among them. "The ponderous reverberations" of the big gun, Gere said, "echoed up the valley as though twenty guns had opened, and the frightful explosions struck terror to the savages," many of whom were killed or wounded. "Completely demoralized by this unexpected slaughter, firing suddenly ceased and the attacking party precipitately withdrew." As the Indians fled, the second battle for the fort ended. Despite the close quarters of the struggle, the defenders' losses in the two fights at the post were only six killed and fewer than twenty wounded. Although Lieutenant Gere asserted in his official report of the battles that the Sioux loss in the two attacks "could hardly have been less than 100," this may have been an overestimate.

Nevertheless, it was a costly defeat for the Dakotas. On their way back to Little Crow's village that night, they camped and held a council. Smarting from their repulse, Little Crow and about half of the warriors decided to appease their anger by attacking New Ulm again the next day and taking vengeance on the German settlers. With some four hundred men, Little Crow left the camp that night for New Ulm. The rest stayed in the camp until morning and then returned to Little Crow's village. At about nine thirty the next morning, Saturday, August 23, the Indians emerged from some woods onto the prairie west of New Ulm. Slowly, they moved along the foot of the bluff above the town, quickening their movement as they formed a line whose ends curved forward to threaten the envelopment of the whites' position. In command of the defense, Judge Flandrau sent skirmishers onto a terrace below the bluff and deployed a large number of his citizen soldiers in a line across the prairie to protect the town's buildings. All of them watched the Indians' maneuvers with nervousness and awe. "Their advance upon the sloping prairie in the bright sunlight was a very fine spectacle, and to such inexperienced soldiers as we all were, intensely exciting," Flandrau related. "When within about one mile and a half from us the mass began to expand like a fan, and increase in the velocity of its approach. . . . Then the savages uttered a terrific yell and came down upon us like the wind."

The sudden charge, accompanied by the wild yells, unnerved Flandrau's men, who broke and ran toward the barricades in the middle of town, passing many of the outer buildings, which the Indians were quick to occupy. Flandrau and his officers gradually ended the panic, rallying the men into retaking some of the buildings and organizing a defense of the inner part of the town. Marksmen were sent scrambling up a stone windmill to snipe at the Indians, and others were ordered to fort up in a brick post office building that commanded an approach to the barricades. To provide a better view of the Indians' movements and help keep them at a distance, volunteers set fire to many of the buildings in front of the defenders' positions and let them burn to the ground. When the Indians did the same thing to buildings in their front, a large, open space was created, which the Dakotas hesitated to cross.

"It got to be," said Flandrau, "a regular Indian skirmish, in which every man did his own work after his own fashion." Although the Dakotas surrounded the town, the whites held them off during several hours of sharp fighting. In midafternoon, the Indians noticed that a wind was blowing toward the town from the river. Concentrating in the lower part of the settlement, they set fire to buildings there and advanced behind a wall of dense smoke toward the barricaded whites. Suddenly a group of some sixty warriors "on ponies and afoot" charged up a street toward the center of town. Despite the memory of his men's panic in the morning, Flandrau rallied the defenders and ordered a countercharge to meet the Indians head-on. "This was the critical point of the day," Flandrau reported. "But four or five hours under fire had brought the boys up to the fighting temperature, and they stood firmly, and advanced with a cheer, routing the rascals like sheep. . . . As [the Indians] fled in a crowd at very short range we gave them a volley that was very effectual and settled the fortunes of the day in our favor."

At dark, having failed to break the whites' resistance, the Dakotas withdrew. A number of them reappeared the next morning, but after some halfhearted skirmishing, abandoned the fight and departed. In the two battles at New Ulm, thirty-six of the defenders had been killed and at least twenty-three wounded. "One young man received three bullets through different parts of his pantaloons, in rapid succession, without being hurt in the least," Flandrau noted in his official report. Again, the Indian losses were not known. Most of the town was destroyed—one hundred ninety buildings were in ashes—and that afternoon Flandrau and his officers decided to evacuate the settlement the next day. Food and ammunition were giving out, and epidemics were threatening the townspeople and refugees. Their long confinement, Flandrau explained, "was rapidly producing disease among the women and children, who were huddled in cellars and close rooms like sheep in a cattle car." Crowding had been so intense in the rooms of some of the buildings that the women had been obliged to provide more space by taking off their hoopskirts. Escorted by a troop of one hundred fifty newly arrived volunteers from Nicollet and Sibley counties, about two thousand people, with one hundred fifty-three wagons loaded with children, old persons, sick, and wounded who rode atop piles of baggage and household goods left New Ulm on the following morning and made their way fearfully downriver, expecting at any moment to be attacked again by Dakotas. When they reached the town of Mankato, thirty miles away, without incident, Flandrau gave a sigh of relief. "Under Providence," he reported, "we got through."

To the Dakotas, the stout resistance of the citizens at New Ulm and, more particularly, that of the soldiers at Fort Ridgely were sobering blows. "We thought the fort was the door to the valley as far as to St. Paul, and that if we got through the door nothing could stop us this side of the Mississippi," said Chief Big Eagle years later. "But the defenders of the Fort were very brave and kept the door shut" to a further Indian advance in that direction. The terrible war, however, that had begun on a red morning less than a week earlier was far from concluded. It would spread north and west, involving other Indians, General John Pope (who was about to lose the Second Battle of Bull Run), and thousands of Union troops, diverted from fighting the Confederates.*

---

* Eds. note: At the end of the Sioux uprising, 309 Indians and mixed-bloods were sentenced to be hanged. President Lincoln had the records reviewed. Most sentences were commuted, but thirty-eight were hanged in an elaborate public execution in Mankato, Minnesota, on December 26, 1862, as the Civil War raged in the East. It remains the largest public execution in U.S. history.

7

The Last Stand of Chief Joseph

Although political and legal battles were to occur over a span of almost one hundred fifty years, until well into the twenty-first century, the Nez Perce War of 1877 could truly be called, as a military event, the last Indian War. In telling the story of that war, Josephy was able once again to bring together familiar elements of a long history of conflict. Bravery, persistence, tactical skills—and luck— on both sides.

Josephy published his account of the Nez Perce War first in American Heritage *in 1958. He then expanded the article to become the final chapter of his 1961 book,* The Patriot Chiefs, *commissioned and published by Viking Press. Without question, this is the archetypical story of American Indian resistance against white encroachment on a land—and a world—held sacred.*

In June 1877, just one year after the Custer debacle, a new and unexpected Indian outbreak flared in the West. To an American public wearied and disgusted with a governmental policy, or lack of policy, that seemed to breed Indian wars, this one, an uprising by formerly peaceful Nez Perce of Oregon and Idaho, was dramatized by what appeared to be superb

Indian generalship. One army detachment after another, officered by veterans of the Civil War, floundered in battle with the hostiles. Western correspondents telegraphed the progress of a great, thirteen-hundred-mile fighting retreat by the Indians, swaying popular imagination in behalf of the valiant Nez Perce and their leader, Chief Joseph, who, as handsome and noble in appearance as a Fenimore Cooper Indian, became something of a combined national hero and military genius.

The government received no laurels, either, as the long trail of bitter injustices that had originally driven the Nez Perce to hostility became known. The war, like most Indian troubles, had stemmed from a conflict over land. For centuries the Nez Perce had occupied the high, grassy hills and canyon-scarred plateau land where Washington, Oregon, and Idaho come together. A strong and intelligent people, they had lived in peace and friendship with the whites ever since the coming of Lewis and Clark in 1805, and it was their proud boast that no member of the tribe had ever killed a white man.

Joseph was the leader of only one of the Nez Perce bands, a group of some sixty males and perhaps twice that number of women and children who lived in the Wallowa Valley in the northeastern corner of Oregon. Isolated on all sides by natural barriers of high mountain ranges and some of the deepest gorges on the continent, the valley's lush grasslands provided some of the best grazing ground in the Northwest, and settlers were particularly anxious to possess it. But Joseph's band of Nez Perce had lived there in security and peace for generations, and just before he died in 1871 Joseph's father, a prominent chief named Wellamotkin, known familiarly to the whites as Old Joseph, had fearfully counseled his son:

When I am gone, think of your country. You are the chief
of these people. They look to you to guide them. Always
remember that your father never sold the country. You must
stop your ears whenever you are asked to sign a treaty selling your home. A few years more, and the white man will
be all around you. They have their eyes on this land. My
son, never forget my dying words. This country holds your
father's body. Never sell the bones of your father and your
mother.

The crisis came for Joseph almost immediately after his
father's death. He was thirty one years old, a tall and powerfully built man with the philosophical bent and strong and
logical mind of a civil, rather than a war, chief. Like most members of his band he had had many friendly contacts with white
men, and he did not fit the typical picture of a hostile Indian
who had grown to manhood hating the Americans. Though
he had come to believe that the Indians and whites did not mix
well, he had a humanitarianism that transcended national loyalty and an understanding of conflicting forces that was rare in
either Indians or whites.

He had been born in the spring of 1840, probably near the
juncture of Joseph Creek and the Grande Ronde River in the
deep, sheltered warmth of the Joseph Canyon, where his father's
people and their herds waited out the winter till Chinook winds
told them that they could ascend to the high, greening mead-
ows and fast-running streams of the nearby Wallowa Valley. At
the time there were some four to six thousand Nez Perce; most
of them lived in small fishing villages that dotted the banks of
the Clearwater and Salmon Rivers and the middle stretches of

the Snake and its tributaries, and were widely spread over a vast expanse of territory. Each village or small concentration of them lived under the leadership of its own chief, and during his youth Joseph visited most of the settlements with his father, learning the tribal lore that held them all together as a single nation. It was a colorful past, filled with dramatic events that spoke of many lands and tribes other than their own.

From their earliest days, the Nez Perce were known to be a traveling people, and at various periods of the year journeyed far and wide from their home settlements. War parties constantly ranged southward through Idaho and Oregon against the Shoshonis, who were the Nez Perce's traditional enemies. Others traveled to northern Idaho and Washington to visit Spokans and Coeur d'Alenes, with whom they sometimes fought and were sometimes friendly, and still others made long excursions across the rugged Bitterroot Mountains to join Flathead Indians on buffalo hunts in western Montana. All the Nez Perce, at one time or another, traveled down the Columbia River to the Dalles to trade with Chinook people who came up from the Pacific Coast, and until the middle of the eighteenth century the western Indians exercised a dominant influence on the culture of the Nez Perce, whose way of life more closely resembled that of the fish-eating Columbia River tribes than the buffalo-hunting Plains Indians of Montana.

Sometime about 1730 the Nez Perce first saw horses in the camps of their Shoshoni enemies to the south. The animals had come overland from the Spanish settlements in New Mexico, via Apaches and Utes, and by trading and raiding the Nez Perce soon had herds of their own. With the animals they began to cross the Bitterroots in larger numbers and move farther east across the plains, assimilating to a greater degree than before the ways of the Plains Indians with whom they traded and fought. At the same time a remarkable event occurred in their own homeland. Perhaps alone among all the Indian tribes on the continent, the Nez Perce learned to practice selective breeding and developed a strong and beautiful type of spotted horse that became known for its speed and endurance. The Nez Perce were already fashioning the most prized bow on the plains, one made from the horn of a mountain sheep, and now they appeared with the handsomest warhorse, a spotted and painted pony, which they festooned with feathers. Known today as the Appaloosa (from "a Palouse," the name of a portion of the original Nez Perce country), the horse is still a favorite of cowmen in the rugged plateau country of the Northwest.*

By the end of the eighteenth century many of the Nez Perce had become essentially Plains Indians, though they continued to return regularly to their home villages on the Columbia River tributaries, where fish and roots still constituted a major part of their diet. But their journeys took them into strange and faraway lands, and they were already in contact with tribes who lived along the upper Missouri River in the Dakotas. From them they heard of white men, and in their camps they saw trade

---

* Eds. note: In his initial research on the Nez Perce, Josephy found and accepted historian Francis Haines's contention that the Nez Perce, building on ancient lines of horses from Asia to the New World, selectively bred the spotted horses as their "warhorse." In 1961 he followed Haines in his article on Chief Joseph in *American Heritage* magazine. In 1962 he was asked to substantiate text provided by Haines to the Amon Carter Museum in Fort Worth for an art exhibit on Appaloosa horses. Haines had been unable to satisfy museum curators—and neither did Josephy. From there he did his own extensive research, publishing articles—responded to ineffectively by Haines—for the New York Westerners *Brand Book* in 1967 and 1968. Josephy owned and loved Appaloosas, and held that the Nez Perce, first among Northwest tribes, selectively bred horses, but bred them for speed and endurance, and not for their distinctive spotted coats.

guns and other goods that made the strangers with beards seem worth meeting. They had already learned of white men from the coastal tribes at The Dalles, who showed them metal goods left along the Northwest Coast. But unlike the Missouri River whites, the sea traders on the Pacific did not give guns to the Indians, and firearms were already becoming a necessity in the hunts and wars on the plains. In the spring of 1805 the Nez Perce sent three of their young men to the Missouri River villages of the Minnitaree Indians in present-day North Dakota to try to purchase guns, and they returned with six of them.

In the fall of that same year, the members of the Lewis and Clark Expedition, bound for the mouth of the Columbia River, struggled through the Bitterroot Mountains and emerged in the Nez Perce country. It was an exciting event for the villagers, who had never seen whites before. The explorers were starving after their ordeal in the mountains, and the Indians welcomed them into their settlements and gave them food. But the natives' kindly feelings for the Americans increased when the captains promised to send them traders who would provide them with more guns and white men's goods. The expedition leaders could not live up to their promise, and the first known white man to arrive within trading distance of the Nez Perce was David Thompson, a member of the Canadian North West Company, who crossed the Canadian Rockies and circulated through the country of the upper Columbia River and its tributaries between 1807 and 1811.

There are indications in Thompson's journals that a mysterious group of Americans was also in contact with the Nez Perce during part of the same time, but history knows nothing else about them, and for a number of years the Nez Perce did most, if not all, of their trading with Thompson and his colleagues.

Thompson called the Nez Perce Sahaptians, which was a Flathead word for them and referred to the geographic location of their homeland, south and west of the Flatheads. But from the Columbia River tribes some of the Nez Perce copied the habit of wearing small pieces of shell in their noses as adornments. They abandoned the custom entirely soon after the arrival of white men in their country, but Thompson's French-Canadian *engagés* saw their pierced noses and found that Nez Perce was easier to say than Sahaptian, so that name soon took hold for all of the tribe. In 1811, American traders of John Jacob Astor's company finally reached the Northwest and opened trade of their own in competition with the Canadians. The American stay was of short duration. The War of 1812 forced the sale of Astoria, and the Americans abandoned the country to Canadian monopoly. The Nor'Westers built inland posts and pursued a vigorous trade through much of Idaho, and the Nez Perce received a growing supply of guns and trade goods. In the early 1810s the North West Company merged with the Hudson's Bay Company, and factors and traders of the big British firm brought new wealth to their Indian clients.

With their horses and guns, the Nez Perce continued to roam eastward, and in the late 1820s their buffalo-hunting parties began to meet American trappers and mountain men as far east as Wyoming's Green River Valley. The Indians liked the wild, free fur men, who helped them fight their mutual enemies the Blackfeet, and who lived with them in their camps as equals and gave them higher prices than the British for their pelts. The Nez Perce whooped and sported with the Americans at the trappers' annual rendezvous, and some of the mountain men took Nez Perce women as their wives.

During the 1820s, also, another influence of the white

men entered Nez Perce lives. Hudson's Bay men began taking Northwest Indian youths to an Anglican mission school
at Red River in central Canada, and when the youths returned
to their villages they stirred an interest in Christianity among
their people. Earlier, many of the Nez Perce and Flatheads had
learned some of the rudiments of the white men's religion
from Iroquois Indians, who had been reared as Roman Catholics in eastern Canada and had followed the Nor'Westers as
engagés and free trappers into the Oregon country. Now, both
the Nez Perce and the Flatheads desired to have the religion
for themselves, regarding it as a power like their own medicine
that would endow them with added wisdom and strength. In
1831 they began to send emissaries to St. Louis with returning
mountain men, hoping to enlist teachers who would come to
live with them.

In the American city they met both Roman Catholics and
Protestants, and missionaries from various churches were
soon racing one another to Oregon to save the Indians' souls.
In 1836 the Reverend Henry H. Spalding and his wife opened
a Presbyterian mission at Lapwai in the heart of the Nez Perce
country near present-day Lewiston, Idaho. At first the Indians were overjoyed to have teachers among them, and they
attended the mission classes with enthusiasm. The Spaldings
taught them reading, writing, and farming as well as religion,
and many of the Nez Perce abandoned their trips to the buffalo plains and settled down to raise grains, vegetables, and
herds of the white man's cows. A few of the leading men were
converted as examples for the rest, and among them was Old
Joseph of the Wallowa band, who became a fast friend of the
Spaldings. On November 17, 1839, Spalding recorded that he
"lawfully" married Joseph and his wife, "Asenoth," and on

April 12, 1840, he noted that he baptized Joseph's new son "Ephraim," who was undoubtedly the future young Joseph.

All did not go well at the mission, however, and in time many of the natives became disillusioned with the white man's medicine, which did not seem to give them the new power in war and hunting that they expected. Other Indians, who had somehow thought that the missionaries would be like the "bighearted" trappers and would be a new source of white men's goods at cheap prices, began to quarrel with the Spaldings and urged them to leave their country. By the late 1840s, when settlers began to stream into Oregon, the situation at the mission had become dangerous. Many of the natives now accused the Spaldings of having brought the white men to steal their country, and when the neighboring Cayuse Indians, with similar fears, heightened by the panic of a measles epidemic, turned on their own missionaries, the Marcus Whitmans, and massacred them in 1847, the Spaldings fled from Lapwai.

Some of the Nez Perce, including a chief named Lawyer who lived on the upper Clearwater River, were loyal to the missionaries and were sorry to see them go. Old Joseph probably also regretted their departure, though Spalding believed that Joseph had turned against him. At any rate, Joseph and his people retired to the isolation of the Wallowa Valley and, like the rest of the Nez Perce, avoided becoming involved in a punitive war which the Americans waged against the Cayuse who had killed the Whitmans.

In 1855, after peace had returned to the country, Joseph and the other Nez Perce leaders signed a treaty that defined a large reservation for the tribe. According to Americans at the treaty Council, the Wallowa chief still carried a Bible and spoke warmly of the Spaldings. His friendship for the whites had apparently not waned, and shortly afterward, when the Yakimas and other Northwest tribes, who had been traditional allies of the Nez Perce, rose up against the Americans, Joseph approved of aid that some of the members of the Nez Perce nation gave to the United States troops. But in 1860, when white trespassers found gold on Nez Perce land and miners overran part of the reservation, his good feeling came to an end. White men cheated, bullied, and murdered Nez Perce in their own country, and there was no redress. New towns sprang up, crowding Indian villages out of existence, and in 1863 commissioners arrived from the East to try to end the turmoil by gathering the Indians into a new and smaller reservation. For a while the Nez Perce chiefs at the council were united in opposition to the Americans' proposal,* but finally, after secret night meetings with individual chiefs, in which the commissioners apparently gave promises of private favors, some of the leaders, headed by Lawyer, agreed to accept the new reservation.

The agreement reduced the Indians' land to less than one-fourth of its previous size, and all the chiefs who signed represented bands whose homes already lay within the boundaries of the new reservation. The Wallowa Valley was part of the huge area being ceded, and Joseph, along with some two-thirds of the tribal leaders, refused to sign the document. Neither Joseph nor his son were regularly practicing Christians at

---

* Eds. note: The background to this new, 1863 treaty is fully explained in the earlier chapter "A Most Satisfactory Council." By 1862 there were over eighteen thousand white miners "illegally" on the Nez Perce Reservation. The Civil War was on, the Union needed the western gold, and in any case removal of eighteen thousand whites would have been impossible. The solution was a new treaty, which divided the Nez Perce into "treaty" and "non-treaty" bands, and led to the War of 1877.

this time, but the aging chief is said to have returned to the Wallowa in anger from the council and to have torn up the Bible the missionaries had given him, exclaiming that he wanted nothing more to do with the white men or their civilization.

From then on, Lawyer and the other Indians on the new reservation lived in close and unhappy relationship with the white settlements that mushroomed about them, while Joseph's people continued their old way of life, unmolested by the Americans, who made no move immediately to claim the Wallowa. But as the settlers edged toward the routes into the valley, the Indians sensed the approaching conflict, and the old chief knew that a crisis was inevitable.

In 1871 young Joseph buried his father in the beloved Wallowa and assumed leadership of the band. Almost at once the emergency arrived. Settlers from Oregon's Grande Ronde found a pass into the valley and moved in, claiming the Indians' land. The new chieftain protested to the Indian agent on the reservation, and an investigation was undertaken by the Bureau of Indian Affairs to determine whether the Treaty of 1863 affected Joseph's band, which had not agreed to it. The inquiry resulted in a decision that the Wallowa still belonged legally to the Indians, and on June 16, 1873, President Grant formally set aside half of the Wallowa "as a reservation for the roaming Nez Perce Indians" and ordered the white intruders to withdraw.

Recognition of their rights brought joy to the Indians. But it was short-lived. Some settlers, refusing to move, threatened to exterminate Joseph's people if they didn't leave the valley. In defiance of the presidential order, more whites rolled in by the wagonload. As friction increased, Oregon's governor, Leonard P. Grover, attacked Washington officials for having abandoned the government's position of 1863 and forced the administration to reverse itself. In 1875 a new and confusing presidential edict reopened the Wallowa to white homesteaders.

The Nez Perce were dismayed. Young Joseph, whom they called Heinmot Tooyalakekt, meaning "Thunder Traveling to Loftier Mountain Heights," counseled patience. He moved the Indian camps from the neighborhood of the settlers and again appealed to the federal authorities. The assistant adjutant general of the Military Department of the Columbia, Major H. Clay Wood, was assigned to make a survey of the conflicting claims, and in his report, forwarded to Washington by his commanding officer, O. O. Howard, the one-armed "Christian" general of the Civil War stated: "In my opinion, the nontreaty Nez Perces cannot in law be regarded as bound by the treaty of 1863, and insofar as it attempts to deprive them of a right to occupancy of any land, its provisions are null and void. The extinguishment of their title of occupancy contemplated by this treaty is imperfect and incomplete."

At first the government took no action, but as harassment of the Indians continued and the threat increased that they might retaliate with violence, a commission of five members was appointed to meet with the Nez Perce in November 1876, with authority to make a final settlement of the matter for "the welfare of both whites and Indians."

The commissioners, Howard, Wood, and three eastern civilians, found Joseph a disquieting figure.* Only thirty-six years old, tall and powerfully built, he seemed strangely amicable and gentle: yet he bore himself with the quiet strength and

---

*   Eds. note: The "easterners" were David H. Jerome of Michigan, A. C. Barstow of Rhode Island, and William Stickney of Washington, D.C. Along with General Howard and his adjutant Major Wood, they were appointed to the commission by Secretary of Interior Zachary Chandler.

dignity of one who stood in awe of no man. And when he spoke, it was with an eloquent logic that nettled the whites, who found themselves resenting their inability to dominate him.

Why, they asked him, did he refuse to give up the Wallowa? He answered by referring to the land as the Mother of the Indians, something that could not be sold or given away. "We love the land," he said. "It is our home."

But, they persisted, Lawyer had signed it away in 1863. Joseph had a ready reply that embarrassed them. "I believe the old treaty has never been correctly reported," he said.

> If we ever owned the land we own it still, for we never sold it. In the treaty councils the commissioners have claimed that our country has been sold to the government. Suppose a white man should come to me and say, "Joseph, I like your horses, and I want to buy them." I say to him, "No, my horses suit me, I will not sell them." Then he goes to my neighbor, and says to him, "Joseph has some good horses. I want to buy them but he refuses to sell." My neighbor answers, "Pay me the money, and I will sell you Joseph's horses." The white man returns to me and says, "Joseph, I have bought your horses and you must let me have them." If we sold our lands to the government, this is the way they were bought.

To all their arguments, Joseph replied with an uncompromising "No" and when the council ended, the exasperated commissioners had made no progress with him. But events were moving against the Indians. The situation in the Wallowa had grown perilous, and the commission was under political pressure. Two excited white men had killed an Indian youth after mistakenly accusing him of stealing their horses. Joseph had had all he could do to keep his people calm, and the settlers, fearing an uprising, were arming and calling for military protection.

To the commissioners, despite the fact that it was unjust and there was no legal basis for it, there could be only one decision, and before they left the reservation headquarters at Lapwai, they rendered it: unless, within a reasonable time, all the non-treaty Nez Perce (the other bands that had not signed in 1863, as well as Joseph's people in the Wallowa) voluntarily came onto the reservation, they should be placed there by force. General Howard, symbolizing the force that would be used, signed the report along with the three easterners. Only Major Wood's name was absent, and it is believed that he submitted a minority report, though it has never been found.

Immediately after the decision, the Indian Bureau defined the "reasonable time" and ordered the Indians to come onto the reservation by April 1, 1877. Unable to move their herds and villages across the rugged canyons in the dead of winter, the Nez Perce appealed for another conference, and, as April 1 came and went, General Howard agreed to one last meeting with all the non-treaty chiefs at Lapwai. It did no good. The die had been cast, and Howard adamantly refused to discuss the commission's decision. As the Indians pleaded in proud but pitiable terms to be allowed to remain in the lands where their fathers were buried, the General finally lost patience and threw one of the most respected old chiefs, a deeply religious war leader and tribal orator named Toohoolhoolzote, into the guardhouse. It broke the spirit of the others. To gain Toohoolhoolzote's release, they capitulated with bitterness and agreed to have their bands on the reservation in thirty days.

All of Joseph's skill as a diplomat had to be called into play when he returned to his people. He had abandoned his father's counsel and trust, and there were cries to ignore him and go to war rather than to move to the reservation. When Joseph argued that the white man's power was too great for them to resist and that it was "better to live at peace than to begin a war and lie dead," they called him a coward. But he received strong assistance from his younger brother, Ollokot, a daring and courageous buffalo hunter and warrior who had won many tribal honors and held the respect of the more belligerent younger element. Eventually the two brothers won agreement to the capitulation from the band's council. With heavy hearts, the Indians prepared to round up their stock and move.

A half year's work was crowded into less than thirty days as the people combed the mountains and forests for their animals and drove them down the steep draws to the Snake. The river was in flood, and hundreds of head of stock were swept away and drowned during the tumultuous crossing. Other portions of the herds, left behind on the bluffs and plateau, were driven away by whites who attacked the guards and harassed the withdrawing Indians. By June 2, with twelve days of grace remaining, the people reached an ancient tribal rendezvous area just outside the border of the reservation. Here they joined the other non-treaty bands and lingered for a last bit of freedom.

It was a fatal pause. On June 12 the Indians staged a parade through the camp, and one of the young men, named Wahlitits, whose father had been murdered by a white man two years before, was taunted by an old warrior for having allowed the slaying to go unavenged. The next morning, his honor as a man impugned, Wahlitits stole away with two companions.

By nightfall, in an outpouring of long-suppressed hatred, the youths had killed four white men along the Salmon River and wounded another one, all notorious for their hostility to the Nez Perce. The young men returned to the camp, announced what they had done, and raised a bigger party that continued the raids during the next two days, killing fourteen or fifteen additional whites and striking terror among the settlers and miners of central Idaho.

Both Joseph and Ollokot had been absent from the camp during the first raid, butchering cattle on the opposite side of the Salmon River. They returned in horror, finding the camp in confusion and the older people crying with fear and striking their tipis, intending to scatter to hiding places. Most of the Indians were certain that there would now be war, but Joseph still hoped to avert it. He tried to calm his people, assuring them that General Howard would not blame the whole tribe for the irresponsible actions of a few of its young hotheads, and urged them to remain where they were and await the troops, with whom he would make a settlement. The situation, however, had gone too far. The warriors rode around the camp, crying out that they would now give General Howard the fight that he had wanted, and the people would not listen to Joseph. One by one the bands departed to a hiding place farther south, in White Bird Canyon, leaving behind only Joseph, Ollokot, and a few of the Wallowa Indians.

Joseph's wife had given birth to a daughter while he had been across the Salmon, and he lingered with her now in their tipi. Several warriors were detailed to watch him and Ollokot, lest these leaders who had so often pleaded for peace would desert the non-treaties and move onto the reservation. But though he had vigorously opposed war, Joseph would not abandon his people; two days later he and Ollokot, resolved to fight now that hostilities seemed unavoidable, joined the non-treaties in the new camp at White Bird.

Back at Lapwai Howard was stunned by news of the Salmon River outbreaks. He had planned all winter against trouble in the Wallowa, and when Joseph had moved out peacefully, he had thought that all danger was past. At the news of the outbreaks, he hastily ordered two troops of the 1st Cavalry, that had been stationed at Lapwai, ninety troopers and four officers under Captain David Perry and Captain Joel Trimble, to round up the hostiles and force them onto the reservation. Eleven civilian volunteers and twelve treaty Nez Perce accompanied the troops, and after a rapid two days' march of almost eighty miles, they learned of the Nez Perce camp in White Bird Canyon and prepared to attack it early the following morning.

Alert Indian spies warned the Nez Perce of the troops' approach. The soldiers would have to descend a long draw of treeless, rolling land, flanked by ridges and hills, to reach the Nez Perce village, which lay behind two buttes at the bottom of the slope. The chiefs were uncertain whether to resist and detailed six men to take a flag of truce forward and try to arrange a peaceful meeting with the officers. At the same time, the old men, women, and children were ordered to drive in the camp's stock, while the warriors, stripping for action and mounting their ponies, sought hiding places to the right and left of the draw to await events. The total manpower of the Indian bands was about one hundred fifty, but many of the men that morning were lying in camp, drunk on whiskey seized during the raids and unable to fight. Others had no weapons or were too old, sick, or frightened to use them. Altogether, not more than forty-five or fifty Indians—armed with bows and arrows; shotguns; old, muzzle-loading, fur-trade muskets; and a few modern rifles—rode out to defend the village.

The nature of the terrain, offering a multitude of hiding places for flanking attacks, should have put the troopers on their guard. Instead they trotted confidently down the draw, ready for a thundering surprise charge. As they rounded a small hill, the Indian truce team appeared directly ahead of them. Behind the men with the white flag were other Nez Perce, sitting on their horses waiting to see what would happen. There was an instant of surprise. Then a volunteer raised his rifle and shot at the truce team. The Indians backed away, unharmed, a Nez Perce behind them fired in return, killing one of Perry's two trumpeters, and the fight was on. As Indians began shooting from all directions, Perry hastily deployed his men in a line across the draw, placing the volunteers on a high, rocky knoll to his left. The company in the center dismounted, letting men in the rear hold their horses, and the company on the right remained mounted.

The battle, fought without plan by the Indians, lasted only a few moments. On the left a small body of Nez Perce swept from behind a hill and galloped straight at the volunteers, sending them flying in panic back up the draw and exposing Perry's whole line. At the same time Ollokot, leading a large number of warriors, emerged from cover on the right and, firing as he came, charged into Perry's mounted troops, frightening the horses and disorganizing the soldiers. The men in the center, seeing Indians and confusion all around them, gave way and made a sudden rush for their horses. In a few minutes the entire command was cut into small groups fighting desperately for their lives. Nineteen men under Lieutenant Edward

Theller tried to make a stand but were driven against a rocky wall and wiped out. The rest of the troop disintegrated into a fleeing rabble and got away, leaving behind them a total of thirty-four dead, a third of Perry's command. The Indians had only two men wounded and none killed; equally important for the future, they retrieved from the battlefield sixty-three rifles and a large number of pistols.

Perry's defeat spread alarm throughout the settlements of the Northwest and angered the rest of the nation, to whom the Custer massacre was still fresh. Howard was shocked and, fearing that the uprising would spread to the treaty Nez Perce as well as other Northwest tribes, called for troop reinforcements from all over the West. Men were started inland from Portland and San Francisco, artillerymen returning from Alaska were diverted up the Columbia, and from as far away as Atlanta, Georgia, infantry units were entrained for the scene of the new Indian outbreak.

Within a week Howard himself took the field. With a force of 227 hastily assembled troops, twenty civilians, and a large group of packers and guides, he marched hurriedly out from Lapwai, intending to punish the hostiles. The Indians, reinforced by a small band that had just returned from the Montana buffalo plains under the leadership of two redoubtable warriors, Five Wounds and Rainbow, had withdrawn from White Bird and, when Howard caught up with them, had crossed with all their equipment and pony herds to the relative safety of the south bank of the Salmon. For a while the two groups faced each other from opposite sides of the wilderness river while Howard planned how to get his troops across the turbulent stream and catch the Indians before they could retreat into the rocky wilds of central Idaho. From his rear he received false information from excited settlers that a large band of hitherto peaceful Nez Perce, under the famous tribal war chief Looking Glass, was planning to leave the reservation and join the hostiles. Accepting the information as true, he divided his forces and sent Captain Stephen Whipple with two troops of cavalry to intercept Looking Glass.

It was a disastrous move. As Whipple departed, Howard received boats and started across the river, only to see the Indians move off into the wilderness ahead of him. For several days he was led on a wearying, frustrating chase through mud and driving rain, up and down steep hills and mountain slopes, and across some of the most rugged terrain in the West. Meanwhile Whipple reached Looking Glass's village on the reservation and, although he found it peaceful, launched a vicious assault upon it. The startled Indians, struck without warning, fled across a river to the shelter of some trees, where they were rallied by their outraged chief. Rumors now came to Whipple that the main band of Indians had somehow evaded General Howard, had recrossed the Salmon, and were between him and the General, threatening his own rear, Howard's supply lines, and all the settlements on the Camas Prairie which he was supposed to be protecting.

The rumors this time were true. With Howard's troops floundering in the wilds, the non-treaties had managed to cross again to the north side of the Salmon. Howard tried to follow them, could not get his men and equipment across the river, and had to go back over the entire dreadful mountain trail to the place of his original crossing, where he had left his boats. Meanwhile Whipple, forgetting Looking Glass in the face of the full Nez Perce force, sent out a reconnoitering party of ten men under Lieutenant S. M. Rains and dug in for an expected attack. The Indians wiped out Rains's party to a man, cut up another group of scouts and several hastily formed bodies of civilian volunteers, and finally, bypassing Whipple and the terrified settlers barricaded in Cottonwood and Grangeville, moved to another hiding place on the South Fork of the Clearwater River. Here they were joined by Looking Glass's infuriated band. It gave the Indians another forty fighting men but also raised the number of women and children, who would have to be carried along and protected from the soldiers, to a peak figure of four hundred fifty.

From the beginning it had been assumed by the whites that Joseph, spokesman for the non-treaties in peacetime, had also been leading them in war. Howard had credited him with skillfully contriving the ambush of Perry at White Bird. Now Joseph was being given grudging praise for the masterful way in which the Indians had evaded Howard in the wilderness and doubled back to get between him and Whipple. In addition, the Nez Perce had been conducting themselves in an unusual manner for Indians "on the warpath," refraining from scalping or mutilating bodies, treating white women and noncombatants with humanity and even friendliness, and otherwise adhering to what was considered the white man's code of war. This too was credited to Joseph, whose dignity and decency at prewar councils were recalled by Howard and the Indian agents.

The truth was that Nez Perce successes were resulting from a combination of overconfidence and mistakes on the part of the whites, the rugged terrain that made pursuit difficult, and, to a very great extent, the Indians' intense courage and patriotic determination to fight for their rights and protect their people. Indian strategy and tactics had also played a role, but at each step of the way these were agreed upon in councils of all the chiefs and were carried out on the field by the younger war leaders and their warriors. Joseph sat in the councils, but since he had never been a war chief his advice carried less weight than that of men like Five Wounds, Toohoolhoolzote, and Rainbow. On the march and in battle Joseph took charge of the old men, women, and children, an assignment of vital importance and sacred trust, while Ollokot and the experienced war chiefs led the young men on guard duty or in combat. The whites had no way of knowing this, and, as events continued to unfold, the legend that Nez Perce strategy was planned and executed by one man, Joseph, was spread far and wide by the hapless army officers opposing him and accepted without question by correspondents and the U.S. public.

On July 11, with a reinforced army of four hundred soldiers and one hundred eighty scouts, packers, and teamsters, Howard was back in pursuit of the Nez Perce. Suddenly he sighted their camp lying below him on the opposite side of the Clearwater River, opened fire with a four-inch howitzer and two Gatling guns, and prepared to launch an attack. The Nez Perce were taken by surprise, but old Toohoolhoolzote and twenty-four warriors raced across the river, scaled a bluff to the level of the soldiers, and, taking shelter behind boulders, engaged the troopers with a fierce and accurate fire that held them up until more Indians could come across and get into the fight. The firing was sharp on both sides, but as increasing numbers of mounted Nez Perce began appearing over the top of the bluff to circle the troops' rear and flanks, Howard hastened his men into a square and ordered them to dig in on the open, rocky ground with their trowel bayonets.

The fighting raged all day and continued in the same spot

the next morning, an almost unprecedented length of time for Indians to maintain battle in one location. The Nez Perce, outnumbered almost six to one and occasionally under artillery fire, kept the troopers pinned down and on the defensive with marksmanship that Howard's adjutant, Major C. E. S. Wood, described as "terribly accurate and very fatal." Several times small groups of Indians darted forward to engage the soldiers in hand-to-hand fights, and once they almost captured Howard's supply train. In addition, the Nez Perce held the only spring in the area and controlled access to the river; under the blazing July sun the soldiers suffered unmercifully from thirst.

By noon of the second day the chiefs had decided that there had been enough fighting without decision. Many of the warriors had become restless and tired and wanted to leave. Holding the line long enough for Joseph to get the families packed and safely away with the herds, the Indians, one by one, ceased fighting and withdrew down the bluff. Howard's troops followed the last of them across the river and through the abandoned camp. It was an anticlimactic and hollow finish to a battle that had cost the army thirteen killed and twenty-seven wounded, two of them fatally. Howard could count four Indians killed and six wounded, but the hostiles had escaped from him again.

The Nez Perce crossed the Clearwater north of the troops and paused at an old meeting ground on the Weippe Prairie to decide what to do next. They had had enough of Howard and thought that if they left Idaho and went somewhere else, the General would be satisfied and would leave them alone. Looking Glass, who many times had hunted buffalo and fought with the Crows in Montana, urged that they cross the mountains and join that tribe. They could then hunt on the plains in peace,

he told them, and the war would be over. It was a harsh proposal, for it meant the final abandonment of their homeland,
but with the people's safety weighing heavily on them Joseph
and the other chiefs reluctantly agreed to the exodus. On July
16, having named Looking Glass as supreme chief for the trek
to the Crows, the bands set off on the arduous Lolo Trail across
the wild and precipitous heights of the Bitterroot Mountains.

Smarting under increasing criticism from Washington, as
well as from the press and public, Howard once more took
after the Indians, doggedly following their trail up through
the thick and tangled forest growth of mountain slopes to the
high, ridge-top route that led from Idaho to Montana. It was a
painful and grueling trip for both pursuers and pursued. The
Indian families, stumbling along over steep and rocky trails,
guarded by the warriors and driving some two thousand
horses with them, managed to keep well ahead of the troops,
who, with their guns and camp equipment, found the going
even rougher. In the meantime word of the Indian flight had
been telegraphed ahead to Montana, and from Missoula Captain Charles C. Rawn, with thirty-five men of the 7th Infantry
and two hundred citizen volunteers from the Bitterroot Valley,
hastened to the eastern end of the Lolo Trail and threw up a
log fort from which to block the hostiles' passage until Howard could catch up to them from the rear.

On July 25, after nine days in the mountains, the Nez Perce
appeared above Rawn's fort, and Joseph, Looking Glass, and
an elderly chief named White Bird came down for a parley.
Explaining that they were on their way to the Crows, the Indians promised to move peacefully through the Bitterroot Valley,
respecting the settlements and paying for any supplies they
needed. It satisfied the volunteers, who, having no stomach for

an Indian fight, deserted Rawn and stole back to their homes. As a federal officer, Rawn was obliged to continue his posture of resistance, but fortunately for his depleted garrison the Indians shrewdly bypassed his fort and, making a noisy feint in front of him, quietly filed around him on another mountain trail that led them into the Bitterroot Valley. The embarrassed Captain withdrew to Missoula, and his log bastion was promptly dubbed Fort Fizzle by the many wags who were beginning to root for Joseph and the apparently unconquerable Nez Perce.

Moving through the heavily settled valley, the Indians scrupulously maintained their promise to commit no hostile act. At Stevensville they paused to buy coffee, flour, sugar, and tobacco and paid the merchants with gold dust and currency. The friendly treatment they received from the Montana citizens made the Indians believe that, now that they were out of Idaho, the war was over and they were safe. They moved leisurely south to the Big Hole Valley and, on an open meadow beside the willow-lined Big Hole River, pitched camp to rest.

Howard was still far back in the Bitterroots, temporarily out of the picture. But, unknown to the Nez Perce, a new force of one hundred sixty-three army regulars and thirty-five volunteers under Colonel John Gibbon was hurrying across country from Fort Shaw, on the Sun River, by forced marches to attack them. On the night of August 8 Gibbon gained a wooded hill above the unsuspecting Nez Perce camp and, the next morning at dawn, launched a surprise attack. Firing volleys into the sleeping village, the soldiers charged down the hill in a long line, forded the shallow river, and swept into the camp, shooting and clubbing men, women, and children. Some of the Nez Perce were able to seize their weapons and ammunition belts and escape to the shelter of the willows. There they were rallied by the aged White Bird, who cried at them, "Why are we retreating? Since the world was made, brave men have fought for their women and children! Fight! Shoot them down! We can shoot as well as any of these soldiers!"

Gibbon's commanding officer on the left had been killed during the opening charge and, without a leader, that part of the line faltered as Indians stood their ground and fought back desperately from the tipis. The troopers were forced toward the right, allowing the Nez Perce in that sector to erect a firing line against them. This brought confusion to the main part of the camp, where Gibbon's men, in complete control, were unsuccessfully trying to set the leather tipis afire. With his milling troops being pushed together and soldiers being struck both by the Indians on the left and by White Bird's snipers on the right, Gibbon, who had been wounded in the leg, ordered a withdrawal across the river to the protection of the wooded knoll from which the attack had been launched. To his chagrin the Nez Perce swarmed after him, and in a few moments he found himself on the defensive, fighting fiercely, his position encircled by well-concealed Indian sharpshooters.

As the soldiers pulled out of the village, the old men, women, and children, directed by Joseph, hurried back in, picked up their dead and wounded, struck the tipis, and, driving their pack strings and pony herds ahead of them, moved off toward the south. The warriors remained behind, continuing the siege on the hill throughout the day and into the night, pinning down Gibbon's men in shallow holes and behind fallen trees, and picking off anyone who showed himself. Cut off and without prospect of relief, the soldiers' position rapidly became desperate. The men ran out of water, and cries from the unattended wounded filled the air. Gibbon's howitzer, ordered to come up after the initial attack, arrived on the scene and was immediately captured by a group of wild-charging Nez Perce, who rolled it over a steep bluff. Another body of Indians seized a packload of two thousand rounds of Gibbon's ammunition. By eleven that night, with their camp safely away, the warriors mercifully decided to break off the engagement and spare the surviving troopers. Backing off slowly to guard against pursuit, they took the trail after Joseph.

Gibbon's men, cut up and dazed, were in no condition to follow. Thirty-three soldiers were dead and thirty-eight wounded. Fourteen of the seventeen officers were casualties. Howard's men, coming up hurriedly the next day, found the troops still in a state of shock, burying the dead and trying to care for the groaning wounded.

The Indians' losses at the Big Hole had also been high. Between sixty and ninety Nez Perce had lost their lives, including Rainbow, Five Wounds, and some of the tribe's most able warriors. Many of the casualties had been women and children, slain during the initial attack on the tipis. Joseph's wife had been among the seriously wounded, and Joseph had been seen fighting his way through the early part of the battle sheltering his new baby in his arms.

The Nez Perce now quickened their retreat across southwestern Montana. Gone were illusions that the whites would let them be. In their desperation to escape, only one haven seemed left to them. Like Sitting Bull, they would go to Canada and seek refuge among the tribes in the country of Queen Victoria. Canada was hundreds of miles away, but they would get there somehow. Looking Glass, blamed for the false sense of security that had led to so many deaths at the Big Hole, was relieved of command, and a tough fighter named Lean Elk, whom the whites had known as Poker Joe, was elevated to supreme chief. The column headed eastward toward Targhee Pass, which would lead the refugees over the Continental Divide to the Yellowstone, where they could turn north to Canada. West of the pass, rear-guard scouts brought word that Howard was catching up and pressing close behind them again. In a bold night attack, twenty-eight warriors led by Ollokot and three other chiefs stole back to Howard's camp and ran off the General's entire pack string. Howard came to a dead halt, forced to scour the settlements for more animals, and the Indians hurried on, unhampered, across the Divide and into the area which five years before had become Yellowstone National Park.

A sight-seeing party, of which General William Tecumseh Sherman was a member, had just left the area, but the Nez Perce swooped up two other groups of campers and took them along. The chiefs insisted on humane treatment for the frightened tourists, who included a number of women. In time, as the Indians continued across the park, past geysers and bubbling mudpots, the sightseers were allowed to escape. On the eastern side of the park, the Indians found themselves harassed by new bodies of troops, coming at them from posts on the Montana plains. One force of the 7th Cavalry under Colonel Samuel Sturgis tried to set a trap for the Indians in the upper Yellowstone Valley, but the Nez Perce fought their way skillfully through a mountain wilderness where the whites thought passage would be impossible and emerged on the Clark's Fork River in Sturgis's rear. Realizing he had been tricked, Sturgis gave chase with three hundred men, following the Indians across the Yellowstone River and down its northern bank past present-day Billings, Montana.

On and on the Indians hurried. Near Canyon Creek they

passed a stage station and captured a stagecoach. Letting its
occupants escape into some nearby willows, the warriors had
a day of great fun, driving the incongruous-looking coach along
in the rear of the column. The sport ended abruptly. At Canyon Creek the bands turned north, and here, on September 13,
Sturgis's hard-riding cavalry overtook them. There was a furious fight. A rear guard of Indians, hiding behind rocks and in
gullies, held off the troopers while the Nez Perce women and
children drove the pack strings and herds to the protection of a
narrow canyon that cut north through rimrock country. Sturgis
ordered his men to dismount, an error that allowed the Indians
to escape into the canyon. Later the cavalry tried to follow the
Nez Perce in a running fight up the canyon, but the Indians succeeded in making pursuit difficult by blocking the canyon floor
behind them with boulders and brush. At darkness, weary and
running out of ammunition and rations, Sturgis gave up the
chase. Three of his men had been killed and eleven wounded.
The Indians counted three wounded, but the long pursuit was
beginning to tell heavily on them. They too were becoming
tired and dispirited, and they were losing horses. Many of the
animals were going lame from the difficult trek and had to be
abandoned. Others were being lost in the hurry to keep moving.

Beyond Canyon Creek their old allies, the Crows, now
in service as scouts for the army, began to attack them. The
Nez Perce fought them off in running engagements and continued across the Musselshell to the Missouri River, helping
themselves to army stores at a military depot on Cow Island
while a frightened sergeant and twelve men looked on help-
lessly from behind an earthwork. Just across the Missouri, the
Indians fought off a halfhearted attack by a small force from
Fort Benton and hastened on across badlands and open, roll-

ing plains to the Bear Paw Mountains. About thirty miles short of the Canadian line, exhausted by the long flight, they paused to rest, confident that they had outdistanced all pursuers.

Once more they were wrong, outflanked again by the telegraph, and this time the pause would end in their last stand. From Fort Keogh in the east, Colonel Nelson A. Miles, with nearly six hundred men that included the 2nd and 7th Cavalry, the mounted 5th Infantry, and a body of Cheyenne warriors, was hastening obliquely across Montana, hoping to intercept the hostiles before they crossed the border. On the cold, blustery morning of September 30, Miles's Cheyenne scouts sighted the Nez Perce tipis in a deep hollow on the plains close to Snake Creek on the northern edge of the Bear Paw Mountains. Miles ordered an immediate attack, and the Cheyennes and 7th Cavalry, supported by the 5th Infantry, charged across the open ground toward the village.

The assault caught the Nez Perce in three groups. Some, including women and children, were on the distant side of the camp and were able to mount and flee to the north, where they scattered on the broken plains, to die from hunger and exposure or to eventually reach Canada in small, pitiful groups. Others, including Joseph, were trapped with the horses at some distance from the camp. A third group, at the village, found protection behind a low-lying ridge. These warriors, hidden behind rocks, opened a deadly fire on the attackers, inflicting heavy casualties and sending the troopers reeling back short of the camp. Two officers and twenty-two soldiers were killed in the assault and four officers and thirty-eight enlisted men wounded.

The 2nd Cavalry, meanwhile, had been sent around the camp to capture the Nez Perce pony herd and to try to cut off escape. This unit had better luck. The troopers crashed into the herd, stampeding the horses and splitting the Indians into small groups that fought back hand-to-hand or sought cover in gullies or behind rocks. A few of the Indians got away on ponies and disappeared to the north. Others, among them Joseph, crawled or fought their way back to the main body of Nez Perce, reaching the camp under cover of darkness. The troopers drove off at least a third of the horses, however, and most of the Nez Perce remaining war leaders, including the brave Ollokot and Toohoolhoolzote, were killed in the fighting.

The heavy casualties Miles had sustained deterred him from ordering another charge, and he decided to lay siege to the village. He made one attempt to cut off the Indians from their water supply by establishing a line between the camp and the river, but the troops detailed to the task were driven back by fierce Indian resistance. As the siege settled down, both sides dug in, continuing a desultory sharpshooting fire between the lines. The weather turned bitterly cold, and the next morning five inches of snow covered the unretrieved bodies of the dead. The Indians, wounded, hungry, and cold, suffered intensely. Using hooks, knives, and pans, the people tried to dig crude shelters in the sides of the hollows. One dugout was caved in by a hit from Miles's howitzer that had been tilted back for use as a mortar, and a woman and child were buried alive.

As the siege continued, Miles grew concerned. There were rumors that Sitting Bull, with a band of Sioux, was coming to the Nez Perce's rescue from Canada. And, even if they didn't show up, Howard was getting closer, and Miles wanted the glory of Joseph's end for himself. Hoping to hurry the surrender, he hoisted a white flag over his trenches and, after negotiations with a Nez Perce who could speak English, lured Joseph across the lines. The two men parleyed amicably for a few moments, but when Joseph began to detail terms for an honorable surrender, Miles had him seized and made prisoner. The same day, however, the Nez Perce captured one of Miles's officers. The next morning an exchange was agreed to, and Joseph was returned to his camp.

The siege went on amid cold and snow flurries, and on October 4 Howard reached the battlefield with a small advance party that included two treaty Nez Perce. The appearance of their old enemy, heralding the arrival of reinforcements for Miles, took the final heart out of the suffering Nez Perce. The next morning the two treaty Nez Perce crossed the lines and told the chiefs that if they surrendered, they would be honorably treated and sent back to Lapwai. The chiefs held a final council. White Bird and Looking Glass still opposed surrender. Joseph pointed to the starving women and children in the shelter pits and to the babies that were crying around them. "For myself I do not care," he said. "It is for them I am going to surrender."

As the council broke up, Looking Glass was suddenly struck in the forehead by a stray bullet and killed. As the surviving warriors gathered around the slain chief, Joseph mounted a horse and, followed by several men on foot, rode slowly up the hill from the camp and across to the army lines where Howard and Miles awaited him. As he reached the officers, he dismounted and handed Miles his rifle. Then, stepping back, he adjusted his blanket to leave his right arm free and, addressing Miles, began one of the most touching and beautiful speeches of surrender ever made:

Tell General Howard I know his heart. What he told me before I have in my heart. I am tired of fighting. Our chiefs are killed. Looking Glass is dead. Toohoolhoolzote is dead. The old men are all dead. It is the young men who say yes or no. He who led the young men is dead. It is cold and we have no blankets. The little children are freezing to death. My people, some of them, have run away to the hills, and have no blankets, no food; no one knows where they are— perhaps freezing to death. I want to have time to look for my children and see how many I can find. Maybe I shall find them among the dead. Hear me, my chiefs. I am tired; my heart is sick and sad. From where the sun now stands, I will fight no more forever.

The fact that neither Joseph nor any other individual chief had been responsible for the outstanding strategy and mas- terful successes of the campaign is irrelevant. The surrender speech, taken down by Howard's adjutant and published soon afterward, confirmed Joseph in the public's mind as the sym- bol of the Nez Perce's heroic, fighting retreat. Although the government failed to honor Miles's promise to send the Indi ans back to Lapwai, sympathy was aroused throughout the nation for Joseph's people. At first the Indians were shipped by flatboats and boxcars to unfamiliar, hot country in the Indian Territory, where many of them sickened and died. But friendly whites and sympathetic societies in the East continued to work for them, and public sentiment finally forced approval of their return to the Northwest. In 1885 Joseph and most of his band were sent to the Colville Reservation in Washington. Joseph made many attempts to be allowed to resettle in the Wallowa but each time was rebuffed. In 1904 he died, brokenhearted, an exile from the beautiful valley he still considered home.

Fishing at Celilo Falls on the Columbia River prior to construction of The Dalles Dam in 1957. (Negative #74928 courtesy of the Oregon Historical Society.)

II

INDIANS AND
THE NATURAL WORLD

Native Endurance—
A Connection to Place

◇◇

A Commentary by Jaime A. Pinkham

Nowhere has any community sacrificed so much in the face of progress and development than tribal communities in the United States. Land and water and the abundant natural resources they harbored were wrestled away. However, in a turnabout, no community has achieved more in the face of adversity to restore and protect the environment than the same tribal communities.

The following writings by Alvin Josephy appeared at an extraordinary pivot point. They lead into the turnabout when tribes, weary of exploitation, began using the modern era of self-determination to protect their rights and those of the environment.

Josephy is no stranger to my native nation, the Nez Perce. His relationship began as an interest in the 1877 Nez Perce War and grew into friendship and a common advocacy. In the 1960s he bought a ranch among our ancestral homelands in northeast Oregon—lured perhaps by the very reason our ancestors lived among those mountains and river valleys for many generations.

Most tribal opening chapters start at "time immemorial." In fact, scholars of anthropology used carbon dating to estimate tribal existence in North America at well over ten thousand years. Either way, America's diverse environment fashioned a mixture of cultures. Each tribe across the landscape maintained an autonomy that could be heard in the distinct languages, observed by the independent movements across exclusive homelands and distinguished by individual styles of customs and governance.

Then and today the natural world is a mainstay of tribal existence and identity: from the Keepers of the Forests in the northern hardwoods of Wisconsin, to the coastal rain forests of Washington where the canoe builders still practice their craft; from the snowcapped Sierra Blanca, birthplace of the Mescalero Apache in New Mexico, to the spruce forests that wrap life-sustaining resources around the village of Galena in the Alaskan Yukon.

It is often said that the American Indian was the first natural resource manager, long before Europeans arrived. There is truth to this statement but I often ask, Who really managed whom? Over those ten thousand years, our ancestors maintained a special relationship with the land, acknowledging that our livelihood depended on bounty provided by the seas, rivers, prairies, tundra, and forests. Land offered up foods to nourish us and medicines to heal us. It provided materials and places that were essential to our education, spiritual connectivity, and recreation.

Our interactions and observations shaped our relationship with the land. We responded to the natural cycles turning upon the land and waters. We did not make the salmon run or the berries and medicines grow. When the salmon returned to the healing waters of their birth, we followed. When the roots and berries returned to the high country, so did we. In other words, nature managed us.

We were vulnerable in our dependency on the natural world. By appearance the environment might be viewed as harsh, with an unpredictable disposition, but it never had a cruel intention. Attempts to defeat nature could place our survival at risk because a healthy, sustainable environment is intimately tied to a healthy, functioning tribal community.

I imagine the early explorers who visited our native homelands took back tales of how the land was full, and empty. Filled with abundant, seemingly limitless resources, yet empty in appearance, with plenty of unused room ready for expansion. It prompted a rush of indulgence that outstripped nature's capacity to deliver. Fish and wildlife were decimated without regard for future generations. Logging, mining, and agriculture tore into the earth, poisoning waters and destroying habitats. Tribes were displaced from their homes and clustered on reservations that shrank over time.

Ironically, the explorers eventually proved right. Lack of restraint left the lands full, but with overflowing toxins, industrialization, and urbanization. And it was becoming empty as resources diminished, some withering toward extinction. Tribes themselves remained targets as non-natives attempted to fleece tribal lands and restrict tribal resource consumption, including uses protected by treaties with the United States.

Josephy outlines the stages of conflict for four tribes. These tribes originally welcomed the newcomers, provided for their security, shared nature's wealth, and collaborated for peaceful coexistence. Unfortunately, the early relations faded quickly. A long winter settled over the tribes, but the connection with their environment never diminished.

In time, this very connection with the environment helped fuel the turnabout that Josephy guides us to. Tribal land-based societies became exhausted by decades of challenges against inherent rights and troubled by the mistreatment of the environment. Tribes responded by reinvigorating their foundations with sovereign powers braced by legal and political capital. They began building a stronger stewardship role, assembling competent institutions with a combined science, technology, and business wisdom that now rivals federal and state counterparts. Here are the four stories Josephy tells.

Cornplanter: Can You Swim?

Nature has been exploited to build bigger cities to support bigger economies. The energy to power both has been siphoned from rivers through dams. Across the country tribal well-being was destabilized as the rivers were dramatically altered and tribes displaced as their homelands were submerged. Evidence of such destabilization is easily uncovered within the Missouri and Columbia River basins and along the Allegheny River as it flows from New York into Pennsylvania.

Along the Allegheny, Cornplanter, a Seneca leader, revered by Americans for his support, was provided a land grant in the 1790s. After his death in 1836, a monument was erected in the cemetery on his land to honor him. Nonetheless, in 1965, the land was submerged by the backwaters of Kinzua

Dam. Kinzua was built through a series of evasive and shady tactics by the federal government. The Senecas' compensation for this loss was not only woefully inadequate but troublesome in acquiring.

Once again, in 2010 the Seneca Nation initiated the first steps in the regulatory process to acquire the license to take over operations of Kinzua Dam's hydroelectric generating facilities. The Nation formed the Kinzua Dam Relicensing Commission in an effort to obtain the license through the Federal Energy Regulatory Commission when the current fifty-year license expires in 2015. If successful, not only can the Senecas diversify their economy but they will also actively begin to offset some of the injustices that occurred when they lost control of their ancestral waters and land along the Allegheny.

Pyramid Lake

Pyramid Lake is a centerpiece for the Pyramid Lake Paiute tribe. When the tribe welcomed non-Indians to their homelands, they introduced them to the lake's bounty: massive Lahontan cutthroat trout. Later, as cities and farms gained a foothold in the region, the tribe found the odds building against them. As a terminal lake, the cumulative impact from all upstream actions, including diversions, sediments, and pollutants, were all negative. The tribe was in conflict with factions representing industries, agriculture, and governments, including the federal government charged with acting on their best behalf.

Yet another turnabout occurred. The tribe exerted its sovereign, legal, and political will to secure much-needed water for Pyramid Lake. Today they are signatory to an operating agreement with federal, state, and local governments. Their task is to balance the demands for fish and wildlife, recreation, and municipal, industrial, and agricultural uses. In 1979 an amazing discovery was made when a remnant population of the Pyramid Lake Lahontan cutthroat trout was located in a tributary. These fish provided the brood stock to replenish the fishery. Key to this success was the tribe's scientific and technological contribution, which has rebuilt harvestable populations enjoyed by all citizens. In addition, they were among the first tribes in the nation to establish water-quality standards under the authority of the Clean Water Act.

Stories become lessons for sharing. History cannot be undone—its scars will always show. But the scars upon the land and the people can sometimes heal. They begin to heal through the courage of the faithful who never relinquished a relationship to the natural world and respect for the vital role it plays in our survival.

Some of the best stories are those tied to the land. The land has the longest memory, holding places that remind us of our victories and sacrifices. It is the birthplace of our legends that are told and continually retold. The land is life. And, just as it holds the remains of our ancestors, our bodies, too, will someday return to the care of the earth, our Mother.

As we labor to save the salmon, save cutthroat trout, save the rivers and our land, we also labor to save ourselves. It is labor because the road ahead will not be easy. We will be addressing expanding populations with increased demands for resources. We will need to prepare a response to changing climate patterns and their impact on the natural cycles.

And we must be ready to negotiate our way through the uncertainty of political gridlock to make timely decisions.

The work will require humility. Nature has been at this game longer, with expertise that is leaps and bounds ahead of us. It is wiser beyond our imagination. We can never fully mimic nature, we cannot repeat her handiwork, we can never take her place; but if we listen and learn we can do a better job of following her lead.

Following in our ancestors' footsteps, the next steps are ours to take. We cannot hide from our history. How we measure up will be recorded by those writers following in the footsteps of people like Alvin Josephy.

Northwest Salmon Wars

Once an icon of abundance, freedom, and wildness, today the salmon are symbolic of conflicts that underscore the weakening balance between civilization and nature. This is evident in the Pacific Northwest. State laws and legal trickery tried to subvert tribal fish harvests. As oppression grew, the Northwest salmon wars became so unsettling that Indians and their allies gathered on the rivers to help spotlight the injustice.

In a turnabout, treaty law began to prevail, including the landmark *U.S. v. Washington* decision. However, to extend their momentum tribes banded together as managers for one of the largest fish restoration efforts in this country. Litigation will always be an option, but the tribes are forging relations along all segments of the rivers traversing backcountry public lands to private lands and through some of the largest municipal and industrial areas in the Northwest. Even in Washington, D.C., the tribes are noted for their political will combined with sophisticated scientific and management skills.

The Hopi Way

Under a 1930s policy the federal government attempted to get tribes to adopt contemporary government practices. Unfortunately, within some tribes this caused a division between traditional forms of governance and the foreign system advocated by the federal government. Such a division arose among the Hopi tribe. As a result, not all decisions of the new governing council went over well in the different villages. Animosity grew over how business and decisions were being conducted. One such deal involved a coal lease to strip-mine Hopi land on Black Mesa and to pump the Hopi aquifer to create a slurry that would carry the coal in more than two hundred seventy miles of pipeline into Nevada.

In a turnabout, the Hopi used their sovereign authority eventually to halt withdrawal of the subsurface water and revoke the mining permit. Today, they are evaluating their own alternatives, grappling with decisions over creating jobs, generating revenues, and protecting their lands. Among the questions: What other ways can coal be shipped? Are there opportunities for renewable energy production? Does coal mining have a place in the future of the Hopi? The big difference today is that now these are their own deliberations: the Hopi call the shots from here forward.

8

Cornplanter, Can You Swim?
The Native Americans' Fight to Hold
On to Their Land Base

◇◇

In the long history of U.S. Army battles against Indians, the following pages describe one that the army—in this case its Corps of engineers—won without firing a shot. In the process it abrogated the government's oldest active treaty, signed with the Seneca Nation in 1794.

This chapter is from Now That the Buffalo's Gone, *Josephy's 1982 book about more recent Indian history. It details the stubborn and protracted legal and political struggle carried on by the Senecas against the Army Corps of Engineers to build a dam on its lands along the Allegheny River in Pennsylvania. Despite the terms of the 1794 treaty, and even an earlier letter from President Washington promising permanent protection of Seneca land, the battle was lost.*

The Kinzua Dam was completed in 1965. Pennsylvania celebrated, but the Cornplanter monument, along with graves of fellow tribesmen, was moved many miles from its original site, which was now underwater. Thus was repaid Cornplanter, the famous Seneca war chief, who had come to the aid of the American Revolution when it was desperately needed.

In a cemetery high on a promontory overlooking the broad waters of the Allegheny Reservoir in northwestern Pennsylvania stands a stone monument to a once powerful and celebrated Seneca Indian war chief, The Cornplanter, who fought with the British against the Americans during the Revolution, and then became a loyal friend of the United States and a steadfast protector of American families settling in the wilderness of the upper Ohio River Basin. The monument has not been at its present site long. In 1964, amid controversy, anger, and the protests of many Seneca Indians, the United States Army Corps of Engineers moved the memorial shaft, together with what was left of the earthly remains of The Cornplanter and more than three hundred of his followers and descendants, from an Indian cemetery ("our Arlington," pleaded a Seneca woman) that was about to be inundated by rising waters behind the engineers' new Kinzua Dam on the Allegheny River.

In the Seneca language, which many of the Indians still speak, *kinzua* means "fish on spear" and refers to a site on the river 198 river miles above Pittsburgh, just south of the New York state line, where the dam was built. Finished in 1965 at a cost of almost $120 million, it is the largest concrete and earthfill dam in the eastern United States, almost 1,900 feet long and 179 feet high. It is designed to help control floods, as well as to regulate the flow of water for navigation and for the dilution of polluting waste matter poured into the river by mills above Pittsburgh. Among the dam's important by-products are hydroelectric power, now being exploited by private developers, and the provision of new recreational facilities for the region. Behind the dam is the new Allegheny Reservoir, whose size changes constantly depending on rainfall and the season of the year. At its maximum, in time of severe flood condi-

tions, the lake would extend thirty-five miles upriver to Salamanca, New York, and would have a water surface of more
than twenty-one thousand acres. But under ordinary conditions it extends in summer twenty-seven miles, more or less,
covers some twelve thousand acres, and has a shoreline of
ninety-one miles. In winter it is a considerably smaller pool,
covering a minimum of about sixty-six hundred acres and
exposing large areas of mud flats. To the summer vacationer,
tourist, and lover of water sports, the reservoir has provided
a large new recreation center in the forested mountain country of western New York and Pennsylvania and has already
borne out the army engineers' promise that the dam and its
lake would result in the development of a relatively untouched
part of the Northeast in the time-honored tradition of American progress.

. But there was a cost beyond the cost of the dam, and the
raising of a moral question that pricked the conscience of the
nation on what has long been an extremely sore point. In creating the Allegheny Reservoir behind Kinzua Dam, the army
engineers gutted the Seneca Indians' reservation, drowning
approximately ten thousand acres of the Indians' only habitable land, which ran along the Allegheny River, and deliberately breaking an Indian treaty in order to do so. In this
instance the violated obligation was the federal government's
oldest active treaty, made in 1794 with Cornplanter's Senecas
and five other Indian nations at a time when the new American republic urgently needed their friendship on the turbulent
northwest frontier, and resting ever since then on solemn guarantees which were given by President George Washington and
which were supposed to endure through the life of the United
States itself.

To many non-Indians who were aware of the engineers' treaty-breaking action, it was, as Florida Congressman James Haley of the House Interior and Insular Affairs Committee said on May 18, 1967, "a horrible tragedy, a horribly tragic thing," underscored especially by the fact that the United States was, at the same time, insisting that the rest of the world honor and respect the sacredness of treaties. To the Senecas and to many other American Indians it was, moreover, another painful reminder that the history of white men's injustices to them had not ended. Indian wars are no more, for the tribes' power to resist with arms has vanished. But their defensive actions still go on, quietly now and with little or no publicity, in courts of law, and the Indians, more often than not, still continue to lose what they are defending. In their sadness they increasingly ask the white man: Why feel guilty and sorry about what happened in the nineteenth century? Pay closer attention to what you are still doing to us.

To the Senecas, the new body of water behind Kinzua Dam is known today as Lake Perfidy. And many a bitter Seneca tells his children and grandchildren that no one knows for sure whose bones lie beneath the transplanted monument above the lake: the way the moving took place, the remains could be those of another Indian from the old cemetery. The great Cornplanter, perhaps, now rests beneath the waters of the reservoir.

From the very beginning, when army lawyers first looked into the problem of acquiring land for the dam and the reservoir, the Corps of Engineers had little concern for the uniqueness of the treaty-secured Seneca position. The Corps is a highly efficient and capable expression of the modern technological age, able to build great dams, move mountains, control roaring rivers, and alter any manner of landscape. But to many persons the Corps exemplifies, at the same time, the big, self-propelled, faceless juggernauts of the world that grind ahead, seemingly unmoved by the outcries of the people whose lives they affect. As an autocratically tinged bureaucracy and one of the most irresistible lobbies in the nation (relying on the "pork barrel" support of political groups everywhere who sooner or later want public works for their own areas), it befriends the American people in the mass and in the abstract, and makes war on the same people when, as individuals or in small numbers, they get in the way. In 1966 a special study group composed of two colonels and a civilian official of the Corps reported that "too often the [engineers'] planning effort is confined to refining the concept and proving the justification for one or a few promising projects. Too few reports contain evidence that adequate consideration was given to alternatives and to all factors pertinent to producing an optimum solution." In the case of the building of Kinzua Dam, an "optimum solution" required that the engineers possess enough of an understanding of, and a concern for, the Senecas' 1794 treaty to deter them from breaking it. The Senecas whom the engineers confronted in the 1950s were descendants of the westernmost of the five confederated Iroquois tribes who for numerous centuries had occupied present-day upper New York State from Lake Champlain to the Genesee River. From east to west they were, in order, the Mohawks, Oneidas, Onondagas, Cayugas, and Senecas. Joined about 1712 by the Tuscaroras, Iroquoian-speaking relatives who had been driven out of North Carolina by the white man, the Iroquois Confederacy became known as the League of the Six Nations. In the mid-1600s, several bands of Senecas had moved southwestward from the Genesee River to the upper Allegheny Valley, and during the next hundred years they established domination over a large area of western New York and Pennsylvania and eastern Ohio, swelling their own numbers and power by absorbing many Indian captives and refugee groups. Both French and English traders were welcomed in the region, but no white settlement was permitted.

Toward the mid-1700s, trouble came for the western Senecas when English and French military groups began to fight for authority over the upper Ohio Valley. The Senecas were caught between the two sides, but when the struggle erupted into the full-fledged French and Indian War, many of the Senecas sided with the French. With the defeat of the latter in 1763, the still powerful Senecas retired up the Allegheny River to their towns along the New York–Pennsylvania border.

With the coming of the American Revolution, pressure was again exerted on the individual tribes, this time by both the British and the colonists. The Oneidas and some of the Tuscaroras sided with the Americans, many of the Cayugas and Senecas joined Joseph Brant and his Mohawks as allies of the British, and other groups remained neutral.

Under The Cornplanter, whom they elected as their war leader and whom the British commissioned as a captain, the western Senecas from the Genesee and Allegheny valleys conducted raids against American posts and settlements. Cornplanter, then about forty years old, was already one of the strongest and best known of the Iroquois war chiefs. Born in a Seneca town on the Genesee near present-day Avon, New York, sometime between 1732 and 1740, he was the half-breed son of a prominent Dutch trader from Albany named John Abeel and a Seneca woman. By the time of the Revolution he was the principal war chief and a leading spokesman of the western Senecas.

The Revolution was disastrous for the Iroquois. In retaliation for their raids and for the help the Indians had given the British, American punitive expeditions invaded the countries of the Senecas and other tribes in 1779, burning towns, destroying crops, and driving the people from their homelands. Many of the pro-British Senecas joined Brant at Fort Niagara. In 1780, following the departure of the Americans, some of the Indians drifted back to their homes. Others formed a large permanent settlement at Buffalo Creek. Cornplanter and the Genesee River Senecas found their country in ruins and moved to the Allegheny River settlements along the New York–Pennsylvania border. There Cornplanter took over the civil leadership of his people from an elderly uncle, Kiasutha.

Under the protection of the British along the Niagara, where English troops and traders remained on American soil until after Jay's Treaty of 1794, the displaced eastern Senecas at Buffalo Creek kept up a bitter hostility to the Americans. And along the Allegheny, Cornplanter and the western Senecas were a threat closer to the Pennsylvania and New York settlements. The danger was acute, for at any time one or all of the disaffected Iroquois groups, under the influence of the British, could join the Ohio country Indians in an all-out, catastrophic war on the settlers.

At this point, Cornplanter was induced to throw in his lot with the Americans, and the Seneca chief's influence was decisive with all the Iroquois. By 1794, when General Anthony Wayne crushed the Ohio tribes with finality at the Battle of Fallen Timbers, Cornplanter had not only immobilized the

Senecas and other Iroquois so that they remained out of the conflict, but had overseen the ceding and sale of large areas of Seneca land in western Pennsylvania and New York to the Americans. His actions had been angrily opposed by many Iroquois chiefs, including Red Jacket, a fiery Seneca orator at Buffalo Creek, but Cornplanter had ignored them, saying, "If we do not sell the land, the whites will take it anyway."

The grateful Americans were not unaware of Cornplanter's friendship and the many good services he had rendered them, often at the risk of his life. In December 1790, he had met President Washington in Philadelphia and had told him that his people were beginning to fear the loss of their own lands to white settlers. On December 29, Washington responded to him in a letter that was to have little meaning to the Army Corps of Engineers when the Senecas presented it to them more than a century and a half later. Washington wrote:

> Your great object seems to be the security of your remaining lands, and I have therefore upon this point, meant to be sufficiently strong and clear. That in future you cannot be defrauded of your lands. That you possess the right to sell, and the right of refusing to sell your lands. That therefore the sale of your lands in the future, will depend entirely upon yourselves.

In 1791 the state of Pennsylvania, in acknowledgment of Cornplanter's services to American settlers, granted him and his heirs "in perpetuity" three tracts of land, each about a mile square, on the upper Allegheny River in Pennsylvania. One of these, near present-day West Hickory, the chief sold in 1795 to a white friend. Another, at what is now Oil City, he sold to two white men in 1818, but claimed he was paid in worthless money and notes. The third tract, an area known since before the Revolution as the Burnthouse, totaled approximately 908 acres and was on the western bank of the Allegheny about three miles south of the New York state line. It included Cornplanter's own town of Jononhsadegen and two islands in the river. Cornplanter made it his headquarters, settling down there with his followers, who in time built thirty houses for about four hundred people on the grant.

In 1794, discontent arose among many of the Iroquois over increased pressure from the settlers. The Battle of Fallen Timbers had not yet been fought, and the federal government, fearing again that the Iroquois might join the Ohio tribes who in 1790 and 1791 had inflicted serious defeats on American armies, sent Timothy Pickering of Massachusetts as commissioner to meet with the chiefs of the Six Nations at Canandaigua, New York, and establish a lasting peace with them. Pickering's mission was successful: on November 11, 1794, he signed a treaty with fifty-nine *sachems* and war chiefs, including Cornplanter, Fish Carrier, Red Jacket, Half Town, and Handsome Lake for the Senecas, establishing what was to be a permanent peace between the United States and the different Iroquois tribes.

Article three of the treaty, which was signed by Washington, applied only to the Senecas: "Now the United States acknowledge all the land within the aforementioned boundaries, to be the property of the Seneca nation; and the United States will never claim the same, nor disturb the Seneca nation . . . but it shall remain theirs, until they choose to sell the same to the people of the United States, who have the right to purchase."

These were the words that the engineers, a century and

a half later, were to brush aside. The solemn promise was "never," and until the 1950s it gave the Senecas security. In their imagery they made it read, "As long as the grass shall grow and the rivers run," and with that contract they lived in peace.

Cornplanter died on February 18, 1836, and was buried on his grant. That small plot of land in the meantime had taken on added meaning for the Senecas, for there, in 1799, Cornplanter's half brother, the prophet Ganiodayo, or Handsome Lake, had had the first of his revelations and had preached the Good Message—a set of new religious beliefs and practices—to all the Iroquois. This new religion, which still permeates Iroquois life, has been described as a blending of old Seneca beliefs with an ethical code borrowed largely from the Quakers. Its birth on the Cornplanter grant, from where it spread, endowed the plot with something of the sacredness of a holy shrine. In ensuing years, the burial of Cornplanter and his followers and descendants on the same grounds added to the grant's significance, a fact acknowledged by the state of Pennsylvania in 1866 when it erected the stone monument over Cornplanter's grave.

Under the tutelage of Quakers, who first came to live among the Senecas on the Allegheny River in 1798, the Indians became rapidly acculturated to the white man's way of living. Indians were educated, and Indian men were induced to farm (the Quakers persuaded families to spread out in homesteads along the river, out of sight of each other, so the men would not be embarrassed by being seen in the fields, doing what had traditionally been considered women's work). Beginning in 1803, factional disputes on the Cornplanter grant resulted in a gradual movement by Senecas to new communities higher up on the Allegheny across the New York border, and by 1806 Coldspring, south of present-day Salamanca, had become a new Seneca center.

As a result of various land sales that they continued to make to settlers and land companies, the Senecas' territory eventually dwindled to four, and then three reservations in western New York. They were the Cattaraugus, close to Lake Erie south of Buffalo; the Tonawanda, slightly northeast of Buffalo; and a long, narrow strip along the Allegheny River, from present-day Vandalia, New York, to the Pennsylvania state line. This became known as the Allegany Reservation, its name evolving with a different spelling from that of the river. South of this reservation, across the Pennsylvania line, descendants of Cornplanter still dwelled on his grant, which they had inherited as his heirs.*

In 1848, after the Ogden Land Company had almost managed to swindle the Senecas out of their last holdings in New York by getting drunken, venal, or bogus chiefs to sign papers of sale, a group of young Senecas on the Allegany and Cattaraugus reservations deposed the hereditary chiefs for incompetence and graft and set up a new, republican form of government on those two reservations. Calling themselves the Seneca Nation, they wrote a constitution that separated church and state; provided for a legislative council of eighteen (now sixteen) members and a president and other officers elected annually (now every two years) by all adult males (women now have the vote, too); established a judiciary of three "peacemakers" for minor crimes; asked that jurisdiction

---

* Eds. note: The Senecas also own but, according to the 2010 census, do not inhabit a small reservation of some 640 acres near Oil Spring in western New York State.

over serious crimes and major lawsuits be transferred to New
York State courts; and detached the two reservations from
the League of the Six Nations, which had continued (and still
continues, in modified form) to hold together in brotherhood
the different Iroquois peoples in the United States and Canada.
Today, one hundred forty years later, the Seneca Nation still
exists; it has the same form of government, the office of the
president rotating every two years between the Allegany and
Cattaraugus reservations.

In the middle of the nineteenth century, the Erie and Pennsylvania railroads, pushing across New York, bought rights of
way from the Senecas and established a junction on the Allegany Reservation. The site grew into a village originally called
Hemlock but renamed Salamanca for Don Jose Salamanca
Mayel, a large stockholder in the Erie Railroad. The rights-of-
way purchases, plus certain leases granted by the Senecas to
private citizens, were confirmed by federal statute in 1875 and
1890, when Congress gave the Allegany Reservation Senecas
the right to grant thereafter ninety-nine-year leases to all white
homeowners and businesses in Salamanca and in four other
white towns established on the reservation. The leases brought
ridiculously small returns to the Indians (even today the entire
city of Salamanca, with a population of a little more than nine
thousand, pays the Indians a total of only about $16,000 a year
in rent), but all the leases were renegotiated in 1991 for an additional forty years with "fairer terms" for the Indians.

As the years rolled on, the different Iroquois peoples in
New York, surrounded by a sea of whites, were all but forgotten. Living quietly on their reservations, they continued to
hunt, fish, and farm, educate their children, and in many cases
take jobs in the white man's world. A large number of Allegany

Senecas worked in furniture factories or for the railroads in Salamanca. Others followed a path pioneered by the Mohawks and became structural steelworkers, traveling to distant cities for periods of time to help build bridges and skyscrapers. While most of the Iroquois became Christians, many continued to observe the beliefs and practices of Handsome Lake, conducting an annual cycle of ceremonies. These were held in longhouses, rectangular frame buildings which served as both social and religious centers, as well as meeting places, for the Handsome Lake followers. But even the Christians, still holding themselves apart from the whites around them, continued to have pride in their Indian heritage, and it was said that every Iroquois still had "one foot in the Longhouse."

In the years after World War II, several of the Six Nations were beset by sudden new threats to their reservations. In 1954, when the St. Lawrence Seaway was under construction, its builders wanted to place some of their facilities on the St. Regis Reservation belonging to the Mohawks. The needed land was condemned, and though the Indians received $100,000 in compensation, they were left with the uneasy feeling that one day their entire reservation could be taken from them.

Three years later the Tuscaroras, whose reservation lies near Niagara Falls, were treated even more highhandedly by Robert Moses, chairman of the New York Power Authority. Part of his plan for the giant Niagara Power Project was a pump-storage reservoir to be located on the Tuscaroras' reservation. Their resistance to his original demand for thirteen hundred acres forced him to scale the reservoir down to five hundred fifty acres and to pay the Tuscaroras $88,000 for the land, plus the costs of relocating the nine Indian families who were living on it.

Considering the amount of land and the number of Indian families involved, however, none of these incursions matched the assault which the army engineers made on the Senecas' Allegany Reservation and the Cornplanter grant.

The idea for Kinzua Dam was born in 1928, following disastrous floods in the Ohio Valley. In 1938 and again in 1941, the chief of engineers asked for and received authorization from Congress to build Kinzua and a number of other dams as part of a general program of flood control for the Ohio River Basin. The Senecas were not informed by the engineers of their proposal to construct a dam that would inundate a large part of their reservation, and the engineers, in turn, were so unconcerned about the existence of a treaty, which they would have to break if they built the dam, that they failed to make much of a point of it in their presentation to Congress. To the Corps, it seems, land is land, no matter who lives on it. Proceeding on the assumption that the acquisition of land, ultimately, would be the usual matter of paying individual owners, engineers appeared on the Allegany Reservation in 1939 and 1940. The president and the council of the Seneca Nation, thinking that the engineers were making some studies of the river, offered no objection when they began to make surveys along the banks.

Interruptions by Secretary of the Interior Harold Ickes, who wanted Pennsylvania to pay part of the cost of the dam, and then by World War II temporarily sidetracked the Kinzua project. Through sources other than the Corps of Engineers, however, the Senecas began to learn of the plan for the dam, and by 1955, when the engineers again appeared before the Seneca council to ask permission to continue their surveys on the reservation, the Indians were nervous. The engineers allayed their fears, however, by assuring them that they did not yet know if they wished to build the dam and would not know until they had completed their surveys. Assuming that the engineers would keep them informed, the Indians once more let them make their studies.

The members of the Seneca Nation by this time numbered approximately 4,300, of whom perhaps 1,800 lived on the Allegany Reservation, 2,200 on the Cattaraugus Reservation thirty miles away, and the rest off the reservations. The Allegany Reservation, on which the engineers were focusing their attention, totaled 30,469 acres in a slender, forty-two-mile-long strip, averaging a mile wide, on both sides of the Allegheny River as it wound through a valley to the Pennsylvania border. Some 12,000 acres of the reservation were occupied by Salamanca and the other white towns or were taken by rights of way for roads and railroads, and much of the rest of the land was steep, rocky, forested hillside and therefore uninhabitable. Most of the Indians lived in frame houses or hemlock-board shanties strung out in a long line in clearings and wooded areas on the lower hills and bottomlands along the river. The average annual income of a family was about $3,000 (as against $5,000 for a white family in Salamanca), but the Indians, generally, lived in contentment, with fish, game, and firewood close at hand, and with a privacy and a closeness to nature that many a white visitor envied. South of the Pennsylvania line and separated from the reservation by three miles, about fifteen of Cornplanter's descendants still lived on his grant, close to the cemetery where his monument stood.

The engineers made their surveys and left, and in 1956 the Senecas were startled to learn that Congress had appropriated funds for plans for Kinzua Dam. Hearings had been held in Washington, and the engineers had testified, but the Indians had neither been invited to the hearings nor been informed that they were occurring. Now thoroughly alarmed, the Senecas and their tribal attorney moved quickly on two fronts. First they sought an injunction to keep the engineers off their land. Next, recognizing the need for flood control, they hired two eminent private engineers, Dr. Arthur E. Morgan, a former chairman of the Tennessee Valley Authority, and Barton M. Jones, who had built the TVA's Norris Dam, to make an independent study of the need for Kinzua Dam and, if possible, to propose an alternative dam site that would not involve the flooding of their lands.

The cat was now out of the bag. Newspapers began to publicize the Senecas' plight, and angry congressmen claimed that the engineers had misled them, that they had not been informed about the treaty. But if the engineers were chagrined, they failed to show it. Ignoring their critics, they got federal courts, early in 1957, to uphold their right to continue to make surveys on the reservation. And that same year, when Morgan and Jones presented an alternative plan for diverting Allegheny flood waters into Lake Erie at what they claimed was a cheaper cost than the Kinzua project, and without inundating reservation land, the engineers testified successfully against it in Congress (with "explicit misstatements and misrepresentations," according to Dr. Morgan) and won another $1 million appropriation to complete the planning and begin the construction of Kinzua Dam.

The Indians had friends, in and out of Congress, but not enough of them. Dr. Morgan produced still another alternative proposal—a dam site that would not involve any Indian lands—but a study sponsored by the engineers concluded that Dr. Morgan's dam would cost more money and take longer to build. Morgan and the Senecas did not agree and sought an independent comparison, but the engineers prevailed on the Senate to turn aside this request. Treaty or no treaty, the engineers were not going to risk a reversal of their plan, which now, it was revealed, would necessitate the condemnation of slightly more than 10,000 acres of the Indians' habitable land (leaving them only 2,300 on which they could live); the moving of 134 families, or about 700 people, more than one-third of the population of the reservation; the relocation of about 3,000 Seneca graves; and the inundation of the Cornplanter grant in Pennsylvania.

Falling back on the 1794 treaty, which promised that the United States would never claim the Senecas' land and guaranteed that it should be theirs until they chose to sell it, the Indians, in a case against the Secretary of the Army, now sought to halt construction of the Kinzua project, hoping to force the adoption, instead, of the Morgan plan. On April 14, 1958, the U.S. District Court for the District of Columbia ruled that the engineers could take reservation land, the same as any other, by the right of eminent domain, implying, in effect (although the court did not condone it), that the government of the United States, which could make a treaty, could also break it if it wished to do so. The case went on to the U.S. Court of Appeals for the District of Columbia and to the Supreme Court, but the judgment stood. Whether by their own ignorance or by the withholding of information from Congress, the engineers had maneuvered Congress into a position of voting, in the 1950s, to break still another Indian treaty, which it had the constitutional, if not the moral, right to do. By the time Congress realized what it had done, it was too late. The engineers had too many friends on Capitol Hill, and there was no one strong enough to induce the bureaucratic wheels within the Corps to reverse themselves.

That this was true became painfully clear to the Senecas when, as a last desperate measure, they appealed to President Kennedy in 1961, hoping that he would use his prerogative to withhold funds appropriated for the dam. On August 9, 1961, Kennedy replied to Basil Williams, the president of the Seneca Nation: "I have now had an opportunity to review the subject and have concluded that it is not possible to halt the construction of Kinzua Dam. . . . Impounding of the funds appropriated by the Congress after long and exhaustive congressional review, and after resolution by our judicial process of the legal right of the Federal Government to acquire the property necessary to the construction of the reservoir, would not be proper."

And so the dam was built. In his letter to Williams, President Kennedy had added that he would direct federal agencies to assist the Senecas by considering the possibility of finding new land to exchange with the Nation for the area it would lose; by reviewing the recreational potential of the reservoir and methods by which the Senecas could share in that potential; by determining the special damages suffered by the Nation's loss of so much of its land; by aiding those Senecas who had to give up their homes; and by preparing recommendations for whatever legislation might be required to achieve those ends. The White House sent a copy of the letter two days later with a covering memorandum to Major General William F. Cassidy, director of civil works, Corps of Engineers, ordering the Corps to "look into these questions without delay."

The letter was bucked down through the Corps, and although meetings, begun two months later, were held with other government agencies such as the Bureau of Indian

Affairs, as well as with representatives of the Senecas, the Corps behaved as if it were thoroughly irritated with the Indians and had no intention of doing anything for them. The Corps did pay the salary of an able and dedicated representative of the BIA, Sidney Carney, a Choctaw Indian who was sent to work among the Senecas. But except for that, two full years later, with the dam nearing completion and the Indians still living in their old homes that were threatened by the reservoir, so little had been done by Cassidy and the engineers to carry out Kennedy's order that some congressmen, moved to anger, introduced bills authorizing payments for the relocation and rehabilitation of the Indians. "Apparently you don't want to try to do anything for this Indian tribe," Congressman John P. Saylor of Pennsylvania berated a stony-faced Corps witness. "Apparently you have become so calloused and so crass that the breaking of the oldest treaty that the United States has is a matter of little concern to you. . . . The Corps of Engineers has never intended to do anything whatsoever with regard to the Seneca Indians, and they have intended from the very beginning to treat this as just any other dam and leave the Indians only their recourse in the courts."

On August 31, 1964, after months of disagreement between the House and Senate over how much to pay the Senecas—a disagreement caused to some extent by the Corps' influence in urging the Senate to cut down the original House figures and not pay the Indians except via the usual court proceedings—Congress passed a $15,000,573 reparations bill for the Senecas. But added to the bill was a disturbing amendment requiring the Secretary of the Interior to present to Congress within three years a plan for the termination of the Senecas' relations with the federal government—in effect bringing to an end such things as the tax-exempt status of the reservation and federal approval of leases and trusteeship of Seneca land.*

Meanwhile, shortly after President Kennedy had shut the final door on them, the Senecas, who had fought hard to save their land, set about determinedly to prepare for the coming disruption. Under the leadership of George Heron, a past president of the Nation, they set up committees to pick relocation areas for new homes and cemeteries, to plan housing and new community centers, and to propose economic development projects that would aid the people in their new situation. When Congress's appropriation became available in September 1964, the Senecas were ready to move quickly. New ranch-type homes of varying designs were built during the wet and wintry months in two tightly compressed areas that totaled five hundred acres. One of them, named Jimerson-town, near Salamanca, was laid out in 145 one-acre plots; the other, Steamburg, near the southern end of the reservation, had 160 plots of the same size. The Corps of Engineers built the streets in both of the new settlements. A family could own as many as three plots, but even so, the shift to suburban-type living, with houses close to each other, was a sharp change for people who had been used to privacy and a closeness to the woods and wild game. Other money was used to move three thousand Seneca graves to two new cemeteries; to build a community center and tribal council headquarters on each reservation; to develop a sixty-acre industrial park on the Cattaraugus Reservation for industry that hopefully would employ

---

*   Eds. note: According to Stephen Pevar, in *The Rights of Indians and Tribes*, Congress last terminated a tribe in 1966, and President Nixon announced the formal end of the Termination policy in 1970. See Josephy's "white paper" in chapter 12 of this book.

Indians; and to set up a $1.8 million educational fund for college and business and vocational school scholarships for young Senecas. In addition, twenty-five public housing rental units on the Allegany Reservation and thirty-five at Cattaraugus were erected with other federal funds.

The hubbub of moving was accentuated by a constant harassment from the engineers, whose plans called for completion of the dam in 1965 and who kept posting deadlines for the Indians to get out of the condemned area. In working with the leadership of the Senecas, the engineers behaved properly and according to orders and regulations, but many Senecas today remember only their cold and officious manner and recall them as the Sioux recall Custer.

It was traditional in the nineteenth century for the government, when it wanted something from the Indians, to promise them anything and then let someone else worry about carrying out the promise—which, more often than not, was never done. In the case of the Senecas, the government revived the tradition. By 1968, with the dam built and the engineers gone from the scene, the Senecas were well on their way to adjustment to a new life on their smaller reservation. But in scores of ways, hopes that the Indians had once held high were still unrealized. Complaints ranged from new homes left unfinished (front steps not provided from the porch to the ground) or already showing signs of shoddy construction to frustrated attempts to bring revenue to the Nation through use of the area's new recreational potential. Although the engineers, in response to President Kennedy's letter, had led the Senecas to believe that they could profit from concessions on the reservoir, the Indians were indefinitely stalled: the water level at their end of the reservoir, the upper portion, rises and falls the most, and through much of the year contains great mud flats. Solving the problem by channeling or other means would have cost much more than the Indians could afford, especially since their concessions would be competing economically with other facilities (some of them free to the public) prepared by the engineers at the taxpayers' expense lower down on the lake, where the water level is more constant.

The owners and residents of the Cornplanter grant, across the state line in Pennsylvania, were treated even more high-handedly by the engineers. Acquiring that plot, sacred to the chief's descendants and to the followers of the Handsome Lake religion, required delicate treatment by the engineers; instead, its owners were treated like any other citizens being ousted from their property. As early as February 1961, the Cornplanter heirs, organized as the Cornplanter Indian Landowners Corpo-ration, accepted the fact that most of the grant would have to be given up to the reservoir and that The Cornplanter's grave and monument would have to be moved. As a means of per-suading the Senecas to accept this decision quickly and with-out a legal contest, the engineers promised Merrill W. Bowen, president of the Cornplanter group, that the cemetery would be moved to a place of the Indians' choice.

The Senecas first selected a site on the highest part of the grant, which would not be flooded, but the engineers turned it down with the argument that they could not build an access road to it. Then, on August 23, 1963, the Senecas were given a sixty-five-acre tract above the level of the reservoir by the family of Latham B. Weber, publisher of the *Salamanca Republican-Press*. The site was ideal. It was on the west side of the river, close to the old grant and contiguous to the southern bound-ary of the Allegany Reservation. But no sooner had the newspaper announced the gift than the engineers informed both Bowen and the Webers that they needed that tract, too, not for the reservoir but for public recreation purposes! "It is essential to the needs of the project," the engineers wrote.

· There then began a protracted attempt by the Senecas to change the engineers' mind, an attempt that floundered in a sea of deafness, evasions, and red tape. On October 1, 1963, despite their original promise to relocate Cornplanter's grave in a place of the Indians' choice, the engineers announced in a newspaper release that all the graves on the grant would be moved to a new cemetery on a hill across the river, which the Indians would share with whites who were losing their cemetery too. More than one hundred fifty Cornplanter heirs signed a petition in protest, but the engineers were unmoved and on March 31, 1964, received authority from a federal court in Erie, Pennsylvania, to relocate the Indian graves wherever they wished. The relocation to the site across the river, which began on August 26, was attended by threats, rumors, and charges. Fearful of trouble (one Indian, it was claimed, did try to stop the work), the engineers were overly secretive about the matter, and on the day that the monument was to be moved and Cornplanter's grave opened, only two heirs were notified to be present as witnesses. Two others showed up, however, and charges later appeared in newspapers and were filed with the engineers and with the office of Senator Joseph S. Clark of Pennsylvania, claiming rough and irreverent handling of the remains, mixing of the bones, and other misdeeds by those carrying out the work. The engineers went to great length to deny the charges, though they did not take affidavits from those who made them. True or not, the charges reflected the state of tension and hostility between the Cornplanter heirs and the engineers.

The conflict was not over, for the Cornplanter heirs still had no land for a memorial and meeting grounds to take the place of the old grant. In December 1964, Senator Clark made a personal appeal to Colonel James C. Hammer, the district engineer in Pittsburgh, to allow the Indians to keep the Weber tract. Hammer first told Clark's office that the Webers had given the land to the Senecas only after they had known it was to be condemned, which was totally untrue and which the Webers and Bowen were quick to deny. Hammer then replied formally on January 27, 1965, suggesting that the Corps meet with the Indians to try to help them find a suitable site, but implying that they could not have the Weber tract, which provided "a prime location for recreational facilities." In February, Curtis F. Hunter, a Corps representative in Warren, Pennsylvania, near the dam site, met with Bowen and the Webers' attorney in Salamanca, proposed certain alternative possibilities, including the Indians' use of the Weber tract by license rather than ownership, and suggested that they all meet with Colonel Hammer the next time that officer was in the area. On March 14 Hunter called for a meeting on the following day. Hammer did not show up, and instead of talking about the Weber tract, Hunter seemed anxious to pressure the Indians into acceptance of the use of an alternative site across the river. When an impasse was reached, he promised to write Colonel Hammer a letter explaining the Indians' reasons for wanting to retain the Weber tract and told Bowen he would send him a copy. He failed to do this; instead, on April 1, one of his colleagues in Warren, a real estate official named Stanley O'Hopp, asked the Senecas for another meeting on April 5. At that conference, O'Hopp told them that they could not keep the Weber property, but he offered them three alternative sites, the biggest of which, across the river, totaled about sixty-three acres. When the Indians again argued for the Weber tract, he told them to state their position on paper and submit it to the Corps for consideration.

On April 21, Bowen followed up the suggestion and wrote to Colonel Hammer, telling him that O'Hopp's alternative proposals did not reflect a "clear understanding" of the needs and desires of the Cornplanter descendants, and then explaining in detail why the Indians wished to retain the Weber tract. On receipt of the letter, Hammer decided that nothing more could come of further discussions with the Cornplanter heirs, and he ordered condemnation proceedings to be started against the Weber property. Withholding this information from the Cornplanters, Hammer wrote Bowen on May 13 a curt note stating, "I have carefully considered the contents of your letter, but I am unable to find a valid basis for changing the determination . . . that the Weber tract in its entirety is essential to the needs of the Project."

When Bowen got the letter, he telegraphed Hammer, asking for a meeting with him personally. On May 21 Hammer's deputy, Lieutenant Colonel Bruce W. Jamison, replied evasively in a letter that "the Corps" would be pleased to be "represented at such conference as you may arrange," and also notified the Senecas, almost as an afterthought, that "in line with" Colonel Hammer's letter of May 13, the Corps was commencing eminent domain proceedings for the acquisition of the Weber tract. "As you know," Jamison concluded, "the negotiations for acquisition by purchase were not productive of a mutually agreeable price." The Indians could not have known such a thing, because there had never been any negotiations with them over a price.

Meanwhile, the Quaker representative living among the Senecas had written President Johnson an appeal for his assistance in behalf of the Cornplanters, who were still being pushed around. The letter was referred by the White House to Lieutenant General W. K. Wilson, Jr., chief of engineers, in Washington, who sent it to Colonel Hammer in Pittsburgh for his comments. On May 27 General Wilson replied to the Quaker representative, passing on several pieces of misinformation supplied him by Hammer, among them that Hammer "had met with Mr. Bowen on several occasions to negotiate the acquisition of the land for the project" (they had not met face-to-face once, despite Bowen's request for such a meeting), and that when the Webers had given the land to the Indians, "it was well known that the 'Weber' tract was scheduled for acquisition by the Corps" (an untruth that Bowen and the Webers had already set straight). "The entire 'Weber' tract is essential to the needs of the project and must be acquired," General Wilson concluded, employing the same words that Hammer had used in his note of May 13 to Bowen.

The Army had its back up, and neither General Wilson nor anyone else in the Corps could see the silliness of their bureaucratic rigidity. Insisting that a small, sixty-five-acre tract for recreation was essential to the success of the Kinzua Dam project would have been farcical had it not been so unhappy for the Indians. Nor did the Army stop there. From its point of view, the Quaker representative had made a grievous mistake in appealing to the president, and now the Senecas would pay for it.

On May 28, in reply to another telegraphed appeal from Bowen, Colonel Hammer let the Cornplanter leader know that there was nothing more to discuss about the Weber property and that the Army had already instituted eminent-domain proceedings. Recognizing that the engineers could not be stopped, the Cornplanter heirs finally surrendered on June 15, writing Colonel Hammer that they would give up the Weber land but wished to discuss use of the sixty-three acres across the river that Hunter and O'Hopp had mentioned the previous March and April. Hammer replied, asking Bowen to set up the meeting, but shortly afterward Bowen's wife died, and the conference did not occur until September 16. It proved to be the last straw. Hunter and O'Hopp appeared for the engineers and announced that, because of the Indians' "procrastination," the offer of sixty-three acres had been reduced to 8.42 acres, almost entirely hillside, covered with trees and brush. The Indians were shocked, but they could get nowhere with the Corps' negotiators. In a last pitiful appeal, Bowen asked if Hunter could get the engineers to tack on another two acres at the bottom of the hill where the ground was level and the Cornplanters could hold their picnics without danger of sliding. Hunter said he would try, but the next day he called back and reported that the answer was no. Some day, he said, there might be a ski development "back in that direction," and the level land would be needed for a road on which to get in.

So the Cornplanters, in the end, accepted an exclusive but revocable license to use the 8.42 isolated acres of steep land. They have not used it yet, and probably will never use it. On September 24, 1965, Bowen wrote a final letter to Senator Clark, who, although an insistent advocate of the building of Kinzua Dam, had also tried to help the Cornplanters. Telling the Pennsylvania senator of the outcome of their struggle, Bowen urged him to make no further effort in their behalf. "We have been informed," he said, "that our prior efforts to obtain your assistance and that of President Johnson have merely irritated the Corps of Engineers and possibly damaged our case. Your intervention now might only bring about some excuse to take away the few crumbs still offered to us."

His reason for writing the senator, Bowen went on, was "to give you the benefit of our sad experience as you may find legislative opportunities to improve the approach of the Corps of Engineers to other people in the future—people who may be as inexperienced, poor, and lacking in shrewdness and legal services as we have been."

Kinzua Dam was formally dedicated on September 16, 1966. Two hundred and eighty-three years after William Penn had signed his famous treaty, Pennsylvania lost the last of its Indians. At a gala luncheon in the local high school after the ceremonies at the dam, a quartet of girls known as the Kinzua Damsels entertained Governor William Scranton and the other guests with the song "This Is My Country." And in California, Montana, Alaska, and elsewhere, the Army Corps of Engineers was already threatening other Indian tribes with plans for more Kinzuas.

9

"Like Giving Heroin to an Addict"

◇◇

The Reassertion of Native American Water Rights

Explorer John C. Fremont called Pyramid Lake "a gem in the moun-tains." The National Park Service has called it "the most beautiful desert lake in the United States." For a small tribe of Northern Paiute Indians, this lake, named by Fremont himself, was their principal means of existence, in large part due to its population of the huge Lahontan (cutthroat) trout, a species known nowhere else in the world. In 1859, recognizing the lake's crucial importance, the federal government set it aside as the main part of an otherwise barren reservation.

In 1905 the Bureau of Reclamation undertook to build a dam on the Truckee River, thus depriving the lake of a large part of its es-sential water supply. This action, taken without consideration of the Paiutes' historic and legal rights, set off a conflict that continues to this day. Pyramid Lake was saved, barely, but its long-term survival is hardly guaranteed.

The following narrative, a chapter from Josephy's Now That the Buffalo's Gone *(1982), is yet another example of an Indian tribe's unshakable devotion to a place and a way of life.*

In the 1970s, a crisis came to the states of the northern Plains. In that semi-arid part of the United States, where water is a fought-over commodity, a sudden burst of coal strip-mining and energy-producing developments, spurred by the international oil shortage, precipitated a new era of fiercely competitive quarrels over possession of the region's limited water resources. Almost overnight, farmers and ranchers were in confrontations with acquisitive, water-consuming energy conglomerates; both contested the worried demands of municipalities and local industrial and domestic water users; and all three threatened the water supplies of the area's numerous Indian reservations.

In the apportioning of western water, the life-and-death needs of the Indians have historically been given short shrift. "Water is our lifeblood. Without it, our homeland is useless, our people will die, and we will cease to exist," more than one western tribal leader has pointed out. Moreover, Indians were there first, the original owners and the first users of the water. Yet, in carrying out the nation's Manifest Destiny policy of opening up the West to white population and development, the federal government, despite its responsibilities as trustee of the Indians' property, for more than a century led the way in taking water from the Indians and giving it to the whites. Many tribes, as a result, were reduced to poverty and suffering, especially in the critically dry Southwest. The record in Arizona, where incoming farmers, with government support, simply dammed rivers above the irrigated fields of such industrious and self-supporting agricultural tribes as the Pimas and Papagos, cutting off their water supply and condemning them to ruin and starvation, was particularly odious. There, today, the attitude behind such callousness is still strong. The contemporary growth of central Arizona, the refusal to meter the groundwater by water-wasteful cotton-growing corporations, and the greed of land and tract-building speculators in Phoenix, Tucson, Scottsdale, and other communities are still supported in large measure by an indifference to the needs of the water-starved tribes and their reservations and by the use of such refined methods of robbery as the stealthy oblique pumping of water from declining water tables beneath Indian reservations for pipeline delivery to the lawns and faucets of burgeoning real estate developments for newly arrived whites.*

But amid the impact of the energy crisis on the northern Plains there were signs that a new day was dawning for Indian water rights. The situation was still, and for a long time to come will be, rancorous and tied in the knots of legalistic procedures (there is no branch of American law more susceptible to complexity and confusion than that of water rights). Nevertheless, as the result of new Indian assertiveness, various tribes by the mid-1970s had managed to expose, and inspire judicial condemnation of, the derelictions of their trustee, impelling the federal government, finally in 1979, to move over to the Indians' side in Montana, where conflicts resulting from energy developments had become the hottest. In that year, the Justice Department filed suits to try to safeguard the threatened

*   Eds. note: Water continues to be an issue in the Southwest, and negotiations among tribes, cities, and the federal government are ongoing. For example, on July 30, 2013, the Department of the Interior released the following: "As part of President Obama's commitment to empower tribal nations, Secretary of the Interior Sally Jewell, on behalf of the United States, today signed an historic agreement at the Department of the Interior guaranteeing water rights for the White Mountain Apache Tribe of Arizona. The agreement will also provide funding for infrastructure to deliver clean drinking water to the Reservation, as well as water security for the City of Phoenix and other downstream water users."

water resources of the Flathead, Blackfeet, Rocky Boys, Fort Peck, and Fort Belknap Reservations by asking a federal court to establish the amount of water to which they had rights prior to all others from the Flathead, Milk, Marias, and Poplar rivers in that state.

The suits surprised both Indians and whites and caused immediate controversy. Many non-Indians foresaw a loss of water to the reservations and were angered. The suits were "unfair to non-Indians and non-federal water users," complained Montana's senior senator, John Melcher. "This strong-arm tactic by the Justice Department must be met with strong resistance by Montanans." It may not have occurred to him that he was upholding Indian sovereignty by implying that the Native Americans were not also Montanans, but the tribes, too, were upset. The Justice Department had filed the suits without adequately consulting them, an affront to their struggle for self-determination and the right to make decisions about their own affairs. Moreover, in view of the federal government's long record of selling out the tribes, of losing Indian rights by the use of second-rate government lawyers and ill-prepared cases, and of forcing injurious settlements on the Indians, the tribes were suspicious of the Justice Department's intent. If there were to be suits, they wished to use their own lawyers and pursue the cases themselves. In addition, they were not sure that they wanted their water rights established, or "quantified"—not yet, anyway. It would limit them to all the water they would get now and forever into the future—for all foreseeable and unforeseeable needs of their children and their children's children. They knew that under already established law they possessed treaty-guaranteed claims to all the water ever required to carry out the function of their reservations. "Quantification," to them, implied another stealing of their property by putting a permanent limit on what water they could claim and use.

But the government went ahead with the suits. Interior Department officials reminded the Indians that representatives from all of Montana's seven reservations had tried to negotiate with the state legislature, but the state had snubbed them and the legislature had passed a bill putting all water users, including the tribes, under state authority. Montana's next step would have been to haul the tribes into a state court for an enforced settlement of their water rights, and the tribes knew, said the Interior Department, that they could not get as fair a hearing in a state court as in a federal court. From experience, the tribes readily agreed with that and recognized, at length, that the federal government had raced the state to litigation and had successfully gotten the issue into a federal court. So the Montana water-rights cases, which would inevitably be drawn out and might land ultimately in the Supreme Court, started toward a decision that would take years to resolve.

How well the government would do for the Montana tribes could not be foreseen. But there was good reason for the Indians to be wary. Courts—not public opinion, and certainly not Congress, a national administration, or state governments—had forced the Justice Department to reach its new, protective position. In particular, a case in Nevada, affecting a small, relatively little-known tribe, the Pyramid Lake Paiutes, was familiar to many of the Indians. More than most other cases, it had dramatized for the courts, as well as for Native Americans throughout the country, the historic role of the trustee as a robber of Indian rights.

There were political and legal backdrops to that history, all of them familiar to tribes that were trying to protect their water rights, but not well understood by most non-Indians. Under the Commerce Clause of the Constitution, the federal government, specifically Congress, is charged with conducting all affairs with Indians. Until 1871, those affairs were generally formalized by treaties, as with foreign powers, which under another constitutional provision were recognized as "the supreme Law of the Land." No state, save by the express authority of Congress, ever had the constitutional right to deal with the affairs of Indians within its borders—nor do they yet have that right. This injunction was sustained forcibly by Justice John Marshall in *Worcester v. Georgia* in 1832 ("all intercourse with them [the Indians] shall be carried on exclusively by the government of the Union") and by numerous subsequent statutes and court decisions. In addition, new states, on acceptance into the Union, were frequently required to accept a congressional reminder that Indian lands within the state "shall remain under the absolute jurisdiction and control of the Congress of the United States." To the Indians, therefore, the question of the settling of their water rights has been considered a matter between them and the federal government, including its judiciary branch, whose courts—not without considerable significance—have been freer than state courts from the anti-Indian political and economic pressures of those whites within a state who covet Indian resources.

During the nineteenth century, many reservations were created, most of them by treaty between the federal government and the tribes, but some (for tribes whose lands had already been overrun) by special executive or congressional order that often gave landless peoples a home in lieu of what had been taken from them. At the same time, and into the twentieth century, statutes and court decisions confirmed treaty rights, as well as services owed to the tribes in return for the lands they had given up or lost, and, also, defined responsibilities of the federal government to the tribes, including the obligation to act as trustee over Indian property. In the face of non-Indian political pressures, the carrying out of the trust function left much to be desired. As a matter of practice, the government acted more often as the agent of non-Indian interests intent on acquiring or using Indian lands or resources, usually at bargain rates, than as protector of what the Indians owned. With the connivance of the government, through the Department of the Interior, tribes were cheated and robbed, their assets were mishandled and subjected to fraud, and it became a habit not even to inform them of developments and agreements made in their name that would adversely affect their resources. Compounding the injustices was a conflict of interest within the Department of the Interior itself. While one agency of the Department, the Bureau of Indian Affairs, was charged with the responsibility for the trust function, other Department agencies, including the Bureau of Reclamation, the Bureau of Land Management, the National Park Service, and the Fish and Wildlife Service—looking out for the interests of the American people as a whole—often appropriated Indian lands and their resources for their own projects or trampled on Indian rights. Having more support from the non-Indian population than the BIA, the latter agencies generally found it easy to persuade Interior's Solicitor and the Department of Justice lawyers to side with them and refuse to go to court in the Indians' behalf, and the BIA, in turn, found it politically expedient to let the Indians lose.

Though the tribes, on the whole, were unable to protect themselves and were not only illegally unrepresented but—

also in violation of the Constitution—were permitted to suffer losses without due process of law, their water interests occasionally did surface in significant law cases, particularly *Winters v. United States* in 1908, *United States v. Ahtanum Irrigation District* in 1956, and *Arizona v. California* in 1963. Those cases established for Indians what became known as the Winters Doctrine (after the name of the first case), which held that when the United States government created Indian reservations, it also reserved, by implication, sufficient water in any streams running through or bordering on a reservation to carry out the purposes of that reservation—that is, to make the reservation livable by reserving, also, whatever water "may be reasonably necessary, not only for present uses, but for future requirements." Moreover, since it was ruled that treaties were "not a grant of rights to the Indians, but a grant of rights from them—a reservation of those not granted," the Indians, rather than the government, had reserved the water, which like the land was their property, and they were generally deemed to possess a paramount and first-priority right, ahead of any rights a state might grant, to all the water necessary for a reservation's purposes.

In theory, this would appear to have been an answer to the tribes' water problems. The Winters Doctrine, dating from as long ago as 1908, seemed to have offered the reservations sound legal grounds to retain, maintain, and safeguard whatever water they required, for then and for the future. But to most tribes whose water rights had already been taken from them or were still being threatened, the difficulty was to make the law of the Winters Doctrine apply to themselves. Waging a long, complicated, and costly water-rights case on their own was beyond the means or capability of impoverished and legally unsophisticated peoples, and there were dozens of reasons—including the prospect of exposing its own culpability and thereby becoming a defendant—why their trustee, the Department of the Interior, refused to have the Justice Department initiate Winters Doctrine suits for them. The years thus went by, with the Department doing little to stem the theft of Indian water resources—until the fate of one body of tribally owned water, Nevada's Pyramid Lake, possessed by a small group of Northern Paiutes, suddenly in the 1960s became too big a national scandal for the government to ignore.

The "Pathfinder," Lieutenant John C. Fremont of the Army's Corps of Topographical Engineers, was the first white man to describe Pyramid Lake. Exploring southward from Oregon at the head of a party of twenty-five men, including the veteran trappers and guides Kit Carson and Tom Fitzpatrick, he reached the summit of a range of barren hills in northwestern Nevada on January 10, 1844, and sighted in the desert "a sheet of green" breaking "upon our eyes like the ocean." "The waves were curling in the breeze," Fremont reported, "and their dark-green color showed it to be a body of deep water. For a long time we sat enjoying the view. . . . It was set like a gem in the mountains."

The explorers found a well-used Indian trail and, following it south along the eastern shore of the great inland lake, passed herds of mountain sheep, flocks of ducks, and odd tufa formations—calcium carbonate deposits precipitated from the water along the lake's edge mostly by the timeless action of algae and waves, and resembling castles, domes, and needles of varicolored stone. One of them particularly, an island rising almost three hundred feet above the surface of the water, caught their fancy. It "presented a pretty exact outline of the great pyramid of Cheops," Fremont said. "This striking feature suggested a name for the lake, and I called it Pyramid Lake."

At the southern end of the lake the explorers came on a camp of Cui-ui Ticutta Indians (eaters of the cui-ui fish, pronounced *kwee-wee*), a band of a widespread Great Basin tribe which called itself Numa (the People), who are known today as Northern Paiutes. The Indians greeted the whites in friendship and supplied them with great quantities of fish—"magnificent salmon trout," said Fremont's cartographer, Charles Preuss, who wrote in his diary, "I gorged myself until I almost choked." The fish were giant Lahontan cutthroat trout, a species found in no other part of the world. "Their flavor was excellent," Fremont reported, "superior, in fact, to that of any fish I have ever known. They were of extraordinary size—about as large as the Columbia River Salmon—generally from two to four feet in length." There were ample supplies of them, taken from the lake and a river that flowed into it beside the Indian camp, and the people, who, Fremont noted, "appeared to live an easy and happy life," gave the visitors "a salmon-trout feast as is seldom seen . . . every variety of manner in which fish could be prepared—boiled, fried, and roasted in the ashes—was put into requisition; and every few minutes an Indian would be seen running off to spear a fresh one."

That was almost a century and a half ago. To the modern-day visitor who catches his first sight of the huge body of water in the desert, Pyramid Lake is still as breathtakingly dramatic as it was to Fremont. Shaped like a partly opened fan, a little more than thirty miles long on its north-south axis, some eleven miles wide at its broadest expanse in the north and less than four miles wide in the south, it lies in a long, hidden basin near the Nevada-California border. Ranges of arid mountains, rising as high as four thousand feet above the water, surround the lake, descending toward it in steep declines and long, sloping benches and flats covered with sagebrush and other desert plants. On the south the mountains conceal the lake from travelers hurrying by on the east-west railroad or Interstate 80, as well as from the busy urban centers of Reno and Sparks, only thirty miles to the southwest.

The color of the lake, deep blue, green, or gray, changes to reflect the hues of the desert sky but depends also on the density and movement of concentrations of plankton in its waters. Along the shore there are still relatively few signs of development or of man's presence, and the great sheet of water and the hills around it are overwhelmingly quiet save for the sounds of wildlife. California gulls, Caspian terns, and blue herons flap and soar across the sky. Ducks ride the swells, and approximately seventy-five hundred white pelicans, probably the largest colony of that species in North America, nest on Anaho Island, a seven-hundred-fifty-acre National Wildlife Refuge three hundred yards off the eastern shore. The curled-horned mountain sheep that Fremont saw are gone, but coyotes, mule deer, jackrabbits, and bobcats are abundant, as are armies of ground squirrels, lizards, and other rodents and reptiles that make their home in the desert cover.

Despite its large size, the lake is fragile. A remnant of a bigger prehistoric body of water known as Lake Lahontan that filled much of the western Great Basin during the Ice Age, it has only one principal source of water, the Truckee River, which starts at Lake Tahoe in the High Sierras on the Nevada-California border, almost one hundred miles to the southwest. The river runs down the eastern slope of the Sierras, through Reno and Sparks, and empties into the southern end of the lake near the

present town of Nixon, on the site of the Indian camp that Fremont visited in 1844. Pyramid has a maximum depth of about
335 feet, and no outlet, but it loses approximately 147 billion
gallons, or about four and a half feet, of water a year by evapo-
ration. It receives a small amount of water from underground
sources, from surface runoff, and from occasional desert rains;
but in the main it is dependent on the Truckee River, whose
replenishments historically kept it at a somewhat fixed level.

The National Park Service terms Pyramid Lake "the most
beautiful desert lake in the United States . . . perhaps the most
beautiful of its kind in North America"; conservationists and
lovers of outdoor beauty have regarded its wild solitude as one
of the few remaining unspoiled natural wonders in the American West; and the state of Nevada touts the lake as among its
prized attractions for tourists and sportsmen. But the lake is
still the property of the descendants of the Native American
Cui-ui Ticutta, who are now known officially as the Pyramid
Lake Paiute tribe. Save for a narrow strip of barren and mountainous country entirely surrounding the lake and a panhandle
of land extending seventeen miles along the lower Truckee, the
lake presently constitutes their entire reservation and all they
possess on which to exist. Since 1905, however, the lake—and
therefore the tribe, numbering today about sixteen hundred
people—has been threatened with wanton destruction.

The Paiutes, occupiers of the area since ancient times, traditionally lived on rabbits, mud hens, pine nuts, seeds, and other
creatures and wild foods of their desert environment. But, as
Fremont noted, fish from the lake—notably the big Lahontan
trout and the cui-ui, the latter a valuable food fish, growing up
to nine pounds and, like the Lahontan trout, found in no other
region in the world—were the band's principal item of diet.

Since the people lived principally on fish, the federal government in 1859 set aside the lake and the lower river for them as the main part of an otherwise almost barren reservation, with the intent that it serve as their major means of life. Through the years, federal courts confirmed the lake as the Indians' property, and the tribe kept it unspoiled and productive.

In 1905, however, the Reclamation Service of the Department of the Interior built Derby Dam across the Truckee River twenty miles east of Reno, diverting approximately half of the flow of the river, considerably more in dry years, away from Pyramid Lake and into a government irrigation project, newly constructed for white settlers in the Nevada desert around present-day Fallon. No one appears to have considered what would happen to Pyramid Lake or to the reservation and the people who lived on it, once their water was taken from them. No one consulted the Indians or asked them for it, and no one, not even in the Bureau of Indian Affairs, told them that the water was going to be taken. Voiceless and powerless in a white man's world at the time, the Paiutes were, in every sense of the word, wards of the government. But when Nevada's political leaders asked Congress to authorize the irrigation project, the Department of the Interior raised not a murmur in defense of the Indians' water. In a conflict between the interests of the Indians and those of the white farmers who were "opening up" the West, the Department's solicitors, as was their habit, turned their back on the "vanishing race," and with the building of Derby Dam, Pyramid Lake began to receive only that water which the dam did not divert for the irrigation project (now known as the Newlands Project, for Nevada's reclamation-minded senator Francis G. Newlands).

The results at the lake were as dramatic as they were predictable. By the 1960s, the great sheet of water had dropped an average of·fifteen inches a year, for a total of more than eighty feet. Its shoreline had receded an average of ten feet a year; a sister body of water, Lake Winnemucca, once also about thirty miles long and fed by overflow water from Pyramid Lake, had entirely dried up and disappeared. Pyramid Lake's length·had shrunk by several miles, and its surface area had contracted by more than fifty square miles. Fremont's pyramid, now rising 365 feet above the lake, had ceased to be an island, being connected to the shore; and Anaho Island, facing the same prospect, seemed destined to lose its famed pelicans once coyotes and other predators could cross on dry land to the rookeries. At the south end of the lake, moreover, sandbars clogged the mouth of the Truckee, and fish could no longer get up the river to spawn. About 1938, the giant Lahontan trout disappeared from the lake, and the cui-ui faced extinction.

The future of the Pyramid Lake Paiutes had clearly become endangered. Gaining new voice, unity, and self-assertiveness, the Indians determined, in the mid-1950s, to commence an eleventh-hour fight to save their lake. The alternative, as they saw it, was the slow death of the tribe, for without the fish, people would have to abandon the reservation to seek homes elsewhere, and the tribe would disintegrate and vanish. "It is a matter of life and death, not just a question of getting what rightfully belongs to us," the elected tribal chairman, James Vidovich, told the people. And, added Vidovich—an electrical worker then in his thirties, and the descendant of a Paiute who had received the family's surname from an employer of Yugoslav origins—"It may be a long, hard fight."

To the Pyramid Lake Paiutes, there was nothing new about that. They were only there, he could have recalled to them,

because of other long, hard fights for their existence that their
fathers had waged in the past. The first whites who came
on them, fur trappers and emigrants to California, before
and after Fremont's visit, had crossed their lands and killed
them. They were then small groups of extended families who
lived in conical brush-covered wickiups, employing the spiritual help of shamans and praying to Numanah, the Creator
of All Things, following seasonal rounds of fishing, hunting,
and gathering wild foods, and in winter combining in larger
band-size groups in sheltered locations. The apparent poverty
of their land, resources, and way of life, together with their
small numbers and weakness as compared to the power and
strength of the Plains tribes, drew the bullying of many whites,
who, with contempt, termed them Digger Indians, for the stick
with which they dug roots, and killed them on sight for sport.

After the discovery of silver in Nevada, miners and settlers
crowded in among them, appropriating their lands, destroying
the wild game and pine-nut groves, and continuing to murder
them. The creation of the reservation for the Indians in 1859
failed to give them security, and in 1860 they fought back boldly
under Numaga, one of their band leaders. They ambushed and
whipped one force of whites on the southern border of Pyramid Lake, but were then outnumbered by a larger, punitive
army and forced to flee for safety among other bands in the
northern Great Basin. Colonel Frederick W. Lander, an Indian
superintendent, at length negotiated a peace, and the Paiutes, winning an end to the armed aggressions against them,
regained their lake and reservation.

But there were other struggles. They resisted missionaries,
government agents, and teachers who tried to stamp out their
religion and culture. Unable to follow seasonal rounds of hunt-

ing and gathering beyond their reservation, they were forced into the white man's cash economy for their necessities and went to work for whites, attempting to steel themselves against prejudice and unfair treatment in their jobs by retaining their dignity and Paiute identity. Their longest fight was waged against white squatters who in 1865 began settling along the lower Truckee River, on the reservation's only irrigable land. That struggle, waged in courts and the Congress, lasted almost one hundred years, but finally ended in partial victory for the Paiutes and the ousting of some of the squatter families in the 1950s. By that time, the town of Nixon at the foot of the lake had become established as their tribal center, and the Indians, outwardly, were largely assimilated. Inwardly, however, they were still Paiutes and were ready for the battle for their lake.

Although most of the Paiutes' land surface was arid, with irrigation, some of the panhandle strip south of the lake could be farmed and grazed. Through the years, the Indians had opened somewhat less than eight hundred acres of bottom-land along the Truckee to irrigation, principally for hay for cattle and horses; but the tribe was unable to afford to irrigate the higher land, and the federal government would not grant them financial assistance, despite promises to do so. Moreover, the Paiutes at heart were not farmers or stockmen.

Thus the lake, with its cui-ui and artificially planted fish that required periodic restocking and produced only a small fraction of the lake's former output, was still in the mid-1950s their major resource, and along with fish for food, provided 75 percent of their tribal income through the sale of fishing and boating permits to whites. Other income was derived from cattle and from part-time jobs on ranches or in the cities. Still, as late as 1967, almost 70 percent of the Pyramid Lake Paiutes were unemployed, and 52 percent of their families had incomes of under $2,000 a year. If the lake could be preserved, there was an additional promise for the future: the orderly development of recreation facilities, strictly controlled by the tribe in limited areas on the lake, could, according to a survey made for the Paiutes, provide steady jobs for the unemployed and make the reservation economically self-sustaining. Outside capital was available for such development, but not for a lake whose shoreline was steadily declining.

The tribe's principal rival for the Truckee's water, the Newlands Project, was originally planned by the government to irrigate 232,800 acres of desert with water from the Truckee, and another 137,000 acres with water from the Carson River, which runs somewhat parallel to, and south of, the Truckee. The available supply of water, as of the soils, however, was grossly overestimated by the Reclamation Service, and from its inception, the project never had more than 50,000 to 65,000 acres under irrigation with water from both rivers. Fifty years after its beginning, the project looked like an old, settled farm area, with many grassy pastures, fields, gardens, and stands of trees, all watered by canals, and new and old barns and farm and ranch houses shaded by trees and fronting on highways and secondary roads that laced the district. Except at its edges, where the project bordered on the dusty sagebrush desert and muddy flats where temporary runoff flooding occurred, a visitor could imagine that he was almost anywhere in the rural Midwest.

Altogether, the water diverted from the Truckee to the project served about 1,025 farms on which dwelled approximately 5,800 people. The farmers produced mainly hay and alfalfa for cattle; some barley, wheat, and other grains; corn silage;

and a small amount of vegetables and fruits, including pota-
toes and melons. In the winter thousands of cattle and sheep
were brought in from the ranges to be fattened for market. In
addition, some farmers maintained dairy herds, raised turkeys
and other poultry, and kept bees. Most of the whites, typically
industrious, middle-income farm families, lived on the lands
of the project, but many who owned uneconomical one- and
two-acre lots with water rights leased their land to bigger oper-
ators and lived in the town of Fallon. The latter, with a population close to three thousand, was the principal shopping
and marketing town on the project and, except for a garish
gambling casino, might, with its wide streets and easy, friendly
pace, have passed for any county seat in the agricultural West.

The average gross crop value of the Newlands Project
amounted to no more than $4.5 million per year, and from
1909 until 1965 the value of all crops produced during those
fifty-six years totaled only $104 million. Those figures assumed
significance when matched as achievements of "progress"
against what was being denied to the Indians. A 1964 report by
a federal task force concluded, for example, that if the decline
of the lake were halted and recreational facilities built on its
shores, recreational income at the lake would soon exceed the
annual crop value of the irrigation project and within fifteen
years this income would increase to more than three times the
annual value of the project. A later National Park Service study
even upped that figure considerably.

Many people on the project were not unsympathetic to
the plight of Pyramid Lake, but they argued bitterly that they
and their families had long since acquired legal rights to the
water, and it was just too bad if there was not enough in the
Truckee for the lake as well. One of the largest landowners

on the project, Carl F. Dodge, a Nevada state senator whose fourteen hundred acres had been owned by his family for fifty years, reflected the attitude of many of the whites when the Paiutes began their fight. If the water was more valuable for the purpose of keeping Pyramid Lake alive than for keeping the project's farms producing, Dodge said, "then let them buy the water rights and take them over. All I can say about it is if they feel that way, money talks."

No one believed that such a course was economically or, in Nevada, politically practicable. Ranchers and farmers formed a powerful element in the state's political life, and with few areas in Nevada able to support agriculture, it was a safe bet that the state would vigorously resist permitting one of its biggest agricultural districts to return to desert. Moreover, the farms were no longer the only users of the project's water. Through the years, excess "tail water" draining off the farms had built up previously existing marshes in the adjoining desert. Like Pyramid Lake, these became the habitat of large flocks of ducks and other waterfowl and attracted gun clubs. At the same time, other waste water created a partly irrigated pasture, which farmers of the project put to use as a common grazing ground. In 1948 the Department of the Interior's Fish and Wildlife Service made a pact with the irrigators on the Newlands Project and Nevada's Fish and Game Commission. Out of the waterfowl marshlands were created the Stillwater Wildlife Management Area (a public shooting ground) and the Stillwater National Wildlife Refuge (a protected area), and the Interior Department's Bureau of Land Management also agreed to develop and improve the pasture. Once established, both the government's wildlife area and the pasture became recognized "users" of Truckee water. The effect, therefore, was to provide water for Stillwater ducks and project cows, while continuing to deny it to the Indians and Pyramid Lake. And in still another development, Lahontan Reservoir, a large storage lake dammed up by the Bureau of Reclamation to feed the Truckee and Carson river waters to the project as they were needed, had begun to thrive as a recreational center. The very water diverted away from the Indians' lake was being used by whites for boating, fishing, and swimming on an artificially created lake less than thirty-five miles away.

All of this had to be reckoned with by the Paiutes in their late-hour attempt to save Pyramid Lake, and it was further complicated by non-Indian users of water upstream from the lake on both the Truckee and the Carson. The number of those users, including other farmers as well as domestic and industrial interests around Reno, had increased greatly since 1905, and not surprisingly their competitive claims to the limited supply of water had grown more complex. A determined Indian fight for their right to water would threaten all non-Indian users, becoming capable of unsettling many, if not all, of the recognized water rights on the two rivers.

On the Truckee those rights were firmly established in 1944 by a federal district court decision known as the Orr Water Ditch Company decree. The Departments of Interior and Justice did represent the Paiutes at that time, but actually worsened the Indians' position by permitting what amounted to the legalization of Pyramid Lake's destruction. The Winters Doctrine by then had been in existence for many years; the government clearly had the opportunity to right an old wrong by insisting on a court grant of adequate water, under the doctrine, for the lake. But the government asked for no water right at all for the lake, and it got none. The decree gave the Paiutes a right to a meager amount of water, but with the provision that it could be used only for irrigation or stock and domestic purposes. Moreover, the amount of water which they could draw in any year was based on how much land they had under irrigation, and since they were never able to irrigate more than the small strip along the lower Truckee bottomlands, they never thereafter had the legal right to draw more than a fifth of the water granted to them—and none of it, legally, could be used for Pyramid Lake!

In actuality, Pyramid Lake continued to receive water from springs and underground sources below Derby Dam, from leaks in the dam and in the first section of the project's canal, and particularly from floodwater from heavy snowpacks in the Sierras, which the Newlands Project did not need and could not divert and which flowed past the dam to the lower Truckee. Under the Orr Ditch decree, however, the Indians had no right even to the unused floodwater, and so in 1955, when the Bureau of Reclamation announced plans to build new dams on the headwaters of the Truckee and Carson Rivers to control and use the floodwaters, it stated specifically that none of the new project's saved floodwater would be made available to the Indians. This was too much for the Paiutes, who, despite their sparse resources, sought local legal help and began their fight.

On their own, rather than relying on the Bureau of Indian Affairs, they took their case to the Interior and Insular Affairs committees of both the House of Representatives and the Senate, which were then considering the Washoe Project, of which the proposed new flood-control dams were a part. Both committees responded with reports that noted officially for the first time that Pyramid Lake's crisis was due largely to acts of the federal government, and that the government had never undertaken compensatory measures to maintain the lake as a fishery and now ought to do so. When the bill authorizing the Washoe Project passed Congress on August 1, 1956, it directed that facilities be provided to increase water releases to Pyramid Lake to restore its fishery.

By 1963, however, when the Bureau of Reclamation finally firmed up its plans for the project, it revealed, on the contrary, that the new dams would cause the lake to go down even more rapidly. In April 1964, responding to protests by the Paiutes, Secretary of the Interior Stewart Udall appointed an intra-departmental task force to examine the claims of everyone, including the Indians. A preliminary report, completed in September, indicated concern over how to increase, rather than decrease, the water going to Pyramid Lake. It proposed certain modifications in the Washoe Project's plan and economies in the use of water by the Newlands Project. But it recommended no specified grant of water to the lake, nor did it guarantee that the lake would not suffer from the Washoe Project. Ignoring the possibility of a Winters Doctrine suit on behalf of the tribe, it said only that the government should exercise "every effort to maintain the greatest practicable flow of water into Pyramid Lake."

When public hearings on the report were held in Reno, the Paiutes and various Indian and white supporters, who were beginning to be attracted to the cause of the tribe, argued angrily against the omission of a guaranteed grant of water to build up and stabilize the lake.

"Why tell us you will give us as much water as possible?" demanded Avery Winnemucca, a descendant of one of the tribe's best-known Leaders after whom Nevada whites, ironically, had named one of their cities. "Why don't you be specific? At least you did that with others. You've got figures to prove that there is so much allocation for this and so much for that, all in figures. But Pyramid Lake, no. You give us as much as possible."

Other pro-lake, pro-Indian speakers went further, telling Udall's task force members that any discussion of the Washoe Project was premature until the government, under the Winters Doctrine, took steps to guarantee the lake's preservation. "Here in Nevada a terrible crime has been committed against Nevada's first citizens," charged the Reverend H. Clyde Mathews, chairman of the Nevada Advisory Committee to the United States Commission on Civil Rights. Then he added what few others in Nevada had previously admitted openly:

> If this property had been owned by six hundred white stockholders in an irrigation company, would this property have been taken without compensation, *or at all?* . . . The United States government itself has been discriminatory on the basis of race, creed, and national origin in the manner in which the Nevada Indians' water and fishery rights have been allowed to be denied, ignored, manipulated, and in effect destroyed.

Despite such pleas, the task force's final report, reflecting the powerful influence of the Bureau of Reclamation, refused to recommend that the government go to court to seek a water grant for the lake. There was no time for a long, complex water-rights case. A water users' vote of approval for the Washoe Project was waiting to be held. In addition, the Department of the Interior feared that litigation on behalf of the Paiutes might lead to an internal conflict of mammoth proportions within the Department: the successful prosecution of the Indians' case could endanger not only the Newlands Project but other reclamation projects that Indian tribes elsewhere might claim had overridden their rights. All the Department could do for Pyramid Lake, the task force noted, was to undertake certain measures—including the salvaging of excess water, the elimination of seepage and waste in the Newlands Project's canals, and the imposition of regulations and controls at the project— that would increase the amount of water available to the lake. The carrying out of the recommendations would guarantee a considerable increase of water to the lake, Udall told the Indians, and with that promise they withdrew their opposition to the Washoe Project. On November 3, 1964, the white voters in the affected Nevada river basins approved it.

The Bureau of Reclamation did make efforts to conserve Truckee River water by setting up certain minimal controls on the Newlands Project, but it soon became questionable whether the Indians would benefit. Despite the Paiutes' appeals for a statement of a legal basis for the water Udall had promised them, the Department of the Interior refused to assert that the United States owned, controlled, and had the right to deliver to Pyramid Lake the water it was going to save on the Newlands Project, and thus left that water open to appropriation by non-Indian users. In 1968 that threat surfaced with a vengeance. Since 1955, California and Nevada had been working on a settlement that would divide between the two states the waters flowing from Lake Tahoe. All the water in question (including the Truckee and Carson) passed through California before entering Nevada, so California, too, had a claim to it. After thirteen years of work, a document was drafted that not only limited the Indians' water to what the Orr Ditch decree gave them in 1944, but *went beyond that by expressly preventing the federal government and the Indians from ever going to court to seek more water for Pyramid Lake.* Henceforth, the Paiutes would have to apply to Nevada for any water saved by the Newlands Project, and the threat of the Winters Doctrine to the whites would disappear.

The compact was too raw even for the Department of the Interior, which did not care to turn over the fate of federal water rights to the states. The Department registered its objections, with the implied threat that Congress would not ratify an agreement that gave up federal rights. But the Nevada legislature took up the document all the same, and after brief hearings, approved the compact. In California it was a different story. Unwilling to risk rejection by Congress, and appealed to by the Northern Paiute Indians, the National Congress of American Indians (the case had now become a national Indian cause), and many Indian and white friends, the California Assembly Committee on Natural Resources and Conservation refused to approve the compact in the form adopted by Nevada.

On July 6, 1969, the new Secretary of the Interior, Walter J. Hickel, met at Lake Tahoe with governors Ronald Reagan of California and Paul Laxalt of Nevada to try to break the deadlock. Their solution, announced to the press after a ninety-minute meeting on the lake in the cabin of a cruiser owned by Reno gambler William Harrah, made matters worse. Without consulting the Indians, they had agreed that engineers should hasten Pyramid Lake's gradual decline by draining it down to a level at which it would stabilize.

As Vine Deloria, Jr., the Sioux Indian author of *Custer Died for Your Sins*, charged at the time: "It was the same logic used by the Army to destroy a Vietnamese village—'We had to destroy the village to save it.' It naturally followed that the only way to save Pyramid Lake was to drain it."

This weird proposal, which would have dropped the lake abruptly by 152 feet and left it a salt lake in a huge basin of mud flats, outraged not only the Paiutes, who could not believe that the three governments would commit such a flagrant robbery of their property, but large numbers of non-Indians in Nevada, who suddenly saw Pyramid Lake as a priceless gem of the desert and an important recreational asset for the whole state. The public outcry forced the three officials to drop the plan hurriedly and, instead, set up another task force of federal and state appointees who would try to satisfy the supporters of the lake so that a new version of the compact could be written. Even that task force got off to a controversial start, when Governor Laxalt claimed the right to name a Paiute representative to the body. Knowing that the group would be dominated by the Bureau of Reclamation and "stacked" against them, and that any Indian on the body would be participating in the tribe's destruction, the Paiutes refused to have anything to do with it. In their view, their only hope lay now in persuading the government to file a Winters Doctrine suit for their water. Repeated appeals to the Department of the Interior to do so, however, fell on deaf ears. Meanwhile, the Bureau of Reclamation hurried ahead with its Washoe Project, and the interstate compact task force worked out a compromise agreement which tried to eliminate some of the most objectionable features of the original document. The Paiutes still opposed it, since it offered no solution to the lake's problem.

By 1970, the Paiutes appeared to have reached the end of the road. A tangle of decrees, statutes, regulations, and water rights and laws had been used by the Nevada and federal governments to ensure the continued taking of their water. They were almost out of money for legal fees and, on their own, could go no further. In January 1970—as a result of a request for some information and advice from their lawyer, Robert D. Stitser of Reno, to the California Indian Legal Services, an Office of Economic Opportunity public service group of attorneys who had worked successfully on cases with California tribes and were knowledgeable on Indian and water law—new help was suddenly offered them. With the assistance of Robert Pelcyger, one of the CILS lawyers, Stitser and the tribe began to prepare a Winters Doctrine suit, which the tribe would file on its own, and to look for money with which to enlist the services of hydrologists and other expert witnesses. In June, financial aid became available when the Ford Foundation in New York gave California Indian Legal Services a large planning grant to develop a national non-profit organization known as the Native American Rights Fund,* which would provide legal services to Indians without charge. On August 22, 1970, the Paiutes, represented by Stitser and Pelcyger, who had become a staff member of the Native American Rights Fund— and also supported by a national Indian-interest organization, the Association on American Indian Affairs—filed a suit in the U.S. District Court for the District of Columbia against the Secretary of the Interior and the Attorney General of the United States, asking that the former be ordered to deliver enough water to Pyramid Lake to stabilize it by eliminating the waste-

---

*   Eds. note: The Native American Rights Fund, which relocated to Boulder the following year, is still an active nonprofit that uses existing laws and treaties to ensure that U.S. state governments and the U.S. federal government live up to their legal obligations.

ful use of water in the Truckee and Carson Rivers, and that the latter be required to seek "a judicial determination" of the Indians' right to Truckee water.

The first priority was to get enough water to the lake as quickly as possible in order to halt its further decline. The suit held that that could be done simply by stopping the waste of Truckee and Carson River waters by the whites and making the saved water available to the lake. The facts concerning the waste were set forth compellingly to the court. For one thing, the tribe's attorneys revealed, the Bureau of Reclamation had for years permitted the Newlands Project to receive up to nine feet of water for each of its acres, when under the Orr Ditch decree and another decree known as the Alpine decree, which related to the use of Carson River water, it should only have received from 2.92 to 4.5 feet per acre. Much of this illegally taken water, which could have gone to the lake, had been wasted. Moreover, Secretary Udall's promise to the Indians to impose regulations and controls on the project to stop the greedy waste and make the saved water available to the lake had been subverted.

It was estimated that to stabilize Pyramid Lake at its present level, the lake needed to receive an annual average of 135,000 acre-feet of water more than it had been getting from the Truckee (an acre-foot being enough water to cover one acre with one foot of water). For approximately fifty years, said the suit, the Secretary of the Interior's agents (the Bureau of Reclamation) had been permitting the waste of up to 200,000 acre-feet of water annually. If the court ordered the Secretary to stop the waste and send the saved water down the Truckee, Pyramid Lake could, at least, be stabilized, without forcing anyone to give up water to which they had a legal right under the Orr decree.

The whites of the Newlands Project saw it otherwise. Orr decree or not, the Bureau of Reclamation had permitted them to receive 406,000 acre-feet of water a year (far in excess of the decree's limitations), and they wanted that figure adhered to. Their pressure, and that of the Nevada state government, which supported them against the Indians, registered strongly in the Interior Department in Washington. At first, Judge Gerhard A. Gesell of the District Court urged the Secretary and the Indians' attorneys to try to settle the Paiutes' suit by negotiation. It proved impossible. The government's lawyers promised that the Department would issue new regulations concerning the Newlands Project's use of water in 1972, after first consulting the tribe. The promise was not observed. In April 1972, without notice to the Indians, new government regulations appeared that made the situation worse than before. All they said was that measures would be taken to ensure that the water would be put to better use. There was, however, no mention of how much water the Newlands Project could receive, thus permitting the irrigators to draw all the water they wanted, without limit.

The Paiutes' lawyers immediately obtained an order from Judge Gesell voiding the new "non-regulations" and, for the moment, reimposing the 406,000 acre-feet limit, which the project had been using. At the same time, the judge decided that the case must now go to trial. But there were other government manipulations. Trying to halt the litigation, Secretary of the Interior Rogers C. B. Morton announced that he had, at last, requested the Attorney General to institute a suit "for the recognition and protection of a water right for the mainte-nance of Pyramid Lake"—after seventy years, the government would finally go to court for the Paiutes' Winters Doctrine water rights. It was obvious to Judge Gesell, however, that such a suit might take ten to fifteen years before a final decree was issued. There was no need to wait, he said, "to resolve what seems to me to be a matter that requires more immedi-ate attention"—the question of saving the lake with water that the government could make available to it. Complaining that the Interior Department's actions in handling the Paiutes' case that was before him had "bamboozled" him—"I suppose that is the politest word," he said—he scheduled the trial for July.

The Department's "bamboozling," in truth, was an attempt to get out of a situation that was beginning to concern the Nixon administration, which prided itself on its good relations with Native Americans. Largely as a result of the Pyramid Lake case, presidential advisors in the White House had recognized the conflict of interest within the Department of the Interior that had worked against Indians, and in 1970 the Administra-tion had sent to Congress a bill to establish an Indian Trust Counsel Authority that would be independent of the Depart-ments of the Interior and Justice, and would be expressly empowered to bring suits for Indians, even against branches of the United States government, in cases involving land, water, or other natural resource rights. With such an Authority, the Paiutes would not have to be dependent for legal action on the Department of the Interior, whose policy makers and solicitors had been torn between them and the Bureau of Reclamation. Congress, however, had done nothing about the Trust Counsel bill, the Administration had failed to press it, and the legisla-tion had been buried and forgotten. But publicity about the

Pyramid Lake case had increased, and the White House and
the Secretary of the Interior were receiving criticism from the
public and the media. In January 1972, Democratic Senators
Edward M. Kennedy of Massachusetts and John Tunney of California had held a public hearing in Nevada on the plight of the
Paiutes and their lake, and their lambasting of the Bureau of
Reclamation had received ample coverage by the press. Moreover, the interstate task force had completed the writing of new
recommendations, which had urged the elimination of waste
to make available about 95,000 acre-feet of water for the lake,
less than it needed, but had suggested, also, that the only way
to solve the Paiutes' problem was to go to court and settle their
right to water.

All this was in the background of Secretary Morton's decision to file a Winters Doctrine suit for the tribe. It did not halt
the Paiutes' case against the Secretary in Judge Gesell's court,
but the Interior Department hoped that it would demonstrate
the good intentions of the administration. In addition, because
of the length of time the suit would take, it would further stall
an unpopular readjustment of the amount of water the Newlands Project could receive and confer on a future administra-
tration the problem of facing the consequences of a decision
that might give the Paiutes water that was now being used by
somebody else.

On June 5, 1972, a month before the District Court trial was
to begin, Secretary Morton announced that new regulations for
the salvaging of water going to the Newlands Project—as well
as a decision about how much water the Project would receive
after the saving and how much, therefore, would be available
to Pyramid Lake—would be made public in September. The
trial was postponed to await these decisions, and in Septem-

ber the Secretary made his announcement. Once more, it was a disappointment to the Paiutes and the court. The regulations were to be voluntary, rather than mandatory, and would only reduce the amount of water going to the Newlands Project from 406,000 to 378,000 acre-feet a year, still much more than the Project's entitlement under the applicable decrees. The total savings for use by Pyramid Lake would be a mere 28,000 acre-feet a year, far short of what it required if it were to be stabilized.

The tribal lawyers' protests to the Secretary met with rebuffs. Instead, the Department went ahead with the Winters Doctrine case. On September 22, the Solicitor General of the United States, going directly to the Supreme Court, asked that body to exercise original jurisdiction and hear a complaint of the United States against the states of Nevada and California, which sought a decree

> declaring the right of the United States for the benefit of the Pyramid Lake Paiute Tribe of Indians to the use of sufficient waters of the Truckee River to fulfill the purposes for which the Pyramid Lake Reservation was created, including the maintenance and preservation of Pyramid Lake and the maintenance of the lower reaches of the Truckee River as a natural spawning ground for fish and other purposes beneficial to and satisfying such use to be with a priority of November 29, 1859.

With the government thus finally pursuing the long-range rights case, the tribe commenced its own action for immediate water for the lake in Judge Gesell's district court. After a four-day trial in October, Judge Gesell, on November 8, ruled decisively for the Paiutes, calling the Secretary's September decision on the amount of water the Newlands Project could have "an abuse of discretion and not in accordance with law," and adding that "the effect was to deprive the tribe of water without legal justification." He ordered the Secretary to submit to him by January 1, 1973, new regulations that would result in the Newlands Project's receipt of an amount of water "wholly consistent with the Secretary's fiduciary duty to the Tribe."

The decision was historic. Not only did it direct the delivery of adequate water to stabilize Pyramid Lake until the Paiutes' full water rights could be ruled upon in the Winters Doctrine case, but it set a legal precedent for all other American Indian tribes in their conflicts with the federal government as trustee of their property. All previous cases against the government had been limited to the seeking of damages after the fact for Indian property that had already been lost, mismanaged, or damaged. This was the first litigation brought by Indians that successfully forced the government as trustee and fiduciary to carry out its obligation to protect Indian property. The government decided not to appeal Judge Gesell's decision, and the Department of the Interior set about implementing the court's directive ordering more thorough and effective waste controls and freeing some of the Washoe Project's water for Pyramid Lake. At the same time, the court ordered the Newlands Project to be limited to the use of 350,000 acre-feet of water in 1973 and 288,129 acre-feet in 1974.

Though the government observed the court's decision, the farmers of the Newlands Project did not. Entering Nevada courts, they contested the limits that the federal court had placed on their water supply, and year after year continued to draw what they wanted. By the early 1980s, they were still receiving up to 400,000 acre-feet annually, and it was clear that they would try to continue to do so until the Winters Doctrine, or some additional litigation in the future, firmly established the amount of water to which they had a right. Nevertheless, the Bureau of Reclamation's measures, together with the good fortune of a series of years in which the volume of water in the Truckee was above average, helped the lake, which remained relatively stable. In the absence of a definitely specified water right of its own, however, its fate continued to be uncertain. In good years, the level of its water rose dramatically—even providing sufficient inflow to the lower river to permit the fish to ascend to their old spawning grounds—but in bad years it fell. Pursuing a fisheries restoration program, the tribe contracted first with the Nevada Fish and Game Department and then with the U.S. Fish and Wildlife Service for the annual planting of the lake with Lahontan trout fingerlings and other species from state and federal hatcheries, and eventually obtained federal funds for two hatcheries of its own on the reservation. The maintenance of the lake as a popular family recreational area and a fishery for sportsmen brought increasing income to the Paiutes through the 1970s and inspired new hope that the reservation could ultimately become self-sufficient. Organizing a Pyramid Lake Indian Tribal Enterprises, the Indians trained tribal members to manage the expanding fisheries restoration program, which included—when there was adequate flow— the maintenance of the lower Truckee as a revived spawning ground for the natural propagation of the fish. The success of that project, however, rested on the fate of the government's suit for their water rights, which they hoped would ensure the spawning grounds enough water each year.

As foreseen, the Winters Doctrine case was a protracted

one. The Supreme Court, which ruled in June 1973, declined to exercise original jurisdiction, saying that the case should be filed in a lower federal court in Nevada. In December, the Justice Department did so, initiating a suit in the District Court against the Truckee-Carson Irrigation District, the state of Nevada, the cities of Reno and Sparks, and approximately seventeen thousand individually named persons, firms, partnerships, and corporations, all users of Truckee river water, to reopen the Orr Ditch decree of 1944 and establish a permanent water right for Pyramid Lake and the lower Truckee River fishery. The tribe, represented by Robert Stitser and the Native American Rights Fund, joined the United States as plaintiff.

The case, however, did not at first go well for the Indians. On December 8, 1977, the court dismissed the suit, holding that the failure of the government to claim a water right for the lake and the fishery during the Orr Ditch adjudications had effectively ended that right, and that the United States and the Paiutes were now barred by the 1944 decree from a right. In other words, the Department of the Interior's dereliction of its trust duty in 1944 had lost the Paiutes their water rights, and it was now too late to reopen the matter. But the government and the tribe appealed to the Ninth Circuit Court of Appeals, and on June 15, 1981, that court upheld the right of the tribe to sufficient water for its fishery, ruling that the Secretary of the Interior was not authorized to take Indian water rights for a reclamation project, and that when the United States represented Indians in litigation, it was obligated to act as a trustee and not compromise the Indians' interests because of conflicting obligations.

The Native American Rights Fund hailed this as a landmark decision for Indians in general, but it was only another step along the road for the Paiutes. Their opponents immediately petitioned the Circuit Court for a rehearing. By early 1982, they had not received an answer, but it seemed certain that, one way or the other, the case would eventually go to the Supreme Court. Meanwhile, facing the prospect of continued litigation and a possibility that in the end they might not be able to reopen the Orr decision, the tribal and government attorneys worked together on what they hoped might become an alternative solution—a final negotiated settlement of all the Pyramid Lake water litigation.

Whatever occurred ultimately, however, one fact loomed large. The doughty fight of the small Pauite tribe in the Nevada desert had not been in vain. At a minimum, it had saved Pyramid Lake, at least for a time, had given its trustee a sobering lesson, and had demonstrated to other tribes that they could put an end to the continuing theft of their water. By 1977, the struggle to regain and preserve tribal water had become one of the foremost phenomena of Indian affairs in the western half of the country. Dozens of tribes were in some type of litigation to hold on to water they owned, or to get back what had been taken illegally from them. Addressing a meeting of tribal leaders in October of that year, the Assistant Secretary of the Interior for Indian Affairs, Forrest J. Gerard, a Blackfoot Indian, read off a list of tribes that were battling with non-Indian society over rights to water. It was an imposing roll call of large and small tribes in every part of the West: the Yakimas, Crows, Arapahos, the Jicarilla, White Mountain, and Mescalero Apaches, the Zunis, Blackfeet, and Northern Cheyenne, the Moapa, Hoopa, Navajo, Cocopah, and Agua Caliente of Palm Springs, the Osage, Colvilles, Duck Valley Shoshone-Paiutes, and Crow Creek Sioux, the Spokans, Muckleshoots, Umatillas, and Pawnees, the Cherokees, Chemehuevis, three Ute tribes in Utah, various Pueblos in New Mexico, the Pimas and Papagos in Arizona, and on and on.

The sudden Indian assertiveness frightened and angered both urban and rural whites in the West, who saw a threat to the water they had been using and the water they planned on having for future needs. The Winters Doctrine for a tribe seemed to imply to non-Indians the disintegration of all western water law, the voiding or clouding of all established water claims, and a new start with new rules and disastrously reduced rights to water. At the same time, corporations, drawn to the West to develop energy resources or for other reasons, as well as military and other branches of the government, with plans for large-scale facilities in sparsely populated parts of the West, viewed the new Indian water claims as obstacles and nuisances that made it harder for them to acquire the water they needed for their operations. The fears and frustrations of all these groups led to political and legal counterthrusts, designed to halt the tribes in their tracks.

As early as 1973, a National Water Commission report foresaw the coming conflict, but recognizing the growing non-Indian municipal, agricultural, industrial, and recreational needs for water in the West, recommended policies that, in effect, justified by expediency the seizure of Indian water rights. Nothing was done with the report, but its recommendations were not forgotten. In 1976, the courts dealt the Indians a setback. A piece of legislation known as the McCarran Amendment (for the Nevada senator, Pat McCarran) had earlier given states the right to litigate against the federal government in state courts in cases affecting *federal* water rights—rights to water that the federal government claimed it owned. In a suit

known as the Akin case, involving some Indian water rights, it
was now established that states, under the McCarran Amendment, could also pursue cases affecting *Indian* water rights
in state courts. To the Indians, this seemed a violation of the
Constitution, but it stuck. Though Indian water cases could
also be tried in federal courts, the right to decide them now
depended, in part, on who got to which court first. But the
possibility of a trial in a state court was a damaging development for the tribes, for, as noted earlier, the odds were that the
Indians would receive less equitable treatment there than in a
more independent federal court.

Opposition to the Indians' water offensives continued, and
in 1977 President Jimmy Carter, aware of the growing competition for the resource, issued a national water management policy. As a step toward its implementation, his Water
Resources Council, headed by Secretary of the Interior Cecil
Andrus, set up a policy committee within the Interior Department, chaired by Guy Martin, Assistant Secretary for Land and
Water Resources, to carry out a nine-point plan. One of the
points was to determine, or quantify, federal and Indian water
rights in the country. The tribes immediately objected, both to
having their water rights lumped again with federal rights and
to having the Department, which experience had taught them
to distrust, quantify their rights for them. Many tribes did not
yet know their future water needs, were not ready to have their
rights declared and made public, and, when they were ready,
preferred to go into a federal court with their own lawyers
and have their rights established under the Winters Doctrine.
Moreover, they were angry that the Interior Department had
not consulted them.

The Secretary's Water Resources Council backtracked

slightly, agreeing to keep federal and Indian water rights sepa- rated (they were "not the same," the Council admitted), and promised not to publish a paper on Indian rights to the use of water. But a presidential water policy message on June 6, 1978, again implied the sameness of federal and Indian water rights and called on the tribes to quantify their rights by nego- tiation with the states. The message further disturbed many tribes, as well as national Indian organizations, showing not only an ignorance of the tribes' constitutional and historical reliance on dealing exclusively with the federal government, but a lack of sensitivity on the part of their trustee by asking them to negotiate with their principal adversaries. Negotia- tions, moreover, they pointed out, would only be about giv- ing up some of the water they then owned, or to which they had a right. In negotiations, the states could only win, and the Indians could only lose. Other tribes, however, believing that negotiation might be the only practical way to obtain federal financial assistance for water development projects, decided to engage in the settlement process, for without such projects their paper water rights would be virtually worthless. In addi- tion, negotiation was working beneficially for some tribes, like the Ak-Chin in Arizona, and was viewed by others, like the Pyramid Lake Paiutes, as perhaps providing the best prospect for getting a maximum of what they sought.

Nevertheless, the pressure of western business, agricul- tural, and political interests to limit the Indians' water rights and establish those limits permanently continued to be felt by the Department of the Interior, and on August 28, 1978, Assis- tant Secretary for Indian Affairs Gerard, one of the Depart- ment's policy committee members, compliantly circulated a memorandum to the tribes, stating that negotiations with the states should proceed, and under the lead of the Department. Tribal resistance forced a temporary shelving of the policy, and on April 5, 1979, the Department again took to litigation, filing suits in the federal district court in Montana, as mentioned at the beginning of this chapter, to determine the Winters Doctrine water rights of five tribes in that state.

Montana scored a temporary victory when, later that year, the federal court dismissed the suits on the ground that they must be heard in the state courts, where Montana had wanted them to be tried in the first place. The federal government, however, appealed to the Ninth Circuit Court, and the cases continued into the 1980s at the federal level. In 1979, also, the Montana legislature created a nine-member Reserved Water Rights Compact Commission whose designated task was to try to settle the state's water conflicts with the tribes, as well as with the federal government, by negotiation rather than litigation. Like many tribes elsewhere, the Montana tribes considered which course would serve them best—litigation, negotiation, or congressional legislation—and four of them (later reduced to three, when the Flatheads backed away) entered negotiations with the state, though with such skepticism of results that they also continued the court cases.

As long as Indians continue to assert their water rights, and courts recognize them as their rightful property, conflict and confrontation will go on. The Indians need their water to survive. The whites want not to keep the water they have, but to secure as much Indian water as they can get for their expanding needs.*

---

* Eds. note: There is now sufficient water in Pyramid Lake to sustain a fish population—something the tribe and the state, in its tourist advertising, are proud of. Nevertheless, water litigation continues. A "landmark" piece of water

And so, the bitterness—and confusion—built. On March 24, 1981, the Supreme Court opened a whole new Pandora's box of potential conflicts with its ruling in another Montana case that the state owned, and could regulate the use of, the bed and banks of the Bighorn River as it flowed through the Crow Reservation. This decision, giving to the state rights to, and jurisdiction over, property within the reservation that the tribe felt was its own according to treaties, raised a storm among the Indians. The state, and not the tribe, could now apparently control the use of the property inside the reservation for fishing, recreation, mining, energy development, and any other activity by non-Indians as well as Indians. The decision, said the Native American Rights Fund, affected tribes everywhere in the country, throwing "the issue of title ownership to riverbeds, lake beds, and tidelands on reservations up in the air, suggesting dozens of treaties nationwide could now be contested by non-Indians desiring control of these waterways." Most immediately threatened were the Flatheads, who were pressing a similar case in Montana over the right of ownership of the bed of Flathead Lake on their reservation.

At almost the same time, in Arizona, where in 1935 protesting Pima Indians had been barred from a Phoenix courtroom in which U.S. attorneys—supposedly representing them as their trustee—shamelessly gave away their water to a copper

legislation passed Congress in September 2014. According to attorneys for the tribe: "Passage of the legislation brings to a close more than eight years of litigation and congressional consideration of a conflict between the Pyramid Lake Paiute Tribe and the Fish Springs Ranch of Carson City, Nev. The dispute centered on a water pipeline constructed by Fish Springs adjacent to the Pyramid Lake Reservation." Fish Springs agreed to pay $7.2 million to the tribe and transfer to the tribe title to several thousand acres of land adjacent to the reservation, in return for the withdrawal of the tribe's legal challenges to the project. Congressional ratification of the settlement was required and obtained.

company and other white users, there was also turmoil. As one of his last acts in office, in December 1980, Secretary of the Interior Andrus made a first gesture of recompense to the Pimas, as well as to the Papagos and other Arizona Indians, who for so long had been callously robbed of their water and reduced to poverty, by signing contracts for annual allocations of a total of 309,828 acre-feet of water to be delivered to their reservations from the mammoth Central Arizona Project when it is completed in the mid-1980s. Among much of Arizona's white population, an explosion of fury followed. The irate protests included a large advertisement in the December 7 issue of the *Arizona Republic*, headlined in bold black letters: "LIKE GIVING HEROIN TO AN ADDICT."

10

The Great Northwest Fishing War

◇◇◇

Unlike many of the Indian–non-Indian struggles described in these pages, the fishing wars in the Puget Sound region during the 1960s and '70s resonated throughout the nation. Key actions in this struggle, whether individual or legal, served as a catalyst for the Red Power movement and a precedent for other Indian actions throughout the nation in defense of treaty rights long ignored but now called into force. The wide-ranging interpretation of the whole episode is deserving of the detailed narrative that follows, in this third and final chapter drawn from Now That the Buffalo's Gone *(1982).*

We read of people and places, and we learn of legal principles and fishing practices in a seemingly endless maze of contention. Finally, one result is clear. Josephy could write with certainty, "The small tribes of the Puget Sound area were no longer forgotten, demeaned, or overlooked peoples. The Indians had come back, proud of their heritage and the chapter they had added to their history."

In January 1961, James and Louis Starr, Jr., two Muckleshoot Indian fishermen in western Washington State, and Leonard Wayne, a Puyallup Indian who had been raised as a Muckleshoot, set their gill nets in the Green River, a stream that flows from the Cascade Mountains into the southern part of Puget Sound. The next morning, they returned and hauled in their catch—a single coho, or silver, salmon. Suddenly, seven Washington game wardens, with drawn revolvers, burst from hiding places along the bank and arrested the three men for the double crime of fishing out of season and using nets. They were taken to a Seattle court, given suspended fines of $250 apiece, and held in jail for two weeks until other Indians managed to bail them out. Their cases were appealed, and twenty-two months later, in November 1962, they were acquitted by Judge James W. Hodson of Washington's King County Superior Court, who decided that they had been fishing legally in accordance with rights contained in a treaty which their ancestors had made with the federal government.

The episode was not unprecedented. Throughout the Northwest, as well as in Michigan and other parts of the United States, fishing-oriented tribes had had histories of tense and inconclusive conflicts with state and local officials over whether their treaties gave them fishing rights not possessed by others. The 1961 Muckleshoot case, however, had a special significance, for despite its outcome, it signaled the start of a determined drive by northwestern state agencies and non-Indian sport and commercial fishermen to end Indian treaty fishing rights in that part of the nation once and for all. The struggle lasted for years around Puget Sound and on the Columbia River and became increasingly sensational. It was marked by violent battles, hundreds of arrests, demonstrations, the intercession of sympathetic non-Indian celebrities, conflicting court rulings, and, ultimately, by landmark judicial decisions that affected not only fisheries in the Northwest but the future of Indian fishing rights everywhere. In a broader

context, additionally, its impact on Indian-white relations was
historic: it helped to give rise to an anti-Indian backlash movement whose political influence was felt by tribes in all parts
of the country. But, also, it became a catalyst for Indian militancy in the late 1960s and the 1970s, feeding the flames of
Red Power activism, ushering in an era of such confrontations
as those at Alcatraz, the Bureau of Indian Affairs building in
Washington, D.C., and Wounded Knee, and providing inspiration and strength to a developing thrust among all tribes for
self-determination and sovereignty.

To those Indians who were involved in it, the fishing rights
struggle was a fight for survival. During its course, they suffered physical attacks and beatings, jailings, the confiscation
of their boats, fishing gear, and other property, the loss of their
livelihood, and bitter persecution and abuse. Though most
of them were members of some of the smallest and weak-
est tribes in the country, they were arrayed against almost the
entire white population and the full power of the administrative and judicial establishments of their states. Sometimes they
were opposed also by the elected leaders and other members
of their own tribes. But they persisted, and in the war of long
odds that was waged against them, they came, in time, to
loom as modern-day Native American patriots.

The issue of Indian treaty fishing rights has often been
attended more by emotion and racist prejudice than by understanding. In the beginning, when abundant fish filled the lakes
and rivers of all the continent, there was enough for everyone, and conflicts over fishing rights between Indians and
non-Indians were rare. But as the number of commercial and
sport fishermen multiplied, as their catch increased, as logging, pollution, dams, and other works of man combined to

deplete the fish population, the competition for what remained became intense. States issued fishing rules and regulations, instituted conservation measures, and embarked on hatchery and restocking programs. Often, those programs, as well as the state fish and game agencies that administered them, were fully or partly financed by the fees and licenses paid by the non-Indian fishermen, who established a close rapport with the agencies and felt a vested interest in the fish for which they were paying. Still, demand exceeded supply, the commercial and sport fishermen competed for what was available, and the agencies struggled to maximize the product for both groups.

In view of modern-day realities, it seemed natural and justifiable to whites to treat Indian fishers like everyone else, making them abide by state regulations as either sport or commercial fishermen. On or off their reservations, it appeared fair that they should respect legal seasons and limitations of catch and employ the same gear that others were forced to use. But the Indians believed differently: because of their special relations with the federal government, they insisted, first of all, that state rules, regulations, and conservation measures did not apply to them when they fished according to their treaty rights. Secondly, they maintained that the validity of those rights stemmed from the fact that in their treaties, by which they had ceded lands, resources, and grants to the government, they had specifically reserved certain rights, including fishing and hunting, for themselves. The treaties had defined the nature of those rights, the government had guaranteed them, and the tribes had clung to them as property, never giving them away. Moreover, as the fish supply dwindled, the Indians felt aggrieved. Knowing that their existence depended on fish, they had always practiced conservation, and they considered themselves instinctively abler and more dedicated conservationists than non-Indian fishermen. It was plain to them who was polluting the rivers and whose dams were cutting off access to spawning beds. Constituting only a small fraction of the total number of fishermen, they not only balked at being made the scapegoat for the disappearing fish, but complained that white men's actions were nullifying their treaties by depriving them of fish to which they had a right. And they felt, by the same token, that the whites had a treaty obligation to maintain a fish supply for them, even by restocking programs.

Their reasoning, however, was not appreciated by non-Indians, and fell on deaf ears. It no longer mattered to whites what the treaties said; in contemporary America, such agreements were out of date—and, besides, whites argued, one could interpret the wording of the treaties any way one wished. In this impasse, and under pressure from non-Indian fishermen, state agencies refused to acknowledge any obligation to a separate Indian fishery. In effect, by ignoring its right to exist, they also helped their own problem, adding the Indians' share of fish to the total supply available for division between the sport and commercial fisheries.

The fight that erupted in the Northwest was a clash of these opposing points of view and centered, initially, on the Muckleshoots, Puyallups, and Nisquallies, three of a number of small tribes whose reservations bordered Puget Sound and the waters of northwestern Washington. By the mid-twentieth century, most whites in the region were scarcely aware of the Indians who lived among them. Many of the tiny tribal landholdings were lost in the industrial and urban developments that sprawled along the shores of the Sound, and most of the tribal members, whose families had been acculturated for generations, could hardly be distinguished from their non-Indian neighbors. They dressed and lived like whites—many of them off their small reservations and in white residential areas—sent their children to public schools, and competed economically with non-Indians for jobs and a livelihood.

Their Indianness and pride of identity as tribal members, however, were still strong. In each tribe, elders, clan members, and traditional teachers kept alive cultural traits and knowledge of their group's language, and spiritual values and beliefs. Only a minority of the Indian families still derived their income from fishing, but among most of the tribal people fish were still important, not only as food but as a symbol of the group's spiritual cohesiveness. Fish had meant survival for their ancestors, who welcomed their seasonal appearances with ceremonies of thanksgiving. The symbiotic relationship between the people and the fish kept the world in harmony, and the Indians' lives, cultures, and spiritual values revolved around that relationship. Despite acculturation and assimilation, the sense of that bond still remained deeply ingrained among them, as if the disappearance of the fish would mean, also, the disappearance of the Indians.

The Muckleshoots, Puyallups, and Nisquallies fished primarily for salmon and steelhead, in pre-white days using canoes of various sizes that were fashioned from cedar logs, and different types of nets, weirs, and traps, as well as spears and hook and line. They caught five species of Pacific salmon: Chinook, the largest, also called king or Tyee, which averaged from twelve to twenty-five pounds but could weigh up to one hundred pounds; silver, or coho; sockeye, or blueback; pink, or humpy; and chum, or dog. The annual runs of the salmon past the Indians' fishing camps on their way up the rivers from the Pacific to the upper-tributary spawning grounds generally occurred between May 1 and November 30, with the Indians gathering in most of their catch from July to early November. The steelhead, a sea-run rainbow trout, made its welcomed appearance the rest of the year and was harvested between the beginning of December and the end of April. The fish were once so plentiful that an early white settler in the Northwest declared that a person could almost walk across a stream on their backs. Though the Indians in aboriginal times also hunted game and gathered berries, roots, and other wild foods in season, the fish were their staple. That part of their catch that was not consumed at once was air-dried or smoked for later use or for trade with other tribes. The fishing sites belonged to the people in whose territories they were located, but social visiting and intermarriage among members of different groups were common, and the sites were usually shared with relatives and friends from other villages, bands, and tribes.

It is estimated that when whites first began to settle in north-western Washington in the 1840s, the total Native American population along Puget Sound was more than ten thousand. While many of the villages seem to have been politically auton-omous, most were culturally, socially, and linguistically associ-ated in bands and acknowledged the leadership of particular headmen who possessed outstanding qualities and capabili-ties. The Nisquallies, whose numbers have been variously esti-mated at between six hundred and two thousand, occupied a large area from the region of present-day Olympia at the south-ern end of the Sound to Mount Rainier in the Cascades. Most of their villages were along the lower Nisqually River, which they shared with their neighbors, the Puyallups. The latter, whose population appears to have been between five hundred and one thousand, were centered along the Puyallup and White Rivers and possessed the country from present-day Tacoma to the heights of the Cascades. There was, at the time, no people known as Muckleshoots. But just to the north of the Puyallups, principally along the White and Green Rivers, lived several bands, including the Skope-ahmish, or Sko-bobch (meaning Green River), whom the whites later called the Muckleshoots, for the name of the region that became their reservation. All of the groups were members of the Coastal Salish language family and were somewhat interrelated among themselves and with other Puget Sound peoples.

In the early 1850s, the white population grew to several thousand, and in 1853 Congress created Washington Territory. Late that same year, Isaac I. Stevens, a former army officer in the Mexican War, arrived as the first governor. Politically ambitious and in a hurry to make a mark for himself by turning Washington into a thriving part of the Union, Stevens hastened to acquire the lush and fertile lands of the Puget Sound Indians for the settlers whom he intended to lure to the territory. With little regard for the rights and sensibilities of the Indians, he and his aides called together the various bands, and in a whirlwind series of treaty meetings with different groups cajoled and threatened their headmen into ceding large parts of their territories and agreeing to cluster together in a number of small, unwanted areas that Stevens had selected for them.

The first treaty, signed at Medicine Creek on December 26, 1854, with the Nisquallies, Puyallups, and seven other tribes and bands, set the pattern for the others. Stevens, drunk and impatient, ordered the proceedings to be conducted in the limited vocabulary of the Chinook jargon, a mixture of some three hundred French, English, Chinookan, and other Indian words used in negotiations between white fur traders and the north-western tribes. It has been maintained that the employment of the jargon instead of the Indians' own tongues was intended to ease Stevens's task of persuasion by obscuring precisely what he was asking the headmen to sign; but it is clear that they understood enough to know that they were being ordered to move away from the fertile, watered valleys of their fishing rivers, which the white settlers wanted, to three small, undesirable areas where it would be hard, if not impossible, to catch fish. Having been apprised, however, that the Indians would insist that their survival depended on the retention of their right to fish, Stevens gave them a guarantee of access to, and use of, their old fishing stations, and the final treaty contained a section specifically reserving that right for the bands, reading: "The right of taking fish at all usual and accustomed grounds and stations is further secured to said Indians in common with all citizens of the Territory." Despite this assurance, Leschi, a principal headman of the Nisquallies, and a number of other Indians refused to relinquish their ancestral lands and sign the treaty. But Stevens bullied the others into doing so and, according to some of those who refused to sign, forged X's and thumbprints next to their names and that of Leschi. Altogether, the bands and tribes ceded about 2,240,000 acres for $32,500 to be paid to them over a twenty-year period. None of them was happy with what had occurred, and they left the council in confusion and anxiety.

On January 22, 1855, under much the same circumstances, Stevens hurried the Duwamish and five other Puget Sound tribes into signing a somewhat similar treaty at Point Elliott. The Duwamish, whose territory included the site of present-day Seattle, were led by Chief Sealth ("Seattle" being a corruption of his name), an imposing and eloquent man who was already well known as friendly to the whites. Among those present, also, were the Skope-ahmish and other bands that later became known as the Muckleshoots. They did not sign, but apparently accepted Sealth as their spokesman and he signed for them. The treaty contained the same words securing their fishing rights that Stevens had included in the Medicine Creek Treaty, but, again, there was unhappiness. Resigned to the white men's dominion, Sealth made an impassioned speech to Stevens and his aides, concluding movingly:

> When the last Red Man shall have perished, and the memory of my tribe shall have become a myth among the white man, these shores will swarm with the invisible dead of my tribe, and when your children's children think themselves alone in the field, the store, the shop, upon the highway, or in the silence of the pathless woods, they will not be alone. . . . At night when the streets of your cities and villages are silent and you think them deserted, they will throng with the returning hosts that once filled them and still love this beautiful land. The White Man will never be alone.

Stevens brushed aside such Indian sentiments and within the following month met three times more with other tribes, signing treaties at two of the gatherings, but tearing up the treaty paper at the final meeting after receiving angry opposition from one of the headmen. Each of the treaties he signed contained the provision assuring the Indians the right to take fish "at all usual and accustomed grounds and stations . . . in common with all citizens of the Territory." Meanwhile, on

December 30, 1854, he sent the Medicine Creek Treaty to Washington for ratification. With it went a letter containing an explanation of the Indians' reservation of their fishing rights and illuminating not only the Indians' dependence on fish but the whites' reliance on the Indian fishermen for their own local consumption and commercial export of fish. "They [the Indians] catch most of our fish," Stevens wrote, "supplying not only our people with clams and oysters but salmon to those who cure and export it . . . their principal food is fish and roots and berries. . . . The provisions as to reserves and as to taking fish . . . had strict reference to their conditions as above, to their actual wants and to the part they play and ought to play in the labor and prosperity of the Territory. It may be here observed that their mode of taking fish differs so essentially from that of the whites that it will not interfere with the latter." The Medicine Creek Treaty, which included agreements with the Nisquallies and Puyallups, was ratified by the Senate on March 3, 1855, and signed by President Franklin Pierce on April 10 of the same year.

In the Northwest, however, trouble was brewing. Impatient settlers, not waiting for the ratification of the treaties, overran the Indians' lands, angering the bands and embarrassing the headmen who had signed Stevens's papers. Fearing conflict, Stevens's Indian agent at the new territorial capital of Olympia rounded up thousands of members of many different bands and tribes and interned them, under the eyes of the militia, in seven temporary holding areas scattered along Puget Sound. This provocative action made the situation worse, and war suddenly broke out in October 1855 when the whites tried to take the Nisqually leader, Leschi, and his brother into protective custody. The two men escaped to the mountains, joined a large group of refugees from Nisqually, Puyallup, and other tribal villages, and commenced to fight back defensively against the whites, even threatening Seattle with a foray that sent frightened settlers rushing to the safety of blockhouses. Employing ruthless measures, Stevens and the militia finally stamped out the Indians' resistance and drove Leschi to the eastern side of the Cascades. Later, when he returned, he was captured, tried for the murder of a white man, and hanged, though many whites considered him innocent of the killing and urged his acquittal.

The conflict effectively ended the Indians' ability to defend themselves against the increasing white population in western Washington, but it convinced the federal government that the tribes had legitimate grievances against Stevens's hasty and high-handed treaties. Under instructions from his superiors, Stevens met with the interned Nisquallies and Puyallups at Fox Island near Tacoma, where they were being held, and re-adjusted the permanent reservations he had previously assigned to them, giving them back many of their old fishing sites. The Nisquallies received 4,717 acres on both sides of the Nisqually River, several miles above its mouth at the southern end of the Sound, and the Puyallups, who had complained that the original site designated for them at the mouth of the Puyallup River was too small to hold all their people, were granted additional land along both sides of the river to form a reservation which, after another change in its boundaries in 1873, comprised about eighteen thousand acres.

At the same time, Stevens took note of the dissatisfaction of the Skope-ahmish and a number of other bands whom Sealth, the Duwamish leader, had represented at the Point Elliott treaty meeting. Those bands resented being forced to move out of their own country and onto a reservation with the coastal Duwamish and wanted their riverine fishing sites restored to them. A military post was being abandoned on the Muckleshoot Prairie in their homeland, and Stevens now returned that site to them, establishing a reservation of approximately thirty-five hundred acres that encompassed portions of the Green and White Rivers. Shared by many of the small bands, it was named the Muckleshoot Reservation after the prairie and post that had stood there. By 1870, all the various groups on the reserve were known collectively to the whites as Muckleshoot Indians. The three reservations, newly defined by Stevens, were duly approved by executive order in Washington, D.C., on January 20, 1857, and the tribes and bands were moved onto them.

In the years that followed, whites continued to stream into the Puget Sound region, and the Indians lost ownership of much of the land within their reservation boundaries. The area at the mouth of the Puyallup River grew into the city of Tacoma (after the Indians' name for Mount Rainier), and in the 1870s, the federal government began eroding the Puyallups' holdings by granting rights-of-way on their reservation to railroads and other industrial and commercial applicants. The Dawes Allotment Act, passed in 1887, was quickly implemented on all three reservations; the Indians were given individual family-size allotments, and the rest of their lands were opened to whites, who poured onto the reservations and established farms and homes on former tribal holdings. In order to protect the Indians, the Dawes Act prohibited the selling of an Indian's allotment for twenty-five years, when presumably the owner would be competent to deal with whites as an equal and defend himself against fraud. The pressure for Indian land

and resources at Puget Sound became so great, however, that many of the Indians' most desirable allotments were permitted to be sold after ten years, and, by fair means and foul, the transference of Indian property into white hands accelerated.

In 1893, Congress helped the expanding city of Tacoma all but obliterate the Puyallup Reservation by specifically ordering the sale of all the reservation's land, save what had been allotted for Indian homes and an Indian school and burying ground. Similarly, in 1917, during World War I, the government condemned all of the Nisquallies' land on the eastern side of the Nisqually River for use by the Army's Fort Lewis. At a stroke, the tribe lost thirty-three hundred acres, or more than 70 percent of its reservation. The ousted Nisqually families were eventually paid a total of $160,840 for their lands and improvements and for the loss of their hunting rights and access to the lakes and streams on the condemned property. Some of the money was used to purchase other land for tribal members who had lost their allotments. A number of them resettled on the west bank of the Nisqually River, and though they were outside of the reservation's boundaries, their new property was given trust status by the federal government, just as if they were within the reservation.

By the 1960s, the continuing inroads on the reservations and the intermixing within their boundaries of Indian and white property owners, together with the acculturation of most of the Indians and the disappearance of traditional tribal and band political structures, made many non-Indians think that it no longer mattered knowing when they were on or off a reservation, or who was and was not an Indian. In their view, reservations were outmoded and would soon disappear entirely, and Indians were, or should be, no different from anyone else.

Actually, at the time, 1,200 acres of the Muckleshoot Reservation were still in Indian hands, and of the total Muckleshoot
tribal enrollment of 340, about 270 lived on the reservation.
The Nisquallies possessed 816 acres and about 190 of them
lived on trust land. The original tribally owned 18,000 acres
of the Puyallups had been whittled down to thirty-three, most
of them used for their cemetery, but another 200 or 300 acres
were privately owned within the reservation by descendants of
the Indian allottees. The total Puyallup tribal enrollment was
about 450, some 170 of whom lived on these old allotments.

The many changes that had come to the region had also
affected the Indians' fisheries. Many of their usual and accustomed fishing sites had disappeared to farms and white settlements or had been destroyed by towns, cities, and riverside
commerce and industry. Others had been ruined by loggers
and pulp mills, municipal and industrial pollution, dams, and
the rearranging of river channels. As whites took over more
of the land the Indians found it increasingly difficult to gain
access to many of the fishing sites that remained. For a time,
after the period of the treaties, the Indians, as Stevens had
observed, had supplied a large share of the fish consumed by
whites. In the 1880s, however, the burgeoning of salmon can-
neries encouraged the growth of commercial fishing among
the whites, and their competitiveness with the tribal fishers
produced the first quarrels. The conflicts became so bad that
in 1886 federal troops were sent to some of the fishing sites to
protect the Indians.

As sport fishing became popular, the Indians faced another
form of competition, and conflicts increased. Treaty rights
became blurred and subject to argument. By the beginning
of the twentieth century, there was a widespread disregard for

Indian rights, which became more prevalent as the fish runs dwindled and competition grew. To conserve the fish, state regulations were adopted applying to Indians, as well as to non-Indians, and state agencies came into existence to enforce the codes. In 1905, when the federal government contested the right of the State of Washington to grant a private company an exclusive license to use a traditional Indian fishing ground, the Supreme Court in *U.S. v. Winans* ruled it a violation of Indian treaty rights, but created confusion by recognizing that the state had some regulatory authority over Indian fishermen, without defining the nature and extent of that authority. On many occasions thereafter, Indians were arrested for violations of state fishing regulations, and three times, twice in 1916 and once in 1921, the Washington State Supreme Court ruled that the Indians had no greater fishing rights than the whites and must comply with the state laws. In none of the cases did the federal government live up to its trust obligation and appeal the decisions to a federal court in behalf of the Indians.

At the same time, there were doubts. In 1941, the Washington Supreme Court upheld the conviction of a Yakima Indian for fishing without a license. This time the federal government appealed, and the U.S. Supreme Court decided that the state could not require Indians to buy a license to exercise their treaty right to fish, though again it left confusion by adding that a state could regulate Indian fishing for conservation purposes. When, however, the state in 1951 tried to stop some Makah Indians from fishing with nets, a federal court ruled that the regulation which the Makahs were alleged to have violated was not necessary for conservation purposes.

The rights of the state versus those of the Indians were thus left unclear throughout the first half of the twentieth century. In actual practice, Washington's Department of Fisheries, which had jurisdiction over salmon as a commercial food fish, and its Department of Game, which enforced the regulations affecting steelhead as essentially a game, or sport, fish (the two agencies were originally one department), viewed the white fishermen as their clients and were contemptuous of any special exemptions claimed by the Indians. Judges of the state's lower courts, also, were susceptible to the pleas and pressures of the non-Indian fishermen and found it hard to accept the argument that Indians could break a state law that everyone else had to obey. If it was illegal to use nets to catch game fish, including steelhead, and to sell or ship game fish, then that was the law, and, as they saw it, it applied equally to whites and Indians.

But when Indians were arrested, there were sometimes perplexing arguments, and it was often apparent that neither agencies nor judges were exactly sure of what, if any, protection the treaties actually gave the Indians from the state's police power in the matter of fishing. Could the state enforce its rules on a reservation? Did "usual and accustomed grounds" mean that Indians could catch fish outside of their reservations with the same disregard for state laws that they evidenced on their reservations? What were the boundaries of the reservations— the original ones established by Stevens, or those of the Indians' present shrunken holdings? Did the treaty phrase "in common with all citizens" mean that the Indians had to accept the same regulations as everyone else, or did it refer to the amount of fish to which they were entitled? Such were among the numerous questions asked, and various judges differed among themselves about the answers, eventually coming to recognize that only the U.S. Supreme Court could settle these issues. But since the Indians were so poor that they often could not raise bail money for themselves, and the federal government only rarely defended them, the likelihood of a definitive, encompassing case ever going that far, helpful as it might be, seemed remote.

Though most white public opinion firmly assumed that the phrase "in common with all citizens" committed Indians to observance of the state laws, the doubts throughout the years were strong enough to inhibit a full-scale campaign to make the Indians accept the state's rules or stop fishing. The fishery officials and game wardens, frustrated by the uncertainty, and frequently exhibiting crude racism in their anger against the tribal fishermen, harassed the Indians on the Green, Puyallup, and other rivers and made just enough arrests to maintain their authority. Occasionally, judges let the Indians go with a warning, but more often gave them a fine and sixty days in jail. Indians frequently did not even attempt to argue that they had been fishing according to their treaty rights; experience taught them that the judges would simply declare they were wrong. As an added penalty, they sometimes lost their boats and fishing gear: the fish and game officers would impound them during their raids to bring to court "as evidence," but no boat was ever brought to a court hearing, and when the Indians were unable to get them back, they had to find another job to scrape up enough money to re-equip themselves.

Such confiscations, to some Indians, seemed part of a plan to drive them off the rivers by taking away their means of livelihood, somewhat as whites had crippled the Plains Indians by killing the buffalo. These suspicions were not without substance. Through the years, the white men's impact, interference, and competition had made many of the Indians

abandon fishing. To the survivors, the loss of gear and boats—
especially their old dugouts, which were irreplaceable—was a
heavy blow. The Indians, generally, were among the poorest
of the state's poor, and every year, some of those who were
arrested could not meet the expense of buying new nets and
outboard motorboats and had to borrow boats, join others, or
else give up fishing.

In 1954, an Indian arrest that was appealed to a higher
court made it appear for a time that the question of Indian fishing rights might be settled. The case involved a rugged Indian
entrepreneur named Robert Satiacum, who was part Puyallup
and part Yakima. He had grown up among whites at Fife, a
suburb of Tacoma, had worked in the construction industry,
and at times ran several fishing boats on the lower Puyallup
River. Satiacum looked and behaved like a two-fisted prize-
fighter and was not afraid of the fish and game officials. He
was arrested and charged with being in possession of game
fish (steelhead) during a closed season, and with having used
fixed gill nets to catch game fish at two locations, one of them
outside the Puyallup Reservation and the other within the original boundaries of the reservation but on land that had passed
into white ownership.

Satiacum had the means and determination to appeal his
conviction to a Washington Superior Court, which ruled in his
favor on the grounds that he had been within his treaty rights
by fishing at usual and accustomed fishing sites of the Puyallups in accordance with the immemorial customs of his tribe,
and that the state regulations illegally deprived him of those
treaty rights. The state appealed the decision to the Washington Supreme Court, which in 1957 sustained the Superior
Court, but split 4–4, half of its members agreeing with the

Superior Court and half saying that the state would have had the right to arrest Satiacum if it had first proved that enforcement of the regulations had been necessary for conservation purposes. Satiacum's case was dismissed, but the split decision left the Indians' rights issues still unsettled.

Proving that the conserving of the Northwest fisheries depended on halting the activities of Indian fishermen was impossible, as well as ludicrous. The total of all the Indian fishers was estimated to be about 800, as against approximately 6,600 non-Indian commercial fishermen and some 283,000 non-Indian sport fishermen. About 4,000 white oceangoing trollers, supplying fish to large packing corporations, as well as huge fleets of commercial charter boats, harvested the largest part of the salmon runs, each year hauling in more than two million tons of the fish offshore before they ever got to the rivers to reproduce. Once in the rivers, the salmon and steelhead runs were cut down by the barriers and pollution of the whites. Moreover, the Indians were as distressed as the whites by the fall-off in fish and were not recklessly trying to speed the depletion, which hurt them as much as the non-Indians. Though the state wardens cultivated the impression that the Indians had no interest in conservation, the opposite, in fact, was true. Most Indian fishermen limited their catches by carefully policing themselves, and on a number of occasions the tribes proposed that the state agencies and white fishermen join them in designing and implementing a comprehensive and effective conservation program. The state agencies refused to take them seriously, or even meet with them for discussions. The truth was that a meaningful program for the restoration of the fisheries was regarded by the state officials as politically and economically unrealistic, since it implied such unacceptable measures as drastically reducing the number of white fishermen and their catch, forcing cities and industries to clean up and clear the rivers, and prohibiting new developments that would further degrade the environmental habitat of the fish. In the wake of the Satiacum decision, therefore, the fish and game authorities realized that they could not build a logical case against the Indians, and for a time they halted their arrests.

Simplistic arguments, however, continued to be used to rouse public sentiment and prejudice against the Indian fishers. Some of the campaign was deliberately furthered by irritated state game wardens who spied on the Indian fishermen and made secret movies of them catching steelhead in nets out of season to show at meetings of sport fishermen's clubs. Such provocations had their intended effect. Anger continued to build, editorial writers and politicians seethed, and in 1961 the atmosphere was right for state officials to move once more against the Indians. This time, they did so with a determination to bring a final halt to their violations of the state laws. The first of a number of arrests and harassments were of the two Muckleshoots and the Puyallup on the Green River who were later acquitted for being within their treaty rights—the same reason that the Superior Court had used in ruling in favor of Satiacum. Soon afterward, the wardens cracked down on Indian fishermen on the Nisqually River. On January 6, 1962, a small army of three-dozen officers with walkie-talkies and a reconnaissance spotter plane overhead closed in on six Indians and, confiscating their boats, motors, and gear, arrested them for fishing with gill nets. Two Seattle attorneys took the case of the Indians, who pleaded not guilty on the grounds that they had been fishing on Indian trust land, which they claimed was part of the Nisqually Reservation, and were thus within their treaty rights. The Game Department then charged that they were not pure-blood Nisquallies and therefore had no treaty rights, and the trial became a "pedigree" case, in which the Indians had to gather a stack of affidavits, with the help of Billy Frank, Jr., the tribe's vice president, to try to prove that they were recognized Nisquallies. In the end, three of the fishermen were freed, but the other three were fined $10 each.

The acquittal of the three men did not deter the fish and game agents. What appeared to be a serious legal obstacle to their efforts, however, occurred suddenly in 1963 with a federal court decision concerning a treaty fishing rights case in the neighboring state of Oregon. In *Maison v. Confederated Tribes of the Umatilla Indian Reservation,* the U.S. Ninth Circuit Court of Appeals in San Francisco echoed Washington's Satiacum decision in favor of the Indians, ruling that Oregon could only regulate off-reservation fishing by Indians at their usual and accustomed sites to the extent that the regulation was necessary for the conservation of fish, but it went beyond the Satiacum decision by adding, also, that the state could only carry out the regulation if it could not attain the conservation objective by *first* resorting to all other methods, including the restriction of the fishing rights of the non-Indians alone. In other words, a state must first prohibit pollution, sport fishing, and everything else depleting the fish before interfering with Indian treaties. Oregon appealed the decision, but the U.S. Supreme Court declined to review it, and the Circuit Court's ruling stood.

The federal court's decision heartened the Puget Sound Indians, but caused only temporary consternation among Washington's officials. If anything, it turned more whites

against the tribal fishermen along the Sound, and the Indians
soon realized that the State of Washington intended to ignore
the Oregon ruling as impractical. On September 27, 1963, the
Fish and Game Departments got a temporary injunction closing the entire Green River to net fishing, and on the same day
arrested fifteen Muckleshoots who had been netting salmon.
The latter were able to raise enough money to get lawyers, and
they pleaded not guilty. Their appeal, *State v. Herman Moses et
al.* (for one of the arrested fishermen), destined to become the
first of a series of test cases, was sent to the King County Superior Court. If Oregon's Umatilla decision had originally raised
the Indians' hopes, another one, this time in Washington, now
thoroughly dashed them and made the tribal fishermen on all
the rivers feel that a real crisis was approaching. On December
17, 1963, the Washington State Supreme Court, appearing to
many to violate the U.S. Constitution by ignoring the federal
court's Umatilla ruling, decided, in a case affecting a Swinom-
ish Indian in Washington who had been arrested for gill netting off the mouth of the Skagit River (the case was *Slate v.
McCoy*), that Washington State did have the power to regulate
Indian fishing for conservation purposes. Nothing was said
about first having to try every other conservation measure possible, including the restriction of non-Indian fishing, and the
decision, in fact, also conflicted with the same court's action
in the Satiacum case, in which four of its members at the time
had decided that the state could not interfere with treaty rights
at all and the other four had said that the state had to prove
that regulations were necessary for conservation. The McCoy
decision gave Washington State fish and game officials a clear
go-ahead. With the steelhead season already under way, the
Indian fishermen knew that the game wardens would soon

be coming after them in earnest. Hopes for their cause now seemed dim. Nonetheless, they decided that they had no alternative but to continue exercising their rights, hoping that public sentiment might eventually support them or that another test case might develop and give them a more favorable decision. Though they faced the prospect of more arrests, jailings, economic hardships, and perhaps physical violence against them, they persuaded themselves that right was on their side and that, in the end, if they kept fishing, they would win.

Measures for resistance were first organized by a determined group of families whose members fished regularly on the Nisqually River at Frank's Landing, a brushy tract that had been purchased years before for Billy Frank, Sr., one of the tribal members whose allotment on the opposite side of the river had been condemned in 1917 for Fort Lewis. Though the new site was outside the original boundaries of the Nisqually Reservation, it had been given trust status, and the Indians— but, by 1963, not the state—considered it to be part of the reservation. Fishing was better there than on the original reservation, where the Nisqually River ran faster and more turbulently, and Frank's location, a usual and accustomed tribal fishing site, was frequented by many Indians. Billy Frank, Sr., a Nisqually elder who lived on the tract with his wife, was still alive, and other fishing relatives and friends included Don and Pauline Matheson; Alvin and Maiselle Bridges and their daughters, Valerie, Alison, and Suzette; Billy Frank, Jr., the tribal vice president; Nugent Kautz; Don George, Jr.; and Donald and Janet McCloud. Don McCloud was a Puyallup who had been reared among the Nisquallies, and Janet, the mother of eight children, was a Tulalip Indian from farther north on Puget Sound and a descendant of Sealth, the Duwamish chief. An

energetic and forceful traditionalist, she believed in brotherhood between Indians and whites, but fought to get Indians to
maintain pride in their Indianness as well. In the nearby town
of Yelm, where the McClouds lived, she crusaded against the
white-run public school system, demanding that the administra-
trators and teachers end their prejudice against Indian students
and include course materials that would encourage understanding and respect for Indian history and culture.

Immediately after the McCoy decision, the Frank's Landing fishers called an emergency meeting. Word of it was circulated along Puget Sound by Dewey Sigo, a Squaxim Indian
who bought fish from Indians to sell to non-Indian commercial markets, and some fifty persons attended the gathering,
including Indians from the upper Skagit River, Nooksacks,
Quileutes, and Puyallups. Deciding, first, to make a direct plea
to the governor, whom they hoped might intervene with the
state agencies in their behalf, they made signs reading "No
salmon—no Santa," and on December 23, just before Christ-
mas, drove to Olympia and demonstrated at the state capitol.
Governor Albert Rosellini invited them in, listened to them
politely, but dismissed them with a patronizing "Nice to hear
your problems. Come back again."

The appeal focused media attention on them, but also
drew the ire of the Fish and Game Departments. On January 1,
1964, George Smallwood of the Game Department appeared
at Frank's Landing, where some of the Indians were fishing for
dog salmon and steelhead, and ordered them to fish only within
the boundaries of the original reservation seven miles farther
up the river, where the state was willing to recognize that it had
no jurisdiction. The Indians insisted that this was part of the
reservation, and an area where Indians had always fished, and

they refused to pull in their nets. It was the start of a war. The state officials got an injunction from Judge Robert H. Jaques of the Pierce County Superior Court, closing the Nisqually River below the state-recognized Nisqually Reservation to net fishing by the twelve male Indians who regularly fished at Frank's Landing, and the wardens immediately moved in and arrested the Indians. The Bureau of Indian Affairs ignored the Indians' plight, and even the leaders of the Nisqually tribe, who thought the fishermen's resistance was foolish and would only breed more anti-Indian feeling, refused to help with defense funds. To raise legal fees and support the families of the arrested men, as well as to strengthen their own fishing families, they formed an organization called the Survival of American Indians Association and put out a mimeographed newsletter, written and edited largely by Janet McCloud, which told their side of the story. By fishbakes and other means, they raised fifty dollars and enlisted the aid of Jack Tanner, a Tacoma attorney and president of the northwestern division of the National Association for the Advancement of Colored People.

After the first arrests, the fishermen called a truce and moved to Medicine Creek, where they continued to fish quietly. The truce lasted only a brief time. They returned to Frank's Landing, and were again arrested, this time receiving suspended sentences. In the meantime, the arrests spread to the Puyallup and other rivers, and once again fishermen like Robert Satiacum were in conflict with the enforcement officials. The newspapers and radio gave coverage to the fishing war, and reports of what was occurring began to reach other parts of the country, raising sympathy for the embattled fishermen of the small, impoverished Washington tribes, whose struggle was likened by some to that of a David against an unjust Goliath. Members of the activist National Indian Youth Council, as well as traditional Indian leaders from other tribes, traveled to Puget Sound, offering to help the fishing families, join protest "fish-ins," and risk being arrested. The struggle made a particular impact on a soft spoken, politically astute young Indian named Hank Adams, who had been born twenty years before on the Fort Peck Reservation in Montana to Assiniboine and Sioux parents, but who had been raised by his mother and her second husband on the Quinault Reservation in Washington. In time, he became a leading figure at Frank's Landing, raising the struggle's level of militancy and making it a symbol of the Native Americans' new determination to stand up against white men for their rights.

Help also came from some non-Indians, including the motion picture actor Marlon Brando, who arrived to lend support to a protest march on the state capitol, which the NIYC planned in behalf of the fishermen. Prior to the march, Brando decided not to join the group at Frank's Landing because of the opposition of the Nisqually tribal leaders, but staged a demonstration fish-in, instead, with Satiacum on the Puyallup River on March 2. He was arrested for net fishing, but was released on a technicality and not tried. The next day, he participated in the march on Olympia with some one thousand Indians, non-Indian supporters, and curiosity seekers. At the capitol, he and some of the Indians had a fruitless meeting with Governor Rosellini, after which Brando left the state.

The actor's presence gave the Indians' cause dramatic nationwide attention, but the arrests continued. At Frank's Landing, on March 11, six fishermen, including Bill Frank, Jr., Don McCloud, Al Bridges, and Nugent Kautz, who had earlier received suspended sentences on condition that they stop fishing, fished again, were rearrested, and were ordered to jail for thirty days. After a hearing in Superior Court, their case was appealed to the State Supreme Court. With their own test case finally under way, the Frank's Landing fishermen, including those whose case was on appeal, staged another series of fish-ins, trying to continue to earn a living, and the war went on. Indians were arrested, received jail terms, and then went back to the river to fish and be rearrested. While the fishermen were in jail, women, children, and other men took their places. The Indians taunted the enforcement officers, and the latter pushed the Indians around and roughed them up. During their arrests, as well as in court, the Indians were subjected to obscenities and racist treatment. "We had the power and force to exterminate these people from the face of the earth, instead of making treaties with them," a Pierce County assistant prosecutor exclaimed during a hearing after one of the arrests. "Perhaps we should have! We certainly wouldn't be having all this trouble with them today." At another time, Judge Jaques was accused of telling the Indians, "They never meant for you people to be free like everyone else." The bigotry and violence horrified old Billy Frank, Sr., who unsuccessfully petitioned a federal court for an investigation of the brutality and disregard for the Indians' civil rights.

During the summer of 1964, Senator Warren G. Magnuson of Washington tried to solve the dispute and end the adverse attention the state was receiving by introducing two measures in Congress. Both of them advocated compromises that would have been unfavorable to the Indian fishermen, and after hearings on them in August, they died in a Senate committee. In the state, the conflict continued, marked by a picketing of the state's fisheries office in Seattle; by vain attempts by the Inter-

tribal Council of Western Washington Indians and the National
Congress of American Indians, representing tribes throughout
the country, to gain support for an impartial study, involving
federal and state agencies, to determine sound methods for
managing and conserving the fish supply; and, in February
1965, by another demonstration at Olympia.

Meanwhile, in December 1964, Judge F. A. Walterskirchen
of the King County Superior Court finally ruled on the test case
of *State v. Herman Moses et al.*, affecting the fifteen Muckleshoot Indians who had been arrested on the Green River in
September 1963. His decision, dealing the Muckleshoots an
unexpected blow, was that the Muckleshoots had no treaty
rights at all: no people listed as Muckleshoots had signed the
1855 Point Elliott Treaty with Stevens, and therefore the Muckleshoots could not claim any fishing rights under the treaty.
He followed this decision by making permanent the injunction against net fishing on the Green River. The Muckleshoots
immediately appealed his decision to the Washington State
Supreme Court on the grounds that the Indians had not been
permitted an opportunity to prove that the Muckleshoots were
descendants of bands like the Skope-ahmish that had been at
the treaty meeting and been represented by Chief Sealth of the
Duwamish, who had signed the document for them, and that
the Bureau of Indian Affairs itself recognized the Muckleshoots
as a treaty tribe.

Thereafter, the issue followed a tortured course of its own,
reflecting to the Indians the lengths to which the state would
resort in order to deprive them of their fishing rights. The State
Supreme Court, on January 12, 1967, dismissed the Indians'
evidence on a technicality and sustained Judge Walterskirchen's opinion. The Muckleshoots, moreover, were barred

from a further appeal, thus ending the case. But in March 1966, in another, and deliberate, test fish-in demonstration, four Muckleshoots gill-netted in the Green River in defiance of the injunction and were arrested. They were convicted in a lower court, but their case was taken by an attorney representing the American Civil Liberties Union, as well as by two lawyers supplied by the U.S. Department of Justice—which had finally been asked by the Interior Department to support the Muckle-shoots' treaty rights—and was appealed to the King County Superior Court, the same one that had ruled that the tribe had no treaty rights. Expert evidence was again introduced, and the court, now presided over by Judge Lloyd Shorett, finally agreed that the Muckleshoots were a federally recognized treaty tribe. But it was not a total victory. Though the Indians had fished in a usual and accustomed place, the court sustained their conviction for using gill nets. The case was appealed to the State Supreme Court, which affirmed Judge Shorett, and then to the U.S. Supreme Court, where it joined other fishing rights cases that by then had reached the highest court.

Amid the confusions of the varied issues that were being raised by the different cases, still other Washington courts in 1965 began to vacillate and render conflicting opinions, all of them making the Indians' struggle more frustrating and difficult. In a case affecting Satiacum and other Puyallup fishermen, who were being arrested for violating state fishing regulations on the Puyallup River and Commencement Bay, Judge John D. Cochran of the Pierce County Superior Court, in May, astounded the Puyallups, as well as the Bureau of Indian Affairs, by ruling that there was no longer a Puyallup tribe or a Puyallup Reservation, and that all Indian fishermen on the river must therefore observe the state's fishing rules and regulations.

The reservation, said Judge Cochran, had, in effect, been abolished by the breakup and loss of tribally owned lands under the Allotment Act of 1887. There were now only thirty-three acres of trust land left, most of it a cemetery, and there was no tribe to succeed in interest to the rights of the Puyallup signers of the 1854 Treaty of Medicine Creek.

The tribe was forced to appeal this remarkable decision to the State Supreme Court, claiming that it still existed and enjoyed federal recognition as a treaty tribe, that its treaty rights still applied to all lands within the original boundaries of the reservation, and that tribal members still had the right to fish at usual and accustomed places. On January 12, 1967, the Washington Supreme Court decided that there was a Puyallup tribe, but not a reservation, that treaty rights were not absolute, and that they did not extend to the right "to take fish with such gear and at such times as would destroy the fishery." In other words, the Puyallups were deemed not to have any on-reservation rights, since there was no reservation, and only the same off-reservation rights as were accorded everyone else. In addition, the court finally noted that it thought the federal judge of the Ninth Circuit Court had been wrong in the Oregon Umatilla case in ordering a state not to infringe on Indian treaty rights unless it was indispensable for conservation, and introduced more puzzlement by differing entirely with its own previous decision in the Satiacum case of 1957, which had declared that the state regulations had deprived Satiacum of his treaty fishing rights. This decision, too, was appealed to the U.S. Supreme Court.

The initial decision of Judge Cochran, meanwhile, had angered the Puyallup fishermen, and conflict erupted off and on throughout the year as they defied his injunction closing the river to their net fishing. Indians, as well as state officers and Tacoma policemen, were bruised and hurt in scuffles, and Satiacum, threatening to use arms to defend his boats, was arrested twice. A sixty-day jail term kept him off the river, but one of the charges against him, tried as a criminal rather than a civil case, ended in his acquittal by a six-member jury. While he was imprisoned, his attractive twenty-three-year-old wife, Suzanne—a fiery Kaw Indian and grandniece of Herbert Hoover's vice president, Charles Curtis—provided sensational headlines, together with a sister-in-law, Clara Satiacum, by continuing to run his fishing boats, taunting the enforcement officials, and engaging in a series of melees with them, including one wild episode on the night of September 21, when the two women, using one of the boats, led eighteen Tacoma police in a frenzied chase up and down the river for an hour and a half. They were finally cornered by police in a commandeered tugboat but, though arrested and given sentences, were released without having to serve time in jail.

The continued resistance of the Indians and their defiance on the rivers frustrated the fish and game wardens and wore down their patience. Hatred for the Indians, whose calm persistence made the wardens' riverbank stakeouts and sudden lunges at the fishermen seem like the antics of Toonerville cops, increased the tension, and violence of an uglier nature finally broke out at Frank's Landing on the Nisqually River. On the night of October 7, the lights of a warden's patrol boat picked up two Indians, Bill Frank, Jr., and Al Bridges, setting their nets from a dugout canoe. Gunning their motor, the wardens rammed the canoe, dumping both men into the river and almost drowning them. Two nights later, about one in the morning, the wardens came on two Indian boys on a logjam

in the middle of the river. As they cornered the youths and
began to harass them, word spread along the shore. Indians
flocked to the scene, surrounded the wardens, and a fight
broke out. More police arrived, including state police and even
Fort Lewis military policemen armed with submachine guns.
A riot, with possible heavy casualties, was averted only by the
forceful intercession of the county sheriff, whom the Indians
regarded as a friend.

The damage, however, had been done. On October 13,
the angry Nisquallies held a widely publicized protest fish-in,
intending to make it the basis for a legal challenge to the state's
injunction against their fishing. Newspaper reporters, photographers, television cameramen, and observers from such
organizations as the American Friends Service Committee
showed up, as did some eighty state game wardens, some of
them carrying nightsticks, blackjacks, and long, seven-celled
flashlights. The wardens stationed themselves on both sides of
the river and waited for the Indians to do something. Finally,
the Indians, who totaled eight men and nineteen women and
children, put a dugout into the river, carrying two Indian fishermen, two little boys, their dog, and a newspaper cameraman.
As the fishermen began to lower a net, a warden hollered, "Get
'em," and a powerboat roared out and crashed into the dugout,
pitching everyone into the water. In an instant, Indians rushed
into the river to save the children, the wardens descended on
them from both banks, and a free-swinging battle was under
way. Rocks were thrown, people were hit with clubs and
sticks, and children were dragged by their hair and knocked
down. When it was over, several people had been hurt, including Indians, white reporters and cameramen, and some of the
wardens. Indian boats and canoes, nets, and outboard motors

were confiscated, and seven Indians, including Janet and Donald McCloud, Alvin and Maiselle Bridges, and Suzanne Satiacum, who had come to give moral support, were arrested for resisting the officers. The newsmen, however, had dramatic stories to write and pictures to show of the wardens' brutality, and some of the non-Indian observers had lurid, pro-Indian accounts to relate (including the smell of whiskey on the breath of some of the wardens). When the Indians were finally tried by jury almost three-and-a-half years later, on January 1, 1969, they were acquitted on the grounds that they had been justifiably defending themselves.

For a long time, the Nisquallies and Puyallups had been trying to get the federal government to help them, both by defending their fishing rights as their trustee and by protecting their civil rights against the state officials. Appeals to the Attorney General for help in February 1965 had been brusquely turned down by Assistant Attorney General John Doar. A new plea to Secretary of the Interior Stewart Udall was now also rejected for much the same reason: pending court clarification of the tribes' treaty fishing rights, the executive branch was too uncertain of the Indians' complicated legal position to intervene. A march on the Seattle federal courthouse to seek help by members and supporters of the Survival of American Indians Association on October 26, after the attack at Frank's Landing, also failed in its purpose. The Indians were still on their own, and the wardens' surveillances and interferences continued. On December 19, Al Bridges was again arrested on the Nisqually, and a few weeks later, two more Indian fishermen were seized.

In February 1966, the black comedian and civil rights figure Dick Gregory and his wife, Lillian, drew more publicity to the

Indians' fight by participating in a series of fish-ins with the Indians. Gregory was arrested and convicted on three counts of illegal net fishing. He appealed his conviction to the State Supreme Court in March 1968, but lost and served forty days in jail, fasting during his confinement, and announcing, on his release, "If more people went to jail for rights, fewer would go for wrongs."

The fishing rights struggle, meanwhile, was spreading to the Columbia River, where in the spring of 1966 Washington and Oregon officials began arresting Yakima Indian fishermen, sometimes at gunpoint and with considerable savagery, for fishing for Chinook salmon with set-nets at a fishing site known as Cooks Landing above Bonneville Dam. After more than thirty-two arrests had been made, with the Yakimas receiving suspended sentences and then going back to fishing, the Yakimas armed themselves for defense. On July 27, when five Washington State wardens tried to make two more arrests, a Yakima named Clarence Tahkeal interfered with the arrest, training his rifle on the wardens until he could turn them over to the state police in a citizen's arrest that charged the wardens with trespassing.

The conflict on the Columbia spelled new problems for Washington State. The Yakimas, unlike the small groups along Puget Sound, were a large and politically powerful tribe. Moreover, they were associated with a number of other large interior tribes, including the Umatillas, the Warm Springs Indians, and the Nez Perce of Idaho, in asserting treaty fishing rights, similar to those of the Puget Sound Indians, stemming from treaties that they, too, had made with Stevens in 1855. The sudden campaign against the Yakima fishermen at Cooks Landing contributed to the raising of questions among all those tribes about the observance of their own fishing rights, and on August 19 and 20, 1966, they held a meeting at the White Swan Long-house on the Yakima Reservation. It was attended by thirty-eight Indian delegates, as well as tribal attorneys, the assistant area director of the Bureau of Indian Affairs in Portland, and a regional solicitor for the Bureau, who announced that the Department of the Interior would now, upon request, have the U.S. Department of Justice defend their treaty rights and assist the tribes in upholding the self-regulation of their own fishing. The promise encouraged the Indians, who formed a Columbia River Indian Fishing Council and prepared to defend their fishing rights on the Columbia and its tributaries.

The solicitor's assurance of federal support, reflecting growing concern by the Interior Department over the conflict in the Northwest, was the beginning of a change in the recognition of its obligation to the fishing Indians. Early in May, Assistant Attorney General Edwin L. Weisl, Jr., arrived in Portland from Washington, D.C., to look into the arrests of the Yakima fishermen and announced that the federal government was "determined to fight in the courts to uphold the solemn obligation" of the treaties made with the Columbia River fishing tribes. He added, however, that the government would furnish counsel only for those defendants who fished in compliance with tribal council fishing rules.

It was a first step, but a second one followed quickly. Having made known its intention to support any Indian arrested by a state while fishing in accordance with treaty rights and tribally approved regulations, the Department of Justice, on May 31, entered, as amicus curiae, the case in which the Puyallups were trying to prove that they were still a treaty tribe and still owned a reservation, which was then before the Washington State Supreme Court. As noted earlier, tribal recognition was won, but despite the government's assistance, the court ruled against the existence of a Puyallup Reservation and supported the state's right to regulate the Puyallups' fishing. If only as an outside supporting friend, however, the federal government had now intervened for the first time in years in a Washington fishing rights case.

The tribe's lawyers appealed the Washington court's decision to the U.S. Supreme Court, and on December 18, 1967, the Court agreed to hear it, but combined it with the Nisqually case, mentioned earlier, that had begun on March 11, 1964, with the arrests of Nugent Kautz, Bill Frank, Jr., Donald McCloud, Al Bridges, and two other Indians for defying the injunction against net fishing at Frank's Landing. In the Washington State Supreme Court, on January 12, 1967, that case had gone against the Indians, and had been appealed to the U.S. Supreme Court. One of the basic issues in both cases—the state's right to regulate treaty Indian fishing at usual and accustomed sites off the reservation—was essentially the same.

On May 27, 1968, the U.S. Supreme Court, in a decision written by Justice William O. Douglas in the combined case known as *Puyallup Tribe v. Department of Game,* agreed unanimously that, while the treaty Indians did have special rights, separate and distinct from those of others, to fish at usual and accustomed places off the reservation, the state had the power to regulate the fishing, providing the regulation was reasonable and necessary and did not discriminate against the Indians. The case was sent back to the state courts to clarify, in accordance with the Court's decision, what was "reasonable and necessary." Moreover, though the Puyallups were confirmed as a recognized tribe, the question of whether their reservation had been extinguished was not settled.

It was an ambiguous and unsatisfactory decision, which, if anything, worsened the Indians' position. The Court had ignored the concept of the earlier Umatilla decision, in which a federal Circuit Court had ruled that Indians should only be regulated after a limitation or prohibition of non-Indian fishing, and which the Supreme Court at the time had let stand by declining to review it. Now, not only could the state set and enforce fishing rules against the Indians, which courts would be willing to accept as "reasonable and necessary" in themselves, without taking other conservation measures, but the Indians, having got their case to the Supreme Court, seemed at the end of their road.

As the Indians feared, the state viewed the decision as vindication of its asserted right to continue regulating Indian fishing as it saw fit, maintaining that its rules were reasonable and necessary and not discriminatory against the treaty tribes. The Puyallup Reservation was still deemed nonexistent, and another injunction again closed the Puyallup River to the Indian fishermen. The Nisqually River was also closed outside the boundaries of the Nisqually Reservation, and at Frank's Landing, whose fishermen were angered by a BIA decision in October that the site was not considered part of the reservation, there were renewed demonstrations and an escalation of violence and tension.

In 1966, Janet McCloud had viewed the fishing rights struggle as only one phase of a larger, overall fight by Native Americans for their rights throughout the United States, and she had left the Survival of American Indians Association to enlarge

the scope of her activities and join Hopi and other Indian traditionalist leaders and teachers. Traveling to other tribes, she
urged their members to revive pride in their Indianness and
return to the traditional values of their peoples. Gradually, as
she became known nationally among Indians, she took up
the leadership of such causes as the just treatment of Indian
inmates in federal and state prisons, and became a member of
the national steering committee of the Native American Rights
Fund. Hank Adams eventually took over the direction of the
Survival Association at Frank's Landing and strove to merge
its struggle with those of activist Indian and non-Indian groups
elsewhere in the country. Early in 1968, after meeting with
Martin Luther King and then attending the assassinated black
leader's funeral in Atlanta, he became one of the leaders of the
Poor People's March on Washington and, with Al Bridges and
a delegation of Puget Sound fishing Indians, was in the national
capitol when the Supreme Court ruled on the Puyallup case.
The decision incensed Adams and the Indians with him, and,
joined by non-Indian members of the Poor People's group, he
led a protest march on the Supreme Court Building. During
the demonstration, a window of the building was broken, and
Adams and the western Washington Indians pledged to return
to their homes and "fish every season every year from now
on," declaring that "no power of the United States, whether
political, administrative, legislative, judicial, or military, may
extinguish these rights so long as an Indian lives."

Adams and the others returned to Frank's Landing and
began fishing again. Their defiance, accompanied by press
releases and fiery broadsides, received wide publicity and
helped stoke a growing militancy among young Indians in San
Francisco—where, in 1969, they occupied Alcatraz Island—

and other parts of the nation. A few of them came to Frank's Landing, among them Sidney Mills, a nineteen-year-old Yakima Indian paratrooper, who had returned from Vietnam for hospitalization for wounds and had become so disturbed by the attack on his own people's fishing rights that he went AWOL. Later, after serving time in a stockade, he received a discharge. He settled at Frank's Landing as a sort of liaison between the Yakima and Puget Sound fishermen, worked with Adams, and eventually married Al Bridges's daughter Suzette (Adams married another daughter, Alison). The fishermen's militancy, at the same time, won considerable support from non-Indian students and counterculture young people in the Northwest, and many of them came to Frank's Landing to try to help the Indians.

The state officials accepted the challenge, and by the beginning of October 1968, after the Supreme Court decision, raids and arrests had begun again. The fishermen established several camps along the Nisqually River and fished at all of them. On October 13, the anniversary of the 1965 battle on the river, fifteen Indians and about two hundred non-Indians staged a protest rally against the new arrests at the Temple of Justice at the capitol in Olympia. The next day, some fifty wardens and sheriffs' officers appeared at Frank's Landing and, after a scuffle with the Indians and their student allies, arrested two non-Indians and seized a net. Anti-Indian sport fishermen were now also showing up, threatening the Indians with violence, and after the raid Adams accused one of them of firing a shot at an Indian. To protect the camp, Adams posted a guard at the perimeter of Frank's Landing, armed himself, Sid Mills, and another Indian, and announced that thereafter the weapons would be used against any trespasser or state officer who interfered with the Indians' fishing. The threat had no effect. Three days later, the wardens and police struck again, this time attacking Indians who were fishing at one of the other sites on the river. They arrested six fishermen, including the indestructible Al Bridges, and manhandled his daughter Valerie. Though Adams waged a tireless press campaign, accusing the state of discriminating against the Indians and violating the Supreme Court decision by not proving that their interference with the Indians' fishing was reasonable and necessary, the conflict and violence went on.

Meanwhile, arrests of Yakima Indians had also continued on the Columbia River, and in July a group known as the National Office for the Rights of the Indigent (NORI) was asked by Edgar Cahn, the executive director of the Citizens Advocate Center in Washington, D.C., and an attorney interested in Indian affairs, to help the Yakimas. NORI obtained the legal-aid services of three lawyers, who filed a case against the Oregon Fish and Game Commissions on behalf of fourteen Yakimas, including members of the Sohappy family, who had been subjected to arrests, seeking to define their treaty fishing rights, as well as the extent to which Oregon could regulate Indian fishing. Two months after the filing of the suit, known as *Sohappy v. Smith*, the Department of Justice followed through on the government's earlier assurance to the Columbia River tribes and filed a suit against the state of Oregon for itself, the Yakimas, the Umatillas, and the Nez Perce, seeking an injunction to enforce Indian off-reservation fishing rights in the Columbia River watershed. Later, the three tribes, as well as the Warm Springs tribe, intervened in their own behalf in the case, which was known as *United States v. Oregon*.

The two cases, which ran concurrently, were filed in the

U.S. District Court in Oregon. The opinion, handed down on July 8, 1969, by District Judge Robert C. Belloni, was an echo of the decision in the Umatilla case of 1963, which had been ignored for so long. Ordering the state to recognize Indian treaty fishing interests as "a subject separate and distinct from that of fishing by others," it upheld the right of treaty Indians to fish at usual and accustomed places and to have an opportunity to take a "fair and equitable share of all fish." Before the state could regulate Indian treaty fishing, moreover, it ruled that it must establish by preliminary hearings that the specific regulations were reasonable and necessary and were the least restrictive that could be imposed. To accomplish conservation objectives, the state was reminded to restrict or prohibit non-Indian fishing before interfering with treaty rights and imposing similar restrictions on treaty Indians. In addition, Indians must be given an opportunity to "participate meaningfully in the rule-making process."

The decision startled Oregon and Washington. Its implications, including those of putting Indian rights ahead of those of whites and giving the Indians a chance to take an "equitable" share of all fish (the court's interpretation of "in common with all citizens"), angered the non-Indian sport and commercial fishermen along Puget Sound, and although Washington State said it would abide by the decision, it failed to implement its rulings. Instead, the fish and game agencies maintained the old injunctions and continued to make arrests. With nothing changed, the Indians went on fishing as a matter of course, both for their livelihood and to assert their rights, and from time to time celebrities like the Indian singer Buffy Sainte-Marie and the actress Jane Fonda came to give them support.

During 1970, violence broke out again on the Puyallup

River, where Satiacum and other Puyallups had been complaining that the state was violating the 1968 Supreme Court
decision. Since the decision, Washington had done nothing to
alter its own opinion that the Puyallups' reservation no longer
existed, and it had kept in force an injunction that closed the
river to Indian net fishermen. The Puyallups finally decided to
fight the injunction as discriminatory against the Indians and
unnecessary for conservation purposes and had again begun
fishing with set nets for steelhead to sell commercially. Satla-
cum had been arrested and had appealed his conviction. The
Indians, meanwhile, kept fishing, and on August 1, during the
salmon season, some of them established a fishing camp and
set up a few tipis on a small piece of remaining Puyallup trust
land along the river. In the following days, the camp's population increased, as fishermen from Frank's Landing, Indians
from different parts of the country, and non-Indian sympathizers joined them.

The blatant net fishing by a large number of people angered
white sport fishermen, who began to mutter threats against the
Indians. Urged on by the whites, state fishery officers raided the
camp twice, on the nights of August 10 and 11, and on August
12, the fishermen, under the leadership of Satiacum, Ramona
Bennett, a Puyallup tribal council member, Charles Cantrell,
another Puyallup, and Sid Mills and Al Bridges, established a
protective armed guard around the site. Largely to defuse the
situation, the state officials offered to let the Indians fish for
salmon two days a week, using nets, between September 21
and October 23. The Indians rejected the offer, and on September 9, about seventy-five state officers and twenty-five Tacoma
policemen in riot helmets and carrying guns, together with a
number of aroused white supporters, showed up at the camp,

which was then occupied by about two hundred Indians and non-Indians. When some of the fisheries men in a small boat tried to interfere in the Indians' nets, somebody fired several shots, and a wild battle began in the camp and on a trestle that crossed the river. The police and state officers swung clubs and threw tear gas, and one Indian hurled a firebomb that set the wooden trestle ablaze. The police finally restored peace and, amid the flames, smoke, and the wreckage of the camp, arrested fifty-five adults and five juveniles. The other occupants were dispersed, the camp was bulldozed, and the following year those who had been arrested began to receive jury trials. Four non-Indians were convicted of unlawful assembly, and three Indians and a white woman were acquitted. After that, the trials were halted because of other, and more significant, developments that had resulted from the riot.

During the weeks that had preceded the battle, the Department of the Interior had watched the tension on the Puyallup River with mounting apprehension. The Supreme Court decision was not being observed, and after Satiacum's conviction, Stanley Pitkin, the U.S. Attorney for Western Washington, had been directed by the Justice Department to enter a case in behalf of the tribe's steelhead fishing rights. The case, *Puyallup Tribe v. Washington Department of Game*, or *Puyallup II* (because it was the second major Puyallup case), went to the State Supreme Court and then the U.S. Supreme Court, which on November 19, 1973, struck down the state's injunction on the Puyallup River as discriminatory against the Indians and returned the case to Washington State courts to determine a formula for the allocation of steelhead between the Indians and the sport fishermen that would be equitable to both. It still did not settle the central issues of the fishing rights conflict, but for Washington State it was another warning that the winds were beginning to blow in favor of the Indians.

Meanwhile, the battle of September 9 took place. In Washington, D.C., President Nixon and Vice President Agnew had just launched a new policy of support for tribal self-determination and the achievement of Indian aims and aspirations. The violent assault on the Indians, shown on national television, shocked officials in the White House and the Department of the Interior, and was a catalyst for the filing of a new, comprehensive suit on which the Justice Department had been working in an effort to settle all the issues affecting the Washington tribes' fishing rights. Fulfilling its obligation at last as trustee for the tribes, the government became the plaintiff, and on September 18, nine days after the fight at the river, U.S. Attorney Pitkin filed the case, *United States v. Washington*, in the U.S. District Court in Tacoma. It was soon perceived that the case could lead to a landmark decision, clarifying what the 1968 U.S. Supreme Court decision had ignored or left ambiguous, and fourteen Washington tribes, to whom the case was relevant, intervened as co-plaintiffs with the United States.

In the wake of the destruction of the Indians' camp on the Puyallup, meanwhile, tempers flared between the Indians, who continued to fish, and local sport fishermen, who harassed them and threatened to take the law in their own hands and drive them from the river. Then, in the early morning hours of January 19, 1971, Hank Adams was shot in the stomach while he was dozing in a car after setting a fish net in the Puyallup River. Though an investigation of sorts was launched, the assailants were not found, and the Indians charged the police with a deliberate cover-up, an accusation that one official rebutted by suggesting that Adams had shot himself. Adams recovered, and in the following months he and Sid Mills strengthened the association of the Northwest fishing rights struggle with other Indian causes being pressed elsewhere in the country. In the fall of 1972, Adams was one of the main strategists of the Trail of Broken Treaties, a caravan trek to Washington, D.C., by several thousand Indians from throughout the country that ended in the occupation of the Bureau of Indian Affairs building. He was one of the authors of the Indians' list of twenty demands, including the restoration of treaty-making between the federal government and the tribes and a review of violations of past treaties, and was then the chief Indian negotiator in the meetings that ended that confrontation, as well as an intermediary in attempts to terminate the siege at Wounded Knee in South Dakota in the following year. In 1977, having become a nationally recognized spokesman on Indian relations with the federal government, he participated in the preparation of the report of the American Indian Policy Review Commission for Congress.

By that time, the case of United States v. Washington, which had suspended the trials of those who had been arrested during the battle on the Puyallup River, was history. During its course, the government attorneys were joined by lawyers for the tribes, including David Getches of the Native American Rights Fund, who represented five of the tribes, and many agencies and organizations that participated as amici curiae. District Judge George H. Boldt, an Eisenhower appointee, now seventy-four years old and nearing the end of his career, worried the Indians. He had once told a tribal attorney, "I don't want to hear any more about these damn Indian fishing cases." But he called in his law clerk and told him "to put on that table every single case from the beginning of the country that per-

tains in any way to the rights of Indians." The two of them then
went through every one of them, working tirelessly through
weekends. One of his most important conclusions came from
his study of nineteenth-century legal dictionaries. The phrase
"in common with," he decided, meant that Stevens's treaties
had agreed that the Indians had a right to an opportunity to
take the same amount of fish as the whites.

On February 12, 1974, he rendered his decision in a series
of rulings that aroused a storm of protest among the whites
in the state. Pointing out that, by the treaties, the Indians had
"granted the White settlers the right to fish beside them," he
upheld the right of the treaty tribes to fish and manage the
fisheries in their traditional fishing places and ordered that they
had to be given the opportunity to take 50 percent of the harvestable fish. He declared illegal all state regulations that went
beyond conserving fish to affect the time, manner, and volume
of off-reservation fishing by treaty Indians at their usual and
accustomed sites, and to see that his orders were implemented
and enforced, he retained continuing jurisdiction.

A court had finally recognized the Indians' fishing rights.
On the Puyallup, Nisqually, Green, and other rivers, the little
people of the tribes, who had had the determination and courage not to give up, but to keep fishing, had won. But it was not
over. Judge Boldt was burned in effigy, vilified, accused of having an Indian mistress, and attacked by white fishermen, who
were spurred on by the anti-Indian rabble-rousing of Washington State's politically ambitious attorney general, Slade Gorton.
Despite threats to Judge Boldt's life, his receipt of a stream of
"loathsome" letters, and the bombing of the Federal Building
in Tacoma, he continued to hand down rulings to implement
his decisions. He decided that only Congress could disestab-

lish or diminish an Indian reservation, and until it did so, the Puyallup Reservation, with its original boundaries, still existed. To help get the Indians started on managing their fisheries and undertaking conservation and restoration programs, he supported the organizing of a Northwest Indian Fisheries Commission, with representatives from all the fishing tribes and staffs of biologists and other technical and scientific experts. Appointing a Fishery Technical Advisor to the court, he oversaw the drafting of an interim to implement the complex elements of his decision. There were many of them, and some would lead to further court cases. Methods, for instance, had to be devised for computing fish allocations and reporting and counting the Indian and non-Indian catch. A "substantially disproportionate" part of the annual fish runs, moreover, were taken by offshore fishermen before they ever got to the Indians' fishing grounds. It prevented the Indians from having an opportunity to take 50 percent of the fish.

From the beginning, the State of Washington refused to accept the decision. The Washington State Supreme Court, holding that the state could not allocate a resource "among races," enjoined the Department of Fisheries from enforcing Judge Boldt's orders, and amid a growing conflict between the state and federal judges, the Boldt decision went to the U.S. Ninth Circuit Court of Appeals. Thirteen more tribes intervened against the state of Washington, and on June 4, 1975, the Court of Appeals upheld Judge Boldt. A month later, Washington appealed for a rehearing, which was denied. The U.S. Supreme Court, on January 26, 1976, declined Washington's petition for a review, and Judge Boldt's decision stood.

Meanwhile, with the state refusing to enforce the decision, the recent history of the South, in which states had refused to enforce integration in defiance of federal court orders, had its counterpart in Washington. Illegal non-Indian fishing, encouraged by Washington's states' rights stance and detrimental to the Indians' interest, was rampant. At one point, the Ninth Circuit Court denounced the machinations of the state and non-Indian fishermen as one of "the most concerted official and private efforts to frustrate a decree of a federal court witnessed in this century," save for some segregation cases. As the state twisted and turned to avoid implementing Judge Boldt's decision, administrative and legal challenges proliferated. Picking up a theme popular with the non-Indian sport fishermen, the state won a ruling by the Pierce County Superior Court that the Puyallups had no treaty right to steelhead that had been produced in hatcheries and must let the artificially propagated steelhead go through their nets, a ruling that was obviously difficult to observe. When the Puyallups appealed the decision to the Washington State Supreme Court, Judge Boldt enjoined the state from carrying out the edict on any other river until the Puyallups' case had been decided.

On April 8, the State Supreme Court upheld the Superior Court decision and asserted the state's right of jurisdiction over Indian fishing, both off and on reservations, to enforce the decision against taking hatchery-produced fish. The decision in the case, known as *Puyallup III*, was appealed, and in 1977 the U.S. Supreme Court held that individual Indians, but not a tribe, could be subjected to regulation by the state both on and off their reservation. It declined, however, to rule on the Indians' right to hatchery fish, and that issue became part of a larger case, known as *United States v. Washington-Phase II*, dealing, also, with another issue that had not been settled by the Boldt decision—the right of protection of fish habitats against environmental degradation so that the ability of the Indians to secure their share of the fish would not be impaired. In September 1980, the two issues were considered by Judge William H. Orrick of the U.S. District Court for Western Washington, who decided against the state on the hatchery issue and ruled that the state had an obligation to protect the Indians' fishery habitats against environmental degradation.

Still, the cases went on. In Oregon, rulings by District Judge Belloni paralleled and supplemented those of Judge Boldt. On May 8, 1974, Judge Belloni allocated 50 percent of the spring Chinook salmon harvest to the Columbia River tribes. Washington and Oregon appealed to the Ninth Circuit Court, which affirmed Judge Belloni's order. The next year, Judge Belloni again directed Washington and Oregon to assure the upriver Indians 50 percent of the harvestable salmon. Washington, in both years, failed to take steps to implement his orders by restricting the offshore commercial fishing of non-Indians so that more salmon would reach the Columbia, and in June 1976, the judge enjoined the state from permitting non-Indian commercial troll fishing until July. Criminal contempt charges were filed against forty-eight Washington trollers who defied the order, but the charges against them were dismissed. At the same time, Judge Boldt extended the rulings of *United States v. Washington* to herring fishing, and in 1978, as defiance continued, he seized control of the Puget Sound commercial salmon fisheries.

The actions of the federal judges inflamed the non-Indian trollers and independent gill-netters and sport fishermen. Supported by Washington Fisheries Department officials, they vented their rage on the Indian fishermen, vandalizing their equipment and boats, ramming their craft at fishing sites, and threatening to shoot them. On a larger scale, they proclaimed a "Revolt Against Boldt," marching on the capitol and declaring a war against any state officers who tried to enforce the orders of the federal courts. The principal targets of Judges Boldt and Belloni were the oceangoing trollers, whose huge catches penalized the non-Indian gill-netters and sport fishermen as much as the Indians; but the heritage of anti-Indian demagoguery fostered the continued placing of all blame on the Indians, and many whites in the state gave their support to the non-Indian fishermen. Their feelings meshed with, and added to, a questioning of Indian treaty rights that was beginning to emerge in many other parts of the country.

Tribes in a number of states were in the news almost daily, pressing claims for land, water, hunting, and mineral rights, and they were winning cases in the federal courts that seemed to give the Indians a disturbing new status and power. Where their victories were not a direct threat to white property owners and vested interests, as in the Maine and Massachusetts land claims cases, there were few complaints, but their resistance to the acquisition of coal, uranium, water, and other tribal properties, as in Utah, Montana, and Arizona, frustrated and angered developers and state officials. Anti-Indian sentiment was already strong in some parts of the country, fostered most notably by an aggressive organization named, ironically, the Interstate Congress for Equal Rights and Responsibilities, with chapters in at least ten states. It was campaigning vigorously for the end of Indian reservations, tribes, and special rights, and wanted the Department of Justice to stop helping the tribes in the courts. It lobbied in Washington, D.C., and state capitals, numbered among its members state attorneys general and county officials, and published books and pamphlets with titles like *Are We Giving America Back to the Indians?* Almost overnight, fourteen organizations of white fishermen and their sympathizers were formed in Washington State and, joining the Interstate Congress, became its most vocal and powerful constituents. Nine anti-Indian bills, with various aims, including the abrogation of Indian treaties and the ending of tribal rights, were introduced in Congress, the most sweeping of them being authored, in reaction to the Boldt decision, by members of the Washington State delegation. One of them, Congressman Lloyd Meeds, had previously been among the Indians' best friends in the House of Representatives. In the elections of 1976, his friendship had almost cost him his seat, and he had turned full tilt against them.

Washington's senators, Henry M. Jackson and Warren G. Magnuson, also felt the fishermen's heat and pressed Attorney General Griffin B. Bell to consider the possibility of ending the government's trustee obligation to defend Indian rights and property in the courts. Nothing came of their proposal or of the bills in Congress, but the concern of both Indians and whites moved President Jimmy Carter to appoint, in April 1977, a special Presidential Task Force to try to find solutions to the different fishing issues. While the task force worked, conflict worsened between Judge Boldt and the Washington State Supreme Court, which issued orders to the state agencies that countermanded those of the federal judge and encouraged the continued defiance of the non-Indian fishermen. The tense situation was not helped by the task force. Its "Settlement Plan," a feeble effort to persuade all parties to compromise, was published in June 1978, but was rejected by the white fishermen as well as the tribes.

The state, meanwhile, was attempting to get the U.S. Supreme Court to reconsider its 1976 decision not to review the Boldt rulings. As the turmoil in Washington increased, the Carter administration, which had little understanding of the issues and tended to blame the Indians for the conflict, joined the state in its request, and on October 16, 1978, the Supreme Court agreed to intervene and review the controversial case. Its climactic decision, on July 2, 1979, sustained Judge Boldt, adding only slight modifications to his rulings, including an order that the Indians' maximum 50 percent share of the fish include their catch on reservations or at places other than their usual and accustomed sites, as well as fish that they took for subsistence or ceremonial purposes.

The decision at long last ended the rebellion of the Washington state courts, which fell in line with the federal courts to implement the Boldt rulings and halt illegal fishing by whites. With the collapse of official resistance, a new era arrived for the Indian fishermen in the state. There were still conflicts, a dragging of feet by some, and continuous efforts to undo the Boldt rulings by others. In 1980, Slade Gorton, who as state attorney general had carried the fight against the Indians for a decade and lost every fishing rights case he had waged in a federal court, was elected to the United States Senate, largely as a result of his war against the Indian fishermen. He did not give up. In the Senate, he got himself named to the Committee on Indian Affairs, introduced a bill of questionable constitutionality to void the Boldt decisions as they applied to steelhead fishing, and continued his crusade against the tribes. In the Northwest, at the same time, defiance of the Boldt rulings flared up again among some of the white fishermen, who seemingly hoped that renewed conflict and violence would induce the Reagan administration and Congress to support

Gorton's efforts. The courts continued to oppose the rebellious fishermen, however, directing the policing of fishing in Puget Sound, and by 1982 Gorton had won little backing from other Senators.

Meanwhile, as Judge Boldt hoped, a new era had also arrived for the salmon and steelhead. Working with the state Fisheries Department rather than against it, the Northwest Indian Fisheries Commission of the Puget Sound tribes, and a similar organization of the Columbia River fishing tribes, set to work to develop long-term management and enhancement programs that would help restore the depleted fish runs. Given an opportunity, the tribes quickly proved that they were capable and committed conservationists who had always known that their own future lay in the survival of the fish. Indians received technical training and assistance from universities and in cooperative programs with scientists of the U.S. Fish and Wildlife Service and individual tribes established experimental stations and hatcheries and began programs of releasing millions of salmon into the Washington streams. Congress, in turn, on December 22, 1980, passed a landmark Salmon and Steelhead Conservation and Enhancement Act to help finance restoration programs to increase the Northwest fish supply and assist both Indian and non-Indian fishermen to work together harmoniously with federal and state officials to achieve the goals of the Boldt decision.

At the same time, there were problems still to be met. The big hydroelectric dams of the Columbia River and its tributaries still interfered with the fish runs, and in years when few salmon reached the upper parts of the rivers, fishing was halted or restricted, and members of the interior tribes like the Nez Perce in Idaho fought for their rights under the Boldt and

Belloni decisions, insisting that they had a right to a share of the year's total harvestable supply. It was still up to the white man to see to it that adequate fish reached their usual and accustomed fishing grounds. In courts, as well as in Congress, new contests would also have to be waged against nuclear power plants, industrial polluters, pro-energy legislation favoring the proliferation of small hydroelectric projects exempt from protecting the fish runs, and other developments on the Northwest's rivers and streams that would degrade the habitat of the fish, cut off access to spawning grounds, or otherwise impair the fisheries.

But the long fight of the Nisquallies, Puyallups, Muckleshoots, and other Puget Sound Indians had had great impact beyond saving their own fisheries and putting them in a position to share in the restoration of the Northwest fish runs. The Boldt decision, which had vindicated them, had pointed the way also to the protection of treaty fishing rights—as well as treasured hunting and trapping rights—that were still important to many other tribes all over the country as a means of survival and a continued way of life. On May 7, 1979, Chippewa tribes, waging the same kind of struggle that had occurred at Puget Sound, won their own landmark decision in the U.S. District Court for Western Michigan (later sustained by the Sixth U.S. Circuit Court of Appeals and, on December 14, 1981, allowed to stand by the U.S. Supreme Court's denial of an appeal by the state of Michigan), which recognized their right to fish free of state regulation in the areas of Lakes Superior, Michigan, and Huron. By a similar insistence on the observance of treaty guarantees, where they applied, tribes noted that hunting and trapping rights could also be protected.

The small tribes of the Puget Sound area were no longer forgotten, demeaned, or overlooked peoples. The Indians had come back, proud of their heritage and the chapter they had added to their history. The white man, as Sealth, the Duwamish, told Stevens, would never be alone.

❊ ❊ ❊

An Update by David Cummings, Attorney, Nez Perce Tribe

Treaties—Federal Courts: Both the *United States v. Washington* and *United States v. Oregon* treaty fishing rights cases remain under the continuing jurisdiction of the federal courts. As Josephy observed, the Columbia River tribes have worked with their state and federal counterparts to develop fishery management and rebuilding plans within the framework of *U.S. v. Oregon*. These plans, as enforceable court orders, have replaced the salmon season with the salmon-season litigation that dominated the late 1970s and early 1980s. In *U.S. v. Washington*, Judge Orrick's ruling in *Phase II* of the case, declaring that the state had an obligation to protect the Indians' fishery habitats against environmental degradation (noted by Josephy), was overturned on appeal by the Ninth Circuit Court of Appeals on the procedural basis that a declaratory ruling must be grounded in a "concrete case or controversy" before the court. In 2001, the Stevens Treaty tribes of Western Washington (immediately joined by the other party to their treaties, the United States) presented the federal court with such concrete facts concerning the impacts of fish-blocking culverts on their treaty-reserved fishing rights. On August 22, 2007, Judge

Martinez issued a definitive order, holding as follows: "The Court hereby declares that the right of taking fish, secured to the Tribes in the Stevens Treaties, imposes a duty upon the State to refrain from building or operating culverts under State-maintained roads that hinder fish passage and thereby diminish the number of fish that would otherwise be available for Tribal harvest. The Court further declares that the State of Washington currently owns and operates culverts that violate this duty." [*U.S. v. Washington (Culverts)*, 2007 WL 2437166]

On March 29, 2013, Judge Martinez granted the remedy requested by the tribes and supported by the United States, requiring the State of Washington to ensure that any new culvert constructed provided fish passage and requiring fish passage at existing culverts owned or managed by the Washington State Department of Transportation to be implemented within twenty years. [*U.S. v. Washington (Culverts)*, 2013 WL 1334391]

As Josephy described with respect to prior treaty rights cases, the State of Washington has "refused to accept the decision" of the federal courts and Judge Martinez's decisions are presently on appeal to the Ninth Circuit Court of Appeals.

Impacts of the Dams on the Columbia River: As Josephy observed, "The big hydroelectric dams of the Columbia River and its tributaries still interfered with the fish runs, and in years when few salmon reached the upper parts of the rivers, fishing was halted or restricted, and members of the interior tribes like the Nez Perce in Idaho fought for their rights under the Boldt and Belloni decisions, insisting that they had a right to a share of the year's total harvestable supply." The Endangered Species Act (ESA) listings of Snake River spring, summer, and fall Chinook, sockeye, and steelhead and additional salmon and steelhead listings in the Columbia River brought additional scrutiny to the plight of the salmon. However, the federal government's administration of the ESA has been reminiscent of the era when the states would open fisheries and then contend that the burden of conservation should be addressed by closing the treaty fisheries. The government's initial biological opinions concluded that the treaty fishery jeopardized the salmon but that the federal dams on the lower Snake and Columbia Rivers posed no jeopardy to these fish, a position that Oregon District Court Judge Malcolm Marsh promptly rejected in 1994. Oregon District Court Judge James Redden rejected the government's subsequently developed 2000 biological opinion for the federal dams because it relied on a flawed mitigation plan that was not reasonably certain to occur. And, after rejecting two more biological opinions on the dams and presiding over the hydrosystem litigation for thirteen years, Judge Redden described the government's approach as "a cynical and transparent attempt to avoid responsibility for the decline of listed Columbia and Snake River salmon and steelhead," which included a "history of abruptly changing course, abandoning previous BiOps, and failing to follow through with their commitments to hydropower modifications proven to increase survival (such as spill)," and ordered that the Court retain jurisdiction over this matter pending development of a new biological opinion "to ensure that Federal Defendants develop and implement the mitigation measures required to avoid jeopardy." The Nez Perce tribe has been actively involved in this litigation over the impacts of the federal dams on the Snake and Columbia Rivers—and has been aligned with the State of Oregon and conservation and fishing groups—is seeking to ensure the impacts of the hydrosystem are addressed, and is involved in the present challenge to the 2014 biological opinion for these dams.

Fisheries Co-Management: Court orders have acknowledged the Stevens Tribes' role as a co-manager of the fisheries resource based on their treaty-reserved rights. Josephy's observations that the Boldt and Belloni decisions ushered in a new era for fisheries management by the Stevens Tribes, and which "given an opportunity, the tribes quickly proved that they were capable and committed conservationists who had always known that their own future lay in the survival of the fish," continue to ring true. Indeed, tribal fisheries programs have eclipsed many of their state and federal counterparts. For example, the Nez Perce tribe's Department of Fisheries Resource Management is one of the largest fisheries programs in the nation, actively working on all issues affecting salmon and steelhead. Many tribal members are engaged in these efforts, many obtaining technical training and academic degrees to advance this work.

11

The Hopi Way

◇◇◇

From the 1970s to the end of his career as a writer and activist, Jose-phy revealed his sensitivity not only to Indian ways of life but also to environmental crises threatening Indian and non-Indian alike.

This article, originally published in American Heritage *in Febru-ary 1973, is a brief but thorough description of the Hopi way of life as it was preferred by the "traditionalists," those tribespeople who did not wish to enjoy the fruits of contemporary American non-Indian society, as opposed to the "progressives," who were more accept-ing of the ways of whites. There is even an unexpected touch of humor in Josephy's account of the interaction between "hippie" and Hopi cultures. While the counterculture of the twenty-first century has gone in directions different from those of various predecessors, the interests of "hippies" did serve to focus wide attention on the spiritual validity of the Hopi Way and Indian spirituality in general. In any case, capitalism did learn an important lesson on the Black Mesa: "A corporation does not tangle lightly with Indians."*

Perched on the edge of a rocky mesa six hundred feet above the desert of northeastern Arizona is the Hopi Indian vil-lage of Hotevilla. A stronghold of Hopi traditionalists—Indians who remain profoundly loyal to the religious teachings and values of their ancestors—the little settlement of fewer than a thousand people is something of an anachronism on the American scene, a remnant of another day and another way of life that defies many of the influences of the white man's modern-day civilization and at the same time challenges it to do as well in providing mankind with enduring answers for an existence of happiness and contentment.

To the visitor Hotevilla appears to have some of the attributes of a true-life Shangri-la. One of twelve Hopi villages that are strung, at an altitude of six thousand feet, for some seventy miles along the southern escarpment of Black Mesa, it is a remarkable center of peace and serenity in a vast, silent land of stone cliffs and canyons, sandy wastes, and huge, dramatic stretches of painted desert. From a distance the town, like all the Hopi villages, seems to be a part of the landscape, the shapes and earth colors of the buildings blending with the rough terrain of the mesa top. The settlement is low and compact. Rows of flat-topped stone buildings, some with two or three tiers, front on narrow sandy streets. In large open plazas are mounds of earth, covering kivas, the Hopis' underground religious and social rooms, which are reached by ladders whose tops protrude from holes in the center of the mounds. Foxskins and bundles of feathers, part of the garb for the annual round of ceremonial dances and rituals, hang from the walls of some of the buildings.

The town is busy but quiet. Men with bangs over their foreheads and with their long hair in back tied up with a string work industriously repairing houses or packing wool sheared from their flocks of sheep into bags for market. Children and dogs romp past them. Women with pails of water or arms full of corn shuffle by. They have come up steep paths that lead from springs and gardens far below the mesa's edge. From the lip of the mesa the view of the green patches of terraced gardens and the broad desert floor stretching into the distance is at once breathtaking and idyllic. Each garden plot, bordered by a stone wall around it, has been given to a family by the *kikmongwi*, the hereditary chief and spiritual leader of the village. The sandy lower slopes and valleys beneath the mesa are dotted with the dark green clusters of growing crops: squash, beans, melons, gourds, and cotton, as well as corn. Among and beyond the plots, extending in isolated little clumps of green across the desert, are peach trees. Summer rains and seepage from springs water the garden plots; winter rains and snow help the fruit trees. Above the gardens, on a bench of land partway down the mesa wall, a spring feeds a large pool from which the village women fill their pails.

All is outwardly quiet, harmonious, and contented. It is the routine of ages, but there is no sign of monotony. Nothing shrill breaks the peace—no quarreling, no anger. In the silence of the humans and the spaciousness of the unspoiled land one is aware of a closeness to nature: the presence of earth and rocks and growing things everywhere; the clambering down to the gardens and the clambering back up; the vastness of the view from the mesa; the dramatic thunderstorms, the dust clouds, and the movement of the sun that brings changing colors to the canyon walls; the rain, the springs, and the pool of water on which everything depends. But there is also a meticulous order here, day upon day, year after year, that comes from an unquestioned devotion to a timeless philosophy and plan of life. The wellspring of the plan was nature. Its author, the traditionalist Hopis say, was a god, and its goal is to help man to be good so that he will not destroy himself.

Several years ago the serenity of Hotevilla was temporarily profaned by the intrusion of some twenty hippies from San Francisco who, high on drugs, rolled into the village in their trucks and vans and proceeded to hold a raucous orgy at the edge of the Indians' sacred pool partway down the mesa. The offended Hopis got rid of them, viewing them patiently as sick members of a stream of more respectful visitors who were coming from all quarters of the world to learn the traditionalists' prescription for a happier and more meaningful life.

The stream since that time has swelled. A new interest in America's minority groups has made the Indians the subject of many books, magazine articles, movies, and television programs, and accounts of their cultures are having an impact on a restless and changing world. To the disturbed and dissatisfied who are searching for new values and lifestyles and for better relationships with their fellow men, the supernatural, and the earth, almost all the original Indian cultures arouse images of a more natural—and therefore a purer and more self-fulfilling—existence. But most of the native cultures have long since vanished, or been changed by the white man. Here and there in the Western Hemisphere tribes exist with much of the content of their original cultures intact, or almost so, but none of them are as accessible to outsiders as the Hopis, whose centuries-old beliefs are still carefully guarded and maintained by the traditionalists.

Today visitors to the mesa villages are coming in large numbers—husbands and wives and whole families, longhairs in vans, single girls and groups of women, professional men fed up with urban life, and television crews from the United States and abroad—trailing to the stone houses of the gray-haired Hopi elders for interviews and discussions and attending the clans' religious observances in the plazas, studying in awed silence the rituals.

What do they want? A young woman real estate agent watching the Flute Ceremony of the Hopis' Gray Flute and Blue Flute societies in the village of Shungopavi last summer drew her two children closer to her. She had driven them in her white Mercedes from Sunset Beach, California, and would return after a week in the villages. "I'm looking for inner peace, and these people seem to have it," she said. "Maybe I can learn something from them." She paused, studying the clan members in their white blankets fringed with red and black who were reenacting the Hopis' emergence and migration myths. "I didn't want my husband to come with me," she added. "He wouldn't understand."

At Hotevilla a young man and his girl, both from Santa Fe, came out of the home of David Monongye, an elderly village spiritual leader. They walked slowly, with the pleased, faraway look of believers who had found what they had come to see. "Did you notice him?" the girl said. "He stopped talking in the middle of a thought and started to pray. And it came from so far down, like it was deep inside of him, like every part of him felt it. We should pray like that. It was beautiful."

Not all the Hopis are traditionalists and participate in the clan ceremonies or pray in the same manner as David Monongye. Government schools and Christian churches established in some of the villages have turned many of the people away from the beliefs and ways of their ancestors. Known as

progressives, to contrast them with the conservatives, or traditionalists, they live like white men and raise and educate their
children to be successful in the white man's world. But many
of them are defensive and know that they retain Hopi values
that they will never shed, and some of their children, becoming militantly antiwhite, have gone over to the traditionalists
and eagerly sought instruction in the old ways.

The traditionalists exist in every village, though they are
strongest at Hotevilla, which they founded in 1906 after a split
in another village, Oraibi, between themselves and those who
wished to follow the ways of the white man. To the outsider
there is ample evidence that the traditionalists themselves have
not found all of those new ways bad. They have welcomed the
material comforts and conveniences of modern civilization
and, as individuals, have made choices of what to accept and
what to reject. Sewing machines, canned foods, automobiles,
and Grand Rapids furniture are among many of the white
man's products that are commonplace on the mesas. But the
people of Hotevilla have kept electricity out of the village and
have no sewerage. To some it makes no sense; to the traditionalists who made the choices, such decisions had a relationship
to what really mattered—not the adoption of material conveniences, but the maintenance of age-old beliefs and values and
the opposition to changes that might tend to undermine and
destroy those values. They will drive everywhere in automobiles, wear sunglasses to protect their eyes, and use dime-store
supplies for a hundred practical needs. Why no electricity in
Hotevilla? It may baffle an outsider. But the traditionalist has
considered, and has rebuffed what he believes to be a threat.
There is only one thing important to him: in his home and clan

kiva the Hopi must keep alive the myths, legends, and prophecies on which rests the pattern of his life. It is an intertwining of religion and philosophy that he calls "the Hopi Way."

The roots of that plan for existence reach far back toward the very dawn of the human habitation of North America. It is known that at some distant period, possibly during the Ice Age, ten thousand years ago or more, the earliest ancestors of all the Pueblo people of the Southwest—of whom the Hopis are one group—migrated from the north. Eventually the groups spread across the rough and arid plateau country that is known today as the Four Corners area, where the present states of Utah, Colorado, Arizona, and New Mexico meet. Other migrants from more developed areas came among them, bringing them new ideas and skills, and they began to live in circular pit houses, often constructed in large caves or in rock overhangs of cliffs.

Slowly their population grew and demanded more complex and sophisticated systems of society. After about AD 700 they began to build contiguous rooms aboveground, constructing them of stone mortared with adobe or of poles and adobe and arranging them in straight lines or crescents. Member families of clans joined their rooms together, and social and religious organizations developed. Pit houses became subterranean ceremonial chambers and meeting places for the men, and gradually as their culture expanded and flourished through a series of advancing stages, there developed an increasingly formalized religious system, centered on nature and agriculture and including a pantheon of deities, many legends, myths, and prophecies, and special rituals and ceremonies. The overall intention is to maintain harmony and order in the universe by keeping everything in balance, thus bringing rain, ensuring crop fertility, and warding off natural disaster.

The culture of all the Pueblo peoples, including the ancestors of the Hopis, reached a radiant climax in the Southwest in the years from about AD 1100 to 1300. Their settlements stretched all across the red rock canyons, valleys, and juniper-covered hills of the Colorado plateau; some like those at Mesa Verde and Canyon de Chelly were built in huge, arched recesses of cliff walls, while others were constructed on mesa tops or in the open valleys. From time to time there were great movements of people, but the greatest occurred during the latter part of the thirteenth century, when groups abandoned their dwellings in one area after another and moved elsewhere. Various theories ascribe the sudden exodus to a twenty-three-year drought, to pressure from hostile neighbors, or to other reasons. Many of the peoples migrated to the Rio Grande and established new towns, where the Spaniards later found them and named them the Pueblos. Others moved elsewhere across Arizona and New Mexico, settling in different sites.

The people who became the Hopis seem to have stayed where they were, for the earliest of their present villages date to well before 1300, and Oraibi, the oldest continuously inhabited town in the United States, is believed to have been first settled in the eleventh century. Both before and after the dispersal, however, the inhabitants of these communities received many newcomers into their midst, including peoples of other tribes and different languages, so that in time the Hopis became something of a mixture of strains. In their isolation, far to the west of the main bodies of Pueblo peoples, they continued their cultural rise and, as the years went by, wove new legends and sacred beliefs and enriched their civilization with additional ceremonies based on fast-receding memories of early migrations and events of a distant age.

The philosophic foundation on which their society rested was by that time ancient. It was an understanding, permeating every phase and moment of their life, that man was only one element in a delicately balanced universe in which every component interacted and interrelated in harmony. Everything that the Hopi people could comprehend—the rain, the rocks, the growing crops, the natural forces around them, the ideas in their heads, the birds, reptiles, and animals, every act and action—was part of a great living power and contained a spirit that existed everywhere. Everything was in balance, but man alone by wrong living or evil deeds could upset this balance and bring disaster. Therefore man had to live a prescribed way of life—the Hopi way—which had been given to their ancestors by a deity when the first people had entered this world.

From that conviction of man's obligation sprang the full richness of the Hopis' religion, including their myths, legends, prophecies, and annual cycle of ceremonies all designed to illuminate and help them follow the proper and pure way of life so that the balance of the universe would not be disturbed. The welfare and good fortune of people everywhere demanded harmonious attunement to the spiritual world, and the Hopi legends made vividly real the origin and nature of that demand. Man, according to the legends, which differ slightly in details from one village to another, had earlier lived in three different underworlds. Each time, some of the people had grown corrupt and evil and by their wrongdoing had caused dissension and social disorder. Disgusted with the people's fighting, the supreme deity had destroyed each of the underworlds, attempting to wipe out the evil ones, and each time some of the good people had escaped and moved on to the next underworld, where the mistakes were repeated.

Finally, those with good hearts had ascended into the present world through a place of emergence known as *sipapu*. They had been welcomed by the deity Massau'u, the earth's lone occupant at the time. Entrusting the care of the universe to them, he had given them instructions in the proper way to live, as well as prophecies of what would come to pass, and had started their different groups on long migrations, at the ends of which they would come to the place where they should settle, the very center of the universe. Further legends told of the migrations and of the arrival of the individual groups of migrants, one after another, at the Arizona mesas, the universe's center, where they finally built their villages. But at the heart of all the legends was the theme of the Hopi way of life, the plan that Massau'u had given them. Its essence, the key to its present-day appeal to peoples other than the Hopis, was simple: brotherhood, love, and peace.

In their own Shoshonean language the word *Hopi* suggests "one who follows the path," or, in the expression of traditionalists, "one who is good." It has also taken on the connotation of peace, and most Hopis consider themselves today "the people of peace." But, more accurately, Hopi implies peace as a value and goal and, like Christianity, which similarly invokes the ideal of peace, has seen violence committed in its name and in its behalf. Throughout their history Hopis have fought, though scarcely ever with aggressive intent. Warfare and war societies among them have been justified traditionally as defensive in aim, and when Hopis killed enemies, they went to great pains to purify themselves of the bloodshed. Similarly, while anger, violence, and crime among themselves have not been unknown, they are generally traumatic to all the people and are considered grave threats to their social order. Their laws are those of their spiritual beliefs, and penalties for infractions are ridicule and social ostracism rather than punishment or imprisonment.

Both the order and the serenity of the life of the present-day Hopi traditionalists reflect their continued faith in the instructions of Massau'u and their spiritual conviction that they are interrelated with, and responsible for the well-being of, nature and everything in the universe. But the legends also tell them that a few of the evil ones managed to enter this world along with the good people, and Hopi history has been darkened many times by conflicts with forces that jeopardized the people's continued observance of Massau'u's plan and threatened the destruction of this fourth world.

In the past such threats came from raiding Utes, Apaches, and Navajos, who had to be fought off, and from Spanish priests who tried unsuccessfully to convert the Hopis to Christianity. In 1700 one of the most contradictory and violent episodes in the Hopis' history occurred when a Franciscan missionary managed to convert almost half the population of the village of Awatovi. This resulted in so much dissension and internal conflict among the Hopis that the future of all Hopi life was considered threatened by those who remained loyal to their ancient beliefs. Finally, in a desperate attempt to save the Hopi way of life, the *kikmongwi* of Awatovi appealed to other villages to wipe out his town and all its people, good and bad, himself included. The towns of Oraibi and Walpi responded and totally destroyed Awatovi, killing all its inhabitants, Christians and non-Christians, and clearing the earth of this threat to the Hopis' well-being. It was a terrible experience for the tribe, and even today no Hopi likes to talk about it.

For many generations after that the Hopis were undisturbed

by whites. Their arid and rugged land possessed nothing deemed valuable by the Spaniards, Mexicans, or Americans who, in succession, held sovereignty over the area, and the remoteness of the villages from the mainstream of white civilization permitted the Hopis to maintain their culture and religious life without serious interference until the latter part of the nineteenth century. Then new threats arrived with the appearance of Protestant missionaries and United States government agents. Since then, the traditional way of life has been steadily on the defensive. Many Hopis have been Christianized and encouraged to jeer at the traditionalists' "idols," the masked kachinas—symbolic representations of the spirits of animals, birds, plants, places, or ancestors who appear among the people from the kivas during the ceremonies and remind the Hopis of the good way in which they must live. Children forced to attend schools run by the Bureau of Indian Affairs have been made ashamed of their people's beliefs, have been whipped and punished for defending their fathers' faith, and have been taught that the only right way to live is the white man's way. On many occasions traditionalists have tried to keep their children out of schools; for their opposition they have had troops called out against them and have been hustled into prison.

The number of people who turned against their ancient beliefs and became known as progressives, or "friendlies," grew during the first half of this century. Competition, vanity, the lust for acquisition of material possessions, individual ambition—all the human characteristics that Massau'u had warned against—took hold in the towns. To the traditionalists the great turning away from Massau'u's plan meant the balance of the universe was in danger. The dissension that had led to the end of the three previous worlds was growing again.

The destruction of this fourth world, which only good Hopis would survive, was drawing near.

As caretakers of the universe, the traditionalists viewed the white man's way of life, with its wars, ruthless exploitation of the land and natural resources, pollution of the air and water, crime, racial conflict, and poverty, as the principal threat to the delicate balance they were trying to maintain. They prayed to their spirits that the whites would learn the way of Massau'u before the evils of their society and their influence in turning Hopis against each other brought disaster to all. In May 1959, and on other occasions both before and afterward, they sent their elders to the United Nations headquarters in New York, to Washington, and to other centers of the white men to try to tell them of the prophecies of destruction and of the Hopi way that could save them. The whites never knew what they were talking about and dismissed them politely as quaint primitives. Meanwhile, the stage was set for what many of the traditionalists have come to fear may be the final disaster that brings on the world's destruction.

In the 1930s the Bureau of Indian Affairs, making use of the progressives, imposed on the Hopis a white man's form of government. Against the will of the traditionalists, a constitution was written for all the tribe by Oliver La Farge at the request of John Collier, Commissioner of Indian Affairs, and authority over non-religious tribal matters was vested by the federal government in a tribal council. Only 651 of the more than five thousand people in the Hopi villages supported the constitution in a referendum, but it was a majority of those who turned out to vote—most of them progressives—and the government declared the constitution adopted. The traditionalists, who still follow the guidance and decisions of the *kikmongwis*, have never accepted or recognized the tribal council, and the council has been something of a farce, out of communication with the people, responsive to the Bureau of Indian Affairs rather than to the villages, and made up of progressives, some of whom appoint themselves or each other to membership. Through the years it has been a divisive agent, carrying out the policies and programs of the bureau and forcing on the people many things they did not want and that disrupted the harmony of their life.*

Nothing the council did, however, compared with a truly horrendous action it took in 1966. Encouraged by the federal government, its members signed a lease with the Peabody Coal Company of St. Louis for the strip-mining of Hopi land on Black Mesa. The mine would supply coal for thirty-five years to two giant power plants in a network of at least four others that are already under severe attack by environmentalists for the devastating pollution with which they threaten a large area of the Southwest, including the Hopi Reservation. The Peabody lease was signed by the Hopi council in such secrecy that the traditionalists in the villages knew nothing about it until 1970, when the coal company moved onto the mesa to begin operations. Since then, a storm of protest has blown up that has gained the Hopi traditionalists the support of many Indian tribes as well as numerous white individuals and organizations, including the Sierra Club, the Friends of the Earth, and the Environmental Defense Fund. But the deed is done, the sacred land to which the Hopis are spiritually bound is being destroyed, and there is little prospect that the strip-mining can be stopped.

---

* Eds. note: This was the situation at the time of the original publication.

The physical threat to the future existence of the Hopis is very real. Billions of gallons of the Hopis' limited underground water reserves that feed their springs will be used by the mine during the course of the lease, and the contract contains no guarantee that the Hopis will always be supplied with water. Hydrologists are divided on whether the Hopi springs will suddenly dry up, and only time will provide an answer to the question. Furthermore, the lease gives no guarantee that acid from spoil-bank run-offs from the mine will not wash across and destroy the Hopis' gardens. Nor does it guarantee that the land ravaged by the mine will be reclaimed and healed satis factorily after the strip-mining ends. Any one of those catas- trophes would force the Hopis to move, severing the sacred attachment between them and the place Massau'u told them to settle, the center of their universe, and thus bringing about their prophesied destruction.

To many of the white visitors who come to the Hopi vil- lages the strip mine on Black Mesa and the air and water pol- lution with which the new power plants threaten to destroy the exquisite beauty of the American Southwest are sobering reminders of man's present suicidal course on earth. Suddenly the gap disappears between the "quaint primitives" and the rational twentieth-century men who believe themselves cre- ated to dominate and control nature. As the visitors listen to the traditionalists in Hotevilla and the other Hopi towns relating Massau'u's life plan and his prophecies of what will happen if that plan is disregarded, they see the pollution of the air and understand clearly, at last, what the Hopis have been trying to tell the world. And those who have come as pilgrims in rest- lessness and trouble sense that they have found the answers for which they have been searching.

Black Mesa is covered with the holy shrines of generations of Hopis, the signs and markings that signified the Hopis'
belief that they were the stewards, not the exploiters, of the
earth, and that everything in nature is interrelated and must be
respected if man is to survive. But the strip-mine drag lines are
already tearing them up.*

---

* Eds. note: The controversies continue, but Indians—and environmental
laws—are stronger today. Mining operations, the state of the aquifer (much
of the controversy was about use of water to ship slurried coal to the power
plants), and tribal rights are all more transparent now than they were in the
1960s, when the original arrangements were made. Black Mesa Mine's last day
of operation was December 31, 2005, with unsuccessful appeals carrying on
until 2010. Operations at Kayenta Mine carry on at time of publication.

Nimíipu (Nez Perce) dance in their Wallowa Valley homeland at the annual Wallowa Band Tamkaliks Celebration and Friendship Feast. L. to R.: Brothers Don and Richard Powaukee (Nez Perce); Victor Kehama (Yakama); Mary Harris (Cayuse, Karuk, Nez Perce); Thomas Gregory (Nez Perce); Larry Campbell (Spokane). (Photography by Joe Whittle, circa 2011.)

III

THE MIRACLE OF
INDIAN SURVIVAL

Let's Make the Deal
Indian Country's History of Success

◇◇

A Commentary by Mark Trahant

The 1960s-era TV game show *Let's Make a Deal* led contestants to a prize hidden behind one of three stage doors. The audience was always in on the secret: we knew where the best prize was and we would shout at the screen, "One! Pick Door Number One!" But of course we couldn't be heard. We were disconnected from the transmission of a television signal faraway. No contestant, ever, could hear us shout which door they should choose. I thought about what was behind those doors when I read Alvin Josephy's 1979 speech at the University of Michigan, because in one critical paragraph Josephy set the American Indian experience in America as woven from three separate threads that could easily reflect this country's version of *Let's Make a Deal*.

The first door opened to the idea of assimilation. Indians "could stop being Indians and turn themselves into whites," Josephy said. "They would have their hair cut, wear white men's clothes, become Christians, live in white men's houses, become farmers or mechanics, and adopt the white men's language, customs, ways of living, values, society, and culture. In other words, they would become assimilated and disappear as Indians."

At that time, most Americans would probably have shouted their support for Door Number One. It seemed to be the ideal. Open that curtain and the guilt of conquest fades away. The Indians, then, are beautiful and the culture is to be appreciated. There is no competition for land, fish, or political authority. The audience just gets to pretend that American Indians are exactly like everyone else, wearing American clothes, working as farmers, mechanics, carpenters, and, of course, Christians. It's a show. Just like America. Of course this ideal was never possible.

Assimilation begins with a false premise. The truth is that even from the very beginning—the first encounter—there were exchanges of ideas, foods, and blood, which make up both America and Indian Country today. Then again, even if American Indians look the part of a farmer, it's clear after a few sentences that the essence of the Indian, the tribal culture, survives and prospers.

America tried Door Number One more than once, with tragic results. There was the 1887 Dawes Act, a law that promoted assimilation by privatizing Indian land. "But," as Josephy said in his Michigan speech, "on the whole, the Indians kept on being Indians." Meanwhile some ninety million acres were stolen from us. It took both Congress and several presidents to figure out that this policy didn't work, so by the 1930s, another policy door was opened, a timid attempt to turn over self-government to tribes. But that did not last long. By the 1950s, the old assimilation saw was back, and this time Congress added another disaster to the script, termination. House Concurrent Resolution 108 called for a quick and final end to tribal governments and treaty promises made by the United States by terminating relations between the two governments at the "earliest possible date." The result was chaos as wealthy tribes were stripped of timber and other natural resources. "The application of the termination policy, which almost immediately resulted in hardships, new problems, and results exactly opposite to what had been intended," wrote Josephy in his 1969 memo to the incoming Nixon administration. Josephy's point was exactly right—and President Nixon's 1970 message rejected termination (and implicitly assimilation) as a policy course, a path that's been followed by every president since. Forced assimilation is a closed door.

So what about the second door? Josephy said that if Indians refused to play the assimilation game, then the indigenous tribes of North America would be "pushed away, westward to a safe distance, where they would have no contact with white society. They would continue as 'wild' Indians, unconquered, but neither a physical nor cultural threat to the whites." This idea may be the most impractical of any idea tried by the United States (or for that matter, the tribes). In every telling of this narrative, the very act of removal is brutal, followed by an all too short period of autonomy and new acts of encroachment. The eighteenth-century Cherokee Nation was one of the most Christian, civilized societies in North America, building schools, an efficient court system, and other institutions. The Nation's tribal literacy rate far exceeded that of most nineteenth-century communities and their neighbors. A few tribal leaders even thought that statehood might be a part of the bargain. But James Monroe unraveled the pledge: in public he vowed to protect the Cherokee homeland while in private he negotiated to kick the Cherokee people off their land. Soon the very idea of Cherokee independence became a tragedy when thousands of Cherokees were force-marched from Georgia to the Indian Territory—what is now Oklahoma. Andrew Jackson, president at the time of removal, said he was acting in the best interests of the civilized tribes. And he offered a new, better promise: this homeland would be permanent. Not so. The Oklahoma Indian Territory was stolen before the beginning of the twentieth century.

Another attempt at isolation took place in the Great Plains. "No tribe fought harder to live its own way, unmolested on its own lands, than the Sioux—the many independent but often allied bands that called themselves Dakotas or Lakotas, depending on their dialect, and roamed the plains after buffalo in Montana, Wyoming, Nebraska, and the Dakotas," Josephy wrote in "The Custer Myth," a 1971 essay for *Life* magazine. So after the Civil War, "the Great Plains were left to take" and Civil War officers were matched against well-trained Sioux warriors. "In 1868 they heaped the greatest possible insult on the army, forcing it out of their hunting grounds in Wyoming and making Gen. William Tecumseh Sherman agree to a treaty acknowledging the sanctity 'forever' of the lands they claimed as their own. Forever lasted six years. In 1874 Custer violated the treaty, invaded and explored the Black Hills, the holiest of lands to the Sioux, and announced to the world that he had discovered gold there." The treaty did not last. Door Number Two was slammed shut.

Josephy's third option was the most unimaginable: extermination. That story is a part of America's dark history, unfolding again and again in waves of murder. So much so that even Congress had to acknowledge the barbarous implications from massacres at Bear River (near the Idaho and

Utah border), at Wounded Knee in South Dakota, at Sand Creek in Colorado. An 1865 congressional investigation called Sand Creek, where dozens of Cheyenne and Arapaho men and women were slaughtered, a "foul and dastardly massacre which would have disgraced the veriest savage among those who were the victims of his [Colonel John Chivington's] cruelty."

These three threads were common in the history of white–Native American relations. "Though it would seem to some that extermination was the strongest of these threads, actually American policy since the founding of the Republic has pursued assimilation unwaveringly as its principal goal for the Native American," Josephy said in that Michigan speech. He continued:

> The 1960s, however, saw the start of something new. Until then, the white man and the white man's government had done all the planning and thinking for the tribes, imposing on them the programs and policies that they wanted the Indians to carry out. Through the years, almost all of the programs had failed because they were unilaterally framed and implemented in wholesale fashion by whites, in and out of government, who had little or no understanding of, or regard for, the particular needs and conditions of the individual Native American peoples, or of their respective histories, cultures, or abilities to accept or adopt what was being imposed on them. With increasing assertiveness, starting about 1961, the Indian peoples began to ask for, and then demand, the right initially to participate in the devising of policies and programs for themselves, and by the end of the 1960s the right to initiate, frame, and implement the

policies and programs themselves. With American Indian
spiritual leaders, traditionalists, and young Indians in the
vanguard, some of them using the term "Red Power," some
getting media attention as militants or activists, the movement grew quickly into one for self-determination and sovereignty.

Red Power was not in the script. It was Door Number
Four. This alternative allowed Native people to decide what's
appropriate in terms of culture, technology, and even government. The United States tried this approach—at least a little
bit—when Congress enacted the Indian Reorganization Act of
1934. That law recognized tribal governments, but with limited
authority, unlike the powers of citizens of a state, or city, or
county, tribal governments were required to authorize the Secretary of Interior to act as the ultimate chief executive, approving ordinances and tribal laws. "The Native Americans are
the only Americans who have governments that have limited
responsibilities to their peoples," Josephy told those Michigan
students. "Their principal responsibility is still to the federal
government, acting through the Bureau of Indian Affairs. The
Bureau has veto power, even today, over almost everything of
fundamental importance to the Native Americans' life."

But that federal veto power was not forever. In the four
decades since that speech, slowly, bit by bit, tribes have been
assuming more authority in a variety of forms. One of the
most significant ways, at least economically, occurred through
casino gaming. This started with high stakes bingo in California and Florida. Those enterprises led to a 1986 Supreme
Court decision that tribes, not states, had the power to regulate

gambling within their borders. The Supreme Court affirmed a power that was already inherent in tribal government: the power to govern.

Some two-and-a-half decades later, casino gambling is a multibillion-dollar enterprise, employing tribal members and citizens of neighboring communities. One of the elements of the gambling story that is particularly intriguing is one of technology. This is important because many tribal cultures have been gambling—essentially running casinos—for thousands of years.* For many tribes, gambling is a part of our mythology and who we are as tribal people. So the bright-light casinos, slot machines, or card rooms are simply a technological application of an old tradition. Native people incorporate the tools of the time—whether that is a slot machine or a cell phone—as we pursue survival.

This is the antithesis of assimilation. It is taking the technology of the modern era and adapting it to Native America. This is audacious. Too many think of Indians stuck on the images from the past, or worse, Hollywood. But true sovereignty means every people has the right to decide what technology is appropriate. Native Americans use what works. Think about this: not one treaty dictates technology; the documents only guarantee rights to lands, to education, or promises made to continue hunting or fishing "usual and accustomed" places.

The tribes in the Pacific Northwest did just that (a topic also discussed in these pages) when they rebelled against the states of Washington and Oregon and fought to protect

---

* Eds. note: The best-known forms of Indian gambling are stick games and horse races.

their treaty rights to fish for salmon in those "usual and accustomed" places. But the states, eager to please commercial fishing interests, or their constituents' sports-fishing hobby, ignored the treaties. Then the story took on a new twist: the United States of America sided with the tribes. *U.S. v. Washington* was huge and the title is sometimes forgotten. Now the case is named after the U.S. district judge who ruled in favor of the tribes' treaty rights, George Boldt. The Boldt decision said the state had no authority over tribal fishing because it was the tribes who welcomed and gave the settlers hunting and fishing, reserving some "in common" for themselves. The practical side of this ruling was that the tribes became "co-managers" of a scarce natural resource. There is no question that the salmon are in better shape today because of this co-management approach. The court forced tribes and states to work together—the real promise of America.

The opening of the Red Power door did not solve all the many problems facing American Indians and Alaska Natives. Poverty, unemployment, substandard education, and many other social ills are stubborn reminders of past failures. But there are also gems, sometimes hidden, that show promise of what Native people can do for themselves.

In 1955, for example, the management of health programs for American Indians was transferred from the Bureau of Indian Affairs to the Indian Health Service. The BIA's management of health care was a disaster; doctors often quit, complaining about the bureaucracy and the lack of basic services. So the new agency, the Indian Health Service, began its operation focusing on public health: drilling wells, building sanitation systems, and public health programs. The result was almost immediate: a nearly 80 percent drop in gastrointestinal diseases among American Indian and Alaska Natives. A few years later, when the Indian Self-Determination and Educational Assistance Act became law, tribes and tribal organizations were able to take over the functions and run clinics and other health programs directly.

Even the name "Indian Health Service" is misleading. It is really the Indian health "system" because about half of the operations are managed directly by tribes and tribal organizations. Katherine Gottlieb, who directs a nonprofit foundation operating a facility in Alaska, calls this true "self-determination." It is the simple idea that patients can help manage their own care. And the data backs up her words. There has been a 40 percent reduction in emergency room, urgent care; a 50 percent decrease in specialty care visits; a 20 percent decrease in primary care visits; and a 35-plus percent decrease in admissions. Staff turnover has dropped dramatically and the overall rating by customers of their care stands with a score of 91.7 percent out of 100.

You would think that success stories like that from Alaska would bring to an end the debate about doors One, Two, and Three. You would think that the success of tribes would call for more investment in ideas from Indian people about how to solve problems.

But that is not the case. The philosophy of austerity—an anti-government ideology—is the same today as was termination a generation ago. It's as if there is still an audience shouting from faraway, "Door Number One!" Or, as Josephy wrote in the *New York Times*, in 1973, poverty must be "attacked and broken without inhibition." The federal government spends billions rehabilitating communities across the globe, so "the same is certainly due its own citizens, the American Indians." All it takes is programs designed and operated by Indian people "who know better than the whites what they need and can carry out successfully." That idea remains true and a twenty-first-century policy path worth pursuit.

12

The American Indian and the
Bureau of Indian Affairs

◇◇

*In 1969, Alvin Josephy was approached by the Nixon administration
to prepare a report on the Bureau of Indian Affairs and to make recommendations on its operation. Alvin is reported to have said that
he was expected to form a committee to study the matter but replied
that there was no need for this and that "enough studies had been
done." He then proceeded to summarize those previous studies and
in a matter of three weeks produced what has come to be known as
the "Nixon White Paper." The core message of his ninety-three-page
report was that the "termination" policy of the Eisenhower administration must be abandoned. It had been set aside as a failure in
the late 1960s, but it was still on the books. Clearly it was time for a
change, and Josephy's "white paper," along with political and other
pressures, led to Richard Nixon's famous statement that "there will
be 'self-determination' rather than 'termination' for Indian peoples."*

*The following pages are an edited version of the original docu-
ment, retaining its essentials and redacting many contemporary references not required for full understanding.*

———

When the Democrats left office in 1969, the record of the preceding eight years showed a steadily intensifying Indian demand for self-determination, beginning with the Chicago "Declaration of Indian Purpose" of 1961 and coming from more and more elements of the Indian population. Save for some lip service, however, and a slight groping in the direction of permitting American Indians to have a greater participatory role in discussing and managing programs that were framed in Washington for them, the eight-year record also showed that both the Kennedy and Johnson administrations had remained, on the whole, indifferent to this trend. The one bright spot, for a time at least, had been the OEO antipoverty programs, but they were special. No important change had occurred in either policy or substance in the more vital relationship between the Bureau of Indian Affairs and the Indian people the agency was supposed to serve. An observer could conclude that the Democrats for eight years had continued the governmental attitudes about American Indians that they had inherited from the past: the assimilation of the Indians was still the ultimate national goal, and Indians were still judged not competent enough to know what was best for them.

In actuality, this is what had occurred in the 1961–69 period. The real rulers of Indian policy were not in the Department of the Interior but in the congressional committees on Interior and Insular Affairs and in the Bureau of the Budget. Both held a whip hand over the Secretary of the Interior and his Bureau of Indian Affairs in regard to direction, thrust, and appropriations for Indian policies and programs, and both had clung stubbornly to the non-Indians' traditional ideas of what was best for American Indians. By 1969 both were still deaf to the Indians' rising demand for control of their own affairs, and had the power to prevent any meaningful response by the Department of Interior to what Native Americans wanted. The result, in effect, was that the Bureau of Indian Affairs, the agency of government responsible for the welfare, was accountable not to the Indians whom it was supposed to serve and protect but to powerful bodies hostile to Indian self-determination—the congressional committees and the Bureau of the Budget.

Thus many native people remembered with bitterness that termination of federal relations with the tribes had been the policy of the Eisenhower regime, the last Republican administration in office, and faced the prospect of the Nixon administration with considerable uncertainty, and even fear. On September 27, 1968, during his campaign for election, Nixon had promised the Indians that termination of tribal recognition would not be "a policy objective" of his administration and that in no case would termination be imposed without their consent. Indians had applauded that statement, but after the election they looked for a more concrete assertion from the president-elect, guaranteeing that the September promise had not been campaign oratory and spelling out for them in specific terms what the new administration's Indian policy would be.

The position of American Indians in U.S. society, in truth, had reached a point where decisive change could occur. In the view of many, the time for the realization of self-determination had arrived. A new administration, willing to assume the initiative in bringing new attitudes to Congress and the Bureau of the Budget, could respond to the Indians' demands for control and power over their own affairs while continuing to observe treaty obligations and to protect the Indians' lands and resources.

On the eve of assuming office, the new administration recognized that at the very least it would have to make a clean break with the termination image it had inherited from the Republicans of the 1950s. But it was out of touch with the Indians of 1969. It took President Nixon many months to find an Indian commissioner of Indian affairs acceptable to the Republican Party. It took him a year and a half to frame and announce his administration's Indian policy. In the meantime, Republican officials conscientiously acquainted themselves with Native Americans and their needs.

The following document was one of the first foundations upon which the new administration developed the Indian policy that it eventually proclaimed in July 1970. The document was written in January and February 1969 at the request of the president-elect and served as a briefing for him on the then-current status of Indian affairs and on events in federal–Indian relations during the Democratic administrations of the 1960s. Such a background, providing orientation as well as recommendations based on American Indians' own expressed desires and proposals for solutions to their needs, was considered necessary before the new administration could proceed to consider its own policy.

The first section of the report, taking note of American Indians' continued opposition to the termination policy and of their fears that the new Republican administration would revive it, recommends that the president re-enunciate his promise on termination given to the Indians in September 1968. This was ultimately done, first by Vice President Spiro Agnew and Secretary of the Interior Walter Hickel to the National Congress of American Indians in October 1969 and finally by the president in his Message to Congress on Indian Affairs in July 1970.

The report's second section, titled "The Context of This

Study," is basically an orientation lesson in history and points of view for non-Indians dealing with federal–Indian relations in 1969. The third section is a chronological recapitulation of studies and major developments in Indian affairs during the 1961–69 period, revealing the steady Indian demand for self-determination and the government's continued deafness to it. It concludes with the admonition that the time has come to make American Indian self-determination a reality but points out that certain governmental obstacles stand in the way. One of those obstacles, the responsibility of the Department of the Interior to interests that competed with the Indians, is dealt with in the fourth section, which proposes transferring the Bureau of Indian Affairs to the Executive Office of the President but suggests, also, several alternative solutions. The second obstacle, deficiencies in the structure of the Bureau of Indian Affairs that worked inherently to prevent Indian self-determination from becoming a reality, is examined in the fifth section, which also suggests how the bureau might be reorganized. The report's final section discusses specific Indian programs and recommends that they be initiated, planned, and carried out under Indian control and direction.

Following are excerpts from the various sections of the report.

I. A First Priority

It is the purpose of this study to provide an understanding of the shape and substance of present-day federal–Indian relationships and the ability of the Bureau of Indian Affairs to serve efficiently as a vehicle for the management of those relations, as well as to make recommendations for a course upon which to embark in 1969. But among the questions to be examined are where, if not in the Interior Department, functions of federal–Indian relationships should be placed; what, if any, restructuring should be considered within the Bureau of Indian Affairs; which programs and their administration require changes? Any proposed alteration from the status quo would obviously stir again the embers of the Indians' fear of termination. . . .

It is not necessary to argue the wrongs versus the motives of the termination period of 1953–58, or review the specifics of the human damage that occurred. Recognition that the policy should not again be enforced is today so widespread that Indians, as well as all non-Indians knowledgeable about Indian affairs, enthusiastically applauded the statement by President Nixon, addressed to the Indian people through the National Congress of American Indians, on September 27, 1968, during his campaign for election: "Termination of tribal recognition will not be a policy objective, and in no case will it be imposed without Indian consent."

This was a clear, reassuring statement, but now that the new administration has assumed office it requires, at the earliest convenient opportunity, reiteration to the Indian tribes and peoples. . . .

It is therefore recommended that the Administration, hopefully through the President himself, find and take advantage of an opportunity to address the Indian people, possibly through the National Congress of American Indians in Washington, re-enunciating the statement given the Indians on September 27, 1968, particularly as it refers to termination, and making clear that the new Administration has no intention of disrupting the Indian peoples by new directions in policy, but will carry out the promises made on September 27, 1968, and make them meaningful.

Such a statement will not only have great meaning for the American Indians and prepare the ground for productive federal–Indian relations in the years immediately ahead, but will receive the approving reaction of all alienated and dispossessed peoples as well as those in the United States and in other nations to whom the treatment of the American Indians is symbolic of the broadest attitudes of the Administration.

II. The Context of This Study

It has been said often enough, and with great truth, that expert knowledge of the cultures and histories, not alone of Indians generally, but of the many separate tribes, is needed to understand Indian needs, desires, actions, and responses, as well as to work intelligently and compassionately with Indians to help frame, administer, and service policies and programs for their benefit.

There is no doubt that many of the failures and frustrations that mark the course of federal–Indian relations, past and present, can be ascribed to deficiencies of knowledge about Indians among non-Indians who are involved in managing Indian affairs. Indians have long complained about officials who listen to them but don't seem to understand them, and many of the complaints and criticisms that Indians level at the Bureau of Indian Affairs result from actions and programs that were imposed by well-intentioned whites, but bear no relation to the realities of what a tribe, fashioned by a particular history and culture, needed, desired, or could accept and carry out with success.

The Peace Corps, which oriented its enrollees in the backgrounds and cultures of the peoples to whom they were being sent, might have taught the Bureau of Indian Affairs a lesson. But even today, little attention is paid to such instruction of Bureau personnel, and in its proper place in this study a recommendation will be made on that subject. In this section, however, it is appropriate to make several general observations as necessary prerequisites for a more vivid understanding of the implications of the findings and recommendations in the following portions of this study. In a sense they provide a basis and context for a realistic approach to federal–Indian relations in 1969 and to what, if anything, requires rethinking and change.

1) In the great mass of treaties, statutes, laws, and regulations that have been built up during the long course of federal–Indian relations, the non-Indian, to use an analogy, often becomes lost among the trees of Indian affairs and too rarely steps back far enough to see the forest whole. He forgets basic truths about Indians that must never be forgotten, if only because they are in the minds of the Indians with whom non-Indians are trying to work. It would appear unnecessary to restate such facts that the Indians were here for thousands of years; that this is their homeland; that they evolved their own distinctive cultures and did not share the points of view, attitudes, and thinking that came to the rest of the American population from Judeo-Christian and Western civilization legacies; that although the Indians were conquered militarily (and are the only portion of the American population that reflects that

experience), they are confirming a lesson of history, namely that no people has ever been coerced by another people into scuttling its own culture; and that although acculturation and assimilation do occur, they occur only on the individual's own terms. The awareness of such generalizations makes clear the implications of a further facet of Indian affairs that has continuing relevancy, and especially to this study, namely the Indians position, and therefore their posture, vis-à-vis the government.

In matters that are of the most importance to them, the Indians, unlike all other Americans, do not yet enjoy self-government. They are still governed not entirely unlike colonial subjects, by strangers whom they neither elected nor appointed and who are not accountable to them. As late as 1934 the rule of the "governor" was absolute; since then, tribal councils, like the legislatures of many modern colonies, have acquired authority over a broadening range of tribal affairs. But the "governor" is still present with the apparatus of management and the powers of direction, influence, finances, and veto to use when and where they really count. The practical meaning of this relationship of the American government to its Indian citizens in this extraordinarily late day and age was noted recently in a study titled "The Indian: The Forgotten American," published in the *Harvard Law Review* in June 1968. Its authors, Warren H. Cohen and Philip J. Mause, commented: "The BIA possesses final authority over most tribal actions as well as over many decisions made by Indians as individuals. BIA approval is required, for example, when a tribe enters into a contract, expends money, or amends its constitution. Although normal expectation in American society is that a private individual or group may do anything unless it is specifically prohibited by the government, it might be said that the normal expectation on the reservation is that the Indians may not do anything unless it is specifically permitted by the government."

The psychological implications of the Indians' status as compared with that of the rest of the American body politic loom with increasing significance in Indian affairs today, especially as larger numbers of young Indians become educated and motivated to seek the full measure of self-government enjoyed by all other Americans. To an extent, the full perspective of this "forest-view" of all Indians is obscured by dilemmas posed by the obligatory trust function of the government. But a banker, exercising a trust function for a non-Indian citizen, applies himself only to the substance of the trust and does not govern the life of his client or necessarily manage his other affairs. One task in Indian affairs is inevitably to narrow the trustee's domain to the substance of the trust (to be discussed later) and to remove his authority from other areas. The logic of attempting to achieve such a goal can, again, only be appreciated in full by viewing the "forest" whole, and not being enmeshed and inhibited among the trees.

2) To the incoming member of a new Administration the questions and problems of federal–Indian relations are of the here and now. Decisions concerning changes or the retention of the status quo will be made largely within the context of today alone. But to the Indian, the context is an immensely broader one and possesses a vividness and influence that often leads to the frustration and failure of policies and programs when the non-Indian administrator fails to comprehend its relevancy. The context is history, the details and individual steps of which may be unknown to the contemporary non-Indian official, but are still intimate and potent in Indian thinking and responses.

To the Indian, 1969 is a continuation of an unbroken narrative of policies, programs, and promises, often abruptly changing, disorganizing, contradictory, and unrealistic, and of people, many of them still personally remembered, who gave promises and orders and who sometimes worked for good and sometimes for harm. In Washington discussions will occur today, and policies and programs will be considered according to the current situation. But the Indian's mind will also be on a legacy of pacification, army and missionary rule, punishments and repression, allotments, treaty sessions and sacred promises, laws and special rights acknowledged in return for land cessions, and orders given by the government in the 1920s, countermanded in the 1930s, countermanded again in the 1950s, and countermanded once more in the 1960s. Specifically, the Indian's response will be conditioned by the knowledge of a Mr. Smith or a Captain Jones who came to the reservation as the agent of a President in the mid-nineteenth century and told the tribal leaders something that their descendants have kept alive from generation to generation. He will color his reactions to a proposal with the evergreen memories of battles won or lost, of injuries and injustices, of land taken from his people by fraud, deceit, and corruption, of lost hunting, fishing, and water rights, and of zigzag policies of administrations that came to office, just like the new one, and then left. . . .

3) Despite the fear of termination and various programmatic and administrative shortcomings, some of which were quite serious and will be discussed in later sections, a number of profound and important improvements did occur in Indian affairs during the last eight years. One of them, fraught with significance for the future direction of Indian affairs, requires the most serious recognition.

Indians had long asserted, but usually to deaf ears, that the individual tribes knew better than the government what kinds of programs they needed and wanted, and that if they could play decisive roles in the planning of such programs, they could, with technical and financial assistance, demonstrate an ability to learn quickly to administer and execute them successfully.

This assertion was stated forcibly in a "Declaration of Indian Purpose" by some four hundred twenty Indian leaders of sixty-seven tribes at a gathering in Chicago in June 1961, but, although endorsed to some extent by Secretary Udall's Task Force the same year, it received no serious recognition or encouragement from the Bureau of Indian Affairs. The Indians were deemed not to know what was best for them, and programs continued to be imposed on them. . . .

4) In the same vein, it must be noted that the non-Indian population of the United States, reacting to a multitude of winds of change abroad in the world in recent years, is beginning to turn away from a long-held view regarding the Indians' destiny and therefore from what were long considered the proper policies and programs for them. From the time of Jamestown and Plymouth, the most benign attitude of the white man concerning Indians was, assimilate or die. Missionaries and agencies of government tried to rush Indians into becoming Christianized farmers, and from the administration of George Washington until the present-day national policy, stated or implicit, has been directed toward the turning of the Indian into a white man, the alternative seeming to be only continued primitivism, economic stagnation, and ultimate obliteration by white society. All programs, actions,

and attitudes of government have supported this policy, which derived its mandate from the non-Indian population and its representatives in Congress.

At the same time, a minority opinion always existed that expressed the view that Indian "progress" and development, far from being assisted, was actually being crippled and delayed by the "either-or" choice, that Indians would resist attempts to force and hurry their assimilation, and that such attempts would not only fail to achieve their purpose but were morally wrong, since no people had the right to strip a culture from another people. Inevitably, the merits of the point of view of the latter group were obscured by superficial and erroneous arguments that they were more interested in seeing Indian cultures preserved than allowing the Indians to develop, and the minority was unable to bring about a meaningful dialogue that might have produced an impact on national policy, which throughout the Kennedy and Johnson administrations continued, in essence, to point toward the ultimate goal of Indian assimilation.

Of late, however, Indian articulateness, studies of Indian education, and changing attitudes among the American people concerning minority groups have combined to pose the acceptance of a different destiny for the American Indians, one in which they would be allowed to develop on their own terms and at their own chosen rate of speed—bi-culturally if they so desired—being assisted to create a viable economic life for their people, but not being pressured to give up any parts of their individual cultures which they wished to retain, and not being urged to take on any of the dominant society's traits which they did not want. The pros and cons of such a policy need not be argued here. But the strength, particularly among the Indians, of those who maintain that Indian self-determination is now the surest road to Indian progress and development, that it will see a new and electrifying rebirth of Indian initiative and vigor, and that its result will be the growth of viable and healthy Indian communities within the nation has grown to the point where the new administration must take note of the areas in which it may soon engender significant confrontations. . . .

The Indians' demand for self-determination will increase steadily, but there will be many ways to move soundly with it. Perhaps the best way, short of the enunciation of an Administration point of view on the subject, will be a clear and purposeful redefinement of the Bureau of Indian Affairs' functions, procedures, and limits of authority, together with a restructuring of the Bureau to accommodate the changes. Though the changes would not be drastic, intentions and effects on the reservations would be altered, and a natural process tending toward increased self-determination would come into play. Any such change from the status quo would, of course, require the support of the Congress and the Bureau of the Budget and would demand that the Administration play a positive persuasive role with both bodies. . . .

III. Studies and Major Developments in the Last Eight Years

"During the last eight years," an Indian leader said recently, "Indian policies and programs have been studied to death. What we need is for someone to begin paying attention to some of the things that the Indians recommended in those studies."

There is no need in 1969 to repeat the experience of the Kennedy Administration in 1961 with another full-fledged, Task Force–type study of Indian affairs, complete with months of hearings and subordinate studies. . . .

A brief conclusion from the . . . record of what has, and has not, occurred during the last eight years illuminates the following:

1) Both the appropriations and functions of the Bureau of Indian Affairs have increased greatly, and many other Federal agencies, including OEO, EDA, BAA, the Office of Education, and the Labor Department now share the reservation scene with the BIA;

2) The BIA's greatest expansion has occurred in the fields of education, vocational training and placement, housing, and industrial and community development, and is evidence that a change in its orientation from the primacy of its trust function to that of development has become an established fact;

3) The obligations conferred by the trust function still require the wielding of authority over other matters by Bureau officials and result in many of the conflicts between the Bureau and the Indians, as well as much of the BIA's negativism and delays. Increasingly, the Indians are requesting the right to assume full responsibility for the management of their income and final authority over such matters as attorney contracts, tribal codes, and constitutional actions while having their lands continue inviolate in trust status;

4) The principle of self-determination has been accepted and is already being applied in small ways on some reserva-

tions. The BIA has begun a trend of negotiating with tribes to permit them, through contracts, to provide some services; this too is encouraging the process of self-determination. But Indian participation and decision-making are still the exception and are being frustrated and denied too regularly by the Bureau's present organization;

5) At the same time, the BIA's structure still leads to a malaise within the Bureau as bad as eight years ago that positively holds back progress;

6) The top priority is for a change in the administration of Indian affairs to accelerate Indian progress and achieve the maximum effective implementation of Indian policies and programs by utilizing, and not impeding, the Indians' development of self-determination.

IV. Positioning Indian Affairs in the Federal Government

This study now addresses itself to specific recommendations for a course upon which to embark in 1969, including:

> The positioning of the administration of Indian affairs within the government;
> The reorganization of the BIA's structure;
> Programmatic approaches.

This section concerns the first of those items. . . .

This study recommends that a meaningful and determined reorganization of the administration of Indian affairs, together with the providing of an effective Administration thrust to go forward to the opportunities of tomorrow and not simply solve the problems of yesterday, can only be accomplished by moving the Bureau of Indian Affairs to the Executive Office of the Presidency, for the objectives of Indian affairs in 1969 require nothing less than the priority, mandate, and visibility which the President himself can give them. . . .

It is recommended, therefore, at the very least, that if the Bureau remains in the Department of the Interior, it should be placed under an Assistant Secretary for Indian and Territorial Affairs, who can give the proper attention to decision-making at the topmost level of the Department.

Wherever the present Bureau of Indian Affairs is positioned within the government, its structure must be thoroughly reorganized.

It is recommended, therefore, that the reorganization of the structure of the Bureau . . . include:

—the elimination of the Offices of the Assistant Commissioners for Community Services and Economic Development, together with all the staffs and Divisions of those Offices;

—the readjustment of the present Offices of the Assistant Commissioners for Administration, Engineering, and Program Coordination as guidance, coordinating, budgeting, administration, and management arms of the Bureau, reporting to the Commissioner;

—a separate structure for the Assistant Commissioner for Education, who would report to the Commissioner, but would retain his present staffs and Divisions, and would have direct line authority to all elements of the educational system, as well as coordinators with area and agency programs, tribes, and state and local school systems;

—the addition of regional coordinating desk officers, reporting to the Commissioner, but without line authority;

—the addition of an Office of Urban Indian Affairs, concerned with the problems of urban Indians and reporting to the Commissioner;

—the retention of area offices headed by Assistant Commissioners, but the elimination of all branches at the area level and the reorientation of the area office's function to that of providing guidance, advice, and assistance to reservations; and

—the focusing of primary operational attention on the reservations by placing all specialists, save those in education, on the reservation and giving the superintendent authority over them and their budgeting, and a direct line via the area Assistant Commissioner to the Office of the Commissioner.

In addition to Bureau reorganization, the following recommendations are also made:

—The National Council on Indian Opportunity, which has already proved its value, should be continued, with its present functions adequately funded;

—Training programs, and adequate orientation seminars in Indian (and tribal) history and cultures, should be set up and carried out systematically for Bureau personnel who work at every level of the Bureau;

—Superintendents, area heads, and the new Office concerned with urban Indian affairs should be directed to seek from the tribes and Indian communities the most effective methods by which information about government programs can be communicated to individual Indians. . . .

—Contracts with tribes must be accompanied by improved payment procedures, a continuity of planning and programming, the ending of unnecessary supervision and requirements, the provision of necessary working capital and equipment, and an agreement that tribes should receive a fair return, not be required to pay sub-standard wages, and be offered projects that will require them to develop their own staffs of skilled personnel. . . .

—Attention should be given, and steps taken, to end the Bureau's deficiencies in the field of research and development; in the lack of meaningful and adequate data on Indians and Indian affairs; in the use of consultants and non-government experts; and in the modernization of its administrative, fiscal, record-keeping, and other management practices.

—Indian Affairs should be headed by an Indian, but he should possess all the qualities of dedication, determination, knowledge, and vigor that the leadership of the federal conduct of Indian affairs now requires. Indians should also be placed in as many policy- and decision-making positions within the Bureau as possible. Moreover, if the Bureau is kept within the Department of the Interior, the Secretary should have an Indian staff assistant primarily responsible for liaison with the new Assistant Secretary for Indian and Territorial Affairs, the BIA, and Indian affairs generally.

V. Programmatic Recommendations

It is certain that the worst problems afflicting American Indians will never be ended without programs that are adequately funded. It is accepted that the Indians do not have the funds themselves and that they do not have access to the sources of credit that are usually available to other Americans. But the actual funding of programs for Indians by the government has never approached the level required by the massive dimensions of the problems.

A few of the facts obscured by the promulgation of intentions in President Johnson's Message on Indian Affairs on March 6, 1968, underscore the point. The Message conveyed proposals for many new or expanded programs which, somehow, were to be financed by only a 10 percent increase in federal expenditures for Indians above the appropriations of the previous year. One of the proposals was for a 10 percent increase in funds for health programs, including a number of items that would make available to the Indians greater numbers of trained personnel to help cope with the many serious health problems on the reservations. Before the year was over, the exact opposite had come to pass, and the Public Health Service was pointing out that, under Section 201 of the Revenue and Expenditure Control Act of 1968, Public Law 90-364, the Division of Indian Health was facing a reduction of almost one thousand employees, or one-sixth of its total staff, principally among nursing personnel and other patient care supportive staff in the field. A reduction in staff is now occurring on reservations and in Indian hospitals, not only nullifying the promise held out in President Johnson's Message, but bringing a new crisis to the Indians. (Corrective legislation, it hardly needs pointing out, is required at the earliest possible moment.)

Again, the inadequacy of funding a program to deal effectively with another pressing problem is evidenced in the field of Indian housing. The Presidential Task Force had reported to the White House that at least three-quarters of all Indian houses on reservations were below minimum standards of decency and that over a ten-year period roughly one hundred thousand units, "of which approximately eighty thousand are new, would have to be provided for the housing needs of the Indian population." The president's response to the Task Force's assertion that this would require a ten-year program costing approximately $1 billion was to propose an increase of only one thousand new Indian homes (for a total of twenty-five hundred) to be built under HUD programs in fiscal year '69.

The American taxpayer may wonder with increasing impatience why Indian problems are not solved, and why expenditures for those problems continue to mount each year. One demonstrable answer is that the expenditures have never been high enough to do much more than keep the problems going. In the years after the Indians' pacification, the appropriations barely met the minimum subsistence needs of the Indians. In more recent years, with an increasing Indian population and a growing complexity of reservation problems, the appropriations have risen, but consistently have stayed well below a level needed to carry out intentions. It may be impossible, because of higher priority needs elsewhere in the federal budget and the consequent requirement for economy in the Indian budget, to attempt to solve the Indians' problems once and for all with the same kind of massive appropriations that have characterized the most ambitious aid programs for some of the under-developed peoples overseas. But it should be emphasized that the Indians are Americans, and that until a similar approach is adopted for them, Indian programs will continue to limp along, and Indian development will proceed at an unsatisfactory pace. In addition, because of the rapid increase in the Indians' population, there is every prospect that their economic, educational, and health levels will drop steadily behind those of the rest of the population, and that each Administration will leave the Indians worse off, in relation to the rest of the American people, than it found them.

Adequate funding, therefore, should be a major concern of every Indian program. . . .

The planning and application of all economic development programs, long- and short-range, should reflect the Indians' own needs, desires, and cultural traits. By bringing the Indians into the planning and decision-making process, programs need not fail, as they have in the past. . . .

With minor exceptions, the Indians desire the federal government to continue to provide its trust protection for their lands, and the government must continue to give that protection. But it should be possible, by amending the Indian Reorganization Act and other pertinent statutes, to reduce the number of ancillary obligations and responsibilities of the trustee. In their drive for self-determination and self-government, tribes will press increasingly for the right to program their judgment funds, have authority over their budgets, and assume full responsibility for the management of their income, the making of contracts with attorneys, and the framing of tribal codes, resolutions, and constitutional actions. Without abandoning the trusteeship protection of lands, the government should be in a position to be able to transfer those other responsibilities, piecemeal or in full, to tribes deemed ready to assume them. For some tribes, that day may already have arrived, and the continued denial to them of rights they are able to exercise for themselves may be viewed as the most stultifying of all the obstacles that inhibit them on their road to development.

13

The Historical and Cultural Context of White–Native American Conflicts

◇◇◇

Originally a speech delivered at the University of Michigan School of Natural Resources on April 16, 1979, the essay that follows was published as "The Historical and Cultural Context of White–Native American Conflicts" in The Indian Historian, *vol. 12, no 2.*

The essay deals primarily with the impact of European ethnocentricity on the American Indian peoples as the white population pressed from east to west, offering three disastrous historical "choices"—assimilation, removal, or extermination. It also touches on the white quest for land and resources, the changing nature of treaties during the nineteenth century, and, finally, the reemergence of Indian cultural awareness and the beginnings of the struggle for civil rights.

Recently I was reviewing the transcript of the hearings before the House of Representatives Subcommittee on Fisheries and Wildlife Conservation and the Environment of the Merchant Marine and Fisheries Committee, held at Petoskey, Michigan, January 13, 1978. The following caught my eye: it was just a sentence or two in the testimony of Dr. Howard Tanner, Director of the Michigan Department of Natural Resources. Sometimes it is unfair and misleading to quote out of context, but this statement really stands on its own and is parenthetical to the thrust and substance of Dr. Tanner's full testimony:

"Based on an everchanging Indian policy and trust responsibility," said Dr. Tanner, "the federal government now is fostering self-determination for Indian people. Put another way, the policy of self-determination translates into the establishment of a separate nation within a nation and superior rights for a small segment of our society."

There are fundamental errors in that statement, but in many ways it is about as relevant as anything can be to the purposes and aims of this symposium—for it reflects the great need of gatherings such as this one—that can cast light on darkness, supplant misinformation with truth, and, by friendly discussion and exchange of opinions and explanations, erode or eliminate contention and adversary relationships that have been based on ignorance, prejudice, or self-interest so strong as to have precluded an understanding of anything save what one has wished to believe. I will come back to Dr. Tanner's statement shortly.

From the viewpoint of white–Native American history, there is nothing unique or unusual in that statement. From the time of Columbus, almost five full centuries ago, until just the last few years, very few whites have either wanted to, or been able to, try to see the world through Native American eyes. Very few have had any motive to try understanding, much less appreciating, the relationship of a Native American tribe, community, or family to its own universe, as that group perceived it to be, or its points of view and needs, usually stemming from that spiritual relationship, as they affected the Native Americans' actions and reactions in any particular aspect of their daily life or contact with whites. Non-Indians, by and large, from 1492 until today, have inevitably viewed Native Americans and interpreted their words, deeds, lifeways, and values from their own Euro-American perspectives. It has led to endless misunderstandings, frictions, and conflicts, including many that are with us today and continue to plague the relationships between Native Americans and the rest of the American population.

Within the present-day United States, such ethnocentricity (if we can call it that) began even before the days of Jamestown and Plymouth. To the Spaniards in the Southeast and Southwest (Ponce de León, De Soto, Coronado, and all their successors) the Native Americans were alien, strange, heathenish, and different, and the Europeans equated being different with being inferior. The Indians were to be converted, conquered, and impressed as inferiors. If they resisted, they were to be exterminated. The French were more benign. Though many of them also viewed the Indians as inferiors, in fact as children of nature, and converted and asserted dominance over them, the dynamics of the fur trade demanded dependent, but relatively content, Indian fur suppliers. Above all other Europeans, the French made the greatest efforts to see the world as the Indians saw it. Many of the voyageurs and trappers, indeed, lived with the tribes and raised half-breed families who became the start of the large present-day Metis population of mid-continental Canada.

Along the Atlantic Coast, however, the Dutch and English traders and settlers carried on the legacy of the Spaniards and immediately established the heritage of misunderstandings, stereotypic thinking, and conflicts that still pervade white–Native American relations within the United States. The first of these, again, was that the Indians, being different, were inferior. But that inferiority often translated into fear, the religious and cultural fear that the wilderness man, the Indian, with his free, seemingly simple, and unChristian way of life would corrupt the European settler and the society the European had come to erect in the New World. A second part of the heritage had to do with land and resources. Divine guidance told the settlers that they were to multiply and replenish the earth. If Indians were not physically dwelling on and planting the earth, it was being wasted. The whites could take it and use it themselves, buying it from Indians if, indeed, they could find Indians who claimed ownership of it. Or, if the Indians refused to sell it, they could take it by force. Much of the land, of course, contained hunting grounds or fishing stations. But the whites came to regard it as wasteland, and the so-called right of the huntsman became secondary to the right of the agriculturalist. So was born the concept of "the highest and best use" of a resource, which is with us yet, especially with regard to the use of water in the arid West of today.

Other long-enduring concepts arose from the first large-scale colonial Indian wars, the Powhatan War in Virginia and the assault on the Pequots in Connecticut in the 1620s and 1630s, both stemming from misunderstandings and white aggressions and aggrandizements. Now the Native Americans' differences became viewed as those of the Children of Satan, brutish and savage. Puritan writings on the Pequot War are not only part of the standard history of the beginnings of New England white civilization, but they created images of Indians which, though largely false, were carried westward from frontier to frontier and persist even to this generation. The skulking savages of the woods who scalped women and bashed babies' brains out against rocks were part of that image. As an example of what Puritan history did not bequeath to us, however, is the fact that Massachusetts Bay settlers, in the New World only seven years, began the war against the Pequots, without any logical reason save a desire to seize control of the supply and value of their currency, wampum, from the Pequots, by attacking a Pequot village and killing men, women, and children. When the bewildered Indians, who up to then had not warred on women and children, asked if the English intended to kill their women and children, the English Lieutenant Lion Gardiner replied fatefully that the Indians would "see that thereafter." From then on, it was total war.

From then on, also, whites gave the Native Americans three options. The first was that they could stop being Indians and turn themselves into whites. They would have their hair cut, wear white men's clothes, become Christians, live in white men's houses, become farmers or mechanics, and adopt the white men's language, customs, ways of living, values, society, and culture. In other words, they would become assimilated and disappear as Indians. If they refused, they would have to be pushed away, westward to a safe distance, where they would have no contact with white society. They would continue as "wild" Indians, unconquered, but neither a physical nor cultural threat to the whites. If they refused to move or become assimilated, they had a third option: extermination.

From the time of the close of the early colonial wars, these three threads run through the long course of white–Native American relations. Though it would seem to some that extermination was the strongest of these threads, actually American policy since the founding of the Republic has pursued assimilation unwaveringly as its principal goal for the Native American. From one administration to the next, changing ideas regarding how to bring about assimilation have caused wild zigzaggings in programs and surface policies. For a long time, the goal was to isolate conquered Native Americans under agents, missionaries, and educators who would work to assimilate the Indians. The Dawes Act of 1887 hoped to speed the process by breaking up the reservations into small allotments on which individual Indian families would become farmers and live like whites.

For decades, repression of almost every sort imaginable was visited on the captive and isolated native peoples. Their traditional governmental and religious structures of society were smashed and obliterated. Their leaders were punished, exiled, or killed. Their religious ceremonies were banned. Their children were shanghaied away from them, sent to white-run schools where they were punished if they spoke their own language. Rations were withheld on reservations for the smallest sign of opposition. Church and State were combined, possibly the only time in our national history, and missionaries and agents, backed by troops, created tyrannies on reservations, unquestioned and unchecked by any organ of government. Indian arts, crafts, legends, lore, music, dance, and other elements of tribal and group culture were discouraged, mocked, or proscribed.

Through the years, there were always some Indians who became assimilated. But, on the whole, the Indians kept on being Indians, and in 1934 when it was seen how the Dawes Act had done little but impoverish tribal groups by taking from them some ninety million more acres of their land, together with water and resources that might have helped make them economically viable, federal policy changed again. The Indian Reorganization Act of that year brought many reforms, including the right to establish limited self-governments, but its end goal was to continue assimilation, though at a slower pace and more in harmony with the Indians' own cultures. In the intervening years, there have been more zigs and zags: in the 1950s, Congress grew impatient again and tried to speed assimilation by demanding the termination of Federal Indian relations—that is, ending all treaties and treaty obligations—and by relocating reservation Indians in cities. This quickly proved to be a tragedy to the terminated tribes, who lost their reservations and recognition as Indians by the outside world. In addition, there were scandals and hardships for states suddenly saddled with welfare loads, and the implementation of the termination policy was aborted in 1958. Then came a period in the 1960s of trying to achieve assimilation by making reservations economically self-sufficient, raising the Native Americans' standard of living, coping with the socio-economic problems on the reservations, and, in short, moving toward termination more slowly by preparing the tribes for the day when they could hold their own with white society.

The 1960s, however, saw the start of something new. Until then, the white man and the white man's government had done all the planning and thinking for the tribes, imposing on them the programs and policies that they wanted the Indians to carry out. Through the years, almost all of the programs had failed because they were unilaterally framed and implemented in wholesale fashion by whites, in and out of government, who had little or no understanding of, or regard for, the particular needs and conditions of the individual Native American peoples, or of their respective histories, cultures, or abilities to accept or adopt what was being imposed on them. With increasing assertiveness, starting about 1961, the Indian peoples began to ask for, and then demand, the right initially to participate in the devising of policies and programs for themselves, and by the end of the 1960s the right to initiate, frame, and implement the policies and programs themselves. With American Indian spiritual leaders, traditionalists, and young Indians in the vanguard, some of them using the term "Red Power," some getting media attention as militants or activists, the movement grew quickly into one for self-determination and sovereignty.

What this means to the tribal leaders and peoples and to the regional and national Indian groups who adopted it, was essentially the right of Native Americans to manage and control their own affairs, rather than to have outsiders, whether bureaucrats of the Department of the Interior, missionaries, or self-styled non-Indian experts, do it for them. To some non-Indians (and I am now back to Dr. Tanner) it seemed to have meant something else, "the establishment of a separate nation within a nation and superior rights," as Dr. Tanner said. In the light of what I have already said, it is certainly not unique to misunderstand Native American aims. And in all fairness to Dr. Tanner, it is not impossible to find some individual Native Americans here and there who equate sovereignty with the idea of independent Indian groups, whether nations or communities. But the self-determination which almost every tribe in the country and almost all Native Americans from Maine to California and from Alaska to Florida earnestly desire today is basically the right to the freedoms that all other Americans enjoy, the right to speak for themselves, to enjoy tribal governments of their own choosing that are responsive, responsible, and accountable to their own lives and resources and, above all, to receive just recognition and protection of their treaty-guaranteed rights.

Let me deal a moment with this question of self-government, for in many ways it is at the heart of the subject of this symposium, the matter of Native American rights. Within the American body politic today, there are dozens of different forms of government. Various towns and cities have mayors, city managers, representative town councils, and so forth. County structures have other forms of government. In each case, the important ingredients are that they do not violate federal and state constitutions and statutes and that they are responsive, responsible, and accountable to their electorates who have the power to get rid of them if they wish to do so. For example, in Ann Arbor, I am sure you have a totally different form of government from that of the three Selectmen and the representative town meeting that govern my hometown of Greenwich, Connecticut. And we in Greenwich, of course, do not have New York City's structure of a Mayor, Borough Presidents, and a City Council. But each government is responsible to those whom it governs.

The Native Americans are the only Americans who have governments that have limited responsibilities to their peoples. Their principal responsibility is still to the federal government, acting through the Bureau of Indian Affairs. The Bureau has veto power, even today, over almost everything of fundamental importance to the Native Americans' life. There is truth in the saying that we non-Indians can do anything we want to do unless there is a law against it; while the Native Americans can only do something if the law says they can do it. The move for self-determination, therefore, has been a move to transfer power over Indian affairs from outsiders to the individual Indian peoples themselves by enabling them to have governments of their own choosing, which will manage and control their own affairs and resources with responsibility and accountability to their peoples.

The shape and form of those governments will be up to the individual tribes that are involved. In that sense, they will be no different from the scores of varying forms of city and county governments already enfolded in our nation. To suggest that they will become independent countries or nations does not square with the developments that have been taking place. It does not square with the Presidential endorsements of Native American self-determination, first supported by President Johnson and then more specifically by President Nixon in his Message to Congress on Indian Affairs in June 1970. Nor does it square with the tentative moves that have been made toward the realization of self-determination, the bills that Congress has passed during the last five years to put more and more of Indian affairs in the hands of the Indian peoples themselves.

Clouding, and even putting obstacles in the path of this development, however, have been the very complex and seemingly tortuous twin questions of Indian treaty rights and the federal government's trust obligation. To examine the nature of these thorny questions, which are today entangling white and Native Americans in many serious conflicts here in Michigan and elsewhere, I would like to try to follow a second avenue of white–Native American history that paralleled the one concerning whites' attitudes toward Indians which I briefly discussed.

From the earliest days of this Republic, beginning with George Washington's administration, it became accepted doctrine that while the United States maintained sovereignty over the territory within its national borders, the American Indians held title to the particular lands, waters, and resources they occupied and claimed. This doctrine was not devised by the United States. It was inherited and adopted from the European nations and was ratified by the very first Congress when it accepted the following article of the Northwest Ordinance, which the Continental Congress had adopted in 1787:

> The utmost good faith shall always be observed toward the Indians; their lands and property shall never be taken from them without their consent; and in their property, rights and liberty they shall never be invaded or disturbed, unless in just and lawful wars authorized by Congress; but laws founded in justice and humanity shall, from time to time, be made, for preventing wrongs being done to them, and for preserving peace and friendship with them.

Since the federal government for many decades received its principal financing by acquiring Indian-owned land and selling it to settlers, government policy intended getting out ahead of the settlers and sending commissioners to buy desired land from Indians, either moving the Indians somewhere else or leaving them part of their land onto which they would all move, then surveying what the commissioners had bought and selling it to non-Indians. That was the way it was supposed to work. By buying land from the Indians, the government would legally extinguish the Indian title. What did that mean? It meant just what it would mean to you and me today. Despite the fact that the United States and the individual sovereign states hold sovereignty over the territories that lie within their respective borders, you and I, if we own homes and property, have title to those possessions, and they cannot be taken from us without due process of law. That doctrine applies to us, and it applied, and still applies, to the Native Americans.

In actual practice, we know that very often the asserted national policy did not work out for the Native peoples. Settlers often got out ahead of government land purchasers, got into conflicts with the Native landowners, and called for help from the government. Frequently, the government then tried to force the Indians into selling land already taken or coveted by whites. When the Indians refused to sell, wars sometimes ensued, and the defeated Natives were coerced into giving up all or part of their lands and going somewhere else. Often, even treaty cessions with government commissioners were concluded by bribery, misrepresentation, trickery, the use of alcohol, or other illegal and unjust methods.

Through the years the government's attitude toward the Indians changed. At first, when the tribes on the frontier were strong and a military threat to our borders, the government engaged in treaty-making with them as with equals. Whatever the frontiersman thought of them, the tribes were nations. Then, in the 1830s, as the nation grew stronger, treaties continued to be made with them, but, accepting Justice John Marshall's definition of the tribes, they came to be regarded as subordinate, dependent nations. Finally, when the tribes were no longer a serious military threat, and the United States had become a continental power, the federal government stopped making treaties with them and dealt with them as wards of the nation, though it was specifically agreed to continue honoring the terms of all treaties previously made.

Those treaties are only one part of what we must deal with today. However they were made, they each contained provisions that have formed the bases of innumerable conflicts and have involved litigation ever since. In effect, under their terms, the Indians, willingly or not, and whether or not the wording was accurately communicated to them and they understood exactly what the white men understood, gave the whites something or all of what they owned in return for something else. In many cases, they gave up large areas of their land and its resources and moved to small parts of their property which were reserved for their sole use, to be protected and held in trust for them by the federal government. Sometimes, whites simply appropriated all of a tribe's land, and the Indians were left landless. In such cases, eventually, special reservations were created for these dispossessed peoples by presidential executive order or by Congress, and the rights of reservations were accorded to their Native American occupants and their descendants.

Several points are worth noting. From the beginning, Congress has held, and still holds, plenary power under the Constitution over all dealings with American Indians. Secondly, reservations, their resources and treaty-promised rights under the law, are the property of the Native tribes (in a special sense), just as your house and property belong to you. Thirdly, what some people call "superior" rights of Native Americans are rights that the Indians always had and never gave up to anyone, rights that ancestors held on to and bequeathed like an heirloom to their posterity, including their present-day descendants, or rights that were given to tribes by the federal government in payment for what the Indians gave to the government. The recognition of those rights is no more charity, and it makes them no more superior rights, than would be the recognition of the fact that you still own your own home and front lawn, which you may or may not have received as a legacy from your parents or grandparents.

The difference lies in the fact that *your* ancestors were not the original settlers and owners of the land, and of course they made no treaties with the United States.

The argument is made quite often today that this is all history, the result of actions, good or bad, by whites long dead and buried, and that it is all irrelevant or crippling to the needs and conditions of our contemporary society, and to the present generation which had nothing to do with the deeds of yesterday. For many important reasons, this notion requires careful scrutiny.

It is quite true that generation after generation of non-Indians in this country have gone about their business building the modern American nation. In the process, they wiped from their minds the actualities of the country's past relations with the Indians. For a century, the Indians were tucked away on reservations, supposedly being cared for and assimilated by the government, but out of sight and out of mind of the rest of the American people. No one, not even reservation agents and superintendents, kept track of the details of treaties, treaty promises, and other past relationships between whites and the individual tribes. No one remembered, that is, except the Indians who had been affected.

On each reservation, the people kept alive the remembrances of specifics, of the promises that a Captain John

Pennypacker had made to their ancestors in behalf of the United States government at some treaty meeting in the 1830s, or rights that three Senators who formed a commission had guaranteed would be theirs forever at a gathering on their lands in the 1860s. The Indians never forgot, and they still remember, all the particulars. It is not "history" to them, not something that was only good in the past, good for a moment or for the life of a single man. It was for their people, for their children and their children's children. It is something still alive, still meaningful, and still sacred, an heirloom, a legacy, a right in law that they still possess.

The fact that history has come back to haunt the white man is not the Indians' fault. What happened is that during all those long years that the Native American went out of sight and out of mind, he was, indeed, a helpless and powerless ward, unable to assert his rights, unable to protect himself, or maintain his rights, unable to make the white man carry out his promises. Through that long period, the Department of the Interior, through the Bureau of Indian Affairs, not only failed to protect and carry out the solemn guarantees made to the Native Americans, but in many episodes colluded in flagrant violations of Indian rights, ignoring laws that supposedly protected Indians and their property, entering into unjust contracts for Indian resources, and waiving Indian interests in actions and adjudications that illegally appropriated Indian property.

Now we begin to understand a little more clearly the move for self-determination. As that drive got under way and gathered momentum in the 1960s and 1970s, the tribes began to push aside their so-called protectors who had failed to carry out their trust obligation, and with the help of lawyers of their own began to act for themselves. Their object was not to assert new rights or expanded rights, but to gain recognition and acceptance of rights that they had always had or that had been promised them and then illegally taken from them. Just because the non-Indian population had forgotten about Indians and their rights did not mean that they were dead. Let us look at a few of them:

Indians of the Northwest had never given up their right to fish at their usual and accustomed places. They remembered how I. I. Stevens had guaranteed that right to them in 1854. But the whites of the 1960s did not even know who I. I. Stevens was. Generation after generation of newly arrived whites had polluted the rivers and overfished, and now told the Indians that they would have to abide by the white men's fishing rules. Sports fishermen, commercial fishermen, and state officials harassed the Indians and subjected them to violence, arrests, and court appearances. The Bureau of Indian Affairs ignored the Indians' rights and failed to protect them. But then the period of Indian self-determination arrived. The Native Americans finally waged a legal battle for what had always belonged to them and won victories that stunned the Northwest. The federal judge who ruled for them seemingly had no other choice. "This matter should have been settled fifty years ago," he said. But fifty years ago, the Indians had no power and no protector. They possessed rights, but they could not assert them.

In Maine, *who*, between 1790 when the Congress ruled that no one could acquire possession of Indian land without U.S. government approval, *who*, between that year and the 1970s, said that land was being taken illegally from the Penobscots and the Passamaquoddies? Was the fact that the land was taken from the Indians evidence that the law did not count, or that the Indians did not mind losing their land? Or was it that the powerless Indians could not do anything about it, and no white man was going to worry about it? The white man eventually forgot about the law, but the Indian, it seems, did not. When the Indian claim was finally asserted, the whites could do little better than declare that it was ancient history. But it was not ancient history to the Indians. It had never been merely "history" to them.

At Pyramid Lake, Nevada, the contested resource was water. In 1905, the Bureau of Reclamation threw a dam across the Truckee River to divert that stream's water to a new irrigation project for whites in the Nevada desert. Pyramid Lake, which received all of its water from the Truckee, began to diminish. The lake constituted practically the entire reservation of a Northern Paiute tribe that existed on fish harvested from that body of water. The Bureau of Indian Affairs said nothing in defense of the Indians' water rights. In 1934, when all the water of the Truckee River was adjudicated among the irrigation farmers, ranchers along the river, the city of Reno, and other white users, the federal trustees of the Indians' rights were again silent. No water was allocated to Pyramid Lake and its fisheries. The lake went down eighty-five feet, and the native trout disappeared.

Finally, in the 1960s, the Indians began to fight for themselves, and the courts have recognized that they always had paramount and primary water rights. Under the Supreme Court's Winters Doctrine, the establishing of a reservation implied that the reservation had the right to all the water from streams rising on it or crossing it that were necessary to carry out the reasons for establishing the reservation; that is, to give life and economic viability to the reservation's people. Is this a case of Indians demanding new rights, or merely trying to gain rights they always owned but were never allowed to possess?

The long years in which the federal government failed to protect Indian rights or live up to promises made to Indians have created great problems for today. The passage of time, the developments of civilization, the growth of population, and the ever-changing needs of an expanding industrial society have made each Indian claim far from simple in current terms. There are multitudes of new non-Indian rights and claims that also vie for justice. The Indian legal victories, where they have occurred, have bewildered and angered whites in many parts of the country. A so-called backlash against Indians has rushed out of the Northwest and across various parts of the nation where whites feel threatened by Indian assertions of their rights. Bills have been introduced in Congress to halt the Indians in their tracks. Some would undo court decisions that favor the Indians; some would revive termination; some would abrogate all Indian treaties, thus arbitrarily ending all the rights and promises that were once given to the Indians. In their effects, as many Congressmen know, such bills might well constitute the taking of Indian possessions without due process of law.

The Native Americans, of course, might have expected the backlash. As long as they had no power and could not assert their rights, they threatened no one. Now, indeed, they are the villains again. Their present-day situation is not helped by the energy crisis. Many reservations of the Plains and southwestern tribes, once considered undesirable wasteland by most whites, sit atop huge stores of oil, coal, uranium, gas, shale oil, geothermal, and other energy sources, now eagerly sought by the large energy companies. In the 1960s, the Bureau of Indian Affairs, still acting on its own for the tribes, leased large amounts of these resources to corporations and speculators at unconscionably low royalty figures, sometimes even permitting abuses and violations of federal regulations by the corporations. In the 1970s, the tribes woke up, realized they had been bilked, and threatened to sue their trustee, the Department of the Interior. In a quandary, the Department ruled that many of the leases would have to be renegotiated for fairer terms for the tribes. In some cases, however, the leases stuck, and the affected tribes are losing their resources for a pittance. In other cases, on the reservations of the Crow, Northern Cheyenne, Navajo, and certain other tribes, the tribal owners seem headed either for fair and just terms, or even for a future in which they, somewhat like the OPEC nations, will retain ownership and control of development for themselves.

In a parallel development, tribes are asserting their rights to adequate water as never before. But, as one would imagine, this contest, centered in the arid West, like the assertion of control over mineral and energy resources, has added to the backlash. The formation of a Native American OPEC-like group called CERT, a coalition of twenty-five energy resource–owning tribes, presents non-Indian America, and particularly the federal government and the energy industry, with just what the opponents of Indian self-determination always feared, Indian control of their own resources.

After all I have said, Indian self-determination has not yet been achieved. When you talk about self-determination, you either have it, or you don't. There is no such thing as a little bit of it or partial self-determination. It has received a lot of lip service, and many persons who see Indians winning court cases jump to the conclusion that it is entirely a result of self-determination. But no Indian tribe yet has full self-government. The Department of the Interior can still veto tribal actions, even of the large and powerful Navajo tribe, and does so. Some of the legislation mentioned earlier made small, tentative moves in the direction of giving tribes bits and pieces of control over various of their affairs. But tribal governments are still something like those of British colonies, and the governor in the person of the Bureau of Indian Affairs is still top boss with a powerful voice and the veto threat.

Despite this reality, the continued assertion of Indian rights and claims is beginning to confront Native Americans with one of the most perilous situations they have faced in this century. Not only does it appear that they have gotten all the self-determination they are going to get for some time to come (unless they simply assume it on their own), but in the places that count in serious ways in the nation's capital, they are now encountering hostility, indifference, embarrassed silence, or signs that something unpleasant is being considered for them. Politically, Indians are no longer "in." They are "out."

The Senate Select Committee on Indian Affairs, formerly headed by the sympathetic Senator James Abourezk, and staffed by people who understood the Native Americans' points of view, has gone through a considerable change in leadership and membership, and many Indians now regard it with apprehension. In the House, the situation, to most Native Americans, is worse. And the Administration, outside of the Department of the Interior, is downright dangerous, according to the Indians' perspective. The powerful Office of Management and Budget is considered to be anti-Indian. The Attorney General is questioning whether the Supreme Court and the entire United States Government, throughout the two hundred years of the nation's relations with Indians, have been all wrong. He has publicly advanced the proposal that the federal government should abandon the trust obligation. That course, on which he is now working, leads in one direction: farewell to treaties, to treaty obligations, to reservations, to tribes, and to Indians. The White House is silent. There is no Indian policy today. The Administration is waiting for the Attorney General to make his case. It is a case that most directly stems from the backlash against Indians which, in turn, has resulted from the Native Americans' vigorous assertion of their rights.*

There is one more aspect of the question to be considered. In most of the present-day contention with American Indians, including the conflict over fishing rights in Michigan, it is either implied or explicitly stated that the Native Americans of today should be treated equally with all other Americans, no better and no worse, because they are, in fact, *now* just like all other Americans. Though by background and heritage, they are Indians, they are somehow really no longer Indians, no longer any different from all the rest of the American people. So let the past be past, and the present be realistic. We are in 1979, says this thinking.

Has the national goal of the non-Indian really been

---

* Eds. note: Although no Indian tribe has full self-government there is a growing nation-to-nation relationship between Washington and Indian Country. Tribes negotiate and operate complex contracts that deliver basic government services once run by the Bureau of Indian Affairs or the Indian Health Service. In Alaska, for example, the entire health system is now operated by Alaska Native organizations, and the IHS, once the only game in town, foots less than half the cost. Foundation grants, insurance, Medicaid, and Medicare make up the balance. Today some tribes are self-sufficient, not only serving their members needs, but contributing significant dollars to local governments, schools, and other tribal communities.

achieved? Are all the Indians at last assimilated? I think not. In fact, I think far from it. On the surface, it may seem so to many people. Most Native Americans appear to live and dress like their non-Indian neighbors. They use and enjoy the material possessions of our society and culture. They have cars, television sets, commercial fishing boats, and whatever else they can afford that makes life easier and more pleasant for them. They speak the national language; they indulge in sports and entertainments; and some of them go to college and graduate schools. But make no mistake about it. The money culture of modern society may have forced the Native American to change his style of life. But in the process, the old has certainly not disappeared. New ways have been added to old ways. Or, if you will, old ways have changed to accommodate the new. But the old has persisted, still deeply ingrained in all those who take pride in the knowledge that they are Native Americans and who know that they are still different from all other Americans.

Different? How different? There is scarcely a Native American community in this country, even in 1979, that is not still basically group-oriented, that shares, that extends clan- or kinship-derived protections over its peoples, that instinctively regards the group's welfare as more important than the ambitions and competitive drive of an individual. Many Native groups still differ from whites in their spiritual understandings of man's relation to man, of his relation to nature, and to the supernatural. Lifestyles have changed, yes, but not necessarily Native American values, beliefs, and standards of conduct. Ceremonies and rituals, often changed but nevertheless directly derived from the past, are still carried out on many reservations. Dances, songs, and lore still have meaning, often spiritual, sacred, and moral. But most important, perhaps, are attitudes, perspectives, and perceptions about daily life.

Even today, the Native American often means one thing, the white man another. The differences affect concepts of conduct, the right and wrong of actions and activities, and almost every question that forms the base of continuing conflict between Native Americans and whites. The deep spiritual attachment of the Native American to his land and the resources which he has traditionally used as a basic part of his way of life is at times almost incomprehensible to whites, for frequently, at heart, the white man is viewing something from the perspective of its economic or money value, and the native is viewing it as a part of the soul and spirit of himself and of his people and his ancestors.

Fish, no less than land, water, air, or anything else provided to people by the Creator, can be, and are, viewed differently. To some Indians, as in the Northwest and on the shores of the Great Lakes, fish were, and continue to be, so important to the life of the people that they are intertwined in the spiritual life and culture of whole groups. If the fish disappeared, the foundations of the groups themselves would collapse and disappear. To the white, it can be seen that the fish provide sustenance and income for the Native American.

But it is difficult for them to see more. It is difficult for them to see that the fish is at the center of the meaning of life of the Indian community and of all that makes life continue in balance with the universe as the Indian needs it to continue. This is not irrelevant and past history. Nor is it the mark of a group bent on achieving separate nationhood, superior rights, or new privileges. It is, rather, the reflection of the fact that Native Americans are still with us and still asserting the rights that were left for them by their ancestors so that they could continue the life of their people in harmony and balance with their world.

The challenges and opportunities presented by these problems can bring together some of those different attitudes and viewpoints. If there is tolerance and patience, there may be new understanding and perhaps amelioration and resolution among the contesting interests.

14

"You Are on Indian Land!"

◇◇

In 1992, at the suggestion of the University of Nebraska Press, Josephy undertook a collaboration with two scholars in the field of American Indian Studies, Troy Johnson and Joane Nagel, to produce a new edition of Red Power *(1971), his "classic work on Indian activism." The 1999 edition, substantially updated and enlarged, is a comprehensive collection of documents, speeches, articles, and other writings reflecting the events and consequences of Indian activism from the 1960s until the 1990s. This introduction to the new edition, also a result of the collaborative effort, is a summary of the important changes in American Indian society, especially in the areas of tribal sovereignty, economic development, and education.*

It has been more than a quarter-century since the first edition of *Red Power: The American Indians' Fight for Freedom* was published in 1971. Much has happened in Indian country since Vine Deloria proclaimed in 1970: "This country was a lot better off when the Indians were running it." The selection of Deloria's article by the same name as the end piece of the first edition of this book marks the point where our work on the new edition begins. When Vine Deloria, Jr., spoke those words,

Alcatraz Island was still occupied by the group called Indians of All Tribes, Deloria himself was just finishing law school, and many things were to come.

Since 1971 we have seen the rise of a widespread protest movement by Native Americans in cities and on reservations, a proliferation of native newspapers, organizations, and associations supporting American Indian interests and representing Indian communities, a series of landmark tribal land claims and reservation resource rights decisions that have reaffirmed Indian treaty rights, a legislative and judicial reaffirmation of tribal rights to self determination and sovereignty that has opened the way for tribal economic development including casino gaming, a blossoming of cultural and spiritual renewal on many reservations and in urban Indian communities, an emerging intertribal urban Indian culture and community in U.S. cities, and an upsurge in the American Indian population as more and more Americans reassert their native ancestry.

Protests

The occupation of Alcatraz Island by Indians of All Tribes from 1969 to 1971 marked the beginning of the decade-long Indian activist movement known as "Red Power." The 1970s were the most intense years of Native American protest during the twentieth century, and the activism occurred both in cities and on reservations. Many protests of the early 1970s followed the model of the Alcatraz occupation, with Indians taking over possession of federal land and claiming it for educational and cultural uses. Most post-Alcatraz protests were much briefer, however, and often took the form of seizures of unused or abandoned federal property or demonstrations at government buildings or in national parks or monuments such as Mount Rushmore or Plymouth Rock. Many of these protest events involved members of the American Indian Movement (AIM).

As the decade proceeded, American Indian protests lasted longer, and some took on a more serious, sometimes violent, tone, revealing the depth of grievances and difficulty of solving problems centuries in the making. Perhaps best known of these later protests was the seventy-one-day siege at Wounded Knee on the Pine Ridge Reservation in the spring of 1973. Other reservation-based protests continued throughout the 1970s and revealed a growing diversity inside Native America—between urban and reservation Indians and within reservation communities—and included two occupations of the Bureau of Indian Affairs in Washington, D.C., the takeover of property on the Menominee Reservation by the Menominee Warrior Society, and a shootout on Pine Ridge followed by the imprisonment of Leonard Peltier.

The "Longest Walk," in July 1978, was the last major event of the Red Power era. Several hundred Native Americans marched into Washington to dramatize the forced removal of Native Americans from their aboriginal homelands, to bring attention to the continuing problems of American Indians, and to expose and confront the backlash movement against Indian treaty rights that was gaining strength in the Great Lakes and Pacific Northwest regions of the United States. Unlike the events of the mid-1970s, the Longest Walk was seen as a peaceful and spiritual event that ended without violence. Red Power had come full circle, from the festive Alcatraz days through a cycle of violent confrontation, to the spiritual unity that marked the end of the Longest Walk. Since 1980 the Native American rights struggle has moved increasingly into the courts and the halls of U.S. and tribal governments. But activists have continued to challenge stereotypes and exploitation of Indians by protesting the use of Indian mascots by athletic teams, to defend tribal treaty rights by protesting the continued failure to return such Indian lands as the Black Hills, and to protest violations of Indian human rights by demanding the repatriation of Indian burial remains and sacred objects and the protection of native burial and other sacred grounds.

Organizational Growth

The Indian protests of the last three decades have been accompanied by a dramatic growth in the number and variety of organizations designed to represent Indian interests, to build bridges among reservation communities, to link together tribally diverse urban Indians, and to provide a communication network to connect Native Americans around the country and around the world. Dozens of American Indian newspapers and periodicals were founded during the late 1960s and 1970s, including the American Indian Historical Society's *The Indian Historian* and *Wassaja*, the National Indian Youth Council's *ABC: Americans Before Columbus*, and the influential *Akwesasne Notes*, published by the Mohawk Nation. The voices of many of the most militant activists were published in *Warpath,* edited by Lehman Brightman. These periodicals joined the ranks of older, more established newspapers and journals such as the *Navajo Times* and the *Indian Leader*, published by Haskell Indian Junior College (now Haskell Indian Nations University) in Kansas. In addition to the growth in publications,

Native American history and culture became a topic of serious study during the 1960s, and this new academic focus was reflected in educational institutions. American Indian Studies centers were established at over one hundred universities around the United States, and over thirty fully accredited colleges or universities on or near universities were established in the decade following the 1968 founding of the first tribally controlled institution of higher education, Navajo Community College.

A number of important legal, political, and economic national organizations were also established during this period. In addition to the National Indian Youth Council (founded in 1961) and the American Indian Movement (founded in 1968), there were the National Indian Education Association (founded in 1969), the Native American Rights Fund (founded in 1970), the National Tribal Chairman's Association (founded in 1971), and the Council of Energy Resource Tribes (founded in 1975). These organizations provided lines of communication among American Indian communities and represented Indian interests at various levels of government. National organizations with members from different Indian tribes and communities contributed to an increasing awareness of common problems and interests shared by many tribes as well as by the growing urban Indian population.

Land Claims and Resource Rights

Many important decisions about treaty rights and land claims were made during the past three decades. In particular, during the 1980s a number of major tribal land claims settlements and resource rights decisions were made by Congress and the U.S. federal courts. While land claims awards varied in amount and in the extent to which they were judged to be fair, the claims-making process encouraged many Indian communities to research their histories as they organized their cases for litigation. As a result of the increased knowledge of and interest in tribal history and the financial resources obtained from land claims, a number of successful claimants were able to reestablish and revitalize tribal community economic and cultural life. For instance, the Passamaquoddies of Maine invested a portion of the proceeds from their multimillion-dollar land claims settlement in a variety of community enterprises including a housing manufacturing firm and timber mill as well as in educational programs in Passamaquoddy language and culture. Decisions to permit tribal control of economic enterprises opened the way for the Mashantucket Pequots of Connecticut to establish the extraordinarily successful Foxwoods High Stakes Bingo and Casino, many proceeds of which have been used to purchase reservation land and to research and reconstruct tribal history and traditions. Despite these and other land claims settlements (e.g., to the Warm Springs, Yavapai-Apaches, Havasupais, Yakamas, Siletzes, Penobscots), all land disputes have not been settled and continue to generate controversy and protest. The occupation of Yellow Thunder Camp in the disputed Black Hills during the 1980s symbolized unresolved land disputes between the Sioux and the United States.

The exploitation of Indian resources has been the most consistent theme marking Indian–white relations since European contact. The acquisition of Indian land by colonial and U.S. governments through the use of Indian treaties was, for the most part, a successful strategy in that it reduced Indian

landholdings to an infinitesimal portion of the continent. Treaties, however, were not without their costs to non-Indian governments. The consequences of the treaty-making strategy for
U.S. political and economic interests manifested itself in the
past three decades in a variety of legislative and court decisions upholding and expanding tribal rights to develop and
control resources and economic development. In addition to
the 1975 Indian Self-Determination and Education Assistance
Act, there were the 1979 Archaeological Resources Protection
Act, the 1983 Radioactive Waste Disposal Act, the 1983 Indian
Land Consolidation Act, and the 1988 Indian Gaming Regulatory Act, all of which extended tribal sovereignty over the decision making and control of reservation land and resources.
We will argue that one legacy of Red Power activism was the
reversal of three decades of post–Second World War federal
Indian "termination" policy in which the federal government
sought to "terminate," once and for all, Indian treaty rights and
tribal trust status. Instead of termination, the 1970s brought to
Indian country a new era of "self-determination."

The 1973 Menominee Restoration Act explicitly reversed
Congress's earlier decision to terminate the Menominee tribe
of Wisconsin and reinstated the tribe's trust status and tribal
government. This was followed by the landmark 1975 Indian
Self-Determination and Education Assistance Act, which
paved the way for tribal governments to contract for services
outside the direct control of the Bureau of Indian Affairs. The
1975 Self-Determination Act was the beginning of a variety of
legislation ushering in the self-determination era, including a
number of laws reshaping the federal–tribal relationship in the
direction of more self-rule. Among these were the 1972 Indian
Education Act, the 1974 Indian Financing Act, the 1976 Indian

Health Improvement Act, the 1978 Indian Child Welfare Act, the 1978 Tribally Controlled Community College Assistance Act, the 1978 American Indian Religious Freedom Act, the 1990 Native American Languages Act, the 1990 Native American Graves Protection and Repatriation Act, the 1990 Indian Arts and Crafts Act, and the 1994 American Indian Religious Freedom Act Amendments.

Linked to these legislative changes, the 1970s, 1980s, and 1990s have been decades of much change on Indian reservations. Tribal government jurisdiction and the assertion of tribal rights have been reaffirmed and expanded. Reservation communities are developing tribal court systems, establishing tribal education systems including tribal colleges, extending tribal sovereignty and control over resources and taxation, securing and enforcing tribal hunting, fishing, and water rights, and building tribal economic development programs, most recently in the areas of gaming, natural resources, and recreation.

Cultural and Spiritual Renewal

The rise of Indian protest and the reaffirmation of tribal sovereignty during the past three decades has a distinct political and economic character. But this is not the whole picture of what has happened in Indian country since the 1960s. The militancy and legal sophistication of Indian leaders has been strengthened and deepened by a reaffirmation of the centrality of spirituality and a recommitment to native traditions. Many court cases have been fought over Indian religious freedom in schools, prisons, and native churches. Legal cases such as

Pollock v. Marshall (1988), *Lyng v. Northwest Indian Cemetery Protective Association* (1988), and *Employment Division, Department of Human Resources of Oregon v. Smith* (1990) are examples of the increasing attacks on native religions, traditions, and cultures. *Pollock v. Marshall* denied Indian prisoners the right to wear long hair. *Lyng v. Northwest Indian Cemetery Protective Association* was a direct assault on the protection and preservation of Indian sacred sites. Despite the American Indian Religious Freedom Act of 1978 and a study which showed that a proposed logging road would have devastating effects on traditional Indian religious practices, the U.S. Supreme Court ruled that the First Amendment's Free Exercise of Religion clause did not prohibit the government from constructing a proposed road through the sacred land. In *Employment Division, Department of Human Resources of Oregon v. Smith,* the U.S. Supreme Court ruled that the First Amendment does not protect the religious use of peyote by Indian people. Four years later, however, President Clinton nullified the impact of the Supreme Court ruling when he signed Public Law 103-344 (the American Indian Religious Freedom Act Amendments of 1994), which guaranteed American Indians the right to use the sacrament of peyote in traditional religious ceremonies. The effectiveness of Public Law 103-344 protection will no doubt be tested soon, since, in 1997, the Supreme Court found unconstitutional the 1993 Religious Freedom Restoration Act—a law that was passed in response to the *Oregon v. Smith* decision in an effort to protect the religious practices of all U.S. citizens. Another major issue of cultural and spiritual renewal is the continuing struggle over the repatriation of Indian ancestral remains. The strongly voiced demand of Indian people for the right to control and protect their cultural heritage indicates a growing spiritual concern and commitment that resulted in the passage of the 1990 National Museum of the American Indian Act and the 1990 Native American Graves Protection and Repatriation Act, which set up procedures for the return of Indian burial remains and sacred objects to Indian tribes.

As a material manifestation of cultural renewal, there has been a flourishing of American Indian art and cultural organizations and activity during the past three decades. Since the 1960s there has been the creation of many new tribal museums, the thriving growth of tribal and urban Indian pow-wows and arts festivals, the establishment of tribal language programs and craft centers, an explosion of Native American literature, music, and film, and the founding of the National Museum of the American Indian (NMAI). The NMAI is an institution that represents an important move away from the past—a museum about Indians controlled by Indians.

Urban Indian Country

Urban Indian communities have grown rapidly during the last three decades. In 1960 just 28 percent of Indians lived in urban areas. This figure rose to 44 percent in 1970, increased to 50 percent in 1980, and by 1990 more than half of American Indians lived in cities. The growth of the urban Indian population, particularly during the period from 1960 to 1980, contributed to the emergence of the Red Power national Indian protest movement. The urbanization of Indian America had just begun to escalate when the first edition of *Red Power* was published; the decades since then have seen the growth of intertribal communities and the blossoming of pan-Indian culture in U.S. cities—a trend that has had profound consequences for American Indian identity and unity.

The last quarter-century has produced an interesting set of countervailing trends in Indian America, the roots of which can be traced to the pre-1970 period. There has been a "detraditionalization" of Indian individuals and communities as Native Americans have moved into the urban American mainstream. However, there also has been a "retraditionalization" of Indian individuals and communities, as many of these urban (and reservation) Indians have returned to reservations and to traditional practices in an effort to reconnect with their native roots. These apparently contradictory trends are partly the result of demographic and social changes in the Indian population: increased levels of intermarriage, urbanization, and education. On the one hand, we can see the emergence of "new Indians," native people living away from reservation communities, often intermarried with non-Indians or with Indians from other tribes, whose children are of mixed tribal and non-Indian ancestry, who do not speak an Indian language, and who are more educated and more likely to be employed than many of their reservation counterparts. All of these changes mark a path toward the creation of an intertribal Indian identity and community, more assimilated into the American mainstream, more "ethnic" than tribal. On the other hand, we can also see the maintenance of "old Indian ways." The reassertion of tribal sovereignty and the building of tribal resources have fostered a continued and strengthened sense of tribal identity and affiliation and a renaissance of tribal culture, spirituality, and community on reservations and in cities.

Thus, a consequence of urbanization and reservation revitalization has been both the "detribalization" and the "retrib-alization" of American Indians. The tension between these two trends has produced many interesting debates in Indian country about issues of tribal membership and rights, individual and collective ethnic authenticity, misrepresentations or fraudulent claims about individual ancestry or tribal affiliation, and legitimate claims to cultural production rights (who can legitimately produce Indian literature or Indian art; who has genuine knowledge of or should be able to teach Indian spirituality), and it has generated debates about the future of Native American social, cultural, political, and economic life.

Indian Population Resurgence

At the beginning of the twentieth century, the American Indian population reached its nadir, falling to fewer than 250,000. During the ensuing century, particularly in the decades after 1960, there was a dramatic growth in the number of Native Americans and an accompanying revitalization of tribal and urban Indian communities. During the Red Power decade of the 1970s, the number of Americans in the U.S. Census who reported their "race" to be American Indian increased from 792,730 in 1970 to 1,364,033 in 1980—a 72 percent increase (an additional five million Americans reported some Indian ancestry in 1980). This growth in the Indian population could not be explained using the usual demographic tools (increased birth rates, decreased death rates, immigration). Researchers concluded that many individuals had changed their primary identities from non-Indian (most likely "white") to American Indian from one census to the next, and that many of these "new" Indians were likely living in urban areas, often away from traditional Indian communities.

While the growth in the number of American Indians assured the continuation of native communities, a continuation that was in doubt at the beginning of the century, the non-traditional origins and mixed ancestry of many native people posed a challenge to tribal communities and native leaders as the end of the twentieth century approached. That challenge involved questions that paralleled those posed by the urbanization of the Native American population: who could make legitimate tribal membership claims, who had a right to participate in tribal decision making, who should share tribal and other Indian resources, who spoke for Indian rights, and who represented Indian interests?

The Future Red Road

The trends and changes in American Indian protest and politics since 1970 that we have outlined above set the agenda for the documents we have selected for the new edition of *Red Power*. We have replaced and added a number of documents, many of them in the voices of native scholars, activists, leaders, and individuals, covering such topics as tribal sovereignty, reservation economic development, protest activism, health, education, environment, religious freedom, repatriation and protection of sacred sites, self-determination and self-governance, urban Indians, Indian identity, native culture and spirituality, and ethnic authenticity.

The post–Second World War era has been a revolutionary period in American Indian history, marked most importantly, we think, by Native American activism. During this period American Indians have organized themselves to articulate and pursue their rights, have educated themselves to seek legal remedies to past injustices, and have mobilized their urban and reservation members to use protest, politics, and the media to ensure that their grievances and demands are heard. The new edition of *Red Power* covers the early, watershed days of this dynamic and important period of recent American Indian history and examines the entire Red Power era and its aftermath. We hope that this updated and expanded edition will extend the saga of Native American activism and capture the spirit of Indian resistance and renewal that flourished in the final decades of the twentieth century and that marked the path forward into the next millennium—the future Red Road.

Epilogue

◇◇◇

Alvin Josephy wrote, and quoted, these words in closing his monu-
mental illustrated history, 500 Nations *(1994). His words serve to*
encapsulate, with passion and understanding, the myriad stories of
Indian America in the preceding pages of The Longest Trail.

At the time of the five hundredth anniversary of Columbus's
landing, tribal leaders of the United States gathered in ceremony in front of the Capitol in Washington, D.C. They gave
speeches not about the shattered dreams of the past nor the
broken hoop of the present, but about new dreams, a mended
hoop, and the possibilities of the next five centuries for spiritually strong and determined peoples who, in the face of every
trial and oppression, survived. That, in essence, was the story
of the 500 Nations. They ended with the following words:

> *We stand young warriors*
> *in the circle*
> *At dawn all storm clouds disappear*
> *The future brings all hope and glory,*
> *Ghost dancers rise*
> *Five-hundred years.*

But that is another story. . . .

Editors' Acknowledgments

The editors jointly wish to thank The Estate of Alvin M. Josephy, Jr., Alfred A. Knopf, the University of Nebraska Press, and Viking Books for their generosity in allowing use of copyrighted selections from the writings of Alvin M. Josephy, Jr.

Thanks to Matthew Bokovoy of the University of Nebraska Press for his support and enthusiasm, and to Anne Eggers of Knopf for her invaluable care and efficiency in the final steps of completing the publishing process. And finally, our warmest expression of gratitude to our editor, Ann Close, whose persistence in the cause of this project and her editorial efforts, on all fronts, went beyond the call of duty. The same must be said of Keith Goldsmith, at Vintage Books, who picked up the baton in the final stages of the editorial process.

Individually, Marc Jaffe would like to thank the following for their participation: First and foremost, Vivienne S. Jaffe, my partner in life, who has made enormous contributions at every stage of the preparation of this book. I also wish to thank my editorial partner, Rich Wandschneider, whose wide knowledge of Alvin Josephy and his work provided the solid foundation on which the book was built. Thanks as well for his patience and understanding in our hundreds of emails back and forth over the past months. I also thank my children, Nina Jaffe Armistead, David Jaffe, Eva Rachel Jaffe, and Ben Jaffe, also Matoaka Little Eagle, Diane Josephy Peavey, and Jeffrey

Welch—all of whom energized and/or assisted my efforts all the way throughout.

Rich Wandschneider thanks the Josephy family for their support and long friendships; mentors on the Umatilla, Colville, and Nez Perce reservations for their teachings; the many folks who worked with Alvin, Marc, and me at Fishtrap over more than twenty years of exploring western writing and culture; and Anne Stephens and the board and staff of the new Josephy Center for Arts and Culture in Joseph, Oregon, for giving me time and space to do this work. In Alvin's later years, when he talked about leaving a library that would encourage others to carry on his work, I didn't understand its magnitude or the patience, personal relationships, deep research, and timely advocacy that marked his efforts to weave American Indians back into the narrative of our history. I hope Indian elders across the land are pleased with this effort.

Notes on the Editors

Marc Jaffe is a longtime editor and publisher. He began his career at New American Library, moved to Bantam Books, where he served as editorial director for nineteen years, then to Random House and Houghton Mifflin, where he had his own imprint, Marc Jaffe Books. Alvin Josephy introduced Jaffe to the world of Indian history in the 1960s, and their working relationship (as well as their personal friendship) continued until Alvin's death. The two collaborated on the editing of Alvin's last book, *Lewis and Clark Through Indian Eyes*. Marc Jaffe lives in Williamstown, Massachusetts, with his wife, Vivienne, and continues his publishing career as head of Editorial Direction, an editorial and publishing consultancy.

Rich Wandschneider came to the Nez Perce country of northeast Oregon in 1971, after five years as a Peace Corps volunteer and staff member in Turkey and Washington, D.C. In 1976, he opened a bookstore, at which he met Alvin Josephy. In 1988, with Alvin's assistance, he launched Fishtrap, an organization that explores and promotes western writing. Alvin brought Marc Jaffe to the first Fishtrap Gathering, and, for twenty years as its director, Wandschneider and hundreds of writers and readers explored western themes. At Alvin's death, Wandschneider began building the Josephy Library of Western History and Culture, where he continues to explore and share Josephy's work and legacy.

Notes on the Contributors

Roberta Conner is an enrolled member of the Confederated Tribes of the Umatilla Indian Reservation. She is of Cayuse, Umatilla, and Nez Perce ancestry, and director of the Tamástslikt Cultural Institute of the Cayuse, Umatilla, and Walla Walla tribes near Pendleton, Oregon. Conner was formerly Chair of the Board of Trustees of the National Museum of the American Indian, and a board member of the Wallowa Band Nez Perce Trail Interpretive Center. She recently served as vice president of the National Council of the Lewis & Clark Bicentennial Board of Directors, and was one of nine Native contributors to *Lewis and Clark Through Indian Eyes*.

Jaime A. Pinkham has been the Native Nations vice president at the Bush Foundation in St. Paul, Minnesota, since 2009. A forester by education, he has spent a majority of his career protecting Native sovereignty and tribal treaty rights. Prior to coming to the Foundation, he directed the congressional affairs and regional coordination efforts for the Columbia River Inter-Tribal Fish Commission in Portland, Oregon. Prior to that, Jaime was at home with the Nez Perce Tribe, where he was twice elected to the Tribal Council and served as treasurer as the Tribe was expanding into gaming. He also managed the Tribe's natural resource departments, where he was involved in wolf recovery, acquiring ancestral lands, water rights negotiations, and salmon restoration.

Clifford Trafzer is the Costo Professor of American Indian Affairs at the University of California, Riverside. He was born to parents of Wyandot Indian and German-English blood, and raised in Arizona, where he earned a BA and MA in history at Northern Arizona University in Flagstaff. Trafzer earned a PhD in American History with a specialty in American Indian History at Oklahoma State University in 1973, and the same year became a museum curator for the Arizona Historical Society. Trafzer taught at Navajo Community College, Washington State University, and San Diego State University before joining the faculty of the UCR in 1991. He is an author and editor of several books on Indian America, including *Earth Song, Sky Spirit*; *The Chinook*; *Renegade Tribe*; and *Native Universe*.

Mark Trahant is a nationally known author, journalist, and educator. He held the Twentieth Atwood Chair of Journalism at the University of Alaska Anchorage in 2013–14 and has also taught at the University of Idaho and the University of Colorado. He served as chairman and chief executive officer at the Robert C. Maynard Institute for Journalism Education in Oakland, California. In 2009 and 2010, Trahant was a Kaiser Media Fellow writing about health care reform, focused on programs such as the Indian Health Service, and worked as a project investigator for the Smithsonian, exploring President Richard Nixon's contributions to American Indian policy. He is the author of *The Last Great Battle of the Indian Wars*, and his book on austerity was a project started after winning a Rockefeller Foundation residency at the Bellagio Center on Lake Como, Italy.

His long career in journalism included the position as editorial page editor of the *Seattle Post-Intelligencer*. He is a member of Idaho's Shoshone Bannock tribe and former president of the Native American Journalists Association. He lives with his wife in Fort Hall, Idaho.

Suggestions for Further Reading

This list is not comprehensive. There has been a flurry of publishing in the area of righting the Indian story in America, in detailing Indians' struggles against assimilation and annihilation, and in listening to tribal people when talking about the natural world. The selections below are a sampling, sometimes following directly on one of the chapters in this book, sometimes providing the kind of overview that Josephy provided to critical acclaim almost fifty years ago in the 1968 *Indian Heritage of America*. The list includes recommendations from editors and contributors.

Aguilar, George W. *When the River Ran Wild!: Indian Traditions on the Mid-Columbia and the Warm Springs Reservation.* University of Washington Press, 2005.

Andrist, Ralph K. *The Long Death: The Last Days of the Plains Indians.* Collier Macmillan, 1964.

Cajete, Gregory. *Native Science: Natural Laws of Interdependence.* Clear Light Books, 1999.

Connell, Evans. *Son of the Morning Star: Custer and the Little Bighorn.* North Point Press, 1984.

Crosby, Alfred W. *The Columbian Exchange: Biological and Cultural Consequences of 1492*, 30th Anniversary Edition. Praeger, 2003.

Deloria, Vine. *Power and Place: Indian Education in America*. Fulcrum Publishing, 2001.

Harvard Project on American Indian Economic Development. *The State of the Native Nations: Conditions under U.S. Policies of Self-Determination*. Oxford University Press, 2007.

Hyde, Anne F. *Empires, Nations, and Families: A History of the North American West, 1800–1860*. University of Nebraska Press, 2011.

Jackson, John C. *Children of the Fur Trade: Forgotten Metis of the Pacific Northwest*. Oregon State University Press, 2007.

King, Thomas. *The Inconvenient Indian: A Curious Account of Native People in North America*. University of Minnesota Press, 2013.

Krech, Shepard. *The Ecological Indian: Myth and History*. W. W. Norton & Co., 1999.

Landeen, Dan, and Allen Pinkham. *Salmon and His People: Fish and Fishing in Nez Perce Culture*. Confluence Press, 1999.

Light, Steven Andrew, and Kathryn R. L. Rand. *Indian Gaming and Tribal Sovereignty: The Casino Compromise*. University Press of Kansas, 2005.

Mann, Charles C. *1491: New Revelations of the Americas Before Columbus*. Knopf, 2005.

———. *1493: Uncovering the New World Columbus Created*. Knopf, 2011.

McWhorter, L. V. *Hear Me, My Chiefs!: Nez Perce Legend & History*. Caxton Press, 1952.

———. *Yellow Wolf: His Own Story*. Caxton Press, 1940.

Miller, Robert J. *Native America, Discovered and Conquered: Thomas Jefferson, Lewis and Clark, and Manifest Destiny.* Bison Books, 2008.

Silko, Leslie Marmon. *The Turquoise Ledge: A Memoir.* Viking, 2010.

Trahant, Mark N. *The Last Great Battle of the Indian Wars.* Cedars Group, 2010.

Ulrich, Roberta. *American Indian Nations from Termination to Restoration, 1953–2006.* University of Nebraska Press, 2010.

———. *Empty Nets: Indians, Dams, and the Columbia River,* 2nd ed. Oregon State University Press, 2007.

Van Develder, Paul. *Coyote Warrior: One Man, Three Tribes, and the Trial That Forged a Nation,* 2nd ed. University of Nebraska Press, 2005.

———. *Savages and Scoundrels: The Untold Story of America's Road to Empire through Indian Territory.* Yale University Press, 2009.

Wilkinson, Charles. *Blood Struggle: The Rise of Modern Indian Nations.* W. W. Norton & Co., 2006.

Wilson, James. *The Earth Shall Weep. A History of Native America.* Grove Press, 2000.

Alvin Josephy often commented on the value of fiction and poetry in transporting us into historical places and times. Most of those poets and fiction writers were in fact friends of Josephy: Sherman Alexie, Paula Gunn Allen, Debra Earling, Louise Erdrich, Diane Glancy, Joy Harjo, Linda Hogan, Thomas King, Adrian C. Louis, N. Scott Momaday, Susan Power, Leslie Marmon Silko, and James Welch.

Permissions Acknowledgments

Grateful acknowledgment is made to the following for permission to reprint previously published materials:

Alfred A. Knopf: "A Continent Awakes" and epilogue from *500 Nations: An Illustrated History of North American Indians* by Alvin M. Josephy, Jr. Copyright © 1994 by Parkways Productions, Inc.; "Cornplanter, Can You Swim?," " 'Like Giving Heroin to an Addict,' " and "The Great Northwest Fishing War" from *Now That the Buffalo's Gone: A Study of Today's American Indians* by Alvin M. Josephy, Jr. Copyright © 1984 by Alvin M. Josephy, Jr.

The Estate of Alvin M. Josephy, Jr.: " 'A Most Satisfactory Council' " from *American Heritage* 16, no. 6, October 1965; "The Hopi Way" from *American Heritage* 24, no. 2, February 1973; "The Historical and Cultural Context of White–Native American Conflicts" from *The Indian Historian* 12, no. 2, Summer 1972; "Indians of the Sound" from *On the Sound* 2, no. 2, 1972; and "The Hudson's Bay Company and the American Indians" from *The Westerners* XVII, nos. 2, 3, and 4, 1971.

The University of Nebraska Press: " 'You Are on Indian Land!' " from *Red Power: The American Indians' Fight for Freedom*, 2nd edition, edited by Alvin M. Josephy, Jr., Troy R. Johnson,

Index

Page numbers in *italics* refer to illustrations.

Hudson's Bay Company, traders and
    officers of:
    alcohol supplied by, 132–33
    blankets supplied by, 131
    education and accomplishments
        of, 137–38
    flogging of Indians by, 139–40
    guns used as trade goods by, 126
    imperialistic attitudes of, 139–41
    Indians' cultural differences with,
        138–39
    Indian skills and crafts adopted
        by, 136–37
    Indians' personal relations with,
        135–37
    Indian wives and families of,
        128, 137
    land purchases and treaties
        made by, 146
    private trade by, 128
    strict rules for, 127–28
Hull, William, 107, 109
Hunter, Curtis F., 286, 289
Huntington, N.Y., 81
Huron, Lake, 387
Hurons, 47
Hutchinson, Anne, 79

Ice Age, 31, 33, 61–62, 301, 398
Ickes, Harold, 276
Idaho, 150, 164, 219, 220, 222, 234,
    237
Incas, 17
"Indian, The: The Forgotten
    American" (Cohen and Mause),
    429–30

Indiana, 88, 89, 93, 94, 95–96, 99,
    100, 103
    Indian land ceded to U.S. in, 100
Indian Health Service, 418–19,
    464*n*
Indian Heritage of America
    (Josephy), 4
Indian Land Consolidation Act
    (1983), 474
Indian Office, U.S., 196
Indian Reorganization Act (1934),
    416, 442, 450
Indian Self-Determination and
    Educational Assistance Act
    (1975), 419, 474
Indians of All Tribes, 469
Indians of the Pacific Northwest
    (Deloria), 136*n*
Indian Territory, 251, 414
Indian Women in Tent
    (Rindisbacher), *12*
industrialization, 257
Inkpaduta (Wahpekute chief), 190–91
Interior Department, U.S., 293*n*, 295,
    297, 303, 310, 328, 329, 362, 368,
    376, 377, 451
    California-Nevada water right
        agreement opposed by, 315
    conflicts of interest in, 313–14,
        320, 325, 425
    lax defense of Indian water rights
        by, 299, 310–11, 325
    and proposal to drain Pyramid
        Lake, 315–16
    Pyramid Lake lawsuit of, 319–20,
        321, 322, 324–26

Sand Creek Massacre, 415

Santa Cruz River, 53*n*

Santees, *see* Dakota Sioux

Sarcis, 122

sarnp (corn porridge), 81

Saskatchewan River, 132

Sassacus (Pequot *sachem*), 72, 74, 75, 76

Satiacum, Clara, 364

Satiacum, Robert, 351–52, 358, 359, 362, 364, 375

Satiacum, Suzanne, 364

Satiacum decision, 351–52, 353, 363, 374

Sauk, 103, 108

Saulteurs, 122

Saybrook, Conn., 73, 74, 80

Saylor, John P., 281

Schwandt, Mary, 178, 183

Scranton, William, 290

Sealth (Seattle; Duwamish chief), 341–42, 344, 361, 388

Secatogues, 68

2nd Cavalry, U.S., 248–49

Sekanis, 122

self-determination, right of, 88–89, 415–20, 422, 423, 425, 429, 432, 434, 435–36, 442–43, 450–53, 458, 462–63

self-government, of Indians, 450, 452–53, 475

Selkirk, Earl of, 146

Seminoles, 99, 105

Senate, U.S., 311, 321

Indian Affairs Committee of, 385, 422–23, 463

see also Congress, U.S.; House of Representatives, U.S.

Seneca language, 264

Seneca Nation, 273–74, 276, 280

alternative flood control plans commissioned by, 278–79

Kinzua Dam and, 259, 276–77

Senecas, 45, 49, 50, 258–59, 268

Allegheny Reservation of, *see* Allegheny Reservation

in American Revolution, 264, 268–69

Cattaraugus Reservation of, 273, 274, 277, 282–83

Cornplanter grant of, *see* Cornplanter Grant

Corps of Engineers' hostility toward, 281, 283–84, 285, 290

JFK's order for government relocation aid to, 280–81, 283

land sales by, 270, 273

in League of the Six Nations, 267

Quakers and, 272

relocation of graves of, 279, 282, 285

reparations bill for, 281–82

1794 treaty with, 265, 267, 271–72

as steel workers, 275

survival of, 274–75

Tonawanda Reservation of, 273

treaty termination policy and, 281

Weber property of, 284–89